IN
WORDS
AND
DEEDS

IN
WORDS
AND
DEEDS

Battle Speeches in History

RICHARD F. MILLER

UNIVERSITY PRESS OF NEW ENGLAND

HANOVER AND LONDON

Published by University Press of New England,
One Court Street, Lebanon, NH 03766
www.upne.com
© 2008 by University Press of New England

Printed in the United States of America
5 4 3 2 1

Library of Congress Cataloging-in-Publication Data

Miller, Richard F., 1951–
In words and deeds : Battle speeches in history /
Richard F. Miller.
    p.   cm.
Includes bibliographical references and index.
ISBN 978–1–58465–731–6 (cloth : alk. paper)
1. Speeches, addresses, etc.—History and criticism.
2. Military history. I. Title.
PN4193.M5M55   2008
a 808.859'358—dc22   2008010979

 University Press of New England is a member of the Green Press
Initiative. The paper used in this book meets their minimum
requirement for recycled paper.

THIS BOOK IS DEDICATED TO MY BELOVED WIFE, ALYSON,
MY FATHER, SAMUEL H. MILLER, AND THE MEN AND WOMEN
OF THE USS *Kitty Hawk*, THE THIRD BATTALION, EIGHTH
MARINE REGIMENT, AND THE THIRD HEAVY BRIGADE
COMBAT TEAM, FOURTH INFANTRY DIVISION

Contents

Acknowledgments

The idea for this book arose on my first stint as an embedded journalist aboard the USS *Kitty Hawk* in March 2003 during the Shock and Awe phase of Operation Iraqi Freedom. This experience was my introduction to the battle speech incarnate. I returned to the theater twice more as an embedded journalist: in 2005 with the Third Battalion, Eighth Marine Regiment, at Camp Fallujah, and in 2006 with the Third Heavy Brigade Combat Team, Fourth Infantry Division, at Camp Warhorse, located near Buqubah. These assignments filled my notebooks with real battle speeches, and as I continued to read the many military histories required for this book, I discovered that battle speeches, like the wars that spawn them, are almost without number.

Because I wanted this book's battle speeches to be publicly accessible, *In Words and Deeds* contains none of the actual words or deeds recorded during my own overseas experiences. However, I wish to express my gratitude to the soldiers, sailors, and marines whose words and deeds informed this work. In ways known only to me, this is really their book—they managed the tactical situations around which this study was organized, and it was how they spoke and acted then that suggested many of my battle-speech genres and conventions used here. In a sense, they wrote the book; I only took notes.

I first wish to thank Commander Roxie Merritt, United States Navy, who facilitated my embedding arrangements for all three trips; Lieutenant Commander Brook DeWalt, then Public Affairs Officer on the USS *Kitty Hawk*; Captain Michael Brown on Admiral Matthew Moffit's staff; and Captain Thomas Parker, commander of the *Kitty Hawk*, whose daily remarks on the 1MC (ship's public address system) amounted to a serialized Pre-Invasion Speech for the crew. Witnessing Lieutenant Commander Victor "Dirk" Bindi review orders with his pilots just before Shock and Awe was an Instructional Speech, first hand. Then there was Vice Admiral Thomas Keating, whom I have never met but whose Pre-Invasion Speech to the *Kitty Hawk*'s crew I heard. It was my first official battle speech, and it is still one of the best.

At Camp Fallujah in 2005, U.S. Marine Corps Public Affairs Officers Colonel Jenny Holbert, Major Francis Piccoli, Captain Donald Caetano, and Sergeant Russ Meade handled the journalists, including the crucial area of their assignments. I am grateful for their kindness and confidence in placing me with active units. It was here that the speeches began to flow. I was fortunate to have been assigned to Weapons Company, led by Philadelphia Eagles fan Captain Edward Nevgloski and his Executive Officer, Lieutenant Richard Lee. I wish to thank them for their kindness, hospitality, and size 11 official-issue desert tan boots. I do not have first names, but on one very difficult patrol, I belatedly wish to express my gratitude to Lieutenant Hunt and Corporal Nichols, both with Weapons Company; they proved that speech and deeds during and after stressful events can make all the difference to morale. One first name I did get on that patrol was Lance Corporal Tyler Davis, the young man who watched my back and had to remind me only once to walk *inside* the tank tracks as we approached an Abrams tank that had been disabled by a mine just moments earlier. I rode next with Gunnery Sergeant Jeffrey V. Dagenhart, a born battle speechmaker, and I wish to thank him for an unvarnished look at life on the MSRs (Main Supply Routes), including checkpoints, patrols, and off-road vehicle and house-to-house contraband searches. Gunny Dagenhart knew how to talk his marines up when desirable and down when necessary.

I wish to thank Public Affairs Officer Major Michael Humphreys and his staff at Camp Warhorse for helping to make my time with the Third Heavy Brigade Combat Team (3HBCT), Fourth Infantry Division, both possible and useful. Major Humphreys and his team produce the *Iron Brigade Chronicle*, a brigade publication that I found brimming with insights about soldiers' lives and duties in today's Iraq. I predict that these kinds of publications—and there are many—will one day become a treasure trove for historians interested in the U.S. Iraq mission. I also want to thank Mike for his willingness to be interviewed for this book, and for some fact-checking that he was kind enough to undertake. The 3HBCT was deployed in various locations between Forward Operating Base Anaconda and Camp Warhorse, and my debt to its members (and battle speechmakers) is immense. Thanks to Captain John P. Sacksteder and Captain Awbrey Lance of the Third Battalion, Twenty-Ninth Field Artillery Regiment (3/29 FA); the former's care and the latter's confidence in assigning me to active patrols are both deeply appreciated. An imperturbable (and many-time improvised explosive device [IED] veteran) Staff Sergeant Donald White was a paradigm of the senior non-commissioned officer, and not coincidentally a superb battle speechmaker. If elections were held, I would vote him all around best delivery for the categories of pre-patrol Instructional Speech and post-IED battle speech. Thanks to Sergeant Kenneth Sargent for his company during the trip to Aldijail, the town brutalized by Saddam. Although this book does not include a category called Speeches in Defense of American Interests Made to the Indigenous Population, Sergeant Sargent would have been tops in this category. Finally, I want to express my gratitude to Lieutenant Colonel Jeffrey Vuono, commander of the 3/29 FA, for his cooperation, and to express my wonder at watching him deliver a difficult speech as he attempted to persuade different Iraqi security forces to work together.

Needless to say, so many golden breadcrumbs had to lead some-where, and with the 3HBCT they did—to the office of its commander, Colonel Brian D. Jones. I wish to thank Colonel Jones for his time and kindness and simply state what he must already know—that 3HBCT's fine reputation must have begun at the top.

None of these stints would have been possible without the support of my extended family. This starts with my cousin Ellen Ratner and cousin-by-marriage Cholene Espinoza. Ellen managed Talk Radio News Service, Inc., which sponsored these trips. Cholene, an Air Force Academy graduate, former U2 pilot, and embed veteran of Operation Iraqi Freedom who now flies heavies around the friendly skies, was generous in offering time- and occasionally life-saving insights both before and after these assignments. And there would have been no assignments without the support of Alyson, my wife. She paid too high a price for these trips but her love and patience never flagged. My children, Eli, Caroline, and Pesha, remained likewise steadfast; nothing says more about the times we live in than finding myself perched over a computer in Balad, helping Caroline with her homework via email as a loudspeaker blared "Incoming!"

Professor William Fowler Jr. of Northeastern University, my colleague at *New England Quarterly,* was helpful in offering excellent advice (as always) and sharing his considerable insight about George Washington. The staff at the Concord Free Public Library was helpful throughout as well; they manage a wonderful resource, and I hope that Concord's residents will continue to give this institution the support it merits. And finally thanks go to my editor, Phyllis Deutsch, at UPNE, who, like a great literary EMT, intervened early, swiftly and decisively and saved this book's life. Additional embarrassments of facts, forms and grammar were avoided with the skillful assistance of copy editor Nils Nadeau. However, any remaining errors of fact, grammar or context are entirely my responsibility.

His truth is an encompassing shield. You will not fear the fright of night, the arrow that flies by day; Pestilence that prowls in darkness, destruction that ravages at noon. A thousand will be stationed at your side, and ten thousand at your right hand; but it will not approach you. You will but gaze with your eyes, and you will see the annihilation of the wicked. For you said, "The Lord is my refuge."

Psalm 91:5–9, *The Book of Psalms: A New English Translation of the Text, Rashi, and a Commentary Digest,* translated and edited by Rabbi A. J. Rosenberg, vol. 3 of 3 (New York: The Judaica Press Inc., 1991), 357

IN
WORDS
AND
DEEDS

INTRODUCTION

The general must be . . . a ready speaker; I believe that the greatest benefit can accrue from the work of a general only through this gift. For if the general is drawing up his men before battle, the encouragement of his words makes them despise the danger and covet the honor; and a trumpet-call resounding in the ears does not so effectively awaken the soul to the conflict of battle as a speech that urges to strenuous valor rouses the martial spirit to confront danger.

Onasander, *The General,* Proemium, 1:13, c. 59 CE

The general should do everything to electrify his own soldiers, and to impart to them the same enthusiasm which he endeavors to repress in his adversaries. . . . Military eloquence is one means, and has been the subject of many a treatise.

Baron De Jomini, article 12, *The Art of War,* 1838

It is by virtue of the spoken word rather than by the sight or any other medium that men in combat gather courage from the knowledge that they are being supported by others. . . . Speech galvanizes the desire to work together. It is the beginning of the urge to get something done.

S. L. A. Marshall, "Why Men Fight," *Men Against Fire,* 1947[1]

IF COMMAND HAS A FIRST PRINCIPLE, it is this: soldiers cannot simply be ordered to die—they must first be persuaded. And the role of battle speeches in persuading soldiers not just to fight but also to enlist, submit to discipline, and take instruction is the subject of this book. As the epigraphs suggest, writers on military doctrine have always recognized the importance of battle speeches in exhorting soldiers to fight. But even if the commentators were silent, the testimony of countless military histories bears witness not only to the importance of battle speechmakers' exhortatory words but also to their inspiring deeds. Herodotus's King Darius the Great knew something about commanding soldiers. "[Many] things can't be shown through words, but through deeds," the Persian king declared, as he weighed the value of one against the other, "while other things are possible in words though nothing clear ever comes of them."[2]

This book's survey of battle speeches cuts a broad swath through history from the sacred time of the Bible to the real time of Operation Iraqi Freedom. A great variety of speeches and deeds has been culled from a tiny fraction of the wars since biblical times to illustrate how commanders, politicians, and ordinary soldiers have used words and deeds to recruit, instruct, or exhort soldiers. *In Words and Deeds* makes several assumptions of which readers should be aware. The first is that there is an irreducible human component to warfare that has survived all of the military, religious, cultural, and political changes from biblical time through modernity. British military historian David G. Chandler has observed that while advances in military technology and increasing "politico-military complexities" have raised swarms of new challenges for commanders, it is nevertheless true that "the essential problems of waging warfare, of exerting leadership and (at a far higher level) generalship under conditions of extreme stress and danger, remain unchanged, just as the essentials of human nature—after all, the essential bedrock or lowest common denominator of all conflicts in whatever age, location or format—are immutable."[3]

In Words and Deeds has only validated this insight. The tensions arising just before a battle or an invasion, the exhortations required during a battle, and the need for a commander to create perspective on a recently ended battle remain much the same today as the evidence suggests they were thirty-five centuries ago. And one can reduce this even further: the similarities include adrenaline-releasing anxieties, the need for camaraderie, and a fact that is seemingly so basic to human existence as to be an autonomic function of consciousness itself—the need to impose narrative on otherwise chaotic events. Battle speeches especially serve this last end by rationalizing war's randomly inflicted death and destruction. War's randomness should not be confused with war's purposes, which, like many human activities, can serve ends that are good or evil and many shades in between. But whatever war's purposes, the apprehensions it creates continue to play on soldiers' minds much as they always have. Soldiers' enthusiasm and interest must still be roused to join an army; roused to take instruction; roused again to perform, both before and during a battle; afterward, soldiers must be comforted and convinced that the battle was worth the price. The ebb and flow of these tensions form distinct patterns that in turn are shaped by the tactical situations that birth them—raising, instructing, and exhorting an army, then explaining to soldiers why they must fight. Battle speeches and the deeds that precede, accompany, and immediately follow them are an important means of accomplishing all of these things.

What Is a Battle Speech?

Colonel Cross, on foot pacing up and down in his nervous way in front of our line, addressed us the following, jerked out as it were: "Men, you are about to engage in battle. You have never disgraced your State; I hope you won't this time. If any man runs I want the file closers to shoot him; if they don't, I shall myself. That's all I have to say." And it's what I call a model speech.

Thomas L. Livermore's recollection of Colonel Edward Cross's speech at the Battle of Antietam, from his memoir *Days and Events, 1860–1866*

[Second Lieutenant William W.] DeWitt said, "I can hear the fire but I can't see it; I guess I must be blind." . . . Then DeWitt said to Johns, "Give me your .45 and guide me to the door; if any Chinks come, I'll let them have it." Johns handed him the pistol and seated him on an ammo case at the CP [command post] entrance. Sightless and still reeling from dizziness, DeWitt sat there while the others beat at the flames.

S. L. A. Marshall, *Pork Chop Hill: The American Fighting Man in Action, Korea, Spring, 1953*

Soldiers of the army of the Mediterranean!

You are a wing of the army of England! You have fought among mountains, in plains, before fortresses; but you had yet to carry out a naval campaign. The Roman legions that you have sometimes rivaled, but never equaled, fought Carthage on this very sea and on the plains of Zama. Victory never forsook them.

Soldiers! Europe is watching you!

Napoleon Bonaparte, Proclamation, May 10, 1798[4]

WHAT IS A BATTLE SPEECH? For the purposes of this book, it consists of the words, deeds, or words coupled with deeds whose purpose is to recruit, instruct, or exhort soldiers for battles. This book further expands the definition of battle speeches to include the words spoken after a battle whose purpose is to explain why it was fought and what it accomplished, as well as speeches made when an army surrenders or declares victory, or when a commander bids farewell to his soldiers. In one form or another, these are all speeches that prepare soldiers either to fight or to endure, to bond with comrades or commanders, or to seal their identification with their unit, country, tribe, or faith. In two words, battle speeches are all about soldiers' *purpose* and *morale*.

Battle speeches may be given by anyone—soldier or civilian—but for this book's purposes, the audience must be exclusively soldiers (or sailors). Thus when the great Puritan divine Cotton Mather (who referred to himself as "neither a Souldier, nor the Son of a Souldier") ascended the pulpit of Boston's Old North Meetinghouse on September 1, 1689, to preach to the Massachusetts Militia, his sermon was really a battle speech. "Gentlemen! It is the War of the Lord which you are now engaged in," he declared as his soldier-audience was about to decamp to fight Indians. The militia was apparently so stirred by his effort that Mather was later asked by its officers to print copies. These words, although spoken by one of the leading clerical lights of his day, were as much an exhortatory battle speech as Admiral Farragut's exclamation from the deck of the USS *Hartford* as it steamed into Mobile Bay: "Damn the torpedoes! Four bells, Captain Drayton, go ahead!" By contrast, speeches like Abraham Lincoln's Gettysburg

Address, while of profound military significance, are excluded here because included in the speechmaker's intended audience was civilian newspaper readers and not just soldiers.[5]

A range of battle speeches featuring words as well as words and deeds are illustrated in the epigraphs. The first was given by Colonel Edward E. Cross to the Fifth New Hampshire Infantry during the battle of Antietam and is easy to classify: a commander's exhortatory words spoken to his unit just before combat. Cross had assembled his men for final instruction and stiffening before assaulting Antietam's Bloody Lane, a sunken road from whose banks Confederate defenders had already repulsed several attacks. Cross "nervously" paced the line and emphasized (probably by shouting) each word to make sure that he could be heard above the din. He informed his soldiers what was happening ("you are about to engage in battle"); he reminded them of their past bravery while stirring their expectations of honor and their fear of shame ("You have never disgraced your state; I hope you won't this time"); finally, perhaps for those soldiers immune to the attraction of honor and not sufficiently averse to the stigma of shame, he made a threat: "If any man runs I want the file closers to shoot him." Cross then concluded by escalating the threat: "If they don't [shoot him], I shall myself." It was, a member of his soldier-audience admiringly recalled, "a model speech."

But battle speeches also consist of deeds (actions) as well as words. The case of Lieutenant DeWitt illustrates how words and deeds conjoin, with deeds serving as speech equivalents. In the Korean War, DeWitt commanded an outpost near Pork Chop Hill. During one Chinese attack, his command post had been struck by artillery and had begun to burn. Filled with dead and wounded men (the latter including DeWitt), the post was soon surrounded by enemy. When DeWitt regained consciousness, he was blind but still able to fight—and command. His speech was simple: "Give me your .45 and guide me to the door; if any Chinks come, I'll let them have it." The words were both instructional ("give me your gun . . . guide me to the door") and exhortatory by personal example ("I'll let them have it"). They carried two messages: I can still command, although I am severely wounded and blind; moreover, I can still fight, despite my wounds. And the words were followed by two simple acts: first, he had himself seated on a crate; next, he pointed his pistol toward the entrance. These deeds carried the same message as his words, and together they worked as Dewitt probably intended. "Afterward the infantrymen paid tribute to the effect on their spirits from the sight of his raised pistol," S. L. A. Marshall wrote upon interviewing DeWitt's men. "Said Johns, 'The guts of that guy steadied us all.'"[6]

The third illustration featured above is an example of a battle speech made with no battle in sight. On May 10, 1798, Napoleon addressed his troops (via printed proclamation) nine full days before they sailed from France to invade Egypt; they would not reach their destination for over five weeks, when perhaps a battle would be fought, or perhaps not. But with characteristic bombast, Napoleon exhorts and challenges his soldiers. He reminds them of their history ("You have fought among mountains, in plains, before fortresses"); he compares them with antiquity's most storied army ("Roman legions") and challenges them to meet the ancient benchmarks ("But you had yet to carry out a naval campaign. The Roman legions that you have sometimes rivaled but never equaled, fought Carthage on this very sea and on the plains of Zama. Victory never forsook them"); finally, he returns his soldier-audience forcefully to the present by asking them to imagine that their deeds are being monitored and perhaps even recorded for posterity, even implying that his soldiers might surpass those of ancient Rome: "Soldiers! Europe is watching you!" he admonished. The enemy was hundreds of miles away and not a shot had been fired, but Napoleon had already begun the work of preparing his army for battle.

In studying battle speeches, one must also pay attention to the *means* by which such speeches reach their soldier-audiences. Speech is usually understood as verbal communication, and battle speeches are thus typically imagined as a speaker personally voicing his words to a soldier-audience gathered within earshot. And in fact all of the ancient battle speeches and many of the more recent examples used in this book are actually (or at least supposedly) voiced by their speakers. Sights as well as sounds can also serve as speech equivalents; it is here that deeds speak. The raised sword or pistol, the standard or color-bearer in the lead, the sight of an officer beckoning his men forward may be, depending on the surrounding noise level, the only "language" possible. Before the invention of printing, hearing the voice and observing the deed were the exclusive means of delivering a battle speech.

As armies expanded not only in size but also in geographical dispersion, antiquity's model of the *strategos* addressing his soldiers while standing on a platform, striding through the ranks, or riding a horse had to be supplemented by other methods of delivering battle speeches. Of course, what made these other methods possible (and thus contributed more than a little to the overall control, and thus the expansion, of armed forces) were advances in communications technology, including such developments as signal towers, marine flag systems, and the printing press. Now commanders could "publish" battle speeches capable of reaching tens of thousands of men (more or less) simultaneously. Later technologies such as telegraphy, telephony, and radio further abetted this process, and at least two battle speeches used in this book—General Jonathan M. Wainwright's surrender speech and General Douglas MacArthur's "I have returned" speech— were broadcast by radio. But the honors for the sheer volume of battle speeches transmitted must be awarded to the printing press and its modern equivalents. Commanders in distant headquarters were now able to convey battle speeches by publishing orders, sending emails, or distributing unit magazines containing the speeches; they could be confident that these publications would be read aloud by subalterns to smaller formations or perused silently by individual soldiers. These new means of distribution and media were only changed methods of circulation, however, and they carried exactly the same genres of battle speeches that Joshua, Alexander the Great, or Julius Caesar might have pronounced in person. Thus *In Words and Deeds* must look beyond the media to examine the message—any communication, be it oral, written, or broadcast, that functions as a battle speech was potentially of interest here. In understanding battle speeches according to their function rather than their delivery, the playing field is leveled between the exclusively oral age of Alexander, Scipio Africanus, and Caesar and the multimedia worlds of later generals George B. McClellan, Dwight D. Eisenhower, and James N. Mattis.[7]

In connection with the printing press, one other development in the history of battle speeches must be mentioned. Arguably the single most important technological innovation in this specific arena were the nineteenth-century inventions of the steam and later the rotary presses, which introduced double-sided, cheap newspapers to an increasingly literate market. (And, in an age of citizen armies recruited on a national basis, a market that was more likely to know someone in uniform.) As newspapers proliferated, so did journalists, who, beginning with William Howard Russell's famous exploits during the Crimean War, began to report from "the seat of the war."[8] This placed on the battlefield itself an auditor who would (almost) contemporaneously report on the events there (or some version of them, at least). Readers now had access to abundant details that had previously been ignored or only briefly summarized—things like the status of the common soldier, the most current maps, and issues great and small relating to strategy, tactics, logistics, casualties, and the relationship between command and political authority. Lastly, and of special importance here, these journalists used a literary technique that has lent color to battle writing from Homer to the *New York Times*: the things soldiers actually *say*. In fact, journalists need battle speeches. First, they confer authenticity and prestige, for to report a live speech is ipso facto proof of having "been there." Speeches became useful for creating heroes, vilifying disfavored generals, providing color and captions, and fleshing out otherwise lean stories and stark maps showing troop movements, weather, or logistics. Indeed, a battle speech researcher soon learns that battle speeches that might go unmentioned in memoirs, letters, formal narrative histories, or official reports can sometimes be found in a newspaper. If only this had been so in antiquity!

BATTLE SPEECHES ARE BEST UNDERSTOOD in the context of the tactical events that prompt their creation, and they are so classified in this book. The science of war, as well as religion, society, and politics, changes over time, but what remains the same from levy to levy, battle to battle, defeat to defeat, and victory to victory are certain broad circumstances of military life. For example, whether one is a Roman citizen, a medieval subject, or an everyman hard-up for adventure, glory, or plunder, the categories of military speech endure. There have always been speeches to enlist recruits, celebrate victories, excuse defeats, surrender armies, or bid farewell. And certain military situations endure too. Whether one thinks of a tribe, squad, platoon, or army corps perched for an invasion or a battle, there has always been an anxious time just beforehand in which soldiers must be steeled for the mission. Likewise, there has always been time after a battle when the outcome must be explained and rationalized. Accordingly, this book will consider battle speeches that are created in connection with the following tactical events:

> Presentation of Items in Recognition of Valor
>   or a Duty Well Done
> Recruiting New Soldiers and Reenlisting Veterans
> Instruction in the Art, Science, and Politics of War
> Pre-Invasion
> Defending against Invasions
> Pre-Battle
> Midst-of-Battle
> Post-Battle
> Assuming Command
> Saying Farewell
> Surrendering
> Final Victory

For example, the speeches featured in the epigraphs can each be placed somewhere on this tactical cycle. Of course, where to place a speech may not always be clear. For example, Colonel Cross's address arguably falls somewhere between a Pre-Battle Speech and a Midst-of-Battle Speech. At the time he spoke, what would soon be known as the Battle of Antietam (or the Battle of Sharpsburg to Confederate historiographers) had been raging for hours. But Second Lieutenant DeWitt is clearly within the Midst-of-Battle category—at the time, not only was the first battle of Pork Chop Hill in its early stages but his unit had been fighting for hours. Napoleon's address is clearly a Pre-Invasion Speech, words to fortify his soldiers' sense of mission by lending historic as well as contemporary importance to what they were about to do.

Predictably, speeches falling into each of these categories share certain features. These are referred to here as "conventions," which one prominent dictionary defines as "a rule, method, or practice, established by rule, custom, agreement or general consent."[9] For example, three conventions that are common to Recruiting Speeches, whether given in antiquity or more recently, are Staging, Family Appeal, and Speechmaker Identity. (Conventions will be capitalized throughout the book to better distinguish them in the narrative.) Staging refers to the visual and sometimes aural background prepared in advance by a recruiter in order to enhance his message. Bands and banners, patriotic posters, smartly uniformed soldiers, a locale of historic or civic importance, free food, and inspiring speeches by dignitaries and religious eminences may all contribute to the figurative stage from which the Recruiting Speech has historically been made. Next is Family Appeal. Throughout history, the ideal recruit has been a young, generally late-adolescent male who in many cases still belongs to a larger household. Recruiting Speeches must not only emphasize things that attract this potential recruit—duty, adventure, glory, or financial reward—but must also offer comfort to his family, especially those whose consent may be necessary or who might influence the recruit's decision to enlist. Finally, there is Speechmaker Identity. The recruiter must have a resume, whether embodied by the uniform he wears, the insignia or medallions he displays, the battle scars he bears, or his combat history or reputation, that will persuade the recruit and his family that the recruiter knows his business and thus also knows how to mitigate the prospects of death, injury, hunger, disease, or exposure; further, that he will take care of his men or represents an entity that will do the same, insofar as *in loco parentis* applies to military situations. Moreover, Speechmaker Identity often goes beyond the perception of competence to reach into social categories—it helps if the recruiter is "like us" in social class, race, politics, or religion. Thus the recruit will be commanded by a leader who is competent but who also shares the same values as the recruit and his family, thus providing even greater comfort.

Each genre of battle speech is characterized by its own conventions, and some of these conventions will cross traditional rhetorical classifications of appeals. As the discussion about Recruiting Speeches suggests, some of these conventions help form the physical background to a speech (Staging) or lend moral authority to the speaker (Speechmaker Identity); other conventions are thematic and characterize the kinds of appeals that are likely to be made, such as Family Appeals. Still other conventions, such as those that typify the Defenders' Speech, may deal with the very tone of the language, as with the Urgency Convention, where the defender must persuade the soldier-audience (or would-be soldier-audience) that the situation is dire and all good persons must rally to the cause—at once. This book essentially asks one question of all battle speeches: What makes the speech work? Classifying speeches by tactical categories and analyzing each category by common conventions provide the analytical tools for the broad survey that *In Words and Deeds* hopes to achieve.

However, something is lost in broad surveys, and this book will prove no exception. First, no claim is made that the conventions assigned to each tactical category of speech are exhaustive; merely that they are typical. Indeed, by referring to them as conventions rather than as hard-and-fast rules, a certain looseness is implied. After all, whether in matters of fashion, art, music, or even history, conventions are made to be broken: the vast number of wars and the speeches they have generated almost guarantees that exceptions to conventions can be found. Nevertheless, the conventions within each tactical category are best imagined as concentric circles that share a common center while leaving outside of themselves considerable room for individuation. With recorded warfare stretching back some five thousand years, the best *In Words and Deeds* can hope to accomplish is to identify these common centers. Likewise, the listing of tactical events also is not exhaustive. For example, limited space precluded consideration of several important tactical events, despite the fact that much source material is available, including speeches that quell mutinies, speeches made at councils of war, and battle sermons.

Certain conventions arguably also apply to every battle speech. For example, the Inspire Confidence Convention is said to characterize Pre-Invasion Speeches. Yet battle speechmakers, who are usually (although not always) commanders, presumably wish to inspire confidence in every speech they make, whether the intention is to attack an enemy or police a campground. Confidence has been singled out as a separate convention for Pre-Invasion and Pre-Battle Speeches because in these categories the stakes—life and death—are enormous. Thus battle speechmakers pay closer attention to confidence when exhorting troops to do something that every gut instinct rebels against—like leaping into the ocean from an amphibious landing craft, then wading in waist-high water carrying a third of one's body weight in a backpack, all the while facing a killing mortar and machine gun fire. Nevertheless, the larger point is that conventions will occasionally blend into more than one category of battle speech. Some degree of imprecision is the bane but also the safe harbor of every would-be classifier.

What Really Was Said or Done?

You will remember that in the hurry and excitement of a charge at a moment when one sees nothing but the enemy, there is no time to note particulars. A man remembers certain phrases or acts, with a blank on each side, just as he does from a dream.

Major Henry L. Abbott, Twentieth Massachusetts Volunteer Infantry, recalling Pickett's Charge at the Battle of Gettysburg[10]

IN CONSIDERING BATTLE SPEECHES, one immediately confronts two questions. First, was a speech made at all? This question has particular importance for antiquity's battle speeches and has been debated from the times of the battles themselves. The issues connected with the existence, not to mention the veracity, of ancient battle speeches are discussed further below. But a second question may be asked of battle speeches from any historical period: assuming that a speech was made, did it occur at the time, in the place, by the speaker, and with the exact words later claimed?

In general, any attempt to answer this question must first surmount two barriers that almost guarantee that claimed battle speeches are not the *ipsissima verba* of what was said; moreover, these barriers also can sometimes obscure the details of the who, when, and where of a battle speech. The first of them is common to the history of any time:

biased sources. Perhaps beginning in the medieval period, the history of war increasingly began to be documented by multiple sources. These have proliferated further to include diaries, letters, official records including midst-of-battle records and after-action reports, newspaper and magazine articles, memoirs, formal narrative histories, documentaries, and raw video and audio feed. It must be remembered that most readers encounter wars, and the battle speeches they generate, only through documents, whether paper, celluloid, or digital. And whether created five minutes or fifty years after the action, these documents are all historical productions and thus carry, virus-like, distortions that can be very contagious to the reader. These distortions result from a compiler's weak memory, social class biases, politics, careerism, outright falsifications, limited access to sources or events, transcription errors, faulty sources, post-facto interpolations, and the like. Thus, a soldier who later records even his own battle speech might be inclined to inflate, edit, or forget what he actually said; moreover, others who heard the speech are inclined toward the same biases, as well as toward conflation—more than one battle speech by more than one speaker might have been made in a relatively short time, and, like the "certain phrases and acts with a blank on each side" that Henry Abbott remembered about remembrance during combat, this tends to jumble chronologies and mix and mismatch words and deeds with speakers and actors. The whole thing relies on malleable and suggestible human memory, the chief means by which immediate experience is converted into memory-text. And aside from intentional falsifications, it is usually human memory and a consciousness impaired by combat stress that presents problems with accurate recall.

The environments in which battle speeches take place must therefore be considered, and the most extreme of these is combat. The din, fear, exhilaration, and chaos of a battle create distortions that act to foreshorten memory, leaving random recollections with much else blurred. A limited sense of topography further corrupts memory—there are few global perspectives for combatants as their worlds shrink to the few yards of ground they happen to occupy or traverse. Who said or did what, and when, and to whom, can become rather interpretive, if it is remembered at all. And fatigue further distorts recollection. The

U.S. Army lists seven consequences from the "prolonged demands of combat" that include "Determinations and calculations become inaccurate," "Reports become faulty," and "Orders are misunderstood/forgotten." Simply put, the combat experience corrupts memory text. Moreover, less studied is how the experience of *post*-combat corrupts combat's memory-text. After-action discussions with comrades and other participants, official interpretations, gradually remembered (and competing memories sometimes gradually repressed or forgotten) can all innocently seep into a soldier's memory-text to produce recollections that transform events from completely individual memories into a consensus account. And beyond these matters, there is an additional complication basic to historians and juries alike: multiple sources can mean conflicting memories, and any two combatants may, in good faith and with no conscious bias, recall the same event quite differently.[11]

To illustrate how distortion can enter memory, consider Colonel Cross's speech given at Antietam: *not* the speech contained in the previous epigraph here, which was a postwar remembrance of subaltern and witness Thomas L. Livermore, but the same speech that Cross recorded in his journal, probably written within a few days of the battle:

> Officers and soldiers, the enemy are in front and the Potomac river is in their rear. We must conquer this day or we are disgraced and ruined. I expect that each one will do his duty like a soldier and a brave man. Let no man leave the ranks on any pretense. If I fall leave me until the battle is won. Stand firm and fire low. Shoulder arms! Forward march.[12]

A comparison of the two Cross speeches reveals many differences, only one of which will be noted here: in his own version of the speech, Cross omits his death threats against his men. Readers are therefore entitled to ask if such a threat was ever made. Of course, no certain answer is possible—the events are long past living memory. However, Livermore's version dates from sometime between 1865 and 1867, two to four years (and many intervening battles—Livermore served throughout the war) after the event. Thus the argument for Cross's own version is very strong—but even here, that version may not be conclusive. There could have been good reasons why Cross did not record (or even precisely remember) "exactly" what he said. First, combat experience was just as likely to degrade his recollection as that of any other witness (and Cross had just sustained a head wound).

Second, Cross's threat to kill his own men, at least as remembered by Livermore, might have been something that, given the successful outcome of his attack (the "Bloody Lane" was successfully captured), Cross felt should go unmentioned. Further complicating matters is that there is good evidence that after the war, Livermore had carefully read Cross's journal but chose to make no changes in his own account. And there is a good chance that neither Livermore's nor Cross's versions are the *ipsissima verba*. Perhaps it was some mix of the two. Regardless, with the exception of speeches that are simultaneously and electronically recorded at the moment of their creation, readers must understand that the battle speeches included in most histories are usually, at best, *approximations* and not certitudes.[13]

With reference to the speeches in this history, some were delivered before the war began, others while it was going on; some I heard myself, others I got from various quarters; it was in all cases difficult to carry them word for word in one's memory, so my habit has been to make the speakers say what was in my opinion demanded of them by the various occasions, of course adhering as closely as possible to the general sense of what they really said.

Thucydides, *The Peloponnesian War*, 1.22.1

Now the special function of history, particularly in relation to speeches, is first of all to discover the words actually used, whatever they were, and next to establish the reason why a particular action or argument failed or succeeded. . . . [But] a writer who passes over in silence the speeches which were actually made and causes of what actually happened and introduces fictitious rhetorical exercises and discursive speeches in their place destroys the peculiar virtue of history.

Polybius, *The Rise of the Roman Empire*, 12.25b

The battle exhortation in ancient historiography is a literary composition and not the historian's report of a speech, which had actually been made. And that was well known in the ancient world.

Professor Mogens Herman Hansen, "The Battle Exhortation in Ancient Historiography: Fact or Fiction?" 1993[14]

BECAUSE THIS BOOK USES EXAMPLES of many battle speeches from antiquity, it is necessary to briefly address the question raised earlier: were the battle speeches that are portrayed in the ancient histories really spoken at all? This question is of intrinsic interest to classicists but is also important to any general consideration of battle speeches. It is more than just a question of pedigree—these speeches were an important means of transmitting a distinctly Western military tradition across the millennia. "The cult of battle, like much else in the classical military tradition, had been passed down chiefly by the classical historians, primarily through the examples of the great commanders," Doyne Dawson has observed. "All educated Europeans knew that Alexander and Caesar had won their reputations by seeking out the enemy, bringing him to battle, and annihilating him." And these "examples of the great commanders" are in part the sum of how classical historians drew their characters, infused them with a particular brand of martial spirit, and had them speak in certain ways about tactics, strategy, the enemy, courage, honor, glory, and war. Thus the ancient battle speeches have almost certainly played an important role in influencing not just later battle speeches but, as Dawson observes, the philosophy of (Western) warfare itself. (Ancient battle-speech appeals are briefly compared with those of modernity in the next section.)

In one sense, accepting Dawson's argument about what "all educated Europeans [and, much later, Americans] knew" renders existential questions or issues of veracity concerning ancient battle speeches almost irrelevant. What really matters over the centuries is not whether Xenophon, Alexander, or Caesar actually uttered the words claimed for them but that generations of subsequent commanders believed, or acted as if they believed, that they did; thus, later students of war studied their words and deeds for insights on achieving victories and avoiding defeats. Nevertheless, readers should be aware that this issue is a contentious one, about which most classicists have an opinion.[15]

This argument falls well outside the scope of this book. However, there are aspects of this debate that do have relevance to later battle speeches. The issue for *In Words and Deeds* becomes not only how particular battlefield tactics influenced the length and content of battle speeches but also whether or not such tactics inherently *required* such speeches. And this study largely concludes that the existence of battle speeches can be practically inferred from tactics by the demands these placed on battle speechmakers and their soldier-audiences.

The larger debate still merits a brief description. It centers mostly on the degree to which ancient battle speeches were embellished or simply invented *ex nihilo* by historians as exercises in rhetoric, meant to dazzle ancient audiences whose acquaintance with such histories usually came from hearing them read aloud rather than reading them silently. Two quotations in the epigraph more or less represent the poles of this larger argument. First comes the famous passage of Thucydides, who claims that, subject to certain limitations ("it was in all cases difficult to carry [the speeches] word for word in one's memory"), the speeches (both battle and non-battle) are, if not the *ipsissima verba* of what was said, at least rendered "as closely as possible to the general sense of what [the speaker] really said." Here Thucydides acknowledges the potential for invention but couched it in terms that link even his acknowledged inventions to "what they really said." Perhaps Thucydides' very acknowledgment strongly suggests, as classicist Mogens Herman Hansen contends, that ancient audiences were already wary of some historians' speeches, and for good reason: in a pre-electronic age, no one historian could reliably remember and accurately reproduce word-for-word all of the speeches given in the course of the twenty-seven-year-long Peloponnesian War. And that Thucydides' methodology survives to the present day is proved by simply switching on a television: his disclosures are eerily similar to those of today's docudramas, which usually present disclaimers stating that the film is "based on" real events or that it contains fictionalized scenes, dialogue, or composite characters. In most cases, modern audiences seem to understand that the "speeches" (or dialogue) contained in such docudramas do not reflect the *ipsissima verba* but instead the screenwriters' attempt, as Thucydides declared, "to make the speakers say what was . . . demanded of them by the various occasions, of course adhering as closely as possible to the general sense of what they really said."[16]

An opposing methodology (in Polybius's opinion) is that of the historian Timaeus of Tauromenion. Polybius declares that Timaeus ignored "the speeches which were actually made" in favor of his own creations, "fictitious rhetorical exercises and discursive speeches" whose use "destroys the peculiar virtue of history." In other words, on the subject of speeches Timaeus is not a genuine historian but rather a fourth-century BCE docudrama producer (only without the disclaimers). And perhaps not surprisingly, Thucydides' own methodology and Polybius's views of Timaeus's have their twentieth-century counterparts, most recently in the persons of classicists Hansen and W. Kendrick Pritchett. As quoted above, Hansen argues that ancient battle speeches were not "the historian's report" of a real speech but rather a literary exercise, a form of entertainment expected by antiquity's audiences. Hansen's view is opposed vigorously, and in my view persuasively, by Pritchett. Adducing a variety of ancient testimonials (and other evidence), Pritchett, while conceding that "ancient historians did not report the *ipsissima verba* of speeches nor necessarily their totality," argues in effect that a Thucydides-type methodology did at least yield a sense of what was said that was, in turn, properly reported by many ancient historians.[17]

But as was previously noted, one aspect of this discussion is especially relevant to the battle speeches of any period: the extent to which particular battlefield tactics influenced (or even created) the need for certain types of battle speeches. It requires little imagination to extend the insights of Dawson, Pritchett, and Victor Davis Hanson (see below) to conclude that tactics determined not only who gave the battle speech but also its length, style, and contents—all of which took shape because of the tactics themselves. Victor Davis Hansen has observed in *The Western Way of War* that the center of battlefield morale and tactical guidance for Greek *hoplites* was embodied in one individual: their commander, the *strategos*. The tactical circumstances of ancient warfare (variations of which persisted for many centuries afterward) frequently had opposing armies facing one another for long periods of time before making contact. Historian Adrian Goldsworthy notes that lengthy pre-battle delays were typical during Julius Caesar's time and resulted in "generals attempt[ing] to build up their men's morale before risking an actual clash with the enemy." Pre-battle apprehension, with all of its physiological consequences, must have soared during these times. Such a tactical environment probably required (and offered the opportunity for) long and perhaps numerous speeches by commanders or their subalterns.

And unlike what is sometimes depicted in films, battle itself did not usually consist of, in the words of Goldsworthy, "a frenzied mass of individual combats, each one ending in death for one of the participants, with the two armies inter-penetrating each other and no trace of units remaining." Instead, Goldsworthy continues, "Real combat appears to have been much more tentative, and occurred in short bursts, after which the two lines separated and, standing a short distance apart, hurled abuse or missiles at each other until one side had built up enough enthusiasm to close once more." Like its Pre-Battle cousin, this kind of Midst-of-Battle environment probably required a commander to continuously exhort by word and deed. Consider Julius Caesar's actions before and during one such battle against the Gauls. First, he delivered a Pre-Battle Speech to his favorite legion, the tenth, "urging them to live up to their traditions of bravery, to keep their nerve, and to meet the enemy's attack boldly." But when the battle unfolded and disaster threatened, Caesar's words (to which he now added deeds) continued: "Caesar snatched a shield from a soldier in the rear (he had not his own shield with him), made his way into the front line, addressed each centurion by name, and shouted encouragement to the rest of the troops, ordering them to push forward and open out their ranks, so that they could use their swords more easily. His coming gave them fresh heart and hope; each man wanted to do his best under the eyes of his commander-in-chief, however desperate their peril, and the enemy's assault was slowed down a little." The example of Caesar is used not only because he was an ancient general but also because he was his own historian. His commentaries appeared during his lifetime, when the living witnesses to these events probably numbered in the thousands. As Pritchett has observed of other classical historians, "It must never be overlooked that Thucydides, Xenophon, and Polybius were military historians writing contemporary history, and their original audiences must have known whether they were lying."[18]

Of course, ancient battle speeches would probably have been subject to the same corruptions of participants' memory-text as their modern counterparts; even if multiple surviving contemporary sources for Alexander the Great or Hannibal existed, it is safe to say that any claimed speeches would raise the same questions as that of Colonel Cross's at Antietam. Once again, whether ancient or modern, battle speeches will always be mere *approximations* of what was said or done. The larger point is that, as even Hansen conceded, "There can be little doubt that a general usually said *something* to his men before a battle."[19] That this was so was a simple function of the pressing tactical necessities connected with morale and instruction, not some later historian's desire to insert inspiriting noise where there had been only silence. Many, if not most, ancient battle speeches were probably buffed and lengthened (although given the timeless proclivity of some veterans to do the same, perhaps historians should not bear all of the responsibility here). But the larger point remains that ancient battle speakers had the time, motive, and opportunity to make these speeches just like their modern counterparts. Because military history has always been the chief study of soldiers, at some point the ancient speeches became the gold standard for military speechifying—with an assist from tactics that in one form or another have continued to vindicate the need to talk to soldiers before, during, and after a battle.

Durable Appeals

We are going to Iraq to liberate and not to conquer. . . . We are entering Iraq to free a people—and the only flag that will be flown in that ancient land will be their own. Show respect for them.

The enemy knows this moment is coming too. Some have resolved to fight and others wish to survive. Be sure to distinguish between them. . . . [As for those who resist] I expect you to rock their world. Wipe them out if that is what they choose. But if you are ferocious in battle, remember to be magnanimous in victory.

Iraq is steeped in history; it is the site of the Garden of Eden, of the Great Flood and the birthplace of Abraham. Tread lightly there. . . .

Don't treat them as refugees in their own country.

The enemy should be in no doubt that we are his Nemesis and we are bringing about his rightful destruction. There are many regional commanders who have stains on their souls and they are stoking the fires of hell for Saddam. He and his forces will be destroyed for what they have done to their people. As they die, they will know that it is their deeds that have brought them to this place. Show them no pity. It is a big step to take another human life. It is not to be done lightly. I know of men who have taken life needlessly in other conflicts. I can assure you that they live with the mark of Cain upon them.

If someone surrenders to you, remember that they have that right in international law. . . . Remember, however, that if you harm your regiment or its history by over-enthusiasm in killing, or cowardice, know that it is your family who will suffer. You will be shunned unless your conduct is of the highest order, for your deeds will follow you down through history. We will bring shame on neither our uniforms nor our nation. . . .

Our business is now north. Good luck.

Excerpts from Lieutenant Colonel Tim Collins's Pre-Battle Speech, spoken to the men of the First Battalion, Royal Irish Regiment, March 19, 2003[20]

As a final matter, it is always important for readers to remember that the battle speeches used in this book are, like all historical artifacts, very much pinned to their moments of creation. *In Words and Deeds* has drawn speeches from the Hebrew Bible through the current Iraq War and grouped them along a single, generic tactical cycle. By plucking battle speeches from their historical context I risk some ahistoricity. It is easy enough to understand that Napoleon's world was a very different place than Eisenhower's, and both were many worlds apart from that of Alexander the Great. But for battle speeches, historical context involves much more than noting differences in weapons and tactics. The rhetorical appeals used in battle speeches are also artifacts, products of specific moments and cultures; thus, while we note historical continuities in speeches, we must also pay careful attention to historical discontinuities—ultimately, we must be sure to retain each speech in its own era. And in noting what has not changed (which is this book's focus), readers may find preserved some ancient traditions of Western warfare, as well as elements of a common humanity even in that most inhumane business of war. To illustrate the kinds of continuities and discontinuities that both join and separate battle speeches from different periods, five categories of rhetorical appeals from antiquity will be briefly compared with those in a recent battle speech: depiction of the enemy, justification for the war, the use of shame, the role of plunder, and religion.

In 1902, Theodore C. Burgess wrote a dissertation titled "Epideictic Literature" that broadly surveyed ancient speeches belonging to that genre that also included battle speeches. From the latter he derived twelve types of battle speech appeals (*topoi*). These were drawn from such historians as Xenophon, Arrian, Caesar, Thucydides, Josephus, Polybius, and Appian; the speeches were "voiced" by such commanders as Julius Caesar, Alexander the Great, Xenophon, Hannibal, Augustus, Scipio Africanus, Fabius, Cyrus, Marc Antony, and Severus. Burgess's list of appeals is as follows (paraphrased in parts):

1. Remember your glorious ancestry, their great deeds, their public spirit, that they have prevailed over this enemy before, and so forth;
2. With such ancestry, do not disgrace your heritage;
3. A comparison of our forces with those of the enemy;
4. In war, it is valor, not mere numbers, that prevails;
5. Great prizes await the victors;
6. The auspices are favorable, the gods are our allies;
7. Death in battle is glorious;
8. Defeat equals disgrace;
9. We have conquered this enemy before;
10. The wrongs suffered from this enemy; the war is just;
11. Patriotism;
12. Our commander is superior to that of the enemy.[21]

Over two millennia separate Burgess's battle speeches from Lieutenant Colonel Tim Collins's Pre-Invasion Speech in the epigraph. At the outset, it should be conceded that comparing the thematic continuities or discontinuities in Burgess's list of appeals with those of Collins is not entirely fair—it places side by side the many speeches

surveyed by Burgess with only one speech given by Collins. Nevertheless, the colonel's speech reveals enough continuities and discontinuities with Burgess's themes to merit a brief comparison.

One theme that survives somewhat intact is Burgess's appeal number 10: "The wrongs suffered from this enemy; the war is just." Colonel Collins certainly believes that the enemy has committed many
grievous wrongs. He speaks of the enemy's "rightful destruction," that
Saddam's subalterns "have stains on their souls" and are "stoking the
fires of hell for Saddam." And in fact the war's justice cannot be separated from the enemy's evil: "We are going to liberate Iraq and not to
conquer," Collins first declares. "We are entering Iraq to free a people." And later he adds: "[Saddam] and his forces will be destroyed for
what they have done to their people. As they die they will know that it
is their deeds that have brought them to this place." What deeds does
Collins refer to? Although he mentions that Saddam has mistreated his
own people and later still predicts that he will probably use weapons
of mass destruction against Coalition forces, Collins does not otherwise provide a bill of particulars. Here one can assume that the colonel had no need to specify particulars—his soldier-audience probably
had an enthymematic understanding of Saddam's crimes, resulting
from at least thirteen years of unfavorable news stories between Iraq's
1990 invasion of Kuwait and the very hour Collins spoke.

Although the enemy has committed wrongs and the war is just, an
important historical discontinuity exists here. The "wrongs suffered
from the enemy" that are captioned by Burgess usually meant wrongs
suffered directly by the country, city-state, or tribe sponsoring the soldier-audience. But in Collins's time, Saddam's wrongs, while tragically
personal to his victims, are injurious to Collins's Coalition sponsors
only in the abstract (Kuwait, a tacit participant, excepted)—Saddam
has not invaded, raided, or pillaged the four Coalition members—
Great Britain, the United States, Poland, and Australia—who composed the invasion force; rather the official thing that was wronged is
a relatively recent construction called the UN resolutions, which in
turn are the products of another only slightly older abstraction—the
United Nations itself. (And both represent the ultimate abstraction:
international law.) And the Coalition, itself a very recent invention,

was not formed to avenge its individual members but to enforce compliance with the other abstractions. That such things could even exist, let alone be good or evil, would have been difficult for Burgess's commanders to conceive.

Consider Burgess's appeal number 2: "With such ancestry, do not disgrace your heritage." By heritage, ancient commanders probably meant to include disgracing one's family group, tribe, city-state, or, at best, nation. Beginning with family disgrace, several of these things are also important to Collins, and he uses them to discourage pusillanimous or extra-legal behavior. "Remember, however, that if you harm your regiment or its history by over-enthusiasm in killing, or cowardice, know that it is your family who will suffer," he warns. "You will be shunned unless your conduct is of the highest order, for your deeds will follow you down through history. We will bring shame on neither our uniforms nor our nation." There is much here that would likely have resonated with Burgess's commanders, who usually meant cowardice on the battlefield when they spoke of disgrace. Although Burgess does not mention shaming the unit ("uniforms") or the state ("our nation"), the Romans in particular were fastidious in demanding that soldiers uphold the honor of the legions to which they belonged as well as the honor of the state. Nevertheless, it is important to note the discontinuity: for Burgess's commanders, the prospect of disgrace was used as a disincentive for battlefield cowardice. But for Collins, the possibility of cowardice actually pales beside his real concern—that his soldiers risk shame if they disrespect Iraqi civilians and their property ("Show respect for them. . . . Tread lightly there"), engage in jingoistic behavior ("and the only flag that will be flown in that ancient land will be their own"), kill unnecessarily, or violate international law governing the treatment of surrendered soldiers. While most of Burgess's commanders could (and sometimes did) show clemency in dealing with adversaries, few of the uses to which Collins sought to apply shame would have resonated in Caesar's time.

Along similar lines, one can see the modern irrelevance of Burgess's appeal number 5: "The most magnificent prizes await the victors." Today, plunder, pillage, and rapine are, like shooting prisoners of war, illegal; taking souvenirs and trophies has been tightly regulated almost to the vanishing point; and soldiers are certainly not paid bounties based on the number of cities captured, enemies killed, or tanks destroyed. By contrast, during the Greco-Roman period (and long afterward), plunder was a routine part of compensation unless specifically prohibited by a commander.[22]

Burgess's appeal number 6—"The auspices are favorable, the gods are our allies"—at first appears to have no counterpart in Collins's battle speech. After all, the words "God" or "gods" appear nowhere in his exhortation, and there is certainly no evidence that before speaking, Collins had a service chaplain slaughter a goat in order to scrutinize its entrails for clues about the invasion's outcome. But what the colonel did do before his speech was take a few moments alone in his tent to pray—which is perhaps one reason why Collins's words are suffused with religiosity, although it is submerged in ways that are consistent with modern, officially secular Western armies. In his brief, 643-word speech, Collins makes no fewer than four direct references to the Hebrew Bible—"Garden of Eden . . . Great Flood and the birthplace of Abraham . . . mark of Cain"—as well as one taken from Greek mythology ("we are his Nemesis"). On a subtler level, these direct references are framed in language with powerful religious overtones: "We are bringing about his *rightful destruction* . . . *stains* on their *souls* . . . *stoking* the *fires of hell* for Saddam . . . will be *destroyed for what they have done* . . . As *they die they will know*" [emphasis added]. (It would have taken only Cotton Mather's four-word conclusion about a "War of the Lord" for Collins's speech to have become a full-blown religious Pre-Invasion exhortation.)[23]

To fully appreciate Colonel Collins's situation, it must be remembered that his battalion was itself a mini-coalition, consisting of "Paddies . . . Micks from England . . . Canadians, Australians, Nepalese, South Africans, Zimbabweans, Fijians . . . [and] U.S. Marines [including] a handful of Mexicans." Thus, not only was his army officially secular, it is likely that this particular soldier-audience worshiped a variety of gods as well as no god at all. Thus, as will be discussed at greater length in the next chapter on the use of religious history *in* battle speeches, Collins needed to submerge or carefully code expressions of religiosity in his Pre-Invasion Speech. While a particular vision of God or ritual could not be mentioned, a generalized biblical literacy was fair game to accomplish one or more of the three usually interconnected reasons why battle speeches favor the invocation of a deity: sanctification, justification, or reassurance. And here, as with other themes used in battle speeches, the use of implication, inference, and enthymeme allows the battle speechmaker to say what he must (but not always explicitly) with the fewest possible words.[24]

1

THE HISTORY IN BATTLE SPEECHES

Soldiers, you have done all that I expected! You have balanced numbers by courage. You have gloriously marked the difference that lies between the soldiers of Caesar and the armed hordes of Xerxes. In a few days we have triumphed in three pitched battles, at Thann, at Abensberg and at Ratisbon. Before another month has elapsed, we shall be in Vienna.

Napoleon, Proclamation to his troops, April 24, 1809

Historical fact, which is so often invoked, to which everyone so readily appeals, is often a mere word: it cannot be ascertained when events actually occur, in the heat of contrary passions; and if, later on, there is a consensus, this is only because there is no one left to contradict. But if this is so, what is this historical truth in nearly every case? An agreed-upon fiction, as has been most ingeniously said.

Napoleon, conversation reported by Emmanuel,
Comte de Las Cases, November 20, 1816[1]

THE ABOVE POST-BATTLE SPEECH by Napoleon was delivered after he captured the town of Ratisbon from the Austrians. It was vintage Bonaparte bombast, excessive in its praise and immodest in its claims. First, he flatters his soldier-audience as he offers a one-line history of the battle: "You have balanced numbers by courage." But then he shifts to another type of historical narrative: "You have gloriously marked the difference that lies between the soldiers of Caesar and the armed hordes of Xerxes." Seven years later, during his final exile on St. Helena, Napoleon reportedly uttered his famous observation that anticipated by almost two centuries the post-modernist attack on so-called objective history. "Historical truth in nearly every case," Napoleon observed, is "an agreed-upon fiction."

If he was referring to his own battle speeches, Napoleon spoke wisely. Consider the Post-Battle Speech above. What were the real differences between the "soldiers" of Caesar and the "armed hordes" of Xerxes? To begin with, about four centuries' worth of changes in tactics, military cultures, and societies, not to mention that breakdowns in discipline occasionally rendered Caesar's soldiers "armed hordes" as well (if a lack of organization is what Napoleon meant by that phrase), and Xerxes' "armed hordes" happened to include the legendary Immortals.[2] All this is true, and Napoleon's comparison is specious in the extreme. Yet this is all entirely beside the point. What mattered was that Napoleon assumed, probably correctly, that his troops would instantly recognize these historical figures, thus making his point concisely and effectively. And here what especially mattered was that the names "Caesar" and "Xerxes" operated as historical icons—metonyms, really—where the former stood for "successful Roman general leading a successful army" and the latter for "unsuccessful Persian general leading an unsuccessful army." One signified Western, familiar, competent, and victorious, the other Oriental, strange, undisciplined, and defeated. That Caesar's battle reports might be self-aggrandizing or that the debate about Herodotus's veracity dates to antiquity is also beside the point. This is the history *in* battle speeches, a history whose chief requirements are that it be usable when uttered and that it be instantly intelligible to the soldier-audience. Of *course* such history is "an agreed-upon fiction"—except when it is not.

Battle speeches usually tell a story, either through a narrative or by using iconic historical persons, places, things, and events. Napoleon's speech above contains two important points applicable to the history in most battle speeches. First, battle speeches are not history lectures; they are not meant to enlighten audiences, ascertain truth, or compare viewpoints. Rather, history is applied to reaffirm what the soldier-audience already believes or would like to believe about themselves, their situation, or their enemy. History is also used to reinforce standards of conduct in which soldiers have already been trained or by which they are expected to abide because of their membership in a certain military unit, religious faith, social group, or political entity. Finally, the past is used to exhort, by exploiting thoughts and emotions closely associated with the iconic histories of certain relevant persons, places, things, and events. The battle speechmaker rarely educates; instead, he organizes and presents historical meanings already familiar to his soldier-audience but amenable to being applied in a new way.

History in battle speeches falls into four very broad categories that are the subject of this chapter. The first category is perhaps the most common: the Unit Historical Narrative. This is the history of some military unit, of any size or type. For example, Napoleon's Post-Battle Speech above uses a Unit Historical Narrative of two such units — Caesar's legions and Xerxes' army — to make its point about a third unit: the Grande Armée.

The second category is the Religious Historical Narrative, a particular favorite of battle speechmakers deeply influenced by Judeo-Christian faiths, which understand human history as being bracketed by seminal events that have already occurred in time (creation and/or revelation) and will occur in time — the messianic period. Between these events God manifests His will in history, usually according to His law, which is set forth in the sacred texts. Powerfully dramatic events like war and emotionally charged moments such as the period just before invasions and battles are times when God's will may usefully appear with special prominence.

The third category is the Social Historical Narrative. Here the battle speechmaker looks to his soldier-audience (or the enemy) and adduces common features of tribal loyalty, social class, family, race, or ethnicity; he then uses or invents a history of these common elements to exhort his audience or diminish the enemy. For example, in these battle speeches races, tribes, ethnicities, and cultures are said to have (or lack) warrior traits; to be naturally faithful (or perfidious); to be naturally inclined to favor certain causes and oppose others. The proof always lies in the battle speechmaker's social history of these groups.

Finally, there is the Political Historical Narrative. Here the history of some political entity under whose authority the soldier-audience (or the enemy) serves is used to inspire loyalty or aggression.

One of the most important features common to all four types of historical narrative is how they are sometimes used to establish (or, when discussing enemies, to anticipate) certain types of behaviors in combat. Thus, a certain military unit's tradition, an article of religious faith, a social trait, or a government's law may require soldiers to behave with special humanity or great violence; likewise, these same factors can be used to explain an enemy's barbarity or cowardice. Thus do historical narratives build confidence, promise victory, anticipate behaviors, and justify the proposed actions.

Unit Historical Narratives

Sergeant Major of the Marine Corps, Carlton W. Kent,[3] told troops on a Sunday visit . . . that the coming battle of Fallujah would be no different than the historic fights at Inchon, in Korea, the flag-raising victory at Iwo Jima, or the bloody assault to remove the North Vietnamese troops who had occupied the ancient citadel of Hue during the 1968 Tet Offensive. Kent went on to say, "You're all in the process of making history. This is another Hue City in the making. I have no doubt, if we do get the word, that each and every one of you is going to do what you have always done—kick some butt." The Marines responded with "Oohra."

> Pre-Battle Speech to the First Battalion, Eighth Marines,
> quoted in Gary Livingston's *Fallujah, With Honor*

The coming offensive in the Guadalcanal area marks the first offensive of the war against the enemy, involving ground forces of the United States. The marines have been selected to initiate this action, which will prove to be the forerunner of successive offensive actions that will end in ultimate victory for our cause. Our country expects nothing but victory from us and it shall have just that. The word failure shall not even be considered as being in our vocabulary.

We have worked hard and trained faithfully for this action and I have every confidence in our ability and desire to force our will upon the enemy. We are meeting a tough and wily opponent but he is not sufficiently tough or wily to overcome us because We Are Marines.

*Our commanding general and staff are counting upon us and will
give us whole-hearted support and assistance. Our contemporaries of
the other Task Organizations are red-blooded marines like ourselves
and are ably led. They too will be there at the final downfall of the
enemy.*

*Each of us has his assigned task. Let each vow to perform it to the
utmost of his ability, with added effort for good measure.*

Good luck and God bless you and to hell with the Japs.

Colonel LeRoy P. Hunt to the Fifth Marine Regiment,
four days before landing at Guadalcanal[4]

T HE "UNIT" OF UNIT HISTORICAL NARRATIVES may be anything—a branch of service, an army, a ship, a battalion, a regiment, a company, or a squad. The Unit Historical Narrative may be
contextualized by a recent event; more commonly, however, an existing unit history will be applied to a current situation or the current situation will be reshaped to fit an existing history. Like most
historical narratives in battle speeches, some Unit Historical Narratives are often constructed from specific historical references, such
as the names of things. Sergeant Major Kent's brief speech from the
epigraphs is an example of how one such unit history—that of the
United States Marine Corps—is derived from the names of battles.
Here Kent uses three historical references, all twentieth-century battles in which marines had fought: Iwo Jima, Inchon, and Hue City. He
strings these names like so many bright lights on a wire in order to illumine a particular narrative about the past: marines always win the
battles they fight, and thus they will also win the battle of Fallujah.
Kent's evidence for this resides in the very names of Iwo Jima, Inchon,
and Hue City: by aggregating them he hopes to create a sense of historical momentum, suggesting that what has been true in the past will
remain true in the future. When Kent says "You're all in the process
of making history," he is doing more than just flattering his soldier-
audience. He wants these young marines to transfer all of the positive emotions associated with the historical victories to the upcoming
battle for Fallujah. In their minds Fallujah must also become a bright
light on a wire to be held up to the gaze of future marines.

The mechanics by which this speech operates is also important because it represents a recurring structural feature of Unit Historical Narratives in battle speeches. Kent is using the names of Iwo Jima, Inchon, and Hue as metonyms: the place (an island and two cities) for events (battles) and outcomes (victories).[5] He does not waste valuable time explaining anything about the history, tactics, or weaponry of these battles. Mentioning their names is sufficient for his purpose, because his soldier-audience will supply the "larger" meanings from their own inventory of knowledge. What were those larger meanings? Iwo Jima probably represented something like "marine victory followed by weeks of bloody fighting against an entrenched, determined enemy"; Inchon may have meant "marines make risky but successful surprise landing followed by bloody fighting for possession of Seoul"; Hue may have meant "marines win last battle of Tet Offensive following weeks of bloody street fighting." But whatever the precise meanings the soldier-audience brought to these battles, the names of the battles themselves served as the opening premises of an appeal.

Where did the soldier-audience derive the associations that Kent was able to rely on? Some U.S. Marine Corps history is taught during basic training; other soldiers may have supplemented their knowledge from selections on the Marine Commandant's Reading List, which features books about all three battles. But all soldiers probably had some familiarity with these battles through popular culture, including television and feature films. Iwo Jima is the easy case. There is the iconic image of the flag raising, featured on two postage stamps (issued in 1945 and 1995); a classic war film starring John Wayne, *The Sands of Iwo Jima* (1949); the U.S. Marine Corps Memorial in Arlington, Virginia; and countless voice-over documentaries featured on various non-fiction cable channels. (Although obviously not relevant to Kent's speech, cinematic treatment of the Battle of Iwo Jima continues, most recently by director Clint Eastwood in *Flags of Our Fathers* (2006), told from the American perspective, and *Letters from Iwo Jima* (2006), as that battle was experienced by the island's Japanese defenders.) Inchon has also been made into a feature film (*Inchon*, 1981) and is the subject of numerous books and documentaries. But for the young men in Kent's audience, the battle that probably summoned the most associations may have been Hue. It was a subject of Stanley Kubrick's film *Full Metal Jacket* (1987), whose haunting, almost surreal images of urban warfare have probably received more mention in Iraq War memoirs than any other war film. However they were derived, these historical understandings of the names of things are what made possible Sergeant Major Kent's speech. And according to the author who included this speech in his history of the battle, it was a success.[6]

Colonel Leroy P. Hunt's Pre-Invasion Speech quoted in the epigraph is also a historical narrative, but one that depends on a more complex understanding of a name. Here it is not the unit's connection with a specific battle but the history of the unit itself: the U.S. Marine Corps. And the understanding that Hunt wants his soldier-audience to derive from his words includes not only reminders of certain traditions and history associated with the corps but also how his marines will be expected to behave in the upcoming battle.

On the afternoon of August 3, 1942, Colonel Hunt, commanding the Fifth Marine Regiment, mimeographed a proclamation for his men aboard a transport ship "somewhere in the Pacific." Four days later this unit landed on Guadalcanal. Hunt's speech contains a key phrase of three words—"We Are Marines"—and it draws its power from the single word "Marines." In fact, this word appears in Hunt's speech three times, always accompanied by other words that imply specific historical "facts" about marines, facts that Colonel Hunt needs his men to remember—not learn, as such, because it is almost certain that his men already knew them. Indeed, some men probably knew these facts before they enlisted—at this point in World War II the marines were only accepting volunteers, and the leatherneck's reputation for tough training and hard service had long been established in the public mind. What was the history of the U.S. Marine Corps that Colonel Hunt wanted his men to remember?

First, he wanted his men to recall that historically the marines have the reputation of being the first to attack America's enemies. He mentions the "coming offensive," which marks "the first offensive," and he continues with "marines have been selected to initiate" this battle, a potential template or "forerunner of successive offensive actions."

Here Colonel Hunt, intentionally or otherwise, insinuates into his speech an important idea also found in the Marine Corps Hymn: "First to fight for right and freedom." Although the words of the hymn were officially adopted in 1929, they had been around unofficially since the mid-nineteenth century. This matters, because the Marine Corps Hymn is itself a historical paean, invoking as it does a select series of historical events: the Mexican War (Halls of Montezuma), the action against the Barbary pirates (Shores of Tripoli), and whatever the "snow of far off northern lands" and "sunny tropic scenes" might have meant to young men in 1942. (The U.S. Marine Corps interventions of the earlier part of the twentieth century, including the Philippines, the Boxer Rebellion, Haiti, Nicaragua, and France, were well within the lifetimes of some members of Hunt's audience.) The hymn, incidentally, takes "first" to an unusual extreme: "If the Army and the Navy/Ever look on Heaven's scenes," the last line of the last stanza declares, "They will find the streets are guarded/By United States Marines." Even in the afterlife, the marines will precede their competitor services. (Of course, why the next world will require marine guards is less clear.)[7]

Colonel Hunt is probably not using the Marine Corps Hymn as the model for his speech. But the hymn arises from the same historical narrative and thus shares many similarities. The first similarity—marines are "first"—implies another one. Being "first" has certain historical obligations, notably the duty to be victorious. "Our country expects nothing but victory from us and it shall have just that," Colonel Hunt declared. "The word failure shall not even be considered as being in our vocabulary." And it is not just "our country" that expects this. "Our commanding general and staff are counting upon us and will give us whole-hearted support and assistance," he states. Moreover, Hunt makes clear that his men have a right to expect the same of other marines. "Our contemporaries of the other Task Organizations are red-blooded marines like ourselves and are ably led. They too will be there at the final downfall of the enemy."

What history is being invoked in the claim that "our country expects nothing but victory" from us? First, in urging that the "word failure shall not even be considered as being in our vocabulary," Hunt alludes to an old idea that haunts many pursuits outside of war as well—that merely contemplating failure is the first step toward actually failing. But for marines, this idea of not failing, or always being victorious, is a historical trope of considerable importance. The enthymematic U.S. Marine Corps motto, *Semper Fidelis,* or "Always Faithful," is one expression of this historical reliability. (Always faithful allows the listener or reader to add her own answer: Always faithful to what? The country? The marines? Each other?) In the section titled "What the U.S. Marine Corps Stands For," *The Marine Officers' Guide* identifies thirteen traits included in the word "marine," and many of these are sourced to a specific historical narrative: "The qualities that the Marine Corps stands for might seem old-fashioned," the *Guide*'s author writes. "Nevertheless, these attributes have shaped the Corps since 1775, from Princeton to Belleau Wood, from Trenton to Chosin Reservoir to Khe Sanh." It turns out that "what our country expects" is specially linked with the absence of "failure" from a marine's vocabulary; conjoined, these notions have a special resonance for marines. (The inclusion of Chosin Reservoir is an indication that success does not always mean victory in a zero-sum sense but perhaps a successful retreat under absolutely horrendous conditions.) The thirteenth trait listed in the *Guide* is "Readiness," and it means something more than simply being prepared—after all, one can be prepared and still lose a battle:

> Above all, the public has maintained a consistent view of the Corps; that
> view is taken for granted. . . . It goes like this: First, that wherever there is
> a crisis demanding U.S. military action, there will be Marines ready and
> able to go there in an instant. Second, once on the scene, those Marines
> will perform in a highly effective manner and restore the situation in our
> favor, without exception. Finally, the public believes that the Corps is a
> good thing to have around and consists of sound, energetic young men
> and women upon whom the national trust can be bestowed.[8]

Both Hunt's speech and the hymn signify that this sense of reliability was understood in 1942 (and long before 1929) to be key to "marines." The hymn declares, "You will find us always on the job—The United States Marines," and "In many a strife we've fought for life / And never lost our nerve."

Both Kent and Hunt's speech illustrates how unit histories work their way into battle narratives by transforming past events (specific battles; the history of the unit) into expected norms of conduct for future events—the battles that loom. Before moving to Religious Historical Narratives in battle speeches, another marine speech will provide an example of how recently concluded battles can be worked into a unit history. The speech below does not rely on iconic references but instead employs a more traditional narrative.

The senior leadership says that Battalion 1/8 . . . will go down in the history books for our contribution to the battle fought in Fallujah. I don't dwell on that, there is still a lot to do. I made a comment to one reporter that uncommon valor is still a common virtue in our Corps. I don't think it ever made the press but I'm firmly convinced of it. . . .

We cut into and crushed the heart of the enemy defense of the city and destroyed a lot of them in the process. By my conservative estimate Battalion 1/8 killed over 600 evil die-hards, out of an estimated 2,000+ (we left some for the other battalions.) It was a tough, close up urban fight, at times 360 degrees, against fanatical Jihads, many of them foreign fighters with a one-way ticket to Allah. . . .

I said that Satan has a face and it's in Fallujah—we found torture chambers, chemical labs and terrorist training facilities. This operation . . . had to take place. Fallujah was the recruiting, training and resource center for terrorism and insurgency throughout Iraq and beyond. Our Marines and Sailors took part in a very noble endeavor in which they can forever take pride. They directly contributed to a safer world and carved out a piece of history in the process.

Excerpts from Post-Battle Speech (read aloud and later posted)
of Lieutenant Colonel Gareth Brandl, First Battalion,
Eighth Marine Regiment [1/8] Marines[9]

THE MEN WHO HEARD Sergeant Major Kent's speech and then survived the battle of Fallujah would have also heard Colonel Brandl's Post-Battle Speech. It is different in one important way from those of Kent and Hunt: it does not rely on iconic historical references for its narration but instead tells its story through a stream of facts. In this way, Brandl's speech probably shaped for his men (and perhaps later historians) some understanding about his unit's place in the battle. Brandl is not interested in giving an exhaustive account—there is no timeline of events or mapping of his companies' movements, no discussion about the quantity of supplies used or casualties suffered, no critique of tactics. *That* version of history will presumably come later and to a different audience when he files his after-action report with headquarters. Instead, Brandl seeks to historicize both the battle and his unit's place in it. Brandl's speech illustrates how some Unit Historical Narratives in battle speeches can assimilate recent history into existing unit histories.

And in fact his unit's history is really what Brandl's speech is all about. He opens with a declaration that the 1/8 Marines "will go down in the history books." Although he disclaims any interest in history ("I don't dwell on that"), he clearly wants to supplement what he believes is the inadequate record of his unit's contribution to the battle, at least as reported by the media ("I don't think it ever made the press but I'm firmly convinced of it"). A stream of facts follows, the results of the 1/8's "uncommon valor," which during the battle had become a "common virtue." (This catchy line was minted by Admiral Chester Nimitz in a Post-Battle Speech after Iwo Jima.)[10] Here enemy casualties are given ("1/8 killed over 600 evil die-hards") and the enemy is characterized ("if Satan has a face . . ."). Indeed, the enemy's evil is best measured by the 1/8's achievements: "we found torture chambers, chemical labs and terrorist training facilities." The fact stream is hardly neutral, not only in the sense that it favors the 1/8's position in its own narrative but also for what it says about the battle of Fallujah itself: that it was a historic fight. (Fallujah was "the recruiting, training and resource center for terrorism and insurgency throughout Iraq and beyond.") For Brandl's understanding of the 1/8's history to have validity, the battle *has* to be historic; otherwise he could not conclude that the unit "directly contributed to a safer world and carved out a piece of history in the process."

In his speech, Brandl has created a new unit history, or more accurately has added several new paragraphs to the unit's sixty-two-year existing history. This battle speech history is an example of the less iconic historical narrative. It relies on a fact-stream derived from a recent battle rather than already understood proper nouns of historical significance. Some of Brandl's history will be transmitted orally, as over time, older soldiers tell newer ones about what "the battle of Fallujah was like." His summary will remain part of their experience. And the passage of time may reveal Brandl's remarks in other recollections as well—memoirs, diaries, letters, or perhaps some future official history of the battle. In this sense, battle speechmakers that create historical narratives of a unit are usually its first historians.

Religious Historical Narratives

Need I speak of our fathers' sojourn in Egypt? They were crushed and subject to foreign rulers for four hundred years; but though they might have resisted with weapons and their own right hand, they committed their cause to God. Who has not heard of Egypt, overrun with every wild beast and wasted by every disease, the barren land, the shrunken Nile, the ten plagues in swift succession, and the consequent departure of our fathers, sent on their way with no bloodshed and no danger, led forth by God to establish his temple-worship? Again, when the Syrians carried off our sacred Ark, did not Philistia and Dagon the idol, did not the whole nation of plunderers rue the day? Their hidden parts suppurated, their bowels prolapsed, they brought it back with the hands that stole it, propitiating the Sanctuary with the sound of cymbals and timbrels and with peace-offerings of every kind. It was God whose generalship won this victory for our fathers, because they placed no trust in their right arm or their weapons but committed to Him the decision of the issue.

> Excerpt from Josephus's speech to the Jewish defenders of Jerusalem, urging surrender to Rome, in *The Jewish War*[11]

TWO TYPES OF BATTLE SPEECH whose historical narrative is derived from religious history will be considered in this section. The first type is featured in Josephus's speech here, delivered by him to his co-religionists, the insurgents defending Jerusalem against Roman encirclement in 70 CE. This speech represents an older tradition in which God and His actions in history are at the core of the narrative. While the purpose of these speeches may be to exhort soldiers to advance, hold, or retreat (or in this case, to surrender), the speech's subject is really God and how His will in history requires the soldier-audience to do precisely what the speechmaker now demands. These speeches are also characterized by an obvious fact of demography: the soldier-audience addressed must be religiously homogeneous, for the simple reason that the religious-historical references used to "prove" the speaker's point would be indecipherable to outsiders. For example, it is unlikely that many Romans had the same intimacy with "our fathers' sojourn in Egypt" or invested the same meaning in already ancient accounts of the Philistines. By contrast, the second type of a Religious Historical Narrative illustrated in the two examples found below is that delivered to more recent soldiers drawn from religiously heterogeneous, increasingly secular Western societies. In these examples, God may or may not exist, but religion appears in a deeply submerged form; code words are used that are calculated to appeal to those who "know" while still being comprehensible to those who may not know or even care; likewise, the code is calculated not to violate legal boundaries separating church from state (now characteristic of most Western societies) and also to avoid offending those who may believe in a different religion or in no religion at all.

FOR MUCH OF THE COMMON ERA, and for Jews long before that, history and religion were inseparable. Since God was also the God of history, of prophecy and revelation, of Mount Sinai and the Resurrection, and of eschatological prospects of a first or a second coming, His will was revealed through time, which, as moments expired, joined the long chain of moments linking the present with creation-in-time. The sum of these moments equals history. God's work in time could be understood through the Bible (used generically here to include the Hebrew Bible and the New Testament), His indispensable sourcebook for interpreting events of the past and present as well as predicting the future. Of course, polytheistic religions that predated or were contemporary with Judaism and early Christianity also had gods that were active in time. Both Hesiod's *Works and Days* and

Homer's *Iliad* and *Odyssey* are partly cosmogonic and theogonic and boast panoplies of divinities with a penchant for intervening in human affairs. But unlike the God of the Bible, the gods of antiquity were not gods of revelation, nor were the works of Hesiod or Homer regarded by polytheists as sacred texts. One reads Homer and Hesiod in vain for something like a Ten Commandments or a Sermon on the Mount that might serve as a guide to how the gods would influence the present or might affect the future. In sum, what paganism lacked was the Law.[12]

By contrast, the excerpt from Josephus's speech above exclusively references sacred texts and is underpinned with references to God's Law, how men should abide that Law, and how that Law will control the future. These are references that Josephus's soldier-audience would have instantly understood, even if they did not ultimately agree with his interpretation. Here (and elsewhere in his speech) Josephus offers his audience some highlights of Jewish military history as recorded in the sacred texts. His examples come from the Torah, the Prophets, and the Writings; together, these contain the Law and the story of how that Law was applied in time.[13]

Few speakers in 70 CE were probably as qualified as Josephus, son of Matthias (born 37 CE), to argue this case. A descendent of the Hasmoneans (Maccabees), he was schooled as a rabbi, trained for the Temple priesthood, and had spent time learning with the Pharisees, the Sadducees, and the reclusive Essenes, the three principal Jewish sects of his day. Josephus's works include two histories, *The Jewish War* (in which the excerpt appears) and *Jewish Antiquities*, and a defense of Judaism titled *Against Apion*. *The Jewish War* is the key source for the war between Rome and the Jews (66–73 CE). In fact, this bitter struggle was as much a civil war between Jews as it was a war of Jews against Rome. By the time it was over, the Temple in Jerusalem lay in ruins and King Herod's mountaintop redoubt at Masada, one of the last strongholds of Jewish opposition, was the scene of a mass suicide of 960 Jewish rebels.[14]

Josephus possessed another important qualification for making this speech, although it was not necessarily recognized by his soldier-audience, most of whom regarded him as a traitor and collaborationist:

he had once battled the Romans and lost. Like Thucydides, Xenophon, and Caesar, Josephus had led troops in battle and survived to write the tale. Assigned to command the defense of the town of Jotapata in the Galilee, Josephus had withstood (by his account, for a surprisingly long time) the siegecraft of Roman general and soon to be emperor Vespasian; eventually the town fell and Josephus was captured. Nevertheless, he made his peace with Vespasian; before the elder Flavian returned to Rome to settle the succession issue, he appointed his son Titus to invest Jerusalem. During that siege, Titus used Josephus as his translator. By the time Josephus spoke to the insurgents on Titus's orders, the siege of Jerusalem was well advanced. The Romans had encircled the city, cutting off food; famine wracked its inhabitants, and the city's outermost walls had been breached.[15]

Other than having to avoid the insurgents' "howls of derision or execration, sometimes with showers of stone," Josephus had few hesitations in making the speech. He genuinely opposed the Jewish rebels' cause, in part because, as he had declared earlier in his speech, Roman domination of the world was God's will. "From every side fortune had passed to them [the Romans]," he shouted to the defenders, "and God who handed dominion over from nation to nation round the world, abode now in Italy." This was certainly a historical argument that implied a historical-religious conclusion: it was God who controlled the fates of nations. But it was also an argument that any run-of-the-mill polytheist might make. And when the argument failed to persuade, Josephus tried a different tack. "As frank advice was lost on them," he concluded, "[I] turned to the story of the nation's past." And certainly by the lights of Jewish theology, there was absolutely no difference between the story of its past and God's history of the world.[16]

Josephus begins this excerpt by posing a rhetorical question intended to focus his audience on the foundational story of the Jews: "Need I speak of our fathers' sojourn in Egypt?" Of course he must, and in the several sentences that follow, he summarizes that history, choosing to emphasize that the present Roman occupation is not the first time that Jews were subject to foreign rule—the two hundred and ten years spent in Egypt was a much longer and harsher experience. But what really differed between then and now was the Jews' relationship with God: "Though they might have resisted with weapons and their own right hand, they committed their cause to God." They were right to do so then—God punished the Egyptians with "the ten plagues in swift succession"—and they would be right to trust God now, rather than their own rebel commanders. Trusting God then, Josephus declares, did no less than continue and make glorious the very history of the Jewish people, "the consequent departure of our fathers, sent on their way with no bloodshed and no danger, led forth by God to establish His temple-worship." Again, Josephus implies that by trusting God now, the Roman siege, with its consequent bloodshed, famine, and anarchy, would cease, and some new future would dawn. (That Josephus is carefully selecting his historical fact-stream may be gauged from the Torah itself—the exodus, for many Egyptians and at least a few Jews, was hardly bloodless.)

Josephus does not end his use of history here. Judeo-Christian religious history is above all predictive: knowing how God's will worked in the past offers human beings guidance about the future. And in Josephus's telling, the future following the exodus from Egypt and extending to the present hour had indeed unfolded predictably—when the Jews' trusted their external affairs to God rather than themselves, God protected them. Thus "when the Syrians carried off our sacred Ark, did not Philistia and Dagon the idol [the god of the Philistines], did not the whole nation of plunderers rue the day?" Josephus answers that they did, and awfully so: "Their hidden parts suppurating, their bowels prolapsed." God had punished these desecrators just as He had punished the Egyptians for failing to heed His demand to free the Jews. And Jewish-Philistine history had proved once again that alone, the Jews could rectify nothing; but with prayer and righteous behavior, God had rallied to their side. He will do so again, now that they face the Romans. "It was God whose generalship won . . . victory for our fathers," Josephus concludes, "because they placed no trust in their right arm or their weapons but committed to Him the decision of the issue." Josephus appeals to the heart of God's Covenant with the Jewish people: that in exchange for obeying His Law (which, Josephus argues, using historical examples, consists of prayer and trust rather than armed rebellion), the Jews will enjoy His grace and possession of the land. But if the Jews persist in refusing to trust God and continue fighting the Romans alone, they will lose both His grace and the land. This, too, can be derived from history—specifically, the destruction of Jerusalem's First Temple by Babylon in 586 BCE. As Josephus argues elsewhere in his speech, "The same portent you saw happen once before at the capture of [Jerusalem], when the Babylonian already referred to marched against it, took the City and Sanctuary and burnt them both, though that generation was surely guilty of no such impiety as yours. So I am sure the Almighty has quitted your holy places and now stands on the side of [the Romans]." If God stands with Rome, the Jewish insurgent cause was hopeless. Josephus argued a syllogism found in other religious battle speeches of the traditional type: "Our" side wins when favored by God, and God favors "us" when we obey His Law. If we are losing the battle, it is because we have not obeyed His Law. In short, God does not favor the strongest battalions but those who are righteous in His sight.[17]

As a final matter, there is an important historical context to Josephus's speech, one that goes unmentioned by him but that must have weighed heavily on the minds of some in his soldier-audience. The argument he made—that Jewish sins would bring God's vengeance upon them in the form of external enemies—was one that had been made by selected Israelites since the time of Moses. This was the history of the Hebrew prophets. "But it shall come to pass, if thou wilt not hearken unto the voice of the Lord thy God, to observe to do all his commandments and his statues which I command thee this day," the Law Giver had warned in Deuteronomy, "[then] all these curses shall come upon thee and overtake thee." In speaking to Jerusalem's defenders, Josephus tried to place himself in that prophetic line. Prophecy is really history, and all prophets are historians: they argue that what was (God's will revealed in history) shall continue to be (the prophecy.) Thus, just as Jeremiah foretold the destruction of the First Temple, Josephus would foretell the destruction of the Second Temple. In sum, Josephus's purpose was to remind Jerusalem's defenders that God's history was in the saddle again (not that it had ever left). And like all Religious Historical Narratives used in battle speeches, Josephus's was meant to prove that that which was will also be.[18]

Soldiers! We congratulate you on an event which insures the liberty of our country. We congratulate every man of you whose glorious privilege it was to participate in this triumph of courage and truth, to fight in the battle of Manassas. You have created an epoch in the history of liberty, and unborn nations will rise up and call you blessed. Continue this noble devotion, looking always to the protection of the just God, and, before time grows much older we will be hailed as the deliverers of a nation of ten millions of people. Comrades, our brothers who have fallen have earned undying renown upon earth, and their blood, shed in our holy cause, is a precious and acceptable sacrifice to the Father of Truth and of Right.

> Excerpt from Post-Battle Speech by Generals Joseph Johnston and
> P. G. T. Beauregard delivered after the Battle of Manassas, July 25, 1861

You are about to embark upon the Great Crusade, toward which we have striven these many months. . . . The hopes and prayers of liberty-loving people everywhere march with you. In company with our brave Allies and brothers-in-arms on the other Fronts, you will bring about the destruction of the German war machine, the elimination of Nazi tyranny over the oppressed peoples of Europe, and security for ourselves in a free world. . . . Good Luck! And let us all beseech the blessing of Almighty God upon this great and noble undertaking.

> Excerpt from General Dwight D. Eisenhower's
> Order of the Day, June 6, 1944[19]

RELIGION, OF COURSE, continues to play a role in battle speeches in modern times. But today's Western militaries are largely secular institutions, served by religiously diverse soldier-audiences; thus, compared with that of Josephus, one finds substantial changes in more recent battle speeches that use Religious Historical Narratives. The two passages excerpted above are examples of how religion tends to appear in coded form in modern battle speeches. The first excerpt, taken from a Post-Battle Speech (a printed proclamation) delivered several days after the Confederate victory at First Manassas, subtly employs references from the Bible to offer its soldier-audience a powerful religious-historical interpretation of the meaning of the victory. The second excerpt is taken from Eisenhower's General Order (printed proclamation), issued as Allied soldiers were heading toward the Normandy beaches. This speech uses the historical metaphor of the Crusades, a reference not drawn from sacred texts but from post-Biblical religious, political, and social history. Both speeches expressly refer to God in a general, non-sectarian way that remains acceptable in battle speeches to this day. But these almost formulaic references to the deity are not the real source of these speeches' power.

Several points require elaboration here. First, in making a speech that used religion and history, Josephus had several advantages over the three American generals quoted in the epigraph. In the Jerusalem of 70 CE, a state's religious neutrality was inconceivable; furthermore, Josephus's very purpose in speaking was the preservation of the Temple Cult theocracy, albeit continuing under Roman authority. His soldier-audience professed the same faith, practiced the same rituals, and shared a common understanding of God and history; they also believed that that history was absolutely genuine—when Josephus mentions Jeremiah, it is unlikely that many (if any) of his listeners doubted that the prophet had once lived, had spoken the words claimed, and had prophesized accurately. By contrast, most of what Generals Beauregard, Johnston, and Eisenhower shared with their soldiers consisted of things not expressly religious: their common American heritage, which instead featured certain ideas about government, popular culture, and their country's history. Religion certainly "informed" some of these ideas, but there were also powerful countervailing influences: freedom of conscience was at least professed to be state policy, and the government was forbidden from endorsing any particular faith; this in turn was supported by a social ethos that often made it impolitic to even publicly inquire about the religious beliefs, or lack of belief, of another. And the base from which the military recruited was religiously diverse, apparent in the backgrounds of the three generals themselves: Beauregard was Catholic, Johnston had Episcopalian roots, and Eisenhower was raised a Jehovah's Witness. In fact, compared with Josephus's shared religion with the Jerusalem insurgents, there was little by way of specific sectarianism to unite Beauregard, Johnston, and Eisenhower with their soldiers other than a common

Judeo-Christian frame of reference that was supported by some Biblical literacy.[20]

But as Generals Beauregard and Johnston's Post-Battle Speech demonstrates, this broad Judeo-Christian frame was more than enough to allow them to imply a powerful Religious Historical Narrative in their speech and thereby explain the battle's larger meaning. Consider several passages from the excerpt. As was the case with Colonel Brandl's Post-Battle Speech, discussed earlier, the historical significance of the battle is usually very important to the speechmaker. "You have created an epoch in the history of liberty," Beauregard and Johnston declare. But what kind of historical "liberty" do they mean? The generals code proof-texts drawn from the Hebrew Bible (Abraham and Moses) in order to assert that the "liberty" referred to evokes the history of a covenanted people rather than anything taken from John Locke or Patrick Henry. For as a result of creating this new "epoch" in liberty's history, "unborn nations will rise up and call you blessed." Considered alone, this is a curious insert for a speech celebrating the preservation of the Confederate government—unless the virtue vindicated by the triumph at First Manassas was really an entire people's virtue—a covenantal people that enjoys a special relationship with God. The source for the generals' statement may have come from any one of a number of Biblical proof-texts. There is God's promise to Abram in Genesis 12:3 (all quotations from the King James Version): "And I will bless them that bless thee, and curse him that curse thee: and in thee shall all families of the earth be blessed." It was repeated again in Genesis 18:18 when Abram had become Abraham and God wondered whether or not to tell him about the destruction of Sodom and Gomorrah: "Seeing that Abraham shall surely become a great and mighty nation, and all the nations of the earth shall be blessed in him?" And perhaps most significantly, there is the promise that God made to Abraham after he had willingly offered to sacrifice Isaac in Genesis 22:18: "And in thy seed shall all the nations of the earth be blessed because thou hast obeyed my voice." God's promise to Abraham was a reward for his willingness to sacrifice his son. And as the generals make clear, the Confederate people too have offered a sacrifice, in the form of battle casualties: "Comrades, our brothers who have fallen have earned undying renown upon earth, and their blood, shed in our holy cause," they declare, "is a precious and acceptable sacrifice to the Father of Truth and Right." Like Abraham, the Confederate people have earned covenantal status by sacrificing in battle some rough equivalent of what Abraham offered to sacrifice in the land of Moriah—their sons.

But just as there was a sequel in the history of Israel, so will there be a sequel in the history of the Confederacy. Beauregard and Johnston promise their men that if they "Continue this noble devotion, looking always to the protection of a just God," very soon ("before time grows much older") "we will be hailed as the deliverers of a nation of ten millions of people." The phrase "deliverers of a nation" is another way of explaining the recent victory in a religious-historical context, as it taps into an enormously important trope drawn directly from the sacred texts. "Deliverer" and "nation" are invariably connected with the story of Moses, invested by God to deliver the Jewish people from Egyptian bondage and into the Promised Land. Although the actual deliverer of the Jews is God (Exodus 3:8), Moses is often credited with being a deliverer, a savior, as when he "delivered" the daughters of Reu'el from the shepherds (Exodus 2:19), or more directly in the New Testament in Acts 7:35, where Moses is described as "a deliverer by the hand of the angel which appeared to him in the bush." Beauregard and Johnston are generals, not theologians; they are not interested in coding some novel Biblical exegesis but instead in linking their victory to commonly held religious ideas in order to create historical meaning: If the soldiers continue to fight and behave well, then "a just God" will also make them "deliverers" of the Confederate nation, as well as God's vessel for transmitting blessings to the future. It is an attempt to transplant the ancient Biblical bargain between God and Abraham into the nineteenth century.[21]

Why code the texts? Why not declare outright that Southern (white) people are God's chosen ones? That they have been ordained by God to transmit His blessings to future nations, and that the Confederate Army has been chosen by God to deliver the Confederacy from Northern bondage? Josephus had little difficulty explicitly charging his narrative of the present with divine meanings. But unlike

Josephus, Generals Beauregard and Johnston operate in a world in which the public discussion of religion is somewhat constrained. To do more than imply religious meaning would transgress important political and social boundaries. First, there was article 9, section 12, of the Confederate Constitution, taken verbatim from its Federal counterpart: "Congress shall make no law respecting an establishment of religion, or prohibiting the free exercise thereof." While no one should confuse today's First Amendment jurisprudence with that of 1861, it is easy to understand why this language was as much a Southern inheritance as that of any other region—after all, the first draft of the Bill of Rights was written by Virginian James Madison. Freedom of religious conscience was accepted by North and South. But there were other considerations. The rebel army was a religiously diverse group. It included Protestants of many sectarian affiliations, Catholics, and even an estimated ten to twelve thousand Jews; moreover (and possibly surprisingly, given certain postwar stereotypes about Civil War religiosity), it seems to have included a significant number of soldiers who may have been only nominally Christian. Finally, there were social and theological prohibitions against blasphemy that would have been violated by direct religious comparisons. Only God, not generals, can choose His people; only God, not generals, can declare who is to be a deliverer of His people or which people will transmit His blessings. Nevertheless, Generals Beauregard and Johnston's use of this imagery strongly suggests that they believed that their army had enough soldiers who were Biblically literate to justify coding their texts. In reaching for a religious narrative to lend meaning to the victory, their challenge was twofold: to touch the persuaded without giving offense to the rest, and to do it in a way that was comprehensible to the entire soldier-audience, not just to those in the know.[22]

Almost eighty-three years later, General Dwight D. Eisenhower issued his General Order of the Day for D-Day, June 6, 1944. Aside from its purpose (it is a Pre-Invasion Speech), it is also differentiated from the others considered here by the type of religious history it employs. Whereas Josephus drew no distinction between religious and secular history, and Beauregard and Johnston referred to the sacred texts in coded form, Eisenhower neither uses God's history nor codes

His words. Instead, the Religious Historical Narrative he employs is drawn from well-known events occurring far into post-Biblical history: the series of medieval military campaigns known as the Great Crusades. These campaigns, a response to papal calls of the eleventh through the thirteenth centuries, were an attempt to restore Christian control to lands conquered by the Muslims. But whatever the Crusades' historical reality, Eisenhower's likely purpose was to incorporate selected features of their medieval (and largely religious) narrative and insert them into the June 1944 invasion of France.[23]

Religious references appear three times in Eisenhower's speech. The first is to the Great Crusade itself: "You are about to embark upon the Great Crusade." The second ("The hopes and prayers of liberty loving people") and third ("And let us all beseech the blessing of Almighty God") might seem formulaic; but in combination with "Great Crusade" they support the very dynamic Religious Historical Narrative that Eisenhower wants to tell. Using real or imagined elements from the actual Crusades, his story might be recast as follows: the Crusades were a combined effort of many peoples ("In company with our brave Allies and brothers-in-arms on the other Fronts"), which resembles the multinational force landing today at Normandy; just like our invasion of France, the Crusades were also an effort to reconquer territory from an ideologically opposed and evil enemy (the medieval Muslims parallel the "German war machine . . . Nazi tyranny"); the Crusades required the same lengthy preparations ("toward which we have striven these many months"); the Crusades required soldiers to cross water on ships, as we cross the English Channel ("embark upon"); Crusaders were liberators, as we are ("the elimination of Nazi tyranny over the oppressed peoples of Europe"). Furthermore, the story goes, both the Crusaders and we have traveled great distances with long absences from home; therefore, as liberators and soldiers fighting in distant lands, the thoughts of those at home as well as those awaiting liberation were with the Crusaders and will likewise be with us ("The hopes and prayers of liberty-loving people everywhere march with you"). Finally, whatever their actual historical reality, the Great Crusades were also a "great and noble undertaking" ("great" meaning of large historical significance or large of heart;

"noble" meaning virtuous or good in God's eyes). Indeed, this under-taking is inherently so great and noble that asking God's *council* is un-necessary—we have only to ask His *blessing* for that which He will obviously approve. As always in battle speeches, historical precision is beside the point. That the real Crusades ultimately failed and some-times hosted reciprocal Christian-Muslim atrocities is irrelevant; what Eisenhower seeks to conjure here are imagined images of knights and nobles, inspired by faith and setting off on a virtuous if dangerous but religiously sanctioned enterprise, not for gold but for God.

Viewed in isolation, this particular narrative is a routine transfor-mation of history into a useful story, probably no better or worse than Napoleon's average "agreed-upon fiction." But words cannot be consid-ered apart from their moment of creation. And in that regard, Eisen-hower's speech was a gem, one perfectly cut for a soldier-audience that was probably as religiously diverse as any in American history. Because "Crusade" (the proper noun) is also "crusade" (the common noun), no sectarian affiliation was required to grasp its meaning. Whether one were Christian, Jewish, atheist, agnostic, or religiously uninterested, only rudimentary English was required to know that "crusade" had an equally relevant and distinctly non-religious meaning that might ap-pear in an ordinary newspaper article about a "crusading prosecutor" or someone's "crusade for reform." But Eisenhower's army was also mostly Christian and doubtless included many believers who under-stood exactly what the Great Crusades were as well as their role in the history of Christianity; the genius of "Crusades" is that it delivers a powerful religious message to the faithful while delivering an equally powerful one to those of no faith or of other faiths; to the latter sol-diers, it is a message that retains the fervent energy, if not the religious associations, of the original event. In sum, this speech was perfectly suited for a secularized, Western military raised on freedom of con-science, and it remains an excellent example of a Religious Historical Narrative that is based on events in historical, not sacred, time.

Social Historical Narratives

The flags which I have the honor to offer for the acceptance of your regiments are the gifts of women, members of some of our oldest fam-

*ilies, whose ancestors came from Germany and settled in this coun-
try before the Revolution. . . . The principle of national unity is a
deeply implanted German sentiment. Gibbon tells us that when the
ancestors of the present Germans first appeared upon the banks of
the Maine [sic], they were made up of distinct tribes, who gradually
coalesced into a great permanent nation, calling themselves by the
name of Allemanni, or all kinds of men, to denote their various lin-
eages and common bravery. From that united condition they became
broken into small nationalities; and to bring them back again, to unite
all speaking the German tongue in one confederated Germany, is an
object for which German patriots have struggled for three hundred
years, and struggled in vain. . . . You are not the first of the German
race who have taken up arms in defense of this country. . . . This detestation of traitors is an old intrinsic German feeling. Tacitus tells us
that the German tribes regarded as among the highest of crimes, and
as a disgrace which could never be wiped out, the voluntary abandonment by a soldier of his shield. . . . What was true then is true now;
for no soldiers have surpassed the Germans in fidelity. . . . You are
American citizens; you are soldiers; you are Germans; you require no
exhortation from me to stand faithfully by your colors. The history of
your country's seventeen hundred years answers for you.*

Excerpt from a flag presentation speech given by Judge Charles Patrick Daly
to the Seventh New York Regiment on May 24, 1861[24]

AMONG THE MOST IMPORTANT historical narratives used in battle speeches are those based on social-group membership, including race, ethnicity, or tribe. Belonging to these groups is usually
regarded as innate; unlike the U.S. Marine Corps, one cannot join
by enlistment, and unlike Christianity or Judaism, one cannot affili-
ate by mere belief. Instead, membership is established by birth and is
further defined by certain traits. These traits may be thought to in-
here biologically or perhaps to have been established by custom for
so long that it makes no practical difference whether they transmit
genetically or represent cultural ideas passed along by each generation. Battle speechmakers seek to rouse certain of these traits when
talking to soldier-audiences belonging to particular groups; con-
versely, when speaking of enemies who belong to other groups, battle

speechmakers sometimes invoke other traits as evidence of inherent evil or weakness.

The traits that Judge Charles Patrick Daly mentions in the excerpted speech are all associated with one such social group—Germans.[25] Indeed, "German" or "Germany" is mentioned eleven times just in the excerpted passages above. Judge Daly certainly faced some special challenges in exhorting the Seventh New York Regiment. "This regiment is composed of Germans, among whom are a number of the veterans of 1848 and '49," a reporter from the *New York Tribune* wrote. "Among the officers are several German noblemen who are exiles in this country, having been driven from their native land on account of their sympathy with and activity in the struggle for German independence in 1848. Many of them have also served in the revolutionary struggles of Hungary and Italy." In short, these men were not only German-born but also political radicals who had earned their revolutionary credentials in several of the era's best-known wars for national autonomy. Many of the men in Daly's soldier-audience had probably immigrated in the decade before the war and may not yet have been American citizens. In his Presentation Speech, Judge Daly sought to convince them that the issues of the American Civil War were also their issues and had always been their issues, not necessarily because of *where* they came from or *what* their experiences had been but rather because of *who* they were—as Germans, they had a "deeply implanted" desire for national unity that was identical to the North's struggle against secession. In making his case, Judge Daly also asserted that Germans possessed unique traits that naturally predisposed them as patriots and loyal men, cleverly reversing the nativist assumptions that had characterized American politics just a few years earlier: then, "German-ness" was deemed foreign to "Americanism"; now, Daly argued, it was everything that America was about—and also what it needed in uniform.[26]

Daly begins by directly connecting Germans with the American Revolution. He declares that the flags being given to the Seventh Regiment are "the gifts of women, members of some of our oldest families, whose ancestors came from Germany and settled in this country before the Revolution." In the very next sentence (not included here) he adds: "Though separated by several generations from those of German birth, the German blood still running in their veins recognizes the promptitude with which the countrymen of their ancestors have taken up arms when the unity of these States is threatened." Daly is not engaging in mere rhetorical flourish here—there were several good reasons why he needed to give his foreign-born soldier-audience a vicarious stake in the American Revolution. First, the consummation of that revolution was the U.S. Constitution, the integrity of which (by Northern lights) was now under attack. Therefore, Daly used a Social Historical Narrative to link his German soldier-audience with their fellow ethnic Germans of the eighteenth century who had already fought and died for American principles. Second, Daly probably realized that unlike some native-born Americans, his audience could have few historic grievances against South Carolinian or Virginian slaveholders, let alone Southern nationalists; indeed, the latter also claimed to be fighting a war for national autonomy, an argument that Daly must have believed some of the Germans would find appealing.[27] And perhaps none of the Seventh Regiment's Germans had direct ancestors who suffered at Valley Forge or triumphed at Yorktown; thus, there could be no argument that these men, based on lineal descent, had any obligation to the men of '76. In short, one might ask: what stake could the Germans of the Seventh Regiment have in this uniquely American war?

Daly answers this question by expanding a Social Historical Narrative that really began the moment he uttered the words "German blood." He argues that the bond between the American Revolution and these Germans exists in German blood, because that blood carries (like hemoglobin) certain character traits that resonate with America's founding principles. The first such trait is the "principle of national unity." Because this principle is inherent to being German, one would expect that it would also be a constant theme in German history. And indeed, Daly finds it to be so, using as proof references from Edward Gibbon's *The Decline and Fall of the Roman Empire*. As Daly reads Gibbon, the ancient Germans at first comprised "distinct tribes" but then became a "permanent nation" and even named themselves "Allemanni, or all kinds of men." (Not surprisingly, Daly asserts elsewhere in the speech that "The American people have presented a similar spectacle on this side of the water—a new Allemanni—a people composed of many races confederated together in one nationality, and having hitherto a common destiny.") And by defending America, Daly asserts that "You are not the first of the German race who have taken up arms in defence of this country," an unsurprising statement given the German predilection for national unity. Daly then dwells at length on the Prussian émigré Baron Friedrich von Steuben's contribution to the American Revolution and urges that the Seventh Regiment follow in their countryman's distinguished footsteps.[28]

What made von Steuben so successful? After a few anecdotes about the old general, Daly concludes that the Revolutionary hero possessed a second trait by virtue of being German: "fidelity," or as Daly phrases it in the negative, "this detestation of traitors." For Germans, this attitude is "intrinsic," an essential quality of being German. And just like the first principle, one would also expect to find this trait manifest throughout German history. Once again, Daly draws his proof-text from ancient history: "Tacitus tells us that the German tribes regarded as among the highest of crimes, and as a disgrace which could never be wiped out, the voluntary abandonment by a soldier of his shield." Finally, Daly succinctly phrases the sine qua non of Social Historical as well as Religious Historical Narratives: "What was true then is true now," he declares, and then he connects this unchanging truth with loyalty. "[N]o soldiers have surpassed the Germans in fidelity," he asserts. "The history of your country seventeen hundred years answers for you."

Our enemies are Medes and Persians, men who for centuries have lived soft and luxurious lives; we of Macedon for generations past have been trained in the hard school of danger and war. Above all, we are free men, and they are slaves.

Excerpt from Alexander the Great addressing his army
before the Battle of Issus, 333 BCE[29]

TO COMPLETE THIS DISCUSSION we will briefly consider the use of Social Historical Narratives that characterize the enemy.

Surprisingly, of the many hundreds of battle speeches and hundreds more references to such speeches surveyed for this book, the vast majority of those that described an enemy did not use a Social Historical Narrative. Instead, the reasons for defeating or destroying the enemy were based on its past actions—it had started the war, or plundered, or raped or killed, or gave no quarter, or behaved cruelly or with gross lawlessness that lay far outside the limits the speechmaker believed were acceptable. Rarely are such reasons linked with the enemy's "blood" or some other racial component. A typical example of this disinclination is Hannibal, whose hatred for Rome was reportedly boundless; nevertheless, he usually characterized his enemy by their actions, as in this exhortatory speech before the Battle of Tinicus in 218 BCE.

> The Romans are a proud and merciless people; they claim to make the world their own and subject to their will. They demand the right to dictate to us who our friends should be and who our enemies. They circumscribe our liberties, barring us in behind barriers of rivers or mountains beyond which we may not pass—but they do not themselves observe the limits they have set.

Here it is possible to imagine Romans behaving differently; in other words, there is nothing in Hannibal's declaration that suggests that Roman "nature" is such that they must behave like bullies or act like hypocrites.[30]

Alexander's Pre-Battle Speech to his men before Issus (see also chapter 6) is a good example of how Social Historical Narratives sometimes operate when demonizing the enemy. Here the negative character imputed to the enemy (as well as the positive traits of the Macedonians) is not a function of nature but of nurture. The Mede and Persian enemy is corrupt because "for centuries [they] have lived soft and luxurious lives"; by contrast, the Macedonians have been victorious and will prevail in this battle because "for generations past [they] have been trained in the hard school of danger and war." Moreover, in an argument that will be made repeatedly across the millennia, Alexander explains to his men that nurture is not only a function of history but also of an existing and superior society— Macedonians are better soldiers because "we are free men and [the Persians and Medes] are slaves." Of course, there is one very practical

and salubrious consequence of fighting an enemy based on his actions or his nurture rather than his nature—one can eventually make
peace with such an enemy. For enemies whose nature is deemed inherently and irremediably evil, the only conclusion to a war is to kill
them all.

Political Historical Narrative

*Young Frenchmen: If you are burning to belong to an army that is in-
tended to bring the wars of the Revolution to a close, by securing its
independence, the liberty, and the glory of the great nation: To arms!
To arms! Rush to Dijon!*

> Napoleon Recruiting Speech, "Proclamation
> to the Youth of France," April 21, 1800

*People of the Philippines: I have returned. By the grace of Almighty
God, our forces stand again on Philippine soil—soil consecrated in the
blood of our two peoples. . . . At my side is your President, Sergio Osmena, a worthy successor of that great patriot, Manuel Quezon. . . .
The seat of your government is now, therefore, firmly re-established
on Philippine soil. The hour of your redemption is here. . . . Rally to
me. Let the indomitable spirit of Bataan and Corregidor lead on. As
the lines of battle roll forward to bring you within the zone of operations, rise and strike. Strike at every favorable opportunity. For your
homes and hearths, strike! In the name of your sacred dead, strike!*

> Excerpt from radio broadcast to the Filipino people by General Douglas
> MacArthur following the landings at Leyte, October 20, 1944[31]

BATTLE SPEECHES USING a Political Historical Narrative will be
familiar to modern readers. Here some aspect of a political entity's history—usually the government under whose authority the soldiers serve—is inserted into a battle speech to exhort soldiers, locate
their current mission within the political entity's history, or provide
historical reasons why the soldier-audience must act as the speaker
insists. Occasionally, Political Historical Narratives are also used to
characterize or vilify an enemy.

The two examples featured in the epigraph demonstrate that battle-speech Political Historical Narratives operate structurally as something of a three-step. First, loyalty is summoned, generally by reference to the political entity the speaker deems entitled to allegiance. Second, a history of the political entity is introduced to "locate" (justify) the battle speechmaker's request for the desired action or emotion. Third, the request for the action or some expectation of future behavior is declared. Napoleon's Recruiting Speech (a printed proclamation) is a straightforward illustration. By saluting his audience as "Young Frenchmen," Napoleon begins by kindling their loyalty—he cares not for young men generally but for young Frenchmen in particular. And his proclamation concludes with a demand for action—"To arms! To arms! Rush to Dijon!" The second step, the actual historical narrative, links the beginning and the end. And that middle is nothing less than Napoleon's abbreviated history of France for the eleven years between the Revolution of 1789 and the issuance of the proclamation in 1800. Master battle speechmaker that he was, Napoleon manages to encapsulate his version of that history in forty-four words. By his retelling, first came the Revolution and its great purposes: "independence, the liberty, and the glory of the great nation." But the Revolution remains unfinished, and the work of Frenchmen, especially young Frenchmen, remains incomplete. All who heard or read this proclamation probably had an enthymematic understanding of what "the wars of the Revolution" were about: attempts by reactionary foreigners and traitors who sought to limit or reverse the Revolution's great gains. Now it is time to consummate the Revolution by concluding these wars ("securing its independence"). If you are one of those especially patriotic or idealistic ("burning to belong") young Frenchmen interested in making history by joining "an army that is intended to bring the wars of the Revolution to a close," then go to Dijon and enlist. Napoleon's appeal is a mix of patriotic and idealistic ("Frenchmen . . . independence . . . glory of the great nation . . . wars of the Revolution . . . liberty"). Aside from its concise summary of recent French "history," it is also utterly typical of how Political Historical Narrative operates in battle speeches: an appeal to loyalty, the historical placement of the desired action, and a request for the action.

With its greater length and typical eloquence, General Douglas MacArthur's radio broadcast to Filipinos illustrates a mix of powerful Political and Religious Historical Narratives in a speech delivered during an actual battle. MacArthur made this live address on October 20, 1944, the same day he famously waded ashore on the Island of Leyte, thereby redeeming his earlier pledge: "I shall return." This is a Midst-of-Battle Speech; not only could "the crack of riflery and the thunder of naval gunfire [still] be heard in the background" as MacArthur spoke, but the speech itself was intended to stir up an already organized Filipino guerrilla force that had been resisting Japanese occupation for almost three years.[32]

Like Napoleon's recruitment proclamation, MacArthur's speech contains its summons to national loyalty in its salutation: "People of the Philippines." But this is not merely imposing on an allegiance to a country's name—there is a powerful, human drama involved, one that MacArthur transmits by not only by noting the redemption of his personal vow ("I have returned") but also by identifying who sits at his side ("your President, Sergio Osmena") and Osmena's intimate relationship with the recent history of the Philippine government: "Sergio Osmena, a worthy successor of that great patriot, Manuel Quezon." And it is the government and its historical continuity with which MacArthur is chiefly concerned, for the next sentence assures his guerilla- and would-be-guerilla-audience that "The seat of government is now, therefore, firmly re-established on Philippine soil."

One source of power tapped by MacArthur's broadcast is a Religious Historical Narrative—its language breathes more than a little of God's grace and redemption, Christ's return, and the apotheosis of Filipino war dead; but what is relevant here is the extent to which this religious theme suffuses a Political Historical Narrative. Elsewhere in the speech MacArthur characterizes the return of the Philippines' lawful government as falling within "The guidance of Divine God" and declares that this government as well as the American invasion force should be "Follow[ed] in His name to the Holy Grail of righteous victory." This religious imagery utilizes long-established Christian symbols of the messianic return of Christ, which, under the circumstances, would have been instantly intelligible to MacArthur's overwhelmingly Roman Catholic Filipino audience. MacArthur, like Josephus, speaks to a religiously homogeneous soldier-audience; however, unlike Josephus, who argued that political submission was a religious duty, MacArthur uses religious imagery here to imply the same about political resistance.

All battle-speech historical narratives must begin with some past event. Since few battle speeches bother with much explanation (there is rarely time), the battle speechmaker essentially wagers that his audience will recognize the past event and provide the desired significances from its own stock of associations. For example, in his Recruiting Speech, Napoleon's history begins with the French Revolution. He uses the name of this iconic event as a metonym in which one intangible thing is a stand-in for other intangible things (the Revolution for the ideas and politics associated with the Revolution), and, like most metonyms, it is enthymematic—Napoleon presupposes that his audience will fill in the blanks for him. In the year 1800 it was probably a safe bet that most young Frenchmen would know both what the French Revolution was and what it meant—that is, they would concur with Napoleon's understanding of its meaning.

MacArthur's history formally begins with two events that happened very close together and that he expresses metonymically: "Bataan and Corregidor." Both Bataan and Corregidor are geographical features of the entrance of Manila Bay, but of course MacArthur wants his guerilla-audience to recall what happened on them—in early 1942, after bitter fighting, American and Filipino forces stationed on the Bataan Peninsula—and shortly afterward, their allies garrisoned on the island of Corregidor—surrendered to the Japanese invaders. There is another association with these metonyms that MacArthur hopes his audience will remember: after the surrender, Allied prisoners of war received brutal, often lethal treatment from their captors. This began during the infamous Bataan death march and continued in prisoner-of-war camps; it also included the brutal Japanese occupation of Filipino civilian areas. For those in the audience who might have been uncertain about how to interpret these metonyms, Mac-Arthur offers an important clue. The "spirit" (that is, the memory of resistance, or the present will to resist, or even the shades of those

who perished fighting or died later under Japanese occupation) invoked by the names of Bataan and Corregidor must be recalled as
"indomitable." To be sure, the flesh of Allied prisoners of war, and by
extension Filipino civilians, was dominated by the enemy, but not the
spirit of "Bataan and Corregidor," which MacArthur demands must
now "lead on."

MacArthur's speech thus holds to the old formula of the Political
Historical Narrative. He first summons loyalty to the political entity;
he then offers a history justifying both why that loyalty is due and why
his present demands are appropriate to and indeed required by the
history provided. And his demands to Filipino insurgents and would-
be insurgents are expressed with typical MacArthurian eloquence,
which one scholar has described as "oratory of the grand style identified with the nineteenth century": "Rise and strike. Strike at every favorable opportunity. For your homes and hearths, strike! In the name
of your sacred dead, strike! Let every arm be steeled." When read in
totality, MacArthur's speech was meant to reintroduce Filipino government to the islands; his use of religious imagery further inspired
and adorned this effort with an extra measure of narrative power.[33]

*Your task will not be an easy one. Your enemy is well trained, well
equipped and battle-hardened. He will fight savagely.*

*But this is the year 1944! Much has happened since the Nazi tri-
umphs of 1940–41. The United Nations have inflicted upon the Germans great defeats, in open battle, man-to-man. Our air offensive
has seriously reduced their strength in the air and their capacity to
wage war on the ground. Our Home Fronts have given us overwhelming superiority in weapons and munitions of war, and placed at our
disposal great reserves of trained fighting men. The tide has turned!
The free men of the world are marching together to a Victory!*

Excerpt from General Dwight D. Eisenhower's
General Order of the Day, June 6, 1944

IN BRIEFLY CONSIDERING how battle-speech Political Historical
Narratives are used to characterize an enemy, it is worth recalling
Eisenhower's Order of the Day for June 6, 1944. The passages featured

above reveals that Eisenhower's real purpose was less to diminish the enemy than it was to build confidence among his own invasion force. However, in arguing for that confidence, Eisenhower chooses to diminish the enemy by way of narrating their history since 1940. What qualifies this as a Political Historical Narrative (and not a Unit Historical Narrative of the German military) is that Eisenhower understands that there are really two enemies and chooses to subsume one within the other. The subsumed one is the German military, and it is formidable ("Your enemy is well trained, well equipped and battle hardened"); after all, German soldiers, not Nazi politicians, will be shooting at the Allied invaders. But Eisenhower also understands that there is a more important enemy: the Nazi Party, a political entity, or at least its formerly successful guiding political philosophy, in whose name and under whose orders the German military had its initial success. Eisenhower therefore refers to the "Nazi triumphs" of 1940–41, following which "much has happened." What he means is that the rise and fall of the German military is really that of the Nazis, the more important enemy here.

As a mature commander addressing a modern, literate citizen-army, Eisenhower will not diminish the enemy to an optical zero; if he had attempted to do so, he would have succeeded only in diminishing his own credibility. By D-Day there had been four years of news reports about the fighting in Europe, while recent battles in North Africa, Sicily, and Italy had also demonstrated the German army to be a well led, experienced, and formidable opponent. And Eisenhower goes further. For those few Allied soldiers who might be feeling overconfident on the eve of the invasion, he offers a bitter pill: the German "will fight savagely."

As will be discussed further in chapter 5, candidly acknowledging an adversary's strength helps morale and reflects trust between the battle speechmaker and the soldier-audience. By giving the Germans their due, Eisenhower has earned some credit with this audience; he now proceeds to spend it via a historical narrative that does diminish the enemy. As with all historical narratives, this one begins with an event—the German Blitzkrieg of 1940 ("Nazi triumphs of 1940–41"). The story also has a plot—the rise, then mostly the fall, of

Nazi Germany's fortunes. And Eisenhower's method is to jar his men loose from the time frame of 1940–41 ("But this is the year 1944!"). Obviously his men know what year it is, but Eisenhower clearly believes that he is battling a "phantom enemy" that exists in the minds of his soldier-audience. That imagined enemy was really an image of invincibility that the Nazis and/or Germans had once enjoyed based on their stunning military achievements of "1940–41." Early in the war, after all, the Germans had occupied an impressive list of countries—Czechoslovakia, Poland, Norway, Denmark, the Netherlands, Belgium, France, Romania, Yugoslavia, and Greece—and in the east they had reached to within twenty miles of Moscow. And they did so by using new and dramatic tactics, especially compared with those of World War I: chiefly, the *Blitzkrieg*, with its crushing air power followed by highly mobile columns of mechanized infantry and armor. It is this image that Eisenhower now sought to diminish.

Eisenhower's rhetorical shove into the present year draws a sharp contrast with "1940–41" because "Much has happened since." Eisenhower the battle speechmaker brackets the beginning and ending dates to his rhetorical history and then fills this space with the story of a German decline. First, the Germans have been reduced by "great defeats," and, in an interesting coda, Eisenhower adds "in open battle, man-to-man." While this serves to place Allied manhood on a par with the enemy's, it may have another, more time-bound significance as well. Many infantrymen stationed in Great Britain during the build-up to the Normandy invasion had experienced the war only by observing overhead bomber flights and reading news reports about the great Allied air offensives of 1943 and 1944. Although often deadly to the men in the planes, few soldiers likely regarded such combat as "proving" that the Germans could be destroyed "in open battle, man-to-man." Moreover, the Allied campaign in North Africa, Sicily, and Italy was fought against both German and Italian soldiers, the latter of whom were regarded as relatively less formidable. But Eisenhower assures his audience that in fact the Germans alone had been defeated in infantry battles, and then he "proves" his case: the "United Nations [including the Soviet Union] have inflicted upon the Germans" these "great defeats." Eisenhower believed it advantageous to remind his men of an important news meme since the German surrender at Stalingrad in February 1943: in a series of offensives or counteroffensives, the Soviet Union had inflicted staggering losses on the German military.

Of course, Eisenhower must also emphasize that British and American forces have not been idle. He explicitly refers to the air campaign, making it the second historical fact in his narrative of German decline: "Our air offensive has seriously reduced their strength in the air and their capacity to wage war on the ground." Besides being additional testimony about German weakness, it is also more reassurance to the invaders—Allied soldiers expected that their air forces would "soften up" the beachheads on D-Day to suppress resistance and an absence of Luftwaffe resistance would make this task easier. Eisenhower then offers the third and fourth historical facts about German decline: the growth in Allied power, via a zero-sum calculation, must imply an automatic reduction in German power. Here, Eisenhower leverages his men's investment in his speech by evoking what they already knew quite well about the Home Front: first, the British and American economies had transformed themselves into enormous engines of defense production; second, beside themselves, many friends and relatives, as well as wives and sweethearts, were now in uniform too. So Eisenhower's declaration that "Our Home Fronts have given us overwhelming superiority in weapons and munitions of war, and placed at our disposal great reserves of trained fighting men" was doubtless greeted by the nodding of tens of thousands of helmeted heads.

Together these "facts" create a narrative demonstrating a three-dimensional collapse in Germany's fortunes: from the air above, the ground below, and the Allied home front behind (and so, hopefully, on the Normandy beaches ahead). "The tide has turned!" Eisenhower assures his soldiers. His use of the metonym "tide" (the rising of ocean water levels as a stand-in for Allied progress in the war) could not have been coincidental. The Americans and Canadians who were poised to invade Normandy had already crossed one ocean to arrive in Britain, and with their British comrades they were now about to cross more saltwater to arrive in France. *They* were the tide, but Eisenhower seeks to even further historicize the mission by globalizing its scope: "The free men of the world are marching together to a Victory!" Thus will the political history of Nazi Germany come to an end. "I have full confidence in your courage, devotion to duty and skill in battle," Eisenhower declares in his penultimate paragraph (not included above). "We will accept nothing less than full Victory!" Thus can a single category of historical narrative, the Political Historical, serve two uses, increasing confidence while diminishing the enemy.

2

THE PRESENTATION AND THE RECRUITING SPEECH

[Presentation of the flag by Charles Tracy] "Col. McQuade and Offi-
cers and Members of the Regiment: The Sons of Oneida County resid-
ing in New York and Brooklyn present to you this regimental color. . . .
Go forth, gallant men. Go with no doubt of your perfect success. Go
assured that you are remembered by us in every thing that can serve
you and not forgotten in our prayers. May the Almighty Upholder of
the Right, the God that Judgeth in the Earth, guard your heads in the
day of battle, and bring you back with the triumphs of victory."

Mr. Tracy thereupon placed the banner in the hands of Col. Mc-
Quade, who responded as follows: "Mr. Tracy and Gentlemen . . . I
can say, sir, we shall ever cherish this color on account of the donors.
We shall defend it in the great and holy cause in which we are em-
barked. I assure you, sir, that those of us who may live to return it
shall return it without blemish, except it may be the blood of traitors
shed in the struggle."

[Col. McQuade] then turned to his regiment, and said: "If there is
any man in the ranks who is not determined to defend the flag to the
last drop of his blood, let him now leave." Not a soldier moved; and
after a moment's silence, a deafening shout of hurrah arose along the
ranks and from the spectators, testifying that all were true.

Excerpts from a flag Presentation Speech by Charles Tracy and reply by Colonel
James McQuade, Fourteenth New York State Volunteers, June 18, 1861[1]

THE PRESENTATION SPEECH is a battle speech that accompanies the giving and acceptance of some object for the purpose

of reward or recognition. It may be a military object, such as a flag, sword, medal, or pistol, or it may be a personal gesture, as for example when the men of the Army of the Potomac's Third Corps contributed a day's pay to purchase, "as an expression of respect," a carriage and horses for General Daniel Sickles, their Battle of Gettysburg–wounded commander. Whatever is given and accepted, the Presentation Speech, like its siblings, usually follows certain conventions.

First, there is the Staging Convention. The spaces in which Presentation Speeches are usually given must be distinguished from ordinary space — for example, where time and opportunity permit, flags, bunting, and music may be provided; under more primitive conditions, the presentation may be marked simply by calling the soldiers to attention. In either case, the scene and mood will be somehow altered to enhance the Presentation Speech's message. In modern militaries, presentation ceremonies — now typically involving the award of decorations or the transfer of authority from one unit to another, have become so important a part of routine experience that they are controlled by highly detailed procedures that have been codified in regulations.[2]

The next and most important convention is the Equivalence Convention. Presentation Speeches must be symmetrical in structure. After all, something intangible — a great or special service, an act of courage, the loss of a limb, or some duty well and nobly performed — is being acknowledged by the presentation of something tangible, and puny in comparison to the service being recognized — a mere thing, a piece of sewn fabric, a bit of ribbon, a few pounds of gunmetal or iron. The first task of the Presentation speechmaker is to endow this presented thing with a symbolic meaning (usually derived from one of the four narratives discussed in the last chapter) that strives for equivalence with the deed being praised.

The Acceptance Convention follows next. Here, the recipient of the thing will reply in some way to the speechmaker. His or her acceptance of the object serves to acknowledge the exchange and simultaneously reaffirms for the soldier-audience the symbolic meanings contained in the Presentation Speech. For example, if the Presentation speechmaker declares that a medal recipient's bravery vindicated

democracy, or the monarchy, or the revolution, or God, then the acceptance of the medal enhances the proposition's truth to the soldier-
audience. (This is especially true for those soldier-audience members
who share the same rank, race, ethnicity, political allegiance, or religion with the recipient.) And this usually completes the presentation "transaction." The last convention, as important as Equivalence,
is Emulation: others should aspire to that deed, service, or standard
for which the recipient is being recognized. Often, the speechmaker
expressly declares that the recipient is himself a successful emulator,
for he has done what other successful comrades have done, or what
praiseworthy historical forebears have done. But whether the Emulation Convention is explicit or not, it can always be derived from the
nature of the presentation ceremony itself.

Although Presentation Speeches continue to this day, their "golden
age," at least in American history, was during the Civil War. This
was true for several reasons. Although that war was not the first U.S.
conflict reported by newspapers, there had never been an American
war covered as extensively. Moreover, even local papers were self-ap-
pointed "papers of record" and thus usually carried speeches of every
kind verbatim. Second, the org charts of Civil War armies made it a
"speech-rich environment." The national army sent some two thousand different units into the conflict, and many of these men heard
Presentation Speeches as they were given their colors. And whenever
medals are presented, speeches will be made. During the Civil War
both the Confederate and the Federal Congresses established medals to be awarded for special acts of bravery. Of these, the Medal of
Honor, established in 1862 and later made permanent, remains the
highest American award for bravery. Major General George Gordon
Meade's speech at the first presentation of this medal appears below.
For all of these reasons, most of the speeches used in this chapter will
be drawn from the Civil War; however, the old conventions still apply,
as a few more recent examples will prove.[3]

The excerpts from Tracy's speech featured above contain the elements of a typical American Civil War Presentation Speech. The
Staging Convention preceded the utterance of any words. The Fourteenth Regiment New York Volunteers, nicknamed the "First Oneida

County Regiment," gathered in Albany and sailed down the Hudson River to New York City before entraining for Washington. More than two hundred members of an organization called "The Oneidas of the Metropolis," all of whom wore "an appropriate badge," met the unit at West Fourteenth Street in the city. Preceded by a "city band of music," the column—which, including civilians, may have numbered up to two thousand people—marched in parade order up Fifth Avenue to the Washington Parade Ground, where a "large concourse of ladies and gentlemen, many of them natives of Oneida country," were present for the flag presentation ceremony. The stage was quite literally set.[4]

Of the several speeches made, the most significant was Charles Tracy's, which accompanied the presentation of the New York state flag. Tracy was an Oneida native, a Yale graduate, and a prominent New York City attorney who was also an important layman in the Episcopal Church; if he held a position in the Oneidas of the Metropolis, it was probably one of importance. For Tracy, the Emulation Convention came first. He devoted half his remarks to a Political Historical Narrative in which he stitched together the military history of Oneida County and the American Revolution. It was replete with stirring historical references that would have been familiar to any good Oneida citizen of that day—the siege of Fort Schuyler and the Battle of Oriskany, both in 1777. Here Tracy gave special emphasis to General Nicholas Herkimer's actions. In a very famous scene from the American Revolution, Herkimer propped himself up under a tree after being shot and issued orders while calmly puffing on his pipe (he would later die from his wound). The spirit to be emulated is clear. Although Herkimer was not, strictly speaking, an Oneida County boy (his birthplace would eventually become Herkimer County), his nativity was still in upstate New York, and close enough to pass him off as a "local boy made good." Much more important to Tracy were the general's actions in battle—he had set aside any concern for his personal safety to perform his duty and thus sacrificed himself to a higher cause. Later in his speech, Tracy articulates similar expectations for the Fourteenth Regiment: "The hazards of camp and battle are before you," he declares. "Great is the sacrifice. Yet deem yourself fortunate that you can devote your lives to such a cause." The men of the Fourteenth have been given the same good fortune as General Herkimer. To personalize the emulative meme, Tracy connects the imagined Oneida boyhood experience of his soldier-audience with the Revolution and the current Southern rebellion. "Anyone familiar with those old [Oneida] battle-fields, who has traced the hacks of the tomahawk, and clambered over the ruins of ancient forts and now witnesses the uprising [the rebellion]," Tracy declares, "may truly exclaim,"

> Again there breathe that haunted air
> The sons of sires who conquered there;
> With arm to strike, and soul to dare,
> As quick, as far, as they.[5]

From Emulation, Tracy proceeds to Equivalence: investing the New York state flag with symbolic meaning. The flag is here presented with fanfare and invested with great meaning because the men of the Fourteenth New York have done something exemplary, albeit intangible—they have voluntarily left their homes, jobs, and dear ones to fight in a war for thirteen dollars a month, and fighting brings with it the possibility of injury and death. That is what the men of the Fourteenth give; in return, they receive a mere piece of colored, stitched fabric bound to a wooden pole. (The ceremony *must* be public, of course, because privately handing them the colors or shipping them by post negates the possibility of Equivalence.) But if Tracy has his way—and based on reports, it appears that he did—the Fourteenth New York is being given no such "thing." Instead, what they get is much more than a flag. In military contexts, flags serve as the archmetonyms of political, religious, or ethnic collectives, the ultimate "stand-ins" for entire armies, populations, monarchs, religions, tribes, and states. (One thinks of the flag-raising atop Mount Suribachi on Iwo Jima as a stand-in for a marine triumph, or Balboa thrusting a flag into the Pacific to represent a "taking" of the world's largest ocean for Spain, or Francis Scott Key's use of the flag as a stand-in for American forces garrisoning Fort McHenry.) Ordinarily, the New York state flag would serve as a metonym for the state of New York. The basic design for this flag was first adopted in 1778; hence, its original meaning could have nothing to do with a war that began eighty-three years later. Thus it is left to Tracy to symbolically reinvent the flag's precise meanings in order to attain Equivalence with what the soldiers have given. This reinvented flag will be Tracy's part of the bargain.

Tracy accomplishes this by linking the theme of "union" with the emblem and motto of the New York state flag: "Upon this flag you see emblazoned, in a single shield, the arms of the Union and the arms of the State of New York—the Stars and Stripes quartered with the rising sun—the morning rays bright with promise, the motto always EXCELSIOR — HIGHER. Well joined!" He then asks: "And what State is more identified with the American Union?"[6]

He answers this question via a new Political Historical Narrative; however, instead of stitching Oneida County together with the Revolution, he uses a stream of facts about the city and state of New York: the first colony-wide Congress convened in Albany; the first federal Congress was held in New York City; George Washington was inaugurated on Wall Street and sworn in by the Chancellor of the State of New York. Moreover, New York's commitment to the Union continued through the War of 1812, when the state "furnished vastly beyond its quota both of militia and volunteers." Indeed, its commitment has continued to the present hour: "And now, to this sacred war of liberty, she sends forty thousand men." Thus, the New York state flag is inherently different from the flags of South Carolina, Georgia, and Mississippi—the flag of the Empire State represents the Union, which, as Tracy next demonstrates, means much more than mere statehood.

Once joined with Union, the meaning of the New York state flag dovetails with the reasons for the present war. "The whole area of the Union is our country [that is, this enlarged version on New York]. Upon every acre of this soil we are at home, until our feet step into the Gulf of Mexico," he announces. "We paid for Florida, and our army will see to it that our national flag again waves over its entire territory." Why Tracy singles out Florida (and not Louisiana, which "we" also paid for) is unclear, but the reasons for the war are perfectly clear, and they have nothing to do with a traitorous cabal of Floridians cheating Uncle Sam out of his real estate deal. "It is a holy war—a war for principles, a war for our kind," Tracy declares. Elsewhere in the speech he gives the reasons why secession is an offense to God:

This country, for three-quarters of a century, has stretched out its hands to the oppressed of all nations. The victims of tyranny and of want have fled hither, and found a place of refuge and an abode of prosperity. What a spectacle is now presented to the world, when traitors rise among us to crush this benevolent Government, and dishearten all men who struggle for liberty! What crime can surpass secession! If it could prevail, the heart of every man sighing for liberty in Europe must sink, and every dungeon of tyranny must deepen its gloom. The time has come, in the affairs of men, when liberty and justice in this country must be maintained. To wage war against such treason is to wage it against the enemies of humanity.

Tracy has now transformed the New York state flag from a parochial banner that formerly served as a metonym for cartographic lines imposed on acreage into a symbol of universal human rights. His logic is clear, simple, and, judging from the reportedly robust reaction of the rank and file, immediately powerful: you fight for the Union, and fighting for the Union is also God's fight; the flag of New York that I present to you this day represents that Union, and thus represents God's cause; you are therefore God's warriors fighting under His banner. Once the theme of holy war is introduced, Tracy's Political Historical Narrative, drawn entirely from secular events in historical times, becomes adorned with religious imagery, which he carries on with throughout the remainder of the speech: "There can never be any great deliverance secured to man except by the sword. . . . The profession of arms is a sacred calling. . . . Great is the sacrifice. . . . You [are] not forgotten in our prayers. May the Almighty Upholder of the Right, THE GOD THAT JUDGETH EARTH, guard you back with triumphs of victory." After this last statement, Tracy "thereupon placed the banner in the hands of Colonel McQuade."

One final convention of the Presentation Speech now needs to be met—Acceptance. Colonel James McQuade accepts the flag on behalf of his regiment and also delivers a short acceptance speech. And McQuade has been paying attention, because his remarks reciprocate those of Tracy. "I can say, sir, we shall ever cherish this flag on account of the donors," he declares, thus acknowledging the Oneida County origins of the presentation ceremony's organizers. "We shall defend it in the great and holy cause in which we are embarked," he adds, embracing Tracy's theme of holy war. "I assure you, sir, that those of us who may live to return it shall return it without blemish, except it may be the blood of traitors shed in the struggle." Here the colonel embraces Emulation—the men of the Fourteenth Regiment will behave as old General Herkimer did, "without blemish," except of course, for the blood of the traitors. And finally, in a parting gesture (and an even tighter embrace of Emulation), the colonel then faces his regiment and announces: "If there is any man in the ranks who is not determined to defend the flag to the last drop of his blood, let him now leave." The reporter then observed, "Not a soldier moved; and, after a moment's silence, a deafening shout of hurrah arose along the ranks and from the spectators, testifying that all were true." With a showman's instinct, Colonel McQuade had sealed the transaction.

I now put into your hands, as I have in the hands of regiments that preceded you, the State ensign of this Commonwealth. You already bear with you the Stars and Stripes, but I would have you recognized wherever you go as coming from this State, where you have your homes. And when you look on the Stars and Stripes you can remember that you are American citizens; when you look on this venerable ensign you can remember your wives and families in Massachusetts.

Excerpt from flag Presentation Speech of Massachusetts Governor
John A. Andrew to the Ninth Regiment Massachusetts Volunteer
Infantry, June 25, 1861[7]

"SAVING THE UNION"—or some other lofty political objective—is not the only meaning with which a flag (or any other thing) can be symbolically invested. The above excerpt from a flag Presentation Speech delivered by Governor Andrew to the departing Ninth Massachusetts Volunteers illustrates another meaning that is exportable to objects. While Charles Tracy invested the New York state flag with God, human rights, the Union, and Oneida County, Andrew takes a different tack: he wants the men of the Ninth, a unit composed principally of Irish immigrants, to associate the state flag with Chapter 222 of the General Laws of the Commonwealth of Massachusetts, officially known as "An Act in Aid of the Families of Volunteers." How many of the Ninth's rank and file could cite the statute's official title is unknown, but it is almost certain that every volunteer understood its terms. Passed one month before the Ninth's departure, Chapter 222 authorized Bay State municipalities to pay, depending on family size, up to twelve dollars a month to a soldier's at-home dependents.[8]

Andrew, like Tracy, had to reinvent a flag whose existing symbols—colors, coat of arms, and motto—were first established in the late eighteenth century, long before Chapter 222 was enacted. Andrew manages this via the word "pledge." By Andrew's lights, the state flag is a pledge. But from this word the governor extracts two different senses, both of which advance the exchange so necessary to the Equivalence Convention. First, Andrew, a prominent attorney before the war, uses "pledge" in its legal sense: a pledge is "something regarded as a security" for a loan or a promise—that is, collateral. Thus, just before the flag was presented to the regiment's color sergeant, Andrew declares, "When you look upon this venerable ensign you can remember your wives and families in Massachusetts." After investing the flag with familial associations, he adds an additional meaning: "Take this [the state flag] as a pledge of affectionate care from the State of your kindred and homes." The flag also becomes the figurative collateral for the state's obligations under Chapter 222. This first use of "pledge" implies a meaning that while you are away you will have this flag to remind you of our promise to care for your families.[9]

But the word "pledge" has a second meaning as well, both in a legal sense and in the vernacular: "a solemn promise to do or refrain from doing something" in the future. Although Chapter 222 was landmark legislation for its day, it was nevertheless subject to the whims of future legislators, and the Ninth Regiment had enlisted for three years. What assurance did the volunteers have that the "Act in Aid of the Families of Volunteers" would continue throughout their term of service? Here Governor Andrew supplies the necessary reassurance via his second meaning of "pledge," as a future promise that is "secured" by the state flag "of the sincere and undying interest which its people [that is, the citizens of Massachusetts] feel and will feel for you." "Will feel" is the key phrase. The flag represents or is symbolic security for the future promise that subsequent electorates will not permit

Chapter 222 to be changed to the detriment of volunteers' families. With these promises in hand, the soldiers may now depart for the war in peace.

Governor Andrew's exchange may be less lofty than Charles Tracy's promise of honor in return for the honorable act of volunteering, but it is practical. Massachusetts offers an expressly economic bargain: men enlisted not only with the risk of death or injury in battle but also for a paltry thirteen dollars a month, a wage that produced considerable financial and often familial hardship. In many cases, the volunteer was either the breadwinner or an important contributor to the family's financial wellbeing. Honor does enter the Massachusetts exchange here, but only as security for the economic bargain—the state pledges its honor, of which its flag may be considered a token. But the honor is really the promise of continued state benevolence. "Take this [the Massachusetts state flag] as a pledge of affectionate care from the State of your kindred and homes, and of the sincere and undying interest which its people feel and will ever feel for you," the governor concluded. Judging by the reaction of the Ninth's rank and file, the bargain was more than acceptable. "This speech of the Governor was received with great enthusiasm and many cheers," reported the regimental historian.

The duties assigned to Hospital Steward Henry Fenton at this place are very arduous and difficult of execution, yet have been performed by him in such a commendable and praiseworthy manner as to please and satisfy all. Accordingly, his many friends concluded to show their appreciation of the good qualities he has ever exhibited, by presenting him with some memorial as a token of their high esteem as a man and a soldier.

One hundred and five dollars were soon subscribed for the purpose, and, thinking that a gold watch would be as serviceable to him, and, therefore, as valuably prized by him, that amount was immediately forwarded to Messrs. Ball, Black & Co., of your City [New York], accompanied by an order for the above-named article, which arrived yesterday. It is an elegant watch, upon which is engaged the following inscription: "Presented to Henry Fenton, Steward, United

States Army, Annapolis, Md., August, 1862, in token of the many noble qualities evinced in his bearing toward his fellow soldiers."

Description of a watch presented to Henry Fenton,
Steward, U.S. Army, August 27, 1862[10]

BEFORE WE TURN to more recent Presentation Speeches, it is worth briefly considering how these speeches work as "unofficial" military discourse, as in the case where a group of soldiers privately decide to honor a comrade by presenting him with a gift. These private presentations may appear to fall outside of the "recruit, instruct, or exhort" function governing the inclusion of speeches in this book; however, the effect of these ceremonies on morale should not be underestimated. Moreover, the Presentation Speech offers a useful window on a comrade's qualities that soldiers value enough to justify spending their hard-earned money.

In the evening of August 27, 1862, at the Church Pavilion located at the United States General Hospital at Annapolis, Maryland, a "large assemblage" gathered to witness the presentation of an engraved gold watch to Hospital Steward Henry Fenton, described by a soldier-correspondent for the *New York Times* as "one of the most genial and good-natured men it was my good fortune ever to meet." Fenton managed a room of hospital clerks; his exact duties are unknown, although the reporter describes them as "arduous and difficult of execution, yet . . . performed by him in such a commendable and praiseworthy manner as to please and satisfy all." But there was soon to be a change. Fenton "had tired of the life there and decided to return to the more active duties of the front." And perhaps in recognition of his work at the Baltimore hospital, Fenton was promoted and would return to battle as an officer.

As the information featured above indicates, this was a non-official ceremony, undertaken voluntarily by the "many friends" of Steward Fenton. Nevertheless, the ceremony was consistent with Presentation Speech conventions and staged as the means of the presenters allowed: a crowd to witness the honor, the presenter's elaborate speech, and a few remarks by the recipient. The watch's engraving contains a cliché that suggests how the presenters understood the exchange that was about to take place: the watch was being given "as a token" of their respect. It fell to Corporal Ambrose E. Sawyer of the Thirteenth New York Infantry to endow that token with Equivalence to Fenton's prior service in his Presentation Speech.

What did Steward Fenton do to merit this gift? Unlike Tracy or Andrew's volunteers (or the medal recipients discussed below), it was not his decision to enlist, or any brave act in particular, that moved comrades to present him with an expensive watch. Rather, Fenton simply performed his daily duties managing other clerks but apparently exceeded their minimum requirements by doing so cheerfully, kindly, and with devotion, in a Civil War hospital whose stark realities of wounds, disease, and death must have surely tried the constancy of lesser men. And in one passage, Sawyer strings these reasons aloft on a meme of Emulation typical of Presentation Speeches:

> [Your comrades] have looked admiringly upon the manner in which you have performed your arduous labors; they have striven to imitate you in the consistent soldierly bearing which has characterized your intercourse with them and others; they have received your favors and kindnesses gratefully, and now we pray you, accept this as a token of our appreciation of those noble, manly qualities.

Hospital Steward Fenton completed the Presentation Speech with his reply and in accepting the watch shed additional light on his admired qualities: "He felt very grateful and happy to learn that his course had merited their approval, and said that he should always try to do in the future what he had endeavored to do in the past, namely, 'his whole duty.'" The *New York Times*'s soldier-correspondent concluded his article by noting that "the obligations of kindness and gentleness are [as] extensive as the claims to manliness, and that coarseness and tyranny are so many forms of brute power, or so many indications of what is man's peculiar glory not to be." Victorian flourishes sometimes obfuscate details; nevertheless, a reader can probably draw some conclusions about the attitudes of Fenton and his comrades: that those who shuffle the papers necessary to wage modern war also serve, although for some, combat is still preferred; that authoritarian, exhausted, or indifferent chief hospital clerks, the implied foil against whom Fenton is compared, must have been a common experience; that unlike these other clerks, Fenton was willing to work with newer staff and teach them proper procedures; that the sights, sounds, and smells of these often overworked medical institutions probably overwhelmed many average men—and may have eventually overwhelmed Fenton (he requested a transfer to the front), although his self-possession was such that he never allowed these stresses to diminish his cheerful willingness to perform his whole duty.[11]

Officers and Soldiers of the 5th Corps: I have today to perform a most pleasant and gratifying duty—to present to certain meritorious non-commissioned officers and privates medals of honor, conferred on them by the War Department, for distinguished conduct on the field of battle, in capturing flags from the enemy. It has been customary in all ages for nations to commemorate and reward the gallantry and devotion of their sons when engaged in the holy cause of defending their country. . . . This is the first occasion on which the men of this army have been so honored; and I have deemed it proper, through your corps commander, to call you together, that the conferring of this distinction might be witnessed by the comrades of their recipients, and that the inducence [sic] of their example might serve to incite others to emulate their worthy conduct. . . . I trust the medals now presented will serve as incentives to urge you to emulate and surpass the deeds of your comrades now about to be honored.

> Excerpt from speech by General George Gordon Meade
> presenting the first Medals of Honor to soldiers of the
> Army of the Potomac, September 13, 1864[12]

SPEECHES THAT ACCOMPANY the award of medals are also Presentation Speeches and follow similar conventions: Staging, Equivalence (investing the lesser object—the medal—with symbolic meaning equivalent to the virtue being recognized), Acceptance, (that is, the pinning ceremony itself and the recipient's acknowledgment of the speaker's meaning), and the hope of Emulation, especially by the soldier-audience that witnesses the ceremony. However, there are two important differences. Unlike the old-style flag presentation ceremonies, where the colors are accepted and receipt is expressly acknowledged, a medal recipient usually remains mute—he or she simply stands at attention and receives the award (though to do so, then exchange salutes, *is* to accept the honor). Additionally, because the focus here is on an individual's courage or achievement, Emulation is given greater emphasis than in other types of Presentation Speech. This was certainly the case when General Meade presented the first Medals of Honor.

Staging for General Meade's Presentation Speech was elaborate, considering the circumstances. Two things about the ceremony are especially noteworthy: its proximity to the actual point in time when the medals were earned, and to the enemy. The valorous actions (the capture of rebel battle flags) occurred on August 21, 1864, at the Battle of Weldon Railroad, only twenty-three days before the award, and the ceremony took place at General Warren's headquarters on the Weldon Railroad itself, apparently within earshot of Confederate soldiers. Both facts must have added considerable drama to the immediate experience of the Presentation Speech. A special stage had been built that was "gaily decked off with flags, among which were the captured Rebel flags." Bands played and no less than nine generals ascended the "impromptu platform." The recipients all belonged to the Fifth Army Corps, and it was appropriate that their corps commander, Major General Gouverneur K. Warren, convened the ceremony.[13] He spoke "in a loud, clear voice, stated the object for which they had thus met together, and called the names of those who were to be honored, desiring them to come forward to the platform." The recipients, one sergeant and two privates, approached the stage. They were ordered to present and then shoulder their arms. General Meade then addressed the soldier-audience, which may have numbered several thousand men.[14]

Meade was aware that this ceremony was not only unprecedented but also likely to be repeated. "Although this is the first occasion of the presentation of these medals of honor," he declared during his speech, "I trust and have reason to believe, the precedent thus made will soon by followed by many other presentations." Thus the meanings with which he seeks to endow these Medals of Honor must also become a precedent for the way soldiers in the future will understand their significance. And so his Presentation Speech attempts to locate the Medals of Honor in a three-millennia-old stream of Religious, Unit, and Political Historical Narrative. "It has been customary in all ages for nations to commemorate and reward the gallantry and devotion of their sons when engaged in the holy cause of defending their country," Meade declares. To justify this statement, he begins with a Religious Historical Narrative drawn from the sacred time of the Hebrew Bible. "In the Word of God some of the most beautiful passages of the Psalmist are devoted to commemorating and praising the deeds of the warriors of old; for even the chosen people of God were, in the execution of His will, compelled to take up arms and battle for their cause." But Meade's history soon enters the secular time of the Greco-Roman period, and he shifts to a Political Historical Narrative of governments rewarding soldiers. The classical histories, he observed, "are filled with accounts of the honors bestowed upon . . . warriors, crowning them with wreaths of laurels, by triumphal processions, in which were exhibited the trophies and prisoners captured in battle." Modern states have followed suit with "military ranks, titles of nobility, estates and appropriations of money . . . medals and other decorations, together with pensions and endowing institutions, where the aged and disabled soldier can live in comfort and quiet."

Before Meade shifts from historical meaning to Emulation, he cleverly concludes his Political Historical Narrative by bringing it into the present. In this way, the soldiers will be reminded that *this* medal is being awarded by an existing government on behalf of live citizens with expectations about *their* soldiers' conduct on the field of battle. "Besides numerous votes of thanks from Congress, the gratitude of our people for the devotion displayed by soldiers on the battlefield has been testified in many ways—States, counties, and cities have presented lands, houses, &c [to deserving soldiers]," he reminds his soldier-audience. "The fairs devoted to raising funds for the Sanitary Commission have been made the means of honoring the brave and distinguished; and during the session before the last Congress passed a resolution authorizing the Secretary of War to confer on distinguished non-commissioned officers and privates medals of honor." Meade's references probably resonated with his soldier-audience. Every citizen soldier had a congressman; most were aware that their states and hometowns honored soldiers, the details of which were usually covered extensively in local newspapers; and every soldier in the Army of the Potomac knew the work of the Sanitary Commission from its activities in the camps. Indeed, there were likely very many soldiers whose at-home relations had attended, contributed to, or worked in one of the many fairs that the Sanitary Commission had sponsored throughout the country in 1864.

As part of Emulation, Meade must first create an imaginary civilian audience that has expectations for his soldiers' conduct in battle. He will arrive here through an observation soldiers seldom enough heard: "Whatever may be the talents or the genius of a commanding general, and however well laid his plans, unless he is sustained by the brave hearts and stout arms of his soldiers, success will not attend his efforts." But this is not faux humility. Empowering the rank and file in this way justifies Meade's next statement about why the imagined civilians have a right to expect great things from their army. "I therefore take this opportunity, while reminding you of how much depends on the individual exertions of one of you, to say to you that our countrymen look to you for renewed exertions to unceasing and persistent efforts to overcome our enemies and bring this war to a close." In sum, Meade names those in the soldier-audience, not the generals, as the real army; it is their soldierly qualities that will end the war, he says, not his own. He is then ready to introduce Emulation:

> I trust the medals now presented will serve as incentives to urge you to emulate and surpass the deeds of your comrade[s] now about to be honored. . . . And now, fellow soldiers of the 5th Corps, let me again urge you to emulate the example of these honored men, and by your future efforts not only deserve similar rewards, but aid in the great work in which we are all engaged—the overcoming of the enemies of your country and the restoration of peace and happiness to the whole land.[15]

As is usual in medal award ceremonies, no verbal acknowledgment by the recipients was made. However, troops cheering generals had long been a tradition in the Army of the Potomac, and it was continued here: "Upon the conclusion of the address," the *Inquirer*'s reporter noted, "General Warren stepped forward and asked the 'boys' to give three cheers to show the General that they had a heart to appreciate his kindness, which was done, and they were given with a will that must have acquainted the 'Johnies' with the facts that something unusual was going on. The band struck up 'Hail Columbia,' the troops were marched off to their quarters, and General Warren invited his guests to partake of a collation, which was not the least agreeable feature of the proceedings."

In the courtyard outside, two soldiers wounded in the Wednesday-afternoon firefight stood on the back of a Gator all-terrain vehicle, waiting to receive their Purple Hearts. A hundred comrades stood at attention in the scorching sun as the medals were pinned on. Petraeus strode to the front of the ranks. "There is no greater commitment than that which is made by putting the American infantryman on the ground," he said. "We're here to honor two soldiers who are being awarded the most noble of decorations our country has.

"You've really walked point for our nation in this particular battle and this part of the campaign. You've performed brilliantly in countless ambiguous situations." [Petraeus's] strong voice rang through the courtyard. . . .

The ceremony ended. A sergeant dismissed the troops. "Hoo-ah!" they bayed. "Hoo-ah!"

General David H. Petraeus awarding Purple Hearts
on April 4, 2003, at Najaf, Iraq[16]

I N HIS PRESENTATION SPEECH, General Meade did not really create new conventions so much as he applied existing conventions to a medal award ceremony (indeed, the whole point of his varied historical narrative was to implicitly acknowledge this.) Lofty, often prolix orations drawing on Biblical and classical sources were the norm for many types of public speaking in the nineteenth century, and one is entitled to ask how these conventions have fared in the modern era. Of course, one must distinguish between the more universal battle-speech *structural conventions* and the timebound *narrative conventions* with which different historical eras paint the structural elements of these speeches. As General David H. Petraeus's speech above illustrates, the short answer for how battle-speech structural conventions have fared is "quite well."

As was the case with General Meade, the medals that General Petraeus presented—two Purple Hearts—were also awarded proximate to a battlefield. The city of Najaf had just been occupied, although the capture of Baghdad still lay ahead. And as was also the case with Meade, these Purple Hearts were presented not at all long after they were earned. Two days before the ceremony, two soldiers had been wounded in the fighting to capture Najaf; now they were in the city to receive their Purple Hearts. Finally, to echo a point made in the introduction about the role of media, speeches, and archives, just as a newspaper reporter preserved General Meade's speech, embedded *Washington Post* reporter Rick Atkinson likewise wrote down Petraeus's remarks. Otherwise, this speech would likely have been lost to the record.

The similarities in Staging between Meade and Petraeus's awards are obvious. Petraeus also used an "impromptu platform"—the rear bed of an M-Gator ATV. A soldier-audience one hundred comrades strong stood at attention as the general re-enacted the old ritual of pinning the medals. The acceptance completed, Petraeus's words followed those of Meade in using historical narrative to endow the medals with a significance equal to the soldiers' sacrifice. However, Petraeus's speech drew mostly from Unit and Political Historical Narratives rather than one derived from God's history or Greco-Roman heroes. And the sum of those histories appears in the first two sentences of Petraeus's four-sentence Presentation Speech: "There is no greater commitment than that which is made by putting the American infantryman on the ground," he declares. This sentence requires the soldier-audience to add additional premises that are derived from history, because the only way to know the truth of the general's statement is to remember past American wars. Of course, the general is not striving for any precise or comparative historical judgments, as, for example, whether the enormous casualties suffered by the Eighth Air Force over World War II Europe represented a "greater commitment" than the proverbial "boots on the ground." (The Eighth Air

Force suffered some 26,000 deaths and over 47,000 total casualties.) All that matters is that the soldier-audience recalls that in past wars, the United States was *really* at war when it committed infantry. Combining Unit and Political Historical Narratives, Petraeus argues that the use of infantry is the surest evidence that the government of the United States intends to fight for victory; launching missiles, ordering air strikes, or dispatching Special Forces for limited objectives all comprise something less than "war."[17]

The second sentence also requires some history, albeit not of an enthymematic nature. "We're here to honor two soldiers who are being awarded the most noble of decorations our country has," Petraeus declared. Of course, by characterizing the Purple Heart as "the most noble of decorations" the general is presuming that his soldier-audience has some historical knowledge about this particular medal. Originally known as the "Badge of Military Merit" when created by George Washington in 1782, the award fell into desuetude after the Revolution. However, it was revived in 1932 to commemorate the bicentennial of George Washington's birth. If one includes the 150-year-long hiatus, the Purple Heart is the army's oldest decoration, and thus arguably the most "noble," where that word is defined as something "that has a special social or political status in a country or a state."[18]

The final comparison involves the Emulation Convention. Meade was explicit about the importance of emulation and actually used the word "emulate" three times in his speech. On the surface there is nothing in Petreaus's words that seems to address the importance of emulation. But Meade made one other observation that bears on how soldiers really derive the meaning of a speech by "reading" the speech, the speaker, and other surrounding cues. "I have deemed it proper, through your corps commander," Meade had declared, "to call you together, that the conferring of this distinction might be witnessed by the comrades of their recipients, and that the inducence [sic] of their example might serve to incite others to emulate their worthy conduct." Thus General Meade decided in 1864 that the Presentation Speech's Emulation Convention could be satisfied by simply giving men the immediate experience of observing their comrades decorated for valor.

When Petraeus exhorts the recipients, he really intends that his words carry to the one hundred comrades standing nearby. ("His strong voice rang through the courtyard," Atkinson wrote.) "You've really walked point for our nation in this particular battle and this part of the campaign," the general declared. "You've performed brilliantly in countless ambiguous situations." Petraeus's "you" has now grown from the two men receiving the Purple Heart to include their comrades in the courtyard.

In conferring recognition beyond the two men being decorated, Petraeus hints at the same considerations that informed Colonel Collins's speech from the introduction. "Walking point" is military-speak for being the lead soldier on a foot patrol; it is the place of greatest personal danger as well as sometimes the first opportunity to strike at the enemy. But in the 2003 invasion of Iraq, striking the enemy carried certain risks for American soldiers that their predecessors may not have faced: While civilians had always been present among historical enemies, it was now a matter of official, urgent policy that those civilians be spared, as much as possible, war's cruelties. Thus does Petraeus's use of the word "ambiguous" become intelligible as a compliment: in the process of fighting for control of Najaf, in which the enemy was threaded throughout the civilian population, his men had conquered without excessive violence — that is, without exploiting numerous grey areas that might have allowed them greater personal protection but only at the cost of killing more civilians. Had they not performed so "brilliantly," one purpose of the invasion might not have been accomplished: to pacify and empower the civilian population, or at least its anti-Ba'athist portion. Moreover, another meaning lurks in Petraeus's words, although it is not one that he would declare publicly: that the soldiers being decorated were wounded (and the others witnessing the ceremony might likewise be wounded) as a result of pursuing that policy of protecting civilians. To wage war and protect civilians, then, requires that soldiers take greater personal risks; more bravery is required when clearing a building room-by-room than when simply demolishing the whole structure with artillery or air strikes from a safe distance. And thus does Petraeus's battle speech "brilliantly" compact "ambiguous" policies into one seven-word sentence.

The Recruiting Speech

But if need be I can show spears, a banner, medals, and other military honors, to say nothing of the scars on my body—all of them in front. These are my family portraits, these my title of nobility, one not bequeathed to me, as theirs were to them, but won at the cost of countless toils and perils. . . .

The lessons I have learnt are such as best enable me to serve my country—to strike down an enemy, to mount guard, to fear nothing but disgrace, to endure winter's cold and summer's heat with equal patience, to sleep on the bare ground, and to work hard on an empty stomach. These are the lessons I shall teach my soldiers. And I shall not make them go short while enjoying the best of everything myself, not steal all the glory and leave them the toil. . . .

I therefore call upon all men of military age to cooperate with me in the service of our country. And no one need fear a repetition of the misfortunes, which your comrades suffered under my arrogant predecessors. I shall be with you on the march and on the field of battle, to be your guide and to share your perils; and I shall claim no special privileges for myself. Rest assured that, with the gods' help, all the fruits of battle are ready to be plucked; victory, spoils, and glory await you—though even if these rewards were doubtful or remote, it would still be the duty of all patriots to rally to the aid of the fatherland. Cowardice will not enable a man to live forever, and no parent ever prayed that his children might have immortality, but rather than they might live virtuous and honorable lives.

Excerpt from Gaius Marius's Recruiting Speech
for the Jugurthine War, 107 BCE[19]

THE RECRUITING SPEECH carries a heavier burden of persuasion than most other types of battle speeches. Even speeches that exhort men to battle where death, injury, or capture are real possibilities do not shoulder this burden; soldiers who have been trained, disciplined, and armed for a fray are already half persuaded and may need only good leadership to proceed. But attempting to enlist civilians who may have never fired a gun or thrown a spear is another matter. At the same time, the role of Recruiting Speeches in raising armies should not be overstated. Throughout the ages most men have been persuaded into an armed service by other means. Aside from conscription and impressment, informal arguments for and against enlisting have probably circled family tables and town marketplaces since the beginnings of organized warfare. And no speeches are usually necessary where oral reports or images of an enemy's evil are the more persuasive recruiting tool. Sometimes success begets success, mixed with other motives. After word spread about a string of King Herod's victories, "He was joined by a steady stream of Jews from Jericho and other places, some through hatred of Antigonus, others impressed by Herod's successes, but most in the grip of an unaccountable longing for change." The more recent example of Army Ranger Sergeant Joseph LeBleu could be a universal stand-in for the ages of this recruiting phenomenon. After the terrorist attacks of September 11, 2001, he said, "[I felt] godawful that this happened, and I knew I had to get in the fight."[20]

Nevertheless, the Recruiting Speech has always been one means of persuading men to join a military. And like other battle speeches, it is also governed by certain conventions. One of the most important of these is Staging. Selling military service has always required special adornments as well as good arguments. Many Recruiting Speeches must also have Family Appeal—both the recruit *and* his family need to be persuaded. Much is made of the suitability of young men for military life, but less attention is given to the fact that male recruits, traditionally the breadwinners necessary for family support, are not the only ones who must be convinced. Because the legal consent or family blessing of parents or other relations may also be necessary, the wise Recruiting Speechmaker knows that his "recruit-audience" consists of the entire family. Who the speechmaker is, what he has done in the past, and how he promotes himself are the keys to persuasion—the words merely provide the twist that opens the lock. The convention of Speechmaker Identity is thus of supreme importance in Recruiting Speeches. Also important are his professions of care for his soldiers' welfare; the going may be tough, the recruiter will concede, but no recruits will be better cared for than those who sign the rolls today.

Finally, there is the recruiting appeal itself. Here a different aspect of Speechmaker Identity becomes paramount: his identification with the audience. For Recruiting Speeches, this often amounts to the use of a (supposedly) shared Religious, Social, or Political Historical Narrative. These appeals often mix practical with idealistic considerations. For example, time spent making war is time away from earning a living or learning a trade; thus, compensation has always been a consideration, whether it is the promise of plunder or one's inclusion under the G.I. Bill of Rights. The principal historical difference in recruiting appeals between professional armies and short-time citizen volunteer groups has been the prominence accorded pecuniary motives in Recruiting Speeches: in longer-serving professional armies, job security matters more than in citizen armies, for which the appeal of money (enlistment bonuses, bounties, and so on), although not absent, tends to be submerged. Yet idealistic themes occur more frequently than pecuniary appeals throughout history. Patriotism—that is, an appeal with a strong Political and sometimes Social Historical Narrative—is the most common theme. It may be a defensive appeal (defend the homeland!); it may be an aggressive appeal (punish the enemy!); or it may be an appeal that is detached from patriotism completely, such as idealistic appeal to spread to all mankind the reputed benefits of a certain religion or political ideology. And then there is the appeal taken up by Gaius Marius that today's military continues to make: enlistment understood as a means of personal growth and development (to which late-twentieth-century militaries have added job training).

Marius's Recruiting Speech wonderfully illustrates these conventions. But his speech merits attention for another reason: it is perhaps the most famous Recruiting Speech in Western history, and certainly the most influential. In this speech, Marius recruits men without regard to the property requirement that had been the basis for service in the Roman militia at least since the reign of Servius Tullius (578–534 BCE) However, after the Marian reforms (named after Marius), the connection between wealth and service was severed, and the Roman legions began their transformation from a part-time militia into a professional, full-time army that provided the military pillar of empire for many centuries.[21]

What occasioned Marius's speech was the Jugurthine War, which began in 112 BCE and was fought between Rome and King Jugurtha over the succession to the throne of Numidia (present-day coastal Algeria). The causes of the war are less interesting here than the immediate circumstances of Marius's Recruiting Speech. After unsuccessful Roman military campaigns against the brilliant, wily, and ruthless King Jugurtha, Marius, reputed to be of common origins, was elected consul and entrusted with management of the war. But by Sallust's account the patrician-dominated senate remained wary of Marius's origins and fearful that he might ultimately field the army to use against them, perhaps in some revolt of the plebeians. Still, when Marius asked for the authority to fill legions weakened by the earlier Numidian campaigns, the senate could not refuse, although in granting recruitment authority it would prove too clever by half. "As to the addition to the strength of the legions, [the senate was] only too pleased to authorize it," Sallust observed, "because the people were supposed to dislike military service, so that Marius would either have to go without the men he needed or forfeit his popularity with the multitude." But the senate patricians, blinded by social prejudice, had underestimated the power of Marius's direct appeals to the proletariat classes, as well as their willingness to enlist.[22]

Staging can only be inferred from Marius's Recruiting Speech. Sallust does not identify exactly where the speech was given other than to say that once Marius received the senate's authority to recruit, "he called a public meeting." It was almost certainly in Rome and must have been well advertised and attended, given its successful results, so it was probably a public forum chosen with great care. Throughout Roman history, the elaborate staging of triumphs, entertainments, festivals, and electioneering was always a part of the city's civic soul. There is no reason to believe that even a rough-and-tumble soldier like Marius would neglect these things; on other occasions, he had campaigned for political office and mounted triumphs with entertainments, and he surely knew the importance of Staging. Although only hinted at here, what little is known of ancient Recruitment Speeches reinforces the importance of staging of some sort, and preferred backdrops were buildings or landscapes of public, patriotic, or religious significance. For example, during Titus's siege of Jerusalem, the high priests of the Temple made an effort to recruit men to fight the Zealots who were holding the sacred city hostage. The high priests' recruiting meeting used the Temple itself as a backdrop, and when "Ananus son of Ananus," a leading member of the Temple priesthood, addressed the crowd, he "stood up in the middle, and turning again and again to the Sanctuary with his eyes full of tears" he pled for volunteers. Plutarch wrote that when Pelopidas needed to recruit, "There was a general assembly of the people" convened; Pelopidas was "brought forth . . . encompassed by the priests, who held out garlands, and exhorted the people to fight for their country and their gods. The assembly, at their appearance, rose up in a body and with shouts and acclamations received the men as their deliverers and benefactors."[23]

More complete records in recent centuries suggest that staging for Recruiting Speeches remains critically important. Props such as flags and patriotic music, and persons including crisply uniformed soldiers, pretty girls, clergy, and local dignitaries, all serve to advance the recruiter's message. In his recruitment drive following his return from Elba, Napoleon issued instructions to General Antoine Drouot: "I have already told you that the officers of the Young Guard must advertise and get to work recruiting in Paris," he wrote. "Send officers to the various town halls, have a band and drummers, and do everything to stimulate the young men." It is worth recalling at length American Civil War soldier John D. Billings's composite and hilarious description of how Recruiting Speeches were staged in 1861:

> Musicians and orators blew themselves red in the face with their windy efforts. Choirs improvised for the occasion, sang "Red, White, and Blue" and "Rallied 'Round the Flag" till too hoarse for further endeavor. The old veteran soldier of 1812 was trotted out, and worked for all he was worth, and an occasional Mexican War veteran would air his nonchalance at grim-visaged war. At proper intervals the enlistment roll would be presented for signatures. There was generally one old fellow present who upon slight provocation would yell like a hyena, and declare his readiness to shoulder his musket and go, if he wasn't so old, while his staid and half-fearful consort would pull violently at his coat-tails to repress his unseasonable effervescence ere it assumed more dangerous proportions. Then there was a patriotic maiden lady who kept a flag or a

handkerchief waving with only the rarest and briefest of intervals, who "would go in a minute if she was a man." Besides these there was usually a man who would make one of fifty (or some other safe number) to enlist, when he well understood that such a number could not be obtained. And there was one more often found present who when challenged to sign would agree to, *provided* that A or B (men of wealth) would put down *their* names. . . . Sometimes the patriotism of such a gathering would be wrought up so intensely by waving banners, martial and vocal music, and burning eloquence, that a town's [enlistment] quota would be filled in less than an hour. . . . [A]t last a perfect stampede set in to sign the enlistment roll, and a frenzy of enthusiasm would take possession of the meeting. The complete intoxication of such excitement, like intoxication from liquor, left some of the victims on the following day, especially if the fathers of families, with the sober second thought to wrestle with; but Pride, that tyrannical master, rarely let them turn back. [emphasis original][24]

Billings's references to the "fathers of families" having enlistee's remorse and the reluctance of the "half-fearful consort" points to the second convention required for a successful Recruiting Speech: the Family Appeal. This ancient appeal can work on two levels. The first is the traditional notion of family, narrowly defined by blood or marriage; the second blends with a social narrative and defines family far more broadly as the community, tribe, race, ethnic group, or nation. Marius's Recruiting Speech addresses his potential recruits' families on both levels. First, and most important, is his appeal to a recruit's immediate family. Here Marius speaks directly to the fathers and mothers, who we might infer were also in his audience. "Cowardice will not enable a man to live for ever, and no parent ever prayed that his children might have immortality," Marius declares, "but rather that they might live virtuous and honorable lives." The idea that military service might be attractive to parents because it instills in young men discipline and accountability continues also to this day. A current U.S. Marine Corps recruiting brochure entitled "A Message to Parents and Family Members" declares, "The transition from childhood to adulthood in a difficult one. . . . [M]any young people lack the discipline and the self-mastery to be successful on their own. The Marine Corps can, and does, change that." What the words "honor" and "virtue" might have meant to Marius's audience cannot be certain, but they very likely implied the traits of discipline, self-mastery, and success.[25]

Sometimes the appeal to family can be subtle. On April 21, 1861, Fletcher Webster, son of the late Massachusetts senator and national icon Daniel Webster, stood on the balcony of Boston's Old State House and gave a Recruiting Speech to raise an infantry regiment that eventually became the Twelfth Massachusetts. Webster implied throughout his speech that had his father ("he whose name he bore") still lived, he would have approved of what the son was doing; just as his father was devoted to the Union, so was Fletcher. The next speaker declared that Fletcher Webster's grandfather, "that hero of the Revolution, Captain Ebenezer Webster," would, were *he* alive, also approve of Fletcher's course. The next speaker declared that the men who had already enlisted in other units did so "to defend the flag of the Union as their fathers did in the former Revolution." The last speaker of the day declared that "the blood of Webster owes something to Boston, and Boston owes something to the blood of Webster," then continued in this vein by praising the example of Fletcher Webster's brother, who had died of disease during the Mexican War. Clearly the Webster family had made itself available to be used as an "every-family" whose example other families in the audience should follow.[26]

Notions of family can work in both directions. Just as an immediate family must be persuaded to permit the recruit to join, an emphasis on military service's benefit to the larger metaphorical family might also persuade the recruit. Thus Marius, too, addresses a recruit's larger "family," signaled by his use of the word "fatherland"—the nation, or a landed people conceived in the abstract and imagined as a patriarch. Recruiting Speeches have used this family metaphor in several guises. After one's blood and marital relations, perhaps the most important "family" in the recruiting process becomes the recruiter himself. For example, in one Recruiting Speech (printed proclamation) in which he attempted to stir up martial enthusiasm after his return from Elba, Napoleon declared, "You are right to call me your Father; I live only for the honor and for the happiness of France." The next level involves an imputed "family" connection to past generations, usually found in

Recruiting Speeches that use Social or Political Historical Narratives. In his Recruiting Speech Fletcher Webster declared, "Let us show the world that patriotism of '61 is not less than that of the heroes of '76. The noble impulses of their patriotic hearts have descended to us." One's place within this larger family is also important. In another Recruiting Speech (printed proclamation), Napoleon promised potential recruits that those who joined him now will earn enhanced community status: "In your old age, surrounded and admired by your fellow citizens, who will listen with respect when you tell of your great deeds, you will be able to say with pride, 'I, too, was part of that Grand Army which twice entered the walls of Vienna, which entered Rome, Berlin, Madrid and Moscow, which cleansed Paris of the pollution of treason and the presence of the enemy had left in it.'" Here the larger community serves as a surrogate family, with fellow citizens taking the places of admiring parents and siblings.[27]

Perhaps more than most speeches, Speechmaker Identity is crucial to the success of a Recruiting Speech. Aristotle himself observed, in *Rhetoric,* that the "moral character [of the speaker] constitutes the most effective means of proof."[28] Marius establishes his moral character in three ways: he emphasizes his lower social class origins, which he claims to share with his proletarian audience; he ventilates common resentments against the patricians and "proves" that his views as well as his birth are "correct"; and he stresses his successful battle experience (by far the more common theme found in Recruiting Speeches delivered by soldiers). What's more, Marius skillfully blends these three themes into one.

The majority of Marius's long speech, not included above, is a Social Historical Narrative in which he bitterly attacks Rome's patrician class for its hypocrisy, indolence, decadence, and spending down of the moral and financial capital that was really earned by past generations. What is striking about his speech is that the enemy, King Jugurtha, is only mentioned twice, and only in passing. The real enemies for Marius (and presumably for his audience) are the Roman patricians; indeed, it is their fault that the first two campaigns waged against Jugurtha have failed. "Hitherto Jugurtha has been saved from defeat by the greed, incompetence or vanity of your generals; but you have now changed all this," he assures the audience, by electing Marius as consul. Why were the other generals poor commanders? Marius answers this question repeatedly, using the image of a decayed nobility as a foil for his own virtues:

> Compare me, the "new" man, with these high and mighty ones. What they know only from hearsay or reading, I have seen with my own eyes or done with my own hands. What they have learned out of books, I have learned on the battlefield. It is for you to judge whether words or deeds are more to the point. . . . Their ancestors left them all they could— riches, portrait busts, and their own glorious memory. Virtue, they have not bequeathed to them, nor could they; for it is the only thing that no man can give to another or receive from another. They call me vulgar and unpolished because I do not know how to put on an elegant dinner and have actors at my table or keep a cook who has cost me more than my farm overseer. All this, my fellow citizens, I am proud to admit. For I was taught by my father and other men of blameless life that while elegant graces befit a woman, a man's duty is to labor; that every good man should live for honor rather than for riches; that the weapons he carries in his hands, and not the furniture he keeps in his house, are the ornaments most worth having.

Aristotle famously noted that speechmakers (including battle speechmakers) avoid lengthy explanations of things by incorporating the audience's existing beliefs into a speech via enthymeme. Here the virtues Marius claims for himself are those he recognizes that his audience *likes to believe* they also possess. The proletariats gathered before him did not have "riches [or] portrait busts," and when Marius offers them a choice to judge "whether words or deeds were more to the point," his listeners were far more likely to opt for actions over high-flown rhetoric. This section works for Marius because, like his audience, he too is "vulgar and unpolished." And there is no need whatsoever to explain to a man who has no furniture *why* "the weapons he carries in his hands, and not the furniture he keeps in his house, are the ornaments most worth having."

Marius's attacks on an effeminate, undeserving elite lay the groundwork for the speech's close. He is about to ask the parents in his audience for their sons, but first he must share one final bit of information about himself, one of the oldest Speechmaker Identity tropes whenever a soldier is doing the recruiting: "I can show spears, a banner, medals, and other military honors, to say nothing of the scars on my body," he declares, "all of them in front." And now Marius can close: "I therefore call upon all men of military age to cooperate with me in the service of our country." Marius's class-based Social Historical Narrative of Rome also provides reassurance in the form of an interesting twist on the Aristotelian dictum of rhetoric that the past predicts the future: he goes on to explain that that which has been true will *not* be true now: "And none need fear a repetition of the misfortunes which your comrades suffered under my arrogant predecessors," he declared. "I shall be with you on the march and on the field of battle, to be your guide and to share your perils."

It is here that Marius segues into the next common recruiting theme, one that is virtually inseparable from Family Appeal: a professed concern for the recruits' welfare. Most Recruiting speechmakers must overcome the obvious apprehensions of parents and recruits in the audience: that training for war and war itself are a dangerous business; that discipline is harsh and punishments (historically speaking) can be as deadly as combat; that field conditions are tough, and hunger, inadequate clothing, and exposure to weather can be deadlier than combat. Marius is acutely aware of these concerns and addresses them with remarkable candor. His appeal on this subject is twofold and begins with an attempt to hide the realities of soldier life in plain view: "The lessons I have learnt are such as best enable me to serve my country—to strike down an enemy, to mount guard, to fear nothing but disgrace, to endure winter's cold and summer's heat with equal patience, to sleep on the bare ground, and to work hard on an empty stomach." He is telling recruits and their families that the conditions are what they are, but in taking instruction from Marius, the odds of surviving the hardships are greater than they might be with other commanders, especially the decadent patrician-commanders who know nothing of such conditions and therefore cannot competently train men to survive them. Marius's second appeal is particularly clever, morally based, and presumably compelling to his proletarian audience: "And I shall not make them [that is, your sons] go short while enjoying the best of everything myself, not steal all the glory and leave them the toil. I shall be with you on the march and on the field of battle, to be your guide and to share your perils; and I shall claim no special privileges for myself." Here is the ancient bargain that endures to this day: the leader shall eat what you eat, fight as you fight, suffer as you suffer; he will share equally with his men the privations, dangers, plunder, and glory of war. It was a coin whose two sides were both reassuring: since I will endure what your sons endure, they will be subject to no greater risks than I am prepared to take for myself (that is, there will be no reckless expenditure of lives as might be made by rich, inexperienced generals distant from the battle), and your sons will not be neglected as to their living conditions, for I will share them. Thus does Marius offer to the parent-audience himself *in loco parentis*.

Few modern Recruiting Speeches are this bold. Recent speakers may rely on the audience's enthymematic understanding of their uniform, medals, and personal or unit military reputations. Before recruiting for the Second Marine Raider Battalion, combat-experienced Major Evans Fordyce Carlson had achieved some fame by accompanying the Communist Chinese Eighth Route Army during the 1930s. After Pearl Harbor, one marine recruit remembered that the wiry, tough-skinned Carlson "got up on stage and told us that all he could offer was rice, raisins, bullets, a blanket, and maybe death, but lots of glory." Most of his recruit-audience was likely familiar with Carlson's public reputation, and thus few had any reason to question his expertise in fighting an Asian war, however it might later turn out. Napoleon's recruiting tack was to cast himself as a tribune of his army's past victories, always speaking in the collective and having only to mention the names of his triumphant battles, which he did often. While still at sea during his escape from Elba, he wrote what was a reenlistment speech that included one of the grander resumes in Western military history: "Put on the tricolor cockade; you wore it in our great days. Here are the eagles you had at Ulm, at Austerlitz, at Jena, at Eylau, at Friedland, at Tudela, at Eckmuhl, at Essling, at Wagram, at Smolensk, at the Moskowa, at Lutzen, at Wurchen, at Monmirail!" What more could a Recruiting Speechmaker possibly add?[29]

Civilian recruiters usually have no military credentials and thus must rely on general reputations for leadership, integrity, and community standing. How Company C of the Third Massachusetts Infantry was recruited in Fall River presents a typical case. By the time this regiment was raised in August 1862, "the cotton business was booming [and the] question was asked, 'How are we to persuade men to leave their lucrative employment and become soldiers?' But the 'Fathers of the City,' rising to the occasion, called a mass meeting at City Hall, Aug. 13, 1862, where inspiring and patriotic speeches were made by several of the leading men of the city. The effort was successful."[30]

Finally, there is the substance of Marius's appeals. That he is a courageous leader, a battle-tested, natural instructor of men, and a fair commander are not, by themselves, reasons to enlist. They are only means to an end, that is, the things that potential recruits *already* desire. Why *do* men volunteer to fight? For the recruit-audience in his time and place, Marius offers four reasons: "Rest assured that, with the gods' help, all the fruits of battle are ready to be plucked; victory, spoils and glory await you—though even if these rewards were doubtful or remote, it would still be the duty of all patriots to rally to the aid of the fatherland."

Here the "duty of all patriots"—in one form or another, probably the most common recruiting theme in history—operates as a default motive in case the more personally appealing prospects fail. The first of these is "victory"—that is, success in battle, from which all the subsequently claimed benefits will flow, among them "spoils," the pecuniary side of war, the compensation for undertaking its risks. Plunder follows victory; it is the promise of sack and pillage, the enslavement and sale of whole populations, the division of the proceeds. Last here is "glory," that is, renown, which for its fulfillment requires an audience separate from the actor. Glory, while earned in battle, is only bestowed afterward; it is how others regard the combatant and what comrades and commanders will say about what he did during the battle. Thereafter, it is how the civilian community will likewise regard the veteran. Glory may have religious overtones—one's name will live forever and the gods always look kindly upon the glorified—but it can also be measured in this world's goods via enhanced status, prestige, and an honored place at the more figurative table of the community. What Marius was really offering to his plebian audience was a chance for wealth and advancement unavailable in their old world—a chance to also become a "new man" like him.

Reenlisting Speeches

The numerous and important successes which have attended the arms of the Union during the present year, should be rendered permanently valuable by timely reinforcements. A temporary check [a recent reversal on the battlefield, probably here referring to Chickamauga] should arouse us to new exertions, and prevent such a delay of action, at this time, as will prolong and embitter the war. Our armies need more men, and if promptly and freely supplied, the necessity of their service must be comparatively short. A few vigorous blows, at this time, will save a long and exhausting struggle hereafter. . . .

To those who have been in the military service, for nine months or a longer period, Massachusetts presents the opportunity of enlisting . . . and of entitling themselves to the bounty of $402 each, which is offered by the General Government, with the bounty of $50 each, offered by the State Government. . . .

Let Massachusetts arouse herself once more, prevent as she can, all further drafts upon her people, devote herself with all the glowing enthusiasm and the fiery zeal of her patriotic hearts, declare with her determined will, THAT THE REBELLION OF TRAITORS SHALL EXIST NO LONGER, GO HERSELF AND PUT IT DOWN.

> Excerpt from Massachusetts Adjutant General William Schouler's
> General Order No. 27 of October 10, 1863

[The Reverend Thomas B. Fox, sent by Massachusetts Governor John A. Andrew to promote reenlistments,] addressed the regiment, which was drawn up on three sides of a square. In an address of wonderful beauty, completeness, and eloquence, he brought the assurance of remembrance at home. When he who had given three sons to the army alluded to the one who had fallen in the line of the second [Massachusetts] at Gettysburg, tears wet the cheeks of the hardy soldiery.

> Reenlistment Speech of the Reverend Fox, made to Second Massachusetts
> Volunteers[31]

THERE IS ONE SUBSET of Recruiting Speeches that merits brief mention because of its historical importance in waging some wars: the Reenlistment Speech. The purpose of these speeches is to persuade soldiers to remain soldiers despite expiring enlistments. These reenlistments—referred to more recently as retentions—have sometimes been credited with victories in cases where the same armies, drained of veterans, might not have had the same success. In American history, the Civil War is the preeminent example of a successful reenlistment program, which is credited by some historians with having given the North an important edge in morale during the war's final year.[32]

For obvious reasons, reenlistment is crucial in any volunteer army whose core consists of specialists or seasoned combat veterans and whose original term of service is relatively short. By comparison, Roman soldiers during the Principate could expect to serve terms of twenty-five years, and reenlistment speeches were hardly relevant to those middle-aged men fortunate enough to have survived that long. Since the advent of all-volunteer armies, the "retention rate" has become an important measure of general morale and one indication of how current operations might be affecting the military mood.[33]

Before considering the conventions governing Reenlistment Speeches, several obvious contrasts between them and Recruiting Speeches should be noted. First, the reenlistee-audience already knows the reality of the military, and promises of good food, caring officers, adequate shelter and clothing, and the joys of a "soldier's life" may fall flat and typically do not appear in the few genuine reenlistment speeches in the record. As one historian wrote years later of his Civil War comrades as they stood in line taking the reenlistment oath: "Each of the men knew just what war was. He had experienced it, had seen his comrades swept away by shot and shell and foul disease and his regiment dwindle until only a remnant of its former strength remained. These veterans did not have in their second enrollment the inspiration and excitement of war meetings or the novelty of new gold-trimmed uniforms to urge them on."[34]

The same goes for assurances that military life will build character or help a young man or woman to mature; as far as the reenlistee-audience is concerned, service has already achieved these things or never will, or the issue has become moot given the sights, smells, and sounds that reenlistees have already experienced, especially in combat situations. Finally, the staging for Reenlistment Speeches is less important. Most Reenlistment Speeches occur in camp or barrack settings, and the audience is a (figuratively) captive one. Modern reenlistment ceremonies can be accompanied by considerable fanfare; however, for the reasons discussed below, the speeches made at these ceremonial events are meant to laud soldiers who have already decided to reenlist *as well as* persuade any fence-sitters.

The conventions that do appear in Reenlistment Speeches are chiefly thematic, with two dominant appeals: Benefits (that is, the promise of pecuniary reward) and Patriotism (highly charged emotional appeals to patriotic, comradely, or "let us finish the job" sentiments). Interestingly, these appeals often coexist in the same speech. For example, Massachusetts General Order No. 27 counts as a battle speech because, like all state general orders, it was distributed to units in the field and read aloud to assembled soldiers. First, bounties are specified: federal and state payments combined with the thirteen-dollar monthly wage meant a significant sum to the reenlisting veteran. But the appeal does not end there. The order contains some very powerful and veteran-specific patriotic themes, though love of country, preserving the union, and abolishing slavery are not among them. Instead, Adjutant General Schouler appeals directly to the frustration, anger, and pride of the soldier-audience: frustration that the war continues to grind on, anger that the *"rebellion of traitors"* still persists despite two years of war, and pride that Massachusetts remains able to *"GO HERSELF AND PUT IT DOWN."* The capitalization and italicization found in the original order should not be dismissed as a mere stylistic flourish; they comprise a cue to assembly readers about what to emphasize when reciting the order at parade. What Schouler offers his reenlistee-audience is a brief Political Historical Narrative of the war from a soldier's perspective: the patriotic fervor that had inspired so many of you to enlist in 1861 and 1862 must be rekindled ("Let Massachusetts arouse herself once more"); as you have defended your families from rebels, now defend your fellow citizens against the shame of being conscripted (rather than volunteering) and uphold the honor of the state for providing volunteers ("prevent as she can all further drafts upon her people"); remember what your enemies really want ("*rebellion*") and what they really are ("*traitors*"); and so you must continue in uniform and finish what you began ("*that the rebellion of traitors* SHALL EXIST NO LONGER"), because manly honor requires you to do this ("[Massachusetts—that is, you, its living representatives—shall] GO YOURSELF AND PUT IT DOWN").

The Reverend Fox's Reenlistment Speech to the Second Massachusetts represents a very different type of appeal. Based on the text of the narrator (the regiment's chaplain), it seems clear that unlike Schouler's general order, Fox has reversed the sequence of appeals—he leads with an emotional appeal, while money issues are dealt with much later and by others. And where General Order No. 27 used a Political Historical Narrative, Fox blends Social and Unit Historical Narratives. He inserts these histories via one word—Gettysburg—and one allusion: to his son, namesake, and former officer with the Second Massachusetts, Thomas B. Fox Jr.—the one "who had fallen in the line of the second at Gettysburg." Just five months before the Reverend Fox pitched reenlistment, the Second Massachusetts had marched into Pennsylvania with 316 men; forty-five of these, including the commanding officer as well as young Fox, would be killed or mortally wounded in making a forlorn charge based on a mistaken order. Recalling this disaster amounted to Social Historical Narrative at its most poignant—in so reduced a unit, these casualties were an instantly felt subtraction from the regimental family. At the same time, the mention of Gettysburg must have provoked awareness that the battle had become an important milestone in the unit's own historical narrative—the Second Massachusetts had earned great fame by obeying the mistaken order to charge against impossible odds.[35]

The Reverend Fox's reenlistee-audience may have been hardened veterans, but he seemed to understand that combining these particular narratives would tap a deep reservoir of feeling—perhaps survivor's guilt about deceased comrades, the pain of loss, devotion to surviving peers, and a need to assign value and meaning to these sacrifices by seeing the war through. The immediate experience of listening to a father discuss his dead son had an obviously powerful effect on his reenlistee-audience, even bringing them to tears. And Fox, like Schouler, also emphasized the dependence between the home front and the front. By bringing the "assurance of remembrance at home," he had also brought a powerful reminder: while "home" may have been thinking of the soldiers—may even have longed for their return—the Reverend Fox was there as an official agent of the State of Massachusetts, sent in part on a reenlistment mission; it is virtually certain that *his* version of "home" included the expectation that the soldiers should reenlist to help bring the war to a successful conclusion.

Fox's effort was a success. Following this speech he was able to "materially expedite the arrangements" by which enough soldiers of the Second Regiment were reenlisted in order to qualify for veteran status. As the regimental history proudly declared, "The Second was henceforth the SECOND REGIMENT OF MASSACHUSETTS VETERAN VOLUNTEERS. It had earned the title." That money mattered to these mostly obscure men is beyond doubt; but money alone could not possibly compensate soldiers who by the winter of 1863–64 understood all too well what personal risks they would bear in the expected spring offensive.[36]

Brig. Gen. Michael J. Terry, commanding general of the 13th Sustainment Command (Expeditionary), led the [reenlistment] ceremony. He said he was proud of the 1744th as he handed each Soldier their certificate. "I feel humbled as I stand among all of you today. You have chosen to continue your service to the Army in a time of war, and that is very admirable." Terry said service members choose to reenlist for many reasons but there must be something deep in a person's spirit that makes them want to stay in the military. "America needs to understand who you are; you have made a greater sacrifice than some people can imagine."

Excerpt from the speech of General Terry, LSA Anaconda, in Iraq, January 6, 2007[37]

AT PRESENT, the Reenlistment Speech as a genuinely persuasive tool is a rarity. Part of the reason is that modern, all-volunteer militaries, often dependent on technical specialists, no longer abandon retention to the whims of oratory. Moreover, modern professional militaries offer a vast array of occupational specialties, financial benefits, educational opportunities, and postings; as potential reenlistees age, marry, have children, and contemplate retirement, the need for advice can no longer be satisfied by any speech, no matter how dazzling its appeals to patriotism or skillful its plucking of the audience's heartstrings. Thus militaries deploy specially trained cadres of "career counselors" who work with soldiers individually; many reenlistment decisions will be influenced by these relationships rather than made on a parade ground after a grand speech.[38]

However, as illustrated by the speech above, reenlistment ceremonies remain common, though they simply reaffirm decisions already made by soldiers. Speeches are sometimes given, and at ceremonies where groups of soldiers reenlist, speakers may be drawn from the senior command. Still, with no need to persuade, the remarks are often laudatory. Thus in General Terry's remarks to the thirty reenlisting soldiers of the 1744th Transportation Company, he expresses pride in his soldiers, recognizes the difficulties of reenlisting during wartime, and, quite interestingly (and in sharp contrast with the Reverend Fox), implies that their sacrifice is enhanced by the fact that "home" may *not* be fully appreciative of their efforts. "American needs to understand who you are," General Terry declares. "You have made a greater sacrifice than some people can imagine." It is possible that with the advent of a professional, all-volunteer army, the connections between the imagined home front and the front have simply grown weaker. This is especially true, of course, during a controversial war.

But considered in a different light, these reenlistment ceremonies may have replaced the Reenlistment Speech as one means of effectively distributing persuasion, especially to other soldiers still contemplating reenlistment. This is clear from the various unit publications provided to U.S. soldiers serving in Iraq, which prominently feature group reenlistment ceremonies, usually with color photographs and quotations from the officers' speeches. For example, in one issue of *The Club* ("The Official Newsletter of the 1st Brigade Combat Team"), two entries feature photographs and descriptions of group reenlistments. When fourteen soldiers of the "Balls of the Eagle Battalion"

(Second Battalion, 320th Field Artillery, 101st Airborne [Air Assault]) reenlisted in Iraq, *The Club* featured a photograph of these men taking the oath around a giant black trefoil, the emblem of the First Brigade Combat Team ("Bastogne"). The article stated, "On February 6, 14 Balls of the Eagle Soldiers pledged to STAY ARMY [the current Army retention slogan] by re-enlisting for continued service in our Army. These Soldiers were able to take advantage of many re-enlistment opportunities offered while deployed in Iraq." The article continued by thanking Second Battalion, 320th Field Artillery's "Re-enlistment NCO" for his "hard work in helping each Soldier realize the opportunities they are afforded." *How* important these speech substitutes have become may be partly gauged by *who* is featured administering the reenlistment oaths. These figures have recently included General George Casey, Commander of Multi-National Forces in Iraq, General Richard Cody, Vice-Chief of Staff of the Army, and General Joseph F. Fil Jr., Multi-National Division Commander—Baghdad. The role of unit publications as modern conveyors of the same genres of battle speeches spoken by ancient generals to their legions will be considered in greater detail in the next chapter. For reenlistments, it is clear that some of the older messages of the Reenlistment Speech—benefits and patriotism—can now be communicated via an article.[39]

3

INSTRUCTIONAL SPEECH

Marshal Ney will command on the right, supporting the position of General Oudinot. Marshal Lannes will be in the centre, from Hein-richsdorf to about opposite Posthenen. The grenadiers of Oudinot will bear a little to the left, to draw the enemy in that direction. Mar-shal Lannes will deploy on as great a depth as he can, and may therefore form two lines. Marshal Mortier will be on the left. General Victor and the Imperial Guard will be in reserve and will form behind Posthenen. I will be with the reserve. The advance must always be right wing forward, and it must be left to Marshal Ney to begin the movement; he will wait for my orders before advancing.

As soon as the right goes forward, the artillery must redouble its fire along the whole line in the proper direction for protecting this wing.

Napoleon's orders to commanders before the Battle of Friedland, June 14, 1807

In the approaching battle the General Commanding trusts that the troops will preserve the discipline which he has been so anxious to enforce, and which they have so generally observed. He calls upon all the officers and soldiers to obey promptly and intelligently all orders they may receive; let them bear in mind that the Army of the Potomac has never yet been checked, and let them preserve in battle perfect coolness and confidence, the sure forerunners of success. They must keep well together, throw away no shots, but aim carefully and low, and above all things rely upon the bayonet. Commanders of regi-ments are reminded of the great responsibility that rests upon them, upon their coolness, judgment and discretion the destinies of their regiments and success of the day will depend.

"General McClellan's Order for crossing the Chickahominy," May 25, 1862[1]

INSTRUCTIONAL SPEECHES probably comprise the vast majority of formal military communications in war or peace. Their purpose is to convey instructions, information, or orders about the *operations* of existing things, or about how things *should* operate in the future. Instructional Speeches can include such varied communications as a drill instructor teaching recruits how to properly stand at attention, an officer issuing orders on camp construction, or a general on the eve of battle instructing his subalterns on troop placement. Instructional Speech is the most basic form of military communication, and while it may be staged, staging is not required for its effectiveness; in general, Instructional Speeches require only three conventions and may include a fourth. Two of these conventions are sensible in the extreme. First, the speaker, whether he is heard, read, or (in the case of deeds) observed, must possess Command Authority. Second, the soldier-audience must feel obligated by law, moral authority, or the press of circumstances to Listen and Obey. The third convention is sometimes express and sometimes implied but is always present as text or subtext; it relates to the future: the Instructional Speech imagines some Idea of military form or practice that it seeks to convey to its soldier-audience by commanding one or more specific actions. For example, in Napoleon's battle order above the troop placements and directed movements together imply an Idea of this army in motion as imagined by the Instructional Speechmaker. It is a model of how Napoleon imagines his various units moving once the battle begins: large bodies of men organized into separate units, each unit like a part of some finely made watch, the whole moving in a precisely scripted battle sequence. Of course, long before the Battle of Friedland Napoleon had learned that real battles are not watches and that parts do not always function as designed. Nevertheless, Instructional Speeches often ask soldier-audiences to imagine models, not reality.

Napoleon's order obviously also demonstrates the first three conventions of Instructional Speech; significantly, it also touches upon the fourth, Rationalization—that is, a form of persuasion. Many such speeches do not simply command but also seek to persuade the soldier-audience by offering reasons, logic chains, or factoids in their support. These various reasons can be exhortatory but are always closely linked to the specifics of the battle, task, or other Idea behind the speech. Napoleon's Instructional Speech above might at first seem free of Rationalization, but in fact it is a closely argued instruction. Marshal Ney is told to "command on the right" and is also told why: to support General Oudinot. Oudinot is ordered to have his grenadiers "bear a little to the left," and he too is told why: "to draw the enemy in that direction." Likewise, the artillery is ordered to increase its fire and where to direct it "for protecting [the] wing" led by Marshal Ney. Napoleon apparently did not believe that preemptory orders alone were sufficient. His generals had to know the reasons for the orders, and here efficiency unites with persuasion: a soldier-audience that understands the reasons for doing a thing is far more likely to do it as the battle speechmaker hopes.[2]

Instructional Speech has many subsets, and several important ones will be considered here. One must first mention Pure Instructional Speeches, which are those containing orders but no Rationalization. Of course these exist, but they may be rarer than imagined. Napoleon's order is an example of a "Pure" Instructional Speech that was actually rather impure—on close scrutiny, it revealed its Rationalization, though it was discreetly inserted. For that reason, the first subset of Instructional Speeches discussed will be just this sort of "Pure" Instructional Speeches, the scare quotes here meant to suggest that on close scrutiny the instructions are also impure—that is, that, like Napoleon's orders before Friedland, they contain Rationalization.

This must be contrasted with the second example featured above, excerpted from General McClellan's orders of May 25, 1862, to the Army of the Potomac for crossing the Chickahominy River. This is also an Instructional Speech, although it contains nothing about troop placements, only a few things about battle tactics, and very little about the operation of formal plans. Instead, by reminding his soldier-audience about the importance of good discipline, prompt obedience, the conservation of ammunition, proper formation, aimed musket fire, and, for officers, the serious responsibilities of combat command, McClellan offers advice (in the form of orders) about what he believes is required to win battles. In effect, he is instructing his men about the components of *morale,* that is, the means that will produce a proper at-

titude for future victories. McClellan obviously believes that good morale is a logical consequence of all of the Instructional Speeches (and
accompanying practice) that his men have thus far received as part of
their training. "Let them bear in mind that the Army of the Potomac
has never yet been checked," he declares, "and let them preserve in
battle perfect coolness and confidence, the sure forerunners of success." For McClellan, "coolness and confidence" is a function of good
instruction remembered at the moment of crisis. Thus, he presents a
balanced equation for the ideal army: instruction plus drill equals the
victories that a properly prepared army should produce.

McClellan's Instructional Speech is also a persuasive speech, embracing the Rationalization Convention by offering his men reasons at
every turn for remaining faithful to their training. He does this principally by attaching adjectives to the model traits he wants his army to
embrace. After all, if one is already disposed to obeying orders, who
would not wish do so *promptly* and *intelligently*? Who would wish to
enter a battle other than in *perfect coolness* and with *confidence*, especially because these are the *sure forerunners of success*? No army would
voluntarily advance in a disorganized fashion, waste ammunition, or
fail to use the bayonet when necessary. And regimental officers are
given every reason to conscientiously discharge their duties, because
few men wearing shoulder straps would argue that being an officer entails minor responsibilities, or that *coolness, judgment, and discretion*
are not their responsibility, or that their actions are not really conse-
quential. Officers and men alike are thus presented with a series of
rhetorically phrased propositions whose "truth," for motivated volunteers, is beyond argument.

Instructional Speech relating to morale closely resembles exhortatory Pre-Invasion and Pre-Battle Speeches, which will be examined in
later chapters; sometimes, instruction cannot be distinguished from
exhortation, as when a commander waves his sword and leads his men
in a charge with the shout, "Forward!" And McClellan's speech *is* exhortatory but is included here because of its insinuation into what appears to be instructions or orders. (The excerpt above is actually the
second part of the order; the first part deals with more prosaic matters
of ammunition supply, wagon trains, and guard details.) McClellan's

speech also illustrates one of the two larger points made in this chapter—that Instructional Speech can be a vehicle for content other than "pure" instruction. In this chapter we will further consider five types of Instructional Speech: "Pure" Instructional Speeches, Instructional Speeches of Morale, Politics, and Religion, and Instructional Speeches containing Rules of Engagement. We will also discuss wordless speech, or Instructional speech-by-deed. This is where some act (beyond the creation of the instruction) complements, replaces, or gives additional force to the Instructional Speech. Unlike traditional Instructional Speeches, which vertically descend through chains of command, the "deed-as-Instructional Speech" actually moves horizontally because (especially in combat) it may be performed by anyone, observed by anyone, and thus instruct anyone without regard to rank.

"Pure" Instructional Speech

Strikers,

Unfortunately, I have to begin this note by offering our collective prayers and condolences for the loss of both Staff Sgt. Marion Flint and Pfc. Grant Dampier from Company B, 1-8 Combined Arms Battalion; may these Fighting Eagles rest in peace. As we all realize, this enemy is both clever and lethal. In this instance, he threw a pitch at us that we had not seen before, and managed to exact a very high price. We will learn from this unfortunate event and respond accordingly.

*As the enemy adjusts his TTPs [Tactics, Techniques, and Procedures], so must we. I would ask everyone to reexamine our current procedures to ensure we are not developing patterns. We have become very comfortable in this lethal battlespace. . . . **It's the kind of confidence that will set us up for a fall if we are not constantly looking at our routines the way the enemy does.** He searches for our weaknesses. He looks for opportunity. He studies our every move. In this very dangerous game of cat and mouse, we must stay ahead of him. Do not let your guard down!*

The evil twin of too much confidence is complacency. One breeds the other. *After nearly six months deployed and five months in the area of operations, we are starting to see some scattered signs of complacency in some isolated incidents.*

It's natural; it's the halfway point. In some cases, PCCs [Pre-Combat Checks] and PCIs [Pre-Combat Inspections] are not being done to standard. A few weapons are no longer being cleaned as often. Some crews are not test firing as frequently. Some drivers are speeding. We are sometimes skipping the use of a second set of eyes in clearing our weapons. Corners are being cut. I think it's time we all reach back into the bottom of our duffel bags and pull out the Striker FARs [Flat-Ass Rules] and remind ourselves how it was that we approached this battlespace in January. We need to get back into that mindset. Some of the bad habits we are witnessing will get people hurt or killed. We can't have that.

> Excerpt from "Complacency Kills!" by Colonel Brian D. Jones, Commander, Third Heavy Brigade Combat Team, Fourth Infantry Division[3]

"PURE" INSTRUCTIONAL SPEECH is what it is, and on the surface it looks to be no more—the voice of command, a soldier-audience disposed to listen and obey, and a message of straightforward requests, orders, or demands, all of which provide direction toward the realization of some Idea of practice or behavior. (In fact, Rationalization lurks in the language and must always be ferreted out to fully understand the instruction.) Most Instructional Speech is delivered as it has been probably since the beginning of organized warfare—commanders verbally instruct subordinates. Since the invention of printing and the expansion of armies in size, bureaucratic complexity, and geographical distribution, much Instructional Speech is just as likely to be printed, showering recipients with the same snowfall of paper (or emails) as one finds in civilian bureaucracies. Yet commanders in combat environments may not be able to personally and regularly address soldiers, and soldiers may not always be able to download the email; while naval captains can use a public address system to speak to their vessel-bound crews, ground units may cover too large an area to permit anything like a daily parade or morning call. Junior officers and noncommissioned officers must then fill these gaps between a senior leader and the ranks. But the senior leader must still be seen and heard from—he remains a critical part of the leadership in whom men and women must retain confidence.

When the Third Heavy Brigade Combat Team of the Fourth Infantry Division was in Iraq, one of several means by which the senior leadership announced themselves was through the *Iron Brigade Chronicle* [*IBC*], a glossy, full-color monthly unit magazine. "Command View," a column written by the brigade commander, Colonel Brian D. Jones, was among *IBC*'s standing features. The above excerpt is typical in that the commander's view often amounted to an Instructional Speech concerning safety—the same speech he might deliver had he been able to assemble his approximately 3,500 soldiers in one room. However, Jones's brigade was dispersed throughout Diyala Province in six major forward operating bases [FOBs] and many smaller ones; in fact, the last time Colonel Jones had been able to make in-person, brigade-wide speeches was stateside at Fort Carson, Colorado, the unit's home base. In Iraq, therefore, he turned to print. Three thousand copies of the *IBC* were printed each month and distributed to the various FOBs; copies could also be obtained online. Though soldiers were not required to read the *IBC,* junior commanders and noncommissioned officers appear to have encouraged wide readership, believing of its content that "Because of its appearance in the *IBC,* and it comes from Colonel Jones, that is as good as a direct, face to face order."[4]

Colonel Jones's speech is mostly a reminder of things that his soldiers have already learned. However, in a combat environment, these matters must be reiterated constantly. Jones's *IBC* column allows us to grasp something of the immediate experience of pure Instructional Speech (at least in a war zone), because he usually discloses the reasons for a particular speech at a given time. Moreover, in doing so Jones allows readers to quickly grasp the Idea—in this case, of ideal soldiers perpetually vigilant, faithful to their training, confident but not overconfident—that he wants for his brigade. "Complacency Kills!" seeks to battle a timeless military vice. Needless to say, no army in history has ever completely conquered complacency and its causes—numbing routine, boredom, and fatigue. But Jones imagines an army that can, and his speech is written accordingly

In the printed piece one's eye is first drawn to Colonel Jones's headshot, which is significantly different from most author pictures, in that his actual features are almost overwhelmed by his fully strapped Kevlar helmet, safety goggles, and Kevlar ballistic vest. This picture, together with the column, conveys a message about morale as well as safety—*everybody* must wear the proper protective gear, and the commander will do as the private does, for rank has no privileges in matters of safety. But in this case, morale, although entwined with safety, remains secondary in his message.

"Complacency Kills!" grips the reader from the first sentence. Two men have died by enemy action since the last issue of *IBC*. While Jones is clear that their deaths were not the result of any negligence ("[the enemy] threw a pitch at us that we had not seen before"), the fact remains that these men were killed in combat. It is the consummate introduction to a speech about the consequences of complacency in combat: death. And so death provides the context for the speech, because death triggers a response ("We will learn from this unfortunate event and respond accordingly"). Indeed, this month's "Command View" column is part of that response.

Whatever the exact circumstances of the two soldiers' deaths, Jones wants to overturn his troops' complacency. First, he communicates a healthy, perhaps life-saving, respect for the enemy: "This enemy is both clever and lethal. . . . [The enemy] looks for opportunity. He studies our every move. In this dangerous game of cat and mouse, we must stay ahead of him." This is important because a smart enemy constantly changes his "TTPs"—tactics, techniques, and procedures for killing American soldiers. In other words, Jones asserts, this enemy can only succeed if American soldiers are complacent. And here he includes his first instruction: "I would ask everyone to reexamine our current procedures to ensure we are not developing patterns." Probably for reasons of operational security, he will not specify in print which procedures he means, but a civilian reader might infer that these include such matters as how patrols are timed and located, how

vehicles drive down roadways (to avoid roadside bombs), or how obstacles are configured at checkpoints. Presumably, this reexamination
of procedures will be left to the junior and noncommissioned officers
that form the chain linking the colonel to the ranks.

Next Jones inserts additional context to explain why complacency
has now become an issue, pointing to a military defect as ancient
as any in the history of recorded warfare: overconfidence. "We have
become very comfortable in this lethal battlespace," he asserts. Of
course, confidence can be a good thing, as Jones at first seems to suggest—it comes from experience, and from a (healthy) belief in oneself,
one's comrades, and the team's resiliency ("to withstand the enemy's
best shot and come out swinging"). But then he throws (and italicizes)
the hook: no thing is so good that it cannot be overdone ("*It's the kind
of confidence that will set us up for a fall if we are not constantly looking
at our routines the way the enemy does*"). After expressing additional respect for enemy capabilities, Jones inserts his second instruction: "Do
not let your guard down!" Then he offers a second reason for this instruction by shifting the topic from overconfidence to its "evil twin,"
complacency. And here he adds a new (and critical) piece of context
for this Instructional Speech: "After nearly six months deployed and
five months in the area of operations, we are starting to see some scattered signs of complacency in some isolated incidents." Simply put,
the brigade has been in one place too long. Something like a "garrison"
mentality has developed. His soldiers have established routines, and
this is dangerous, for reasons he has already specified here.

In detailing these "scattered signs of complacency" Jones is actually
issuing instructions, although the words "I order/command/instruct"
do not appear. Such words are unnecessary, in fact, because a commander's prestige and authority is (or should be) such that merely to
publicly observe a defect is to order its remedy. And the defects that
Jones wants corrected are many: inspections of equipment and supplies are not being properly performed before combat patrols; weapons are too infrequently cleaned and test-fired; weapons are not being
properly cleared, presumably before reentering the base; lastly, "drivers are speeding," although Jones does not specify whether this is inside the FOBs or on Iraq's roads. By themselves, these might be "small"

matters; however, in a combat zone any one of them might have cat-astrophic consequences: when needed against the enemy, weapons might malfunction; a failure to perform pre-combat inspections can mean insufficient (or the wrong kind of) supplies just when a unit en-counters an enemy; accidents from wholly preventable causes such as speeding and discharges from "unloaded" weapons are just as deadly as combat events. "Corners are being cut," Jones declares. And with this summary diagnosis comes the final instruction:

> I think it's time we all reach back into the bottom of our duffel bags and pull out the Striker FARs and remind ourselves how it was that we approached this battlespace in January. We need to get back into that mindset. Some of the bad habits we are witnessing will get people hurt or killed. We can't have that.

Jones's fulfillment of the Rationalization Convention is obvious: it is death. This begins with the column's title, "Complacency Kills!" It continues with the opening paragraph, containing the proto-eulogy for two comrades. Proximate to every instruction and admonition is the text or subtext that death or injury must be avoided when it can be. After the eulogy, Jones notes that "we" will learn from their deaths in order to avoid more death. The "opportunity" the enemy seeks is your death. The reason why you must not "let your guard down" is to avoid your own death or the death of your comrades. Worse still are deaths caused by negligence—bad driving, a failure to perform some inspection, or an "unloaded" weapon. Jones's speech is pow-erful instruction, because its principal persuader, death, allows few rebuttals.

Never "chase an Apache into the rocks . . ." think before you act!

FAR #6, Colonel Brian D. Jones[5]

BEFORE CLOSING THIS DISCUSSION of "Pure" Instructional Speech, a reader must imagine Jones's "Command View" con-joined with the appropriate FAR or "Flat-Ass Rule" referred to in the preceding section. Each FAR includes a one-line axiom conveying some piece of combat wisdom. FARs are the quintessence of "pure" Instructional Speech—succinct, dramatic, and, at least in combat environments, ignored only at great peril. Before deployment, these FARs *were* Instructional Speeches—Colonel Jones personally presented them to his entire command over several meetings in the movie theater at his unit's home base. He had written twelve FARs, which were printed on cards and distributed to his soldiers (hence his suggestion of review). Each issue of the *IBC* reprints a FAR, together with a discussion illustrating how the rule should be adapted to the unit's actual deployment experience. It was perhaps a coincidence that FAR #6 is reprinted in the same *IBC* as Jones's speech about the dangers of complacency.[6]

Not "chasing Apaches into rocks" is another way of discouraging soldiers from too hastily engaging an enemy under conditions more friendly to them.[7] "Iraq is an area we are not intimately familiar with," Colonel Jones declares in his discussion accompanying FAR #6. "[It] remains an area we are still only getting to know." This is why reprinting FAR #6 is only a continuation of the speech entitled "Complacency Kills!": as a mindset, complacency rests on the acceptance of unexamined assumptions that are not connected with immediate reality. As Jones explains to his soldier-audience:

> The insurgents who call these areas home know every knook [*sic*] and cranny out there. You do not. No matter how familiar you think you are with an area, always pursue cautiously, you never know what lurks around the corner. If you are attacked, and the insurgent flees into a covered area or encourages you to follow him, do not. This could be an attempt to lure you into an ambush. . . . They want us to chase them into an area where they have the advantage. Do not allow the enemy to put you into that position. Think about where you are and what you doing. . . . If you must follow the enemy, remain aware of your surroundings and stay vigilant in your defenses. Rely on your training, remember your experiences and follow your leaders—they know what they're doing.

FAR #6 read in combination with the "Command View" column now yields a more complete picture of how Jones's speech meets the third convention of Instructional Speeches, that of aspiring toward some Idea of behavior or practice. In part, he seeks a return to the "status quo ante deployment," when his soldiers were more compliant with various safety procedures. But he also demands a change of attitude toward the job: a hyperawareness of danger, and a greater humility about the enemy and his environment. The twin assumptions here are that soldiers who understand themselves to be in the constant presence of death are less likely to be complacent, and soldiers who respect an enemy's capability, especially on his home turf, are less likely to be (fatally) trusting.

Instructional Speech: Morale

Cobain, a grenadier, has committed suicide because of a love affair; he was, however, a good soldier. This is the second incident of this nature in the regiment within a month. The First Consul [Napoleon] directs that there shall be inserted in the Guard's orders: That a soldier must overcome grief and the melancholy of love; that there is as much courage in supporting with firmness the afflictions of the soul as there is in standing steady under the grape of a battery of guns. To give one's self up to grief without resistance, to kill one's self to escape it, is to abandon the battlefield defeated.

Napoleon, May 12, 1802

TO THE OFFICERS OF THE MARINE CORPS: I feel that I would like to talk to each of you personally. This, of course, is impossible for me to do. Consequently, I am going to do the next best thing, by writing letters from time to time, which will go to all the officers.

You are the permanent part of the Marine Corps, and the efficiency, the good name, and the esprit of the Corps are in your hands. You can make or mar it. . . .

You should never forget the power of example. The young men serving as enlisted men take their cue from you. . . .

Be kindly and just in your dealing with your men. Never play favorites. . . .

The prestige of the Marine Corps depends greatly on the appearance of its officers and men. . . .

A compliance with the minutiae of military courtesy is a mark of well-disciplined troops. . . .

In conclusion, I wish to impress on all of you that the destiny of our Corps depends on each of you. . . . An inefficient organization

is the product of inefficient officers, and all the discreditable occur-
rences are usually due to the failure of officers to perform their du-
ties properly.

Let each one of us resolve to show in himself a good example of vir-
tue, honor, patriotism, and subordination, and to do all in his power,
not only to maintain, but to increase the prestige, the efficiency, and
the esprit of the grand old Corps to which we belong.

Excerpt from letter of Major General John A. Lejeune,
Thirtieth Commandant of the Marine Corps, September 19, 1922[8]

DEFINING MORALE IS EASY—according to one dictionary, morale is the "emotional or mental condition with respect to cheer-
fulness, confidence, zeal, etc., esp. in the face of opposition, hardship, etc."—but applying this formula to specific military situations is
trickier. Morale is a profound factor not just in this subset of Instructional Speeches but also for most of the battle speeches considered in
this book. Therefore, it is worth quoting the great nineteenth-century
German theorist of warfare Carl Von Clausewitz at some length on
this subject. Morale is an indispensable part of what he calls the "military virtue of an army"; in a discussion of how morale is manifested,
Von Clausewitz also begins to define it:

> An Army which preserves its usual formations under the heaviest fire,
> which is never shaken by imaginary fears, and which in the face of real
> danger disputes the ground inch by inch, which, proud in the feeling
> of its victories, never loses its sense of obedience, its respect for and
> confidence in its leaders, even under the depressing effects of defeat;
> an Army with all its physical powers, inured to privations and fatigue
> by exercise, like the muscles of an athlete; an Army which looks upon
> all its toils as the means to victory, not as a curse which hovers over its
> standards, and which is always reminded of its duties and virtues by the
> short catechisms of one idea, namely *the honor of its arms*; Such an Army
> is imbued with the true military spirit. [italics original][9]

Morale, then, is the ability of any army to retain its sense of self—
"We are Marines," the Immortals, "the Fighting Sixty-ninth"—amidst
the chaos and distractions of combat and hardship. Put another way,
morale can be measured by the degree to which a group retains its
identity and to which individuals belonging to the group fulfill their

obligations toward it in a given circumstance. Of course, Von Clause-witz's imagined army is just that—the Idea of an army, which in his place and time meant one that held its positions under fire, never pan-icked, always bloodied an attacking enemy, obeyed orders, believed in its leaders, understood that even drudgework was important to victory, and was animated by "*the honor of its arms*." It is the desire to produce ideal armies (each age will have its own notion here) that links the two very different Instructional Speeches by Napoleon and General Lejeune that are featured in the epigraph. While Napoleon's orders that lovesick soldiers must not commit suicide might strike some read-ers as foolish and may have been of limited efficacy, the better ques-tion is why the subject even mattered to the First Consul of France. The answer is obvious: lovesickness in the ranks was costing Napo-leon good soldiers for a bad reason and thus negatively impacted his army's morale. Any situation that degrades morale requires attention from commanders via instruction. And the ability to render competent instruction or deliver or write a comprehensible Instructional Speech is one functional synonym for leadership.

Napoleon's attempt to deal with his soldiers' depression and suicide may have been flawed, as there was little science available to him on which to base a remedy. (In fairness, it is quite possible that given the cultural assumptions of his times his appeals might have actually pre-vented some suicides.) He applied what remedial paradigms he did have, mostly through a "bringing men to their senses" approach that appealed to the hypermasculinity of soldiering. Thus his speech twins thematic opposites, the manly soldier versus the more effeminate mel-ancholic: "must overcome" vs. "melancholy of love"; "courage . . . sup-porting with firmness" vs. "the afflictions of the soul"; "standing steady under the grape of a battery of guns" vs. "to give one's self up to grief without resistance, to kill one's self to escape it . . . to abandon the bat-tlefield defeated." Napoleon equates suicide with cowardice and de-moralization, the last two items being matters that by 1802 he had had considerable battlefield experience in managing. But of supreme im-portance here is that Napoleon is not simply ordering good morale (as if such a thing were possible); instead, he is attempting to correct an underlying condition that adversely affects morale. His Instructional

Speech is in fact exhortatory; hinting at a theme of shame, Napoleon implores his audience to act the part of "men" and "soldiers" and exercise greater self-control. (If one were to substitute cowardice for lovesickness, his speech could just as easily have been given on a battlefield to a soldier-audience that was afraid to fight.) While his remedial paradigm for depression might strike readers as antique, one can safely assume that a modern general, fearing a plague of suicides, would also deliver an exhortatory Instructional Speech to the ranks— "the army cares for your well-being and the military has chaplaincy and psychiatric services that can help"—and almost certainly some "pure" instruction to his medical staff: "you must address the rash of suicides in this command . . ." But for both Napoleon and the modern general, the end remains the same: whether one chooses to call it the honor of arms or the combat effectiveness of an army, it amounts to keeping soldiers tuned to and interested in performing as well as those described in Von Clausewitz's imagined army.

Major General John A. Lejeune's letter of September 19, 1922, is a much more explicit instance of an exhortatory Instructional Speech whose principal object is morale. Unlike Napoleon, whose exhortations were premised on connecting notions of masculinity, soldiering, and war, Lejeune's efforts to inspire seem derived from a Unit Historical Narrative. They are in fact based on the U.S. Marine Corps— what the corps has been, is, and should be, though the past here is not explicit but enthymematic ("our beloved Corps"). Anything "beloved" is historical; Lejeune has no need to specify why the corps is beloved, because his officer-audience, being familiar with the corps, its traditions, and its history, already knows the answer. Like the uses of "marines" examined elsewhere, merely mentioning the name here suffices to summon its history.

General Lejeune's phrasing might appear informal: the words "I order," "I instruct," or "by command of" do not appear in his letter. Instead, he explains that because the U.S. Marine Corps has become too large for a tête-à-tête with each officer, "I am going to do the next best thing, by writing letters from time to time." But there is nothing informal about his voice or the message it conveys. First, as the marine commandant, he is already accorded enormous respect within the corps; second, there is no mistaking the voice in this communication—it is that of Command Authority, albeit inserted against a backdrop of wise and considered reflection.

Before reviewing Lejeune's specific admonitions to his officers, we should really consider why he bothers to write at all. The answer is that like McClellan and Clausewitz, Lejeune also has an ideal military (that is, U.S. Marine Corps) in mind, one whose outlines he gladly shares with his officer-audience: "Let each one of us resolve to show in himself a good example of virtue, honor, patriotism, and subordination, and to do all in his power, not only to maintain, but to increase the prestige, the efficiency, and the esprit of the grand old Corps to which we belong." Of course, there is no suggestion that the foregoing exhausts Lejeune's conception of the ideal corps, but it certainly emphasizes how central he believes officers to be within it ("You are the permanent part of the Marine Corps, and the efficiency, the good name, and the esprit of the Corps are in your hands"). And it also suggests that Lejeune understood that a good officer arose in part as a function of character (virtue, honor, patriotism) and in part as a function of military indoctrination (subordination). While these qualities might appear platitudinous, they are in fact very timebound concepts. For example, the Condottieri (chiefly Italian mercenaries) of late medieval and renaissance Europe would have not have considered "patriotism" of much account, nor presumably would they have valued later bourgeois conceptions of honor or virtue. Moreover, Lejeune's notion that a U.S. Marine Corps would even have a "permanent part" is, over the long haul of history, unusual; after the fall of Rome, genuinely permanent military establishments did not reoccur for a millennium. Indeed, Lejeune's introduction of an enthymematic historical narrative ("the grand old Corps") is itself unusual—between the fall of Rome and the seventeenth century (and often afterward), military organizations were often ad hoc, formed for a single campaign and then dissolved.

General Lejeune, of course, cannot simply order good morale and efficient officers, so like other Instructional speechmakers, he addresses the components of good morale, confident that, like adding a column of numbers, the sum will equal the parts. First, the "you" and "your" that he uses throughout his speech operate both individually and collectively: "I want each of you to feel that the Commandant of the Corps is your friend and that he earnestly desires that you should realize this." Here, "you" is the individual officer-recipient reading the letter. But Lejeune then moves to address his officers collectively, and the letter accordingly shifts from horizontal instruction (friend to friend) to vertical (commander to subordinate): "At the same time, it is [my] duty to the Government and to the Marine Corps to exact a high standard of conduct, a strict performance of duty, and rigid compliance with orders on the part of all officers." In fact, this weaving between horizontal and vertical, the comrade-to-comrade address and the voice of collective command, continues throughout Lejeune's review of the qualities and behaviors he believes are important for marine officers. And it is this blend of personal and command voices that both gives the letter its power as an Instructional Speech and makes it interesting to read. For example, after reminding his men that they are "the permanent part of the Marine Corps" (command voice), he counsels them as individuals: "You can make it or mar it." The very next paragraph begins as a personal communication by Lejeune-as-friend: "You should never forget the power of example. The young men serving as enlisted men take their cue from you." Then comes the voice of command, spoken to a collective on behalf of a collective: "If you conduct yourselves at all times as officers and gentlemen should conduct themselves, the moral tone of the whole Corps will raised, its reputation, which is most precious to all of us, will be enhanced, and the esteem and affection in which the Corps is held by the American people will be increased." Once again, in a famous sentence, General Lejeune speaks in a personal voice: "Be kindly and just in dealing with your men," to which he adds, "Never play favorites. Make them feel that justice tempered with mercy may always be counted on." Then comes the command voice: "This does not mean a slackening of discipline. Obedience to orders and regulations must always be insisted on, and good conduct on the part of the men exacted."

Of course, this speech's thematic destination is morale—the morale of officers upon whom the morale of the whole corps depends.

For Lejeune, the ideal U.S. Marine Corps is a body of men coexisting on two levels—the impersonal level of rank, order, and discipline and the personal level of individuals who may wear uniforms but who also form a unique human society. Thus he complements the "small" picture ("A compliance with the minutiae of military courtesy is a mark of well disciplined troops") with the large: "We are all members of the same great family, and we should invariably show courtesy and consideration not only to other officers but of their personal families as well." If marines are a metaphorical family, then real families also must merit these courtesies. Lejeune's unstated reason is enthymematical: discourtesy to a Marine's real family is likely to create morale problems with the metaphorical family.

Small matters include those that concern personal relations. Salutes "between officers and men should not be overlooked"; moreover, "officers should be equally careful to salute each other." A similar spirit should prevail with uniforms, which is the first thing seen of a comrade before the distance has closed for a personal salutation. "Officers should be . . . exceedingly careful to be neatly and tidily dressed, and to carry themselves in a military manner," Lejeune instructs. This is not just a professional matter but also one whose strictures extend into personal space. Even while on liberty, officers must be careful with their own appearance as well as that of their men and "should endeavor to instill into their minds the importance of neatness, smartness, and soldierly bearing." Likewise, courtesy matters even when men are off duty: "On all occasions when officers are gathered together, juniors should show their esteem and respect for their seniors by taking the initiative in speaking to and shaking hands with their seniors." Lejeune emphasizes exactly how personal this is by imagining how the "seniors" will feel about it: "The older officers," he reassures the junior members of his officer-audience, will "appreciate greatly the attention and friendliness on the part of the younger officers." His conclusion works from small to large: "The destiny of our Corps depends on each of you," he begins, then changes his focus: "Our forces, brigades, regiments, battalions, companies, and other detachments are what you make them." Finally, he arrives at the largest picture of all, presented entirely in collective terms:

> An inefficient organization is the product of inefficient officers, and all
> the discreditable occurrences are usually due to the failure of officers to
> perform their duties properly. Harmonious cooperation and teamwork,
> together with an intelligent and energetic performance of duty, are es-
> sential to success, and these attributes can be attained only by cultivat-
> ing in your character the qualities of loyalty, unselfishness, devotion to
> duty, and the highest sense of honor.

Here collective traits of cooperation and teamwork are balanced by individual traits of intelligence and energy, all of which are merged into
duty and success.

It is not difficult to extract from General Lejeune's letter the third
convention of Instructional Speech, the Idea toward which he seeks to
move his officer-audience. In these final paragraphs Lejeune's equation balances the parts that derive from individuals: loyalty, unselfishness, devotion to duty, honor, virtue, patriotism, and subordination.
Their sum is the "prestige, the efficiency, and the esprit of the grand
old Corps to which we belong."

IT IS USEFUL to briefly compare the "visibility" of General Lejeune's
concept of a military ideal with Colonel Jones's thoughts on the
matter. Lejeune's ideals are patent; the words he uses—virtue, honor,
patriotism, subordination, cooperation, teamwork, loyalty, unselfishness, duty, and honor—speak for themselves and define an officer's
character. Written over eighty years ago, these qualities would in some
form or another resonate with Julius Caesar just as they do with contemporary readers. This is true of most exhortatory speeches, whether
designed to instruct about proper courtesies or inspire soldiers before
a battle. The ideals they articulate are usually patent and if not genuinely universal at least long familiar. By contrast, "pure" Instructional
Speeches such Colonel Jones's, or Napoleon's from the beginning of
this chapter, offer ideals that are far less visible to outsiders. This subset of instructional speech is a true creature of context, and often of
fact-specific situations, whether applying FARs to experience or dictating instructions from an operating manual. While Caesar would
immediately grasp the perils of overconfidence and complacency, he
would likely have to wade through considerable explanation about the

tactics and procedures of Jones's times in order to fully understand how these perils are manifest in that world. In short, to exhort is to ostentatiously reach for common ideals widely understood; while "Pure" Instructional Speeches also have ideals at their core, they are usually densely wrapped in manuals that must be comprehended before the Idea is reached.

Political and Religious Instructional Speeches

He [Josephus] explained all that contributed to toughness of body or fortitude of spirit. Above all he trained them for war by stressing Roman discipline at every turn: they would be facing men who had conquered almost the entire world by physical prowess and unshakable determination. He would feel certain of their soldierly qualities even before they went into action, if they refrained from their besetting sins of theft, banditry, and looting, from defrauding their countrymen, and from regarding as personal gain the misfortunes of their closest friends. For if those who went to war had a clear conscience, victory was certain; but men whose private life was smirched had not only human enemies but God to contend with. To this effect he exhorted them continually.

   Josephus describing his own efforts to train a Jewish citizen army
   for the defense of the Galilee, 66 CE[10]

INSTRUCTIONAL SPEECH can also use Political and Religious Historical Narrative to reinforce its demands. These speeches feature the same three basic conventions found in other kinds of Instructional Speech; but unlike them the Idea Convention included here is likely to be filled with examples drawn from history books or holy texts rather than FARs or operating manuals. As is true in other battle speeches, patent Religious Historical Narratives are less likely to be found in addresses to modern, secular armies; however, it is almost certain that the modern emphasis on character traits as a component of successful militaries is a direct descendent of the ancient biblical insistence that strength alone is insufficient for success in battle, and that victory belongs to those who are righteous in God's sight. Political

Historical Narratives do appear in modern Instructional Speeches, and one especially famous instance will be considered below. The above excerpt from Josephus has been selected by way of introduction because it conveniently combines both a Political and a Religious Historical Narrative.

Josephus's advanced credentials for making Religious Historical Narratives have already been noted; but the young priest was also something of an ancient cosmopolite. More than a decade before the destruction of the Second Temple, he had traveled to Rome on a diplomatic mission to free several Temple priests being held on charges whose specifics have not survived; nearly drowning in the Adriatic when his ship sank, Josephus nevertheless made it to Rome and promptly befriended Poppea, Caesar Nero's wife (from whom "I obtained many presents"). She helped him accomplish his diplomatic task, and Josephus likely remained in Rome for several years. It was this acquaintance with the Roman Empire that also qualified him to make the kind of Political Historical Narrative featured above. What occasioned that speech occurred after his return from Italy. The political situation in Israel had changed, and Jewish radicals were preparing for a full-scale revolt against Rome. As noted earlier, Josephus, having learned something of Roman power, opposed "with vehement exhortation" what he considered "the madness of desperate men." (Fearing the politics, after first returning from Rome, Josephus "retired into the inner court of the Temple" to devote himself to priestly duties.) However, as a member of the elite with considerable experience in matters Roman, he was perhaps inevitably returned to the secular world in the ensuing whirlwind of events. In 66 CE the Jerusalem authorities appointed him governor of the Galilee, and one of his tasks was to prepare the region for a possible war with Rome. For Josephus this meant fortifying towns and, with a core force of some 4,500 "professional soldiers," he molded the eligible male civilian population into an army that (he claimed) boasted 60,000 infantry and 250 cavalry.[11]

In describing the Instructional Speeches he made to his Galilean recruits, Josephus creates a Rome vs. Jerusalem/this world vs. world of heaven dichotomy that parallels the two qualities he seeks to instill in his soldier-audience: "[I] explained all that contributed to toughness of body or fortitude of spirit." For "toughness of body" he takes Rome as his model; but for "fortitude of spirit" his model was Jerusalem, or more specifically the Law. Josephus believes that he is waging a struggle simultaneously in this world and before the Heavenly Court: his recruits must be better than Romans with spears, siegecraft, and infantry formations, but they must also be righteous in the sight of God.

The Political Historical Narrative is obviously drawn from the history of the Roman Empire. The fact that Josephus's recruits "would be facing men who had conquered almost the entire world by physical prowess and unshakable determination" provided the foil against which he would train them. The implication here is that he not only aspired to Roman combat methods but also may well have exhorted his recruits—frightening them, challenging them, and spurring them on—by reminding them of their enemy's military prowess and perhaps even offering specific historical examples. Yet, although Josephus remembered that "Above all [I] trained them for war by stressing Roman discipline at every turn" and that part of Rome's success lay in "unshakable determination," it is not to the empire that he looks for *spiritual* power.

For Jews without righteousness, even the most exacting imitation of Roman combat techniques will be to no avail. Instead, Josephus instructs his recruits to aspire to spiritual purity through obedience to the Law. Referring to himself in the third person, Josephus recalls that "He would feel certain of [his men's] soldierly qualities even before they went into action, if they refrained from their besetting sins of theft, banditry, and looting, from defrauding their countrymen, and from regarding as personal gain the misfortunes of their closest friends." Before Josephus's arrival, the Galilee had been the scene of considerable internecine fighting; not only were many crimes committed but the mere existence of these quarrels was itself a violation of the Law, specifically Leviticus 19:16–18 [KJV], which famously concludes, "Thou shalt not avenge, nor bear any grudge against the children of thy people, but thou shalt love thy neighbor as thyself: I *am* the Lord." This bloody factionalism had to cease, and not just because it impaired the military unity of the Galilee. Here Josephus applies the history of the Jews to the crisis confronting the Galilee in as clear a statement as was ever uttered about the connection between personal sanctity and military victory: "For if those who went to war had a clear conscience, victory was certain," Josephus instructed his would-be soldiers, "[but] men whose private life was smirched had not only human enemies but God to contend with."

Josephus was not the first Jewish soldier (nor would he be the last) to fill an Instruction Speech with exhortations connecting spiritual purity with victory in battle. Indeed, in his *Antiquities of the Jews*, written after the fall of Jerusalem, Josephus gives Judah Macabbee an Instructional Speech that in one form or another had been heard by the Hebrews since the days of Moses:

> And when Judas saw [the enemy] camp, and how numerous their enemies were, he persuaded his own soldiers to be of good courage; and exhorted them to place their hopes of victory in God, and to make supplication to him, according to the custom of the country, clothed in sackcloth; and to show what was their usual habit of supplication in the greatest dangers, and thereby to prevail with God to grant you the victory of your enemies.[12]

In this connection it is useful to think about General Lejeune's Instructional Speech to his officers. Here personal righteousness (whose modern, secularized counterparts are the adjectives used by General Lejeune [loyalty, unselfishness, virtue, honor, etc.]) is connected with victory, or at least with a well-led military force that can produce victories. Perhaps the connection is not ironclad—nowhere in his letter does General Lejeune mention God, and it is certainly conceivable that atheistic or agnostic marine officers could successfully embody the desired traits; also, it is likely true that whether derived from religion or not, the desirability of these traits is also rooted in utilitarian concerns (few would deny that an army of sunshine patriots, cowards, thieves, and murderers would, on average, not consistently produce victories). Nevertheless, throughout history the traits noted by Lejeune (and Josephus) have been rhetorically derived from or linked to religious values. Thus for Josephus and a good many soldiers after him, Instructional Speech using Religious Historical themes, themes derived from religion, or even religious instruction (that is, sermons) are as central to the morale of armies as any other type of battle speech.

A proclamation of such grave moment to the nation, officially communicated to the army, affords to the general commanding an opportunity of defining specifically to the officers and soldiers under his command the relation borne by all persons in the military service of the United States toward the civil authorities of the Government.

The Constitution confides to the civil authorities—legislative, judicial, and executive—the power and duty of making, expounding, and executing the Federal laws. Armed forces are raised and supported simply to sustain the civil authorities, and are to be held in strict subordination thereto in all respects. This fundamental rule of our political system is essential to the security of our republican institutions, and should be thoroughly understood and observed by every soldier. The principle upon which, and the object for which, armies shall be employed in suppressing rebellion, must be determined and declared by the civil authorities, and the Chief Executive, who is charged with the administration of the national affairs, is the proper and only source through which the needs and orders of the Government can be made known to the nation.

Discussions by officers and soldiers concerning public measures determined upon and declared by the Government, when carried at all beyond temperate and respectful expressions of opinion, tend greatly to impair and destroy the discipline and efficiency of troops, by substituting the spirit of political faction for that firm, stead[fast], and earnest support of the authority of the Government, which is the highest duty of the American soldier. The remedy for political errors, if any are committed, is to be found only in the action of the people at the polls.

> Excerpt from General George B. McClellan's General Orders No. 163, instructing the Army of the Potomac on obedience to the Preliminary Emancipation Proclamation, October 7, 1862[13]

MOST INSTRUCTIONAL SPEECHES that use politics do so by resorting to historical narrative, drawing on the past to inform their soldier-audience. In constitutional democracies that rigidly adhere to civilian control over the military, battle speeches that are expressly *political*, in the sense of intending to influence elections or policy formation reserved to civilians, are usually unwelcome and often against regulations. Yet war *is* politics, and soldiers are political instruments in the hands of civilians entrusted with managing war. And any war that depends on short-time citizen volunteers will be more political than other wars, if for no other reason than that the "politics" of the war—that is, the main purposes of the war—must broadly accord with the reasons why the volunteers volunteered. As I noted in the introduction, soldiers cannot be ordered to fight but must be persuaded to do so. One could add that persuasion is not a single event but an ongoing process: soldiers must be continually persuaded, in fact, for wars and their purposes are notoriously fickle.[14]

The purpose of the federal government in waging the Civil War changed on September 22, 1862, when President Abraham Lincoln issued the Preliminary Emancipation Proclamation. What had been exclusively a war for the Union now became a war for the abolition of slavery as well. How the federal army and especially soldiers loyal to its then-commander, General George B. McClellan, would receive the prospect of emancipation was a matter of intense concern to President Lincoln and his advisors. McClellan inspired fierce loyalty among all ranks of the Army of the Potomac and was a Democrat who opposed the proclamation (while opposing slavery as well) because he believed that it would harden Southern attitudes and thus foreclose the possibility of sectional reconciliation. But among several senior members of Lincoln's cabinet, there was also the belief that McClellan's political opposition could result in the general marching on Washington to establish himself as a dictator.[15]

Based on rumors and secondhand accounts, the concern about McClellan's loyalty proved unfounded and probably reflected a paranoia that far exceeded McClellan's personal opposition to the proclamation. In truth, McClellan was under pressure from fellow Democrats to announce his support for the proclamation, which then came in the form of the above speech. This order has divided historians as sharply as it did many of McClellan's contemporaries. By noting that "the remedy for political errors, if any are committed, is to be found only in the action of the people at polls," did it indeed contain what historian Allan Nevins has called "a pregnant hint" about the desirability of the

defeat of Lincoln's Republican Party in the upcoming state and federal elections? Or was McClellan's speech just what it seems to be, an
eloquent civics lesson given to armed men amidst the searing hatreds
unleashed by civil war? I tend to agree with recent scholarship that
McClellan was far too conservative, too devoted to the country and its
institutions, to countenance a coup. Instead, it is more likely that the
objectionable sentence about polls was added to remind the army's opponents of emancipation—and they were likely a minority, although
a heartfelt one—that the "remedy for political errors, if any are committed, *is* to be found only in the action of the people at the polls"
[emphasis added]. Thus General Orders No. 163 comprises one of the
more well-written statements in American history explaining why the
military must remain neutral in matters political and offering guidance as to the appropriate channels (and limits) of any opposition. For
Americans, this speech should be considered a historical landmark in
civilian-military relations.[16]

McClellan believes that the proclamation is a radical departure in
war policy ("of such grave moment to the nation"); therefore, in more
recent parlance, he will use its issuance as a "teachable moment" for
the army ("[it] affords to the general commanding an opportunity of
defining specifically to officers and soldiers . . . the relation borne
by all persons in the military service . . . toward the civil authorities
of the Government"). Now McClellan commences a syllogistic civics
lesson in constitutional law beginning with a broad proposition from
which he will shortly construe specific guidance for his soldiers. First,
the premise: "The Constitution confides to the civil authorities—legislative, judicial, and executive—the power and duty of making, expounding, and executing the Federal laws." What follows next is the
second premise: the military exists to support the civil authorities and
is "held in strict subordination thereto in all respects." He then derives
from these his conclusion—that is, the instruction: civil control of the
military is a "fundamental rule of our political system . . . essential to
the security of our republican institutions, and should be thoroughly
understood by every soldier." In short, whatever a soldier's personal
views on emancipation, it is the policy of the legitimately elected government and thus must be supported by the army. But McClellan

understands that Lincoln issued the proclamation pursuant to his war powers; it was not passed by Congress, declared law by the judiciary, or voted on by any electorate. Thus McClellan is careful to explain that in particular the president is entitled to obedience, not only because he is the commander-in-chief but also because he is the key link in the entire constitutional scheme of government. It is "the Chief Executive who is charged with the administration of the national affairs" and thus is the "proper and only source through which the needs and *orders* of the Government can be made known to the nation" [emphasis added]. In short, disobeying the president and refusing to enforce the proclamation would not be some principled act of insubordination on a matter of conscience—it would be tantamount to denying the whole scheme of constitutional government. And McClellan's use of the word "orders" is not coincidental. It must be remembered that although the intended audience for this proclamation was the whole world, its "legal" audience—that is, those upon whom it would be binding by force of law—was the military. The proclamation might have mentioned two earlier congressional acts that had broad consequences for the freeing of slaves; but these acts, important as they were in bolstering Lincoln's arguments for emancipation, were *not* emancipation proclamations. Only the proclamation was the proclamation, and for it Lincoln expressly invoked his war powers, beginning the document as follows: "I, Abraham Lincoln, President of the United States of America, and Commander-in-Chief of the Army and Navy thereof." Any soldier reading the proclamation itself also found the following sentence: "And I do hereby enjoin upon and order all persons engaged in the military and naval service of the United States to observe, obey, and enforce, within their respective spheres of service, the act and sections above recited." Legally, it was as if Abraham Lincoln himself had suddenly appeared around a company campfire, called the men to attention, and issued a direct, face-to-face order.[17]

Given this legal relation, McClellan next intrudes into his soldiers' private spaces, although in doing so he interestingly mimics the same principles that Lincoln used in issuing the proclamation. Just as the president rationalized the issuance of his proclamation as a strictly military measure, so the general uses a military rationale to moderate or even curtail his soldiers' political conversations, even in private. First, he defines an acceptable conversation. Although McClellan does not foolishly use the word "prohibit," he strongly implies that any discussions "carried at all beyond temperate and respectful expressions of opinion" are not acceptable and presumably will have negative consequences. And like the president, McClellan rationalizes this as a matter of military authority: these unacceptable conversations "tend greatly to impair and destroy the discipline and efficiency of troops by substituting the spirit of political faction for that firm, stead[fast], and earnest support of the authority of the Government, which is the highest duty of the American soldier." Dissenting members of McClellan's soldier-audience could discover the consequences of such intemperate political conversations by reading the *Revised U.S. Army Regulations of 1861*, including article 1:1 (inferiors required to obey lawful orders of superiors), or the Articles of War, specifically article 5 (prohibition of contemptuous language against civilian leaders) or article 7 (mutiny, sedition, requirement of inferiors to obey lawful orders). But as McClellan makes clear to any soldiers miffed at this curtailment of their right to free speech, the right to vote remains: the remedy for discontent is ultimately at the polls.[18]

The last two paragraphs of General Orders No. 163, omitted above, contain an interesting rhetorical device and an important appeal worth considering as examples of how Unit and Religious Historical Narratives can bolster battle-speech messages dealing with other topics (in this case, politics). In the first of these paragraphs, McClellan is very careful not to criticize the Army of the Potomac. "In thus calling the attention of this army to the true relation between the soldier and the Government," he assures his men, "the general commanding merely adverts to an evil against which it has been thought advisable during our whole history to guard the armies of the Republic, and in so doing he will not be considered by any right-minded person as casting any reflection upon that loyalty and good conduct which has been so fully illustrated upon so many battlefields." This sentence is convoluted because the message conveyed is so delicate: soldiers must not infer from McClellan's civics lesson on military submission to civilian authority that they or the army did or said something that justified a

rebuke. On the contrary, McClellan assures them that his speech is
not a rebuke but a routinely didactic message, one that is often made
"during our whole history to guard the armies of the Republic" against
the ancient evil of usurping constitutional government. Here McClellan seems hypersensitive to the army's self-esteem, something he was
largely responsible for creating; those who might have taken offense
to this speech are mistaken and have only to consider the unit history
of the army to which they belong, an army whose "loyalty and good
conduct" have already been "fully illustrated on so many battlefields."
Sometimes bad tasting medicine must be sweetened.

McClellan's final appeal is especially interesting, given his supposed use of this speech to undermine the Republican Party. The
paragraph consists of one seemingly unnecessary sentence: "In carrying out all measures of public policy, this army will, of course, be
guided by the same rules of mercy and Christianity that have controlled its conduct toward the defenseless." First, McClellan could
have satisfactorily ended his speech after the preceding paragraph,
which argued that nothing he said shall be construed as a slight upon
the army. By adding this explicit reference to Christianity, McClellan seeks to broaden his *favorably disposed* soldier-audience to include
something close to 100 percent of the Army of the Potomac, most of
whose members were at least nominally Christian. Of course, these
would have included those who might be considering disobeying or
undermining the proclamation. (Such actions could include many
things beyond mounting a coup—for example, resignation, desertion,
partisan politicking, or a simple failure to abide by the proclamation
by returning slaves to bondage or otherwise mistreating them.) And
the few who were not Christian (Jews, atheists, and so forth) would
be hard pressed to deny the merits of any policy based on "mercy . . .
toward the defenseless."

Next, the way in which McClellan invokes Christianity is very curious, given his personal opposition to Lincoln's proclamation. Had
he sought simply to use Christianity to justify obedience to Lincoln's
order, he could have used the same argument as many biblically literate Northerners routinely did on the subject of rebellion: cite Romans 13:1–3, which was often invoked to confer divine sanction on

obedience to established government.[19] But McClellan chose another
aspect of Christianity to explain why obedience to the proclamation
was religiously sanctioned, even if vehemently disputed in the political arena. He asserts that mercy and Christianity are equivalent and
that both must control "conduct toward the defenseless." The defenseless are of course slaves, particularly fugitive slaves who had been escaping to the federal lines with growing frequency since the first days
of the war. McClellan's implication is clear: Christian mercy exists in
obeying the law (cited by Lincoln in his proclamation) that prohib-
its soldiers from returning slaves to bondage; it likewise exists in de-
priving rebellious masters of their slaves, another law referenced in
Lincoln's proclamation. Indeed, whatever McClellan's personal religion (he happened to be an evangelical Presbyterian), one could easily infer his conviction that slavery was un-Christian. Therefore, his
final appeal, probably intended for anti-proclamation diehards, was
that common religious values of both abolitionists and anti-abolition-
ists compel minimum standards of behavior that happen to be embodied in the proclamation. In short, for McClellan, Romans 13:1–3 was
inadequate to the occasion, but the Sermon on the Mount apparently
sufficed. Christian love has always had a wider appeal than "the powers that be are ordained of God."[20]

Instructional Speech and Rules of Engagement: Politics as a Continuation of War with a Mixture of Other Means[21]

*The men were reminded of the mission they were on, to annihilate
all enemy personnel, destroy as many military installations as they
could, and to gather intelligence. There would be no room for any
prisoners. They were also told that there must be no cruelty or disfigurement or mutilation of the enemy, alive or dead. The password
would be "Gung" and the countersign was "Ho."*

Colonel Edward F. Carlson's Pre-Invasion Speech to the Second Marine
Raiders Battalion before the landing on Makin Island, August 1942

*"The enemy will try to manipulate you into hating all Iraqis," [General
James N.] Mattis wrote to his troops. "Do not allow the enemy that*

victory. With strong discipline, solid faith, unwavering alertness, and undiminished chivalry to the innocent, we will carry out this mission. Remember, I have added, 'First, Do No Harm' to our passwords of 'No Better Friend, No Worse Enemy.'"

The Marines would knock on doors, Mattis said, not kick the door down and put a boot on a man's neck. There would be no bulldozing of houses or arrests of the relatives of insurgents. If shot at, no fusillade would be loosed in response. Mattis emphasized marksmanship—one shot, one kill. The hope was that restraint in attitude and firepower would lead to more toleration of U.S. troops and less toleration of the armed resistance.

General Mattis preparing his command for duty in Iraq, 2004[22]

INSTRUCTIONAL SPEECHES containing rules of engagement (ROE) are worth considering for purely historical reasons—no subset of the battle speech genre better illustrates the recently changed nature of Western warfare than do these. (Readers will recall from my introduction Colonel Tim Collins's Pre-Invasion Speech, which articulated the guiding spirit behind one set of ROE.) Few Instructional Speeches are as critical to individual soldiers as those that contain ROE: they specify the "if, when, where, and how" an enemy can be "engaged"—that is, avoidance of the enemy or force applied and the enemy damaged or completely destroyed. Some famous examples of one-line ROE battle speeches from American history include Colonel William Prescott's reported instruction to his men at the Battle of Bunker Hill ("Don't fire/shoot until you see the whites of their eyes") or Admiral George Dewey's instructions to his flagship's captain on entering Manila Bay ("Gridley, you may fire when ready"). But whether very short or exceedingly long (see note 23), these ROE can mean life or death to soldiers, their enemies, and noncombatants. Too much force is overkill that consumes innocents as well as enemies; too little force or the imposition of overly restrictive ROE is underkill that can mean a longer (and therefore bloodier) conflict or higher "friendly"-force casualties, which has its own unpleasant effects on domestic politics and military morale. Driving these concerns today is a global media that has transformed Western warfare into a spectator event, albeit one in which the observers are not passive: they vote, pray, demonstrate, and riot in their respective countries, manage transnational bureaucracies, and in general can influence the willingness of other governments to lend assistance or create obstacles for the war-sponsoring state. As a result, ROE increasingly reflect a consensus politics in which a surprisingly large number of constituencies must be accommodated: international law, the morale of friendly fighters, the war-sponsoring country's domestic population, the host country's civilian population, transnational monitors, various ethnic and religious constituencies, and, of course, the enemy.[23]

Lieutenant Colonel Carlson's Pre-Battle Speech featured above was delivered over the submarine *Nautilus*'s public address system to members of his Second Marine Raiders Battalion shortly before they attacked the Japanese-held island of Makin. This speech was given as much for information as for instruction or exhortation (although information is almost never given for its own sake, instead serving the Rationalization Convention). The men were mostly told about what was not known—the exact number of Japanese defenders—and briefed about the presence of enemy armor and the possibility that the Japanese might attack by air or reinforce Makin from nearby islands. But at some point, Carlson decided to include some ROE about taking prisoners as well. He began by reciting the marines' mission—"to annihilate all enemy personnel, destroy as many military installations as they could, and to gather intelligence"—and noted that because of what was not known about enemy strength or reinforcements, this mission would have to be completed quickly. But in case anyone had missed the meaning of "annihilate all enemy personnel," this ROE was rephrased: "There would be no room for any prisoners." Interestingly, Carlson did impose some limitations—no "disfigurement or mutilation" of the enemy—probably because he deemed torture ("alive") or posthumous cutting to be morally repugnant and unprofessional conduct but also a time-wasting distraction, and time was short because of the possibility that the enemy might reinforce. Besides, there could be no room for prisoners because his soldiers would leave the island as they had arrived, in two tightly packed submarines. In earlier instructions, men had been assigned to squads; some were designated as a reserve force, others to advance. Once on the beach, the hope was to reach the island's treeline before engaging the enemy. But once the shooting began, there were no restrictions on ROE: the men were free to use any weapon they had against any Japanese target.

Of course, Carlson's ROE regarding prisoners contravened international law. The First and Second Hague Peace Conferences of 1899 and 1907, respectively, had made the murder of prisoners illegal, and there was no "secret mission" exception. Carlson's instructions are offered here as one of the infrequent instances in American military history where we discover "a take no quarter policy" (and in fairness to Carlson, there is no evidence that any surrendered Japanese were killed); in that sense, Carlson's speech serves as a useful foil to the very different and far more complex ROE given in General Mattis's instructions to his troops. These were issued, apparently in written form, before Mattis returned to Iraq (he had commanded troops in the 2003 invasion) and sometime before the first, ultimately aborted battle for Fallujah began in April 2004. Mattis's ROE do nothing less than redefine the object of war (at least as traditionally understood), principally by how he defines what "victory" means for the enemy. "The enemy will try to manipulate you into hating all Iraqis," he declared. "Do not allow the enemy that victory." In other words, the enemy's goal is political, not military; the enemy seeks to drive a wedge between American soldiers and the civilian population. Such an enemy does not operate within the traditional Western paradigm of "kill-or-be-killed"; indeed, hypothetically, it is possible that such an enemy could achieve victory without killing any American soldiers. All this enemy would have to do is succeed in provoking Americans to brutalize or kill real or claimed Iraqi civilians. Victory for the enemy is the complete alienation of Iraqi civilians from the American soldiers.[24]

Thus does General Mattis suggest that his soldiers may be functioning like heavily armed community police rather than the more historically ample model of enemy-killers with only a secondary regard for the lives or opinions of civilians. When applying force, then, Mattis instructs his soldiers to use a political strategy to fight an enemy whose chief offensive strategy is likewise political. He surely recognizes that he is asking his soldiers to exercise a non-traditional restraint in combat against a declared but hidden enemy. And making the task even more difficult to manage is the fact that the enemy will not reciprocate. Thus, to be more comprehensible to his marines, General Mattis must dress his insistence on restraint in the garb of traditional soldierly virtues. And these martial virtues (emphasis added) are brightly strung out and preceded by flattering adjectives: "strong *discipline,* solid *faith,* unwavering *alertness,* and undiminished *chivalry* to the innocent." If his men embody these virtues, "we will carry out this mission."

But how exactly is the mission to be fulfilled? In what may have been a confusing charge to some soldiers, Mattis declares that "the mission" rests on two pillars, beginning with "First, Do No Harm." This is an odd motto for a soldier, since it is normally associated with the Hippocratic Oath, the ancient pledge of healers, not warriors. But if the marines are tasked with a political mission, then "Do No Harm" is entirely comprehensible, because "doing harm" is equivalent to a politician's gaffe during an election campaign—gaffes do not kill people but they do alienate voters. And Bing West, the historian-journalist who reported Mattis's instructions, did provide considerable context for the general's concerns: "There were hundreds of thousands of potential recruits for the insurgents in Anbar Province," West observed. "Americans by themselves couldn't win an insurgency." But they could commit gaffes. Mattis had been told about "rough treatment by American soldiers stationed in Ramadi and Fallujah—doors smashed in, cars banged aside by Bradleys, an us-versus-them attitude." Therefore, and in sharp contrast to Carlson's ROE, Mattis's ROE were in reality more political than military.[25]

The mission had a second pillar that Mattis summarized in a motto, famously associated with the U.S. Marine Corps: that the marines make "No Better Friend, No Worse Enemy." This phrase is the military equivalent of political sloganeering, a form of "motto morale" that boosts unit esteem and identification but ultimately ill serves a soldier-audience looking for real guidance about a mission. (For example, Mattis's motto begs a question central to all counterinsurgency warfare: how do uniformed combatants know whom to befriend and whom to treat as an enemy?) But Mattis does provide some concrete guidance in his ROE: Marines would knock on doors, not kick them down; they would handle detainees humanely; they would not punitively destroy insurgents' houses or arrest their relatives; enemy gunfire would be answered by carefully directed fire ("one shot, one kill"). Again, the strategy here is political. "The hope was that restraint in attitude and firepower," West notes, presumably paraphrasing or guessing about Mattis's intentions, "would lead to more toleration of U.S. troops and less toleration of the armed resistance."[26]

Deeds as Instructional Speech

Just as we were going into battle General Wadsworth—that gray-haired old veteran whom the soldiers all loved—rode up. He held a revolver in one hand and with the other he caught the edge of the colors and said, "Follow me, boys." [Color Sergeant Frank] Head replied: "General, I'll follow you anywhere."

From *General Wadsworth: The Life and Times of Brevet Major General James S. Wadsworth,* by Wayne Mahood

Ackerman picked the first house in a row of houses south of Phase Line Blue to get his beleaguered platoon into. His Marines were strung out along a wall, seeking protection from the incoming enemy rounds. He screamed to his men to follow him into the house. No one heard him with all of the noise of the firing going on. The Marines in Haji alley were now caught up in the total chaos of the battle.

"Get in the F***ing . . . house!" Ackerman shouted again.

Once more no one heard him over the noise of the fighting. He started waving his arms to catch his Marines' attention and still no one saw him. Ackerman thought, "What the F***!" He now began waving both hands above his head and pointing to the house to get his men's attention. Finally he barreled his way through the gate and pushed into the two-story house. His 1st and 2nd Squads finally followed their lieutenant in the safety of the building.

Second Lieutenant Elliot Ackerman, First Platoon, Alpha Company, First Battalion, Eighth Marines[27]

INSTRUCTIONAL SPEECH, interestingly, needs no words to instruct; actions alone, or actions conjoined with words, can also
suffice. Thus far, the speeches considered have all been products of
composition aforethought—deliberate prose, good metaphors, and
the benefit of revision. Such speeches may have been composed in
comfortable libraries or at least behind-the-lines headquarters, and/
or printed in carefully edited unit magazines intended to reach remote comrades days later. But sometimes the most important Instructional Speeches are made at times and in places where words cannot
be heard above the din, where a single gesture is far more instructive
than the most eloquent speech, and where the circumstances requiring the instruction arrive without warning, exist for a moment, and
then disappear.

Like Instructional Speeches that consist of words, those that communicate by deed also require a "voice" of command as well as a compliant soldier-audience. Consider the case of a squad of soldiers led
by an NCO that is pinned down in a firefight. If one of the privates
suddenly and wordlessly bolts for an undisclosed location, the others
may or may not follow him—some might even assume that he is fleeing the scene without orders. But if the NCO is seen to do the same
(see Second Lieutenant Ackerman in the above example), the rest of
the group will almost certainly follow. In sum, indispensable to the
deed-as-speech's efficacy is *who* performs the communicative action.
In the second example featured above, it obviously mattered that it
was the distinguished-looking *General* Wadsworth (the anecdote was
misremembered; he was only a major at the time) who was seen to
raise a pistol in one hand and the folds of the colors in the other.
However, unlike Instructional Speeches of words, the instructional
deed-as-speech does not necessarily communicate some ideal military standard of performance or behavior. Its point is usually to induce
some immediate action that may appeal to ideals but itself requires
no reflection; whether the deed appeals to larger ideas (for example,
General Wadsworth's) or to plain survival (Lieutenant Ackerman's), it
will always have the following goal: to motivate a mass of men to move
from one point to another, and to do so quickly.

Instructional deeds-as-speech have other similarities as well, arising from the immediate environment in which they are performed.
Usually, this environment will render ineffective most words beyond
a shout or exclamation. This might be because the sounds of combat
are deafening or the soldier-audience is too large, so that a gesture of
instruction will be seen by far more soldiers than would be able to
hear a speech. And environment is everything. If a commander on a
calm parade ground tries to instruct his soldiers by some silent act as
opposed to a speech, he risks appearing ridiculous. Yet the same gestures under fire might well spur men willingly to their deaths.

Consider the environment in which Lieutenant Ackerman found
himself at one point during the Battle of Fallujah. Moving through a
maze of hotly contested streets and alleys, First Platoon had already
suffered seven casualties, and with no aid station nearby; the wounded
had to move when the unit moved. This meant that too many un-
wounded men, otherwise necessary to suppress enemy fire, were required to assist disabled comrades. And the sounds of that enemy
fire—mostly from rocket-propelled grenades and small arms—was
deafening. So when Ackerman ordered his men to enter a nearby
house for cover in order to stabilize the wounded and reorganize his
unit, his commands went unheard. In fact, no one could see his first
attempt to gesture—the waving of his hands—as an instruction to
enter the house. Finally, he used his entire body-in-motion as the instruction. When he moved out of position and into the house, his men
saw and followed. No words were necessary. The immediate environment made it easy for Ackerman's men to infer their lieutenant's instructions from observing his actions.[28]

Combat circumstances suggest that if words are used, they will
of necessity be few. This does not mean that abstractions and ideals
have no place in instructional deeds-as-speech; quite the contrary, as
the example of General Wadsworth suggests, idealism can be central in wordlessly bolstering the importance of the few words that are
spoken. Wadsworth's use of the props of flag and pistol conveyed the
ideals he believed were necessary to motivate his men. (Note that such
spontaneous or impulsive acts should not be confused with staging,
which requires preset scenes and some planning.) Seizing the colors

and holding them aloft for all to see was a symbolically charged gesture of profound power that probably summoned many feelings in the
observers—patriotism, unit pride, hatred of the enemy, and a desire
for victory. And the pistol simultaneously raised in Wadsworth's other
hand signified that the moment had arrived to unleash great violence
on behalf of these feelings. The three-word instruction—"Follow
me, boys"—was now framed by imagery that totaled an Instructional
Speech of enormous power, appealing at once to the highest ideals
and the most elemental emotions. Nevertheless, the ideals were inci-
dental to the speech's central message, which was an instruction as
to movement. However, that the color sergeant replied "General, I'll
follow you anywhere" suggests that Wadsworth's symbolic appeal to
his men's idealism was effective. After all, the general was not asking
his men follow him "anywhere" but rather into battle at First Manassas. This incident with Wadsworth will be discussed in greater detail
in chapter 6.

*The Teutones could not contain themselves till the Romans should
come down and fight them on equal terms, but hastily arming themselves charged in their fury up the hillside. [Gaius] Marius, sending
officers to all parts, commanded his men to stand still and keep their
ground; when they came within reach, to throw their javelins, then
use their swords, and joining their shields, force them back; pointing
out to them that the steepness of the ground would render the enemy's blows inefficient, nor could their shields be kept close together,
the inequality of the ground hindering the stability of their footing.*

    *This counsel he gave them, and was the first that followed it; for
he was inferior to none in the use of his body, and far excelled all in
resolution.*

    "Gaius Marius," from Plutarch's *Lives*[29]

GAIUS MARIUS (whose Recruiting Speech was featured in the preceding chapter) uses a blend of words and deeds above that offers
an opportunity to consider how the personal example can instruct, especially when combined with Rationalization. Whereas General Wadsworth and Lieutenant Ackerman through their words and/or deeds

wanted soldiers to follow them across some piece of ground, Marius uses his words and deeds to convince soldiers to apply his *ideas*, or to follow him about or in the use of *things*—tactics (stand still, keep the ground), the required distance before the enemy may be engaged (they must come within reach), the sequence of deploying weapons (javelins, then swords), and the use of defensive measures (shields to force them back). Marius's instructional mix of ROE, training, and battle tactics is far too complex to be silently performed. Words were therefore required too.

Perhaps because the army was too dispersed or too large, or the topography was not conducive for an assembly, Marius did not personally deliver his own message (at least not the second time): "Sending officers to all parts [of the army], [Marius] commanded his men." This implies an officers' conference at which the original Instructional Speech was made that obviously included ordering his subalterns to repeat the speech to the larger army. Next, characteristic of the Rationalization Convention found in many Instructional Speeches, Marius gives reasons for his orders, "[Marius or his junior officers] pointing out to them that the steepness of the ground would render the enemy's blows inefficient, nor could their shields be kept close together, the inequality of ground hindering the stability of their footing." Here the enemy (the Teutones) was attacking uphill, and it is easy to visualize the practicality of Marius's tactics. At first, his explanation to the soldiers is harder to understand—why not simply issue the orders and omit the reasons? As we have discussed already, however it *is* persuasion, not simple orders, that keeps soldiers in line of battle. Marius's Instructional Speech was made as the impulsive ("they could not contain themselves") Teutones charged up the hill, and Marius wanted his men to adopt tactics that in a few short moments would mean life for some and death for others. Reasons had to be given so that his men understood why they were being asked to take what might have struck some as unnecessary risks—for example, waiting to hurl their javelins until the enemy was "within reach" (which in this case probably implies a closer distance than one might ordinarily allow for) or waiting before closing to the more intimate space required for swordfights.

In Marius's case, it is likely that no sooner were the explanations and orders delivered than the Teutones began to close on the Roman lines. But the window for instruction had not closed; instead, what came through the window simply shifted from the spoken word to the sight of Marius demonstrating by personal example what he had just said. It must always be remembered that soldiering is a craft as well as a science, and that physical dexterity, an agility with objects, and various movements and motions *require* personal demonstration. And at that moment Marius concluded that instructions alone were insufficient to meet the crisis. Plutarch declares that Marius was the first to follow the "counsel he gave them . . . for he was inferior to none in the use of his body, and far excelled all in resolution." While it may well have been the case that Marius the soldier pitched in because he was spoiling for a fight, it is just as likely that Marius the commander wanted to personally demonstrate his orders, personally embodying the third convention of Instructional Speeches—the military Idea that he wishes his men to follow.

In ancient warfare, a shift such as Marius's from verbal Instructional Speech to instruction-by-deed was sometimes expected and often critical to victory. Victor Davis Hanson's observation about why ancient Greek *hoplites* fought probably applies to Marius's actions here: "Along with regimental esprit," Hanson observes, "an even better incentive for *hoplites* to stand firm was the sight of their own commanding officer, the *strategos*, fighting alongside them in the very front ranks of the army." Here I have simply added additional evidence for Hanson's insight—the word-and-deed as instruction as well as inspiration. In more recent armies, of course, instructional words and deeds are far more likely to be made by junior officers or NCOs.[30]

One such recent example can be found in the words and deeds of U.S. Marine Corps Gunnery Sergeant Jason K. Doran during Operation Iraqi Freedom. The instructions he sought to impart included the importance of remaining task-focused while under fire, as well as the need to control one's fear. At one point, although his soldiers were "still receiving fire from all around," Doran insisted on walking along the line of his mortar men.

As I walked by the Marines lying down in the shit trench, they would stop firing and look at me. I knew what they were thinking—that I was crazy for walking around and not taking cover. I told them as I walked by, "Don't look at me, look at the enemy," or "I am not the one shooting at you, they are over there," and "I know I am good looking, you can look at me all you want when we get to the other side of the city. Until then, kill them." You might think this was stupid but it made a lot of scared faces laugh. For a lot of Marines this was their first shooting match. I couldn't give them a pep talk like in the movies, with that magical lull in the fighting and the background music. It was my way of letting them know that all this chaos was normal.

Gunnery Sergeant Doran's instructions are easily inferred: he is— quite literally—walking the walk as he talks the talk. And both walk and talk suggest a series of important instructions: despite the distractions of being shot at, keep shooting; despite the fear of death, it is not inevitable (today, at any rate); and he (Doran), a veteran marine with as much reason to live as any of them, can walk upright amidst the gunfire and still perform his job coolly. If Doran's soldiers were not persuaded by their sergeant's one-line verbal instructions, they were probably convinced by what in combat is the most eloquent speech of all—personal example under fire. And this merger of words and deeds will become more apparent as the battle speech moves closer to the battle.[31]

4

PRE-INVASION SPEECHES

Soldiers! You are about to attempt a conquest, the effect of which will be incalculable on civilization and the commerce of the world! You are about to deal England the most certain telling blow she can suffer, until the time comes when you can strike her death-stroke. Not many days after our arrival, the Mameluk beys, who have exclusively favored English commerce, who have injured our merchants and tyrannized over the wretched inhabitants of the Nile, will have ceased to exist.

The people among whom we are going are Mahometans; the chief article of their creed is: God is God, and Mahomet is his prophet. Do not contradict them; deal with them as we have dealt with the Jews, with the Italians; show respect for their muftis and their imams, as you have for rabbis and bishops. The legions of Rome protected all religions. You will meet with customs different from those of Europe; you must learn to accept them.

The first city we shall see was built by Alexander. Our every step will evoke memories of the past worthy of the emulation of Frenchmen.

Napoleon, June 22, 1798, proclamation to his army
written at sea before the invasion of Egypt[1]

NEXT TO THE PRE-BATTLE SPEECH, the Pre-Invasion Speech is probably the most familiar of the battle-speech genres. The reasons likely reside in the dramatic circumstances that surround the Pre-Invasion Speech: whole armies, sometimes years in the recruiting, training, and transporting, gather briefly on a precipice of apprehension to listen to their commander's words before plunging into a dangerous future that all but promises unspeakable violence. It is an unrepeatable moment for no better reason than that this exact soldier-audience will never exist again—invasions mean battles, which in turn will mean death and maiming for some members of the audience. The commander who speaks and the soldiers who listen understand well these eventualities; thus, this literal, or in the case of widely dispersed soldier-audiences, figurative assembly is a knowing moment of dramatic contradictions. Here the emotions of fear of the unknown and of death and physical maiming clash with the military training and group socialization mastered thus far by the soldier-audience—holding true to a cause, maintaining self-control, retaining confidence in comrades and officers, and struggling to remain faithful to training. For many soldiers, invasions will be their first experience with war. Even for grizzled veterans, and especially for commanders, the invasion is the moment when apprehensions peak—there are few military operations with as many exotic variables as invasions, including weather, the capabilities of both an unmet enemy and one's untried comrades, the reliability of weapons and machines, the uncertainty of transport over seas and lands never traversed in quite the same way before, and the attitude of occupied populations. Finally, no plan, however carefully drawn, can allow any thinking soldier to peer into this future and not become his own theologian, whether he worships luck, accepts chaos, believes in inexorable just causes, or trusts in God.

For these reasons, invasions have always demanded a special recognition, at least since Joshua delivered an early Pre-Invasion Speech to the Israelites before they crossed the Jordan River: "Sanctify yourselves," he commanded, "for tomorrow the Lord will do wonders among you." He had no need to say more; the mere assurance of God's favor accomplished everything that later and longer Pre-Invasion Speeches would likewise attempt. The Pre-Invasion Speech must respond to the emotional stressors, the ambivalences and contradictions precipitated by the invasion, and somehow resolve them, dampen the uncertainty, and restore a sense of order. How Pre-Invasion Speeches do this is the subject of this chapter. First in line will be two examples of Pre-Invasion Speeches, followed by a discussion of two important but less frequently encountered variations of the genre. Lastly an example of the Defender's Speech—the Pre-Invasion Speech's counterpart, made by those who are being invaded—will be discussed.[2]

Before examining particular Pre-Invasion Speeches, though, we need to consider several definitional issues. First, Pre-Invasion Speeches must be distinguished from Pre-Battle Speeches. After all, these genres bear some resemblance: both are speeches made just before a military force applies great violence, sometimes meticulously planned aforethought, in order to achieve some military or political objective. But there are critical distinctions between invasions and battles. True invasions typically inaugurate new phases of wars, while battles are merely continuations of fighting, usually of a type that is, or in places that are, already familiar to the soldier-audience. Thus, invasions are military watersheds in ways that battles, no matter how titanic, may not be. And the particular conventions that characterize most Pre-Invasion Speeches derive from this distinction: in battles, the enemy is close, perhaps even in view; a fight is certain; even the specifically contested patch of ground or stretch of sea is certain, and the time remaining before contact is probably short. But invasions are typically distant in time and space from an actual battle. The invasion may promise a battle but the main enemy is not yet in view. If battle does occur, it is usually later in time and distant geographically from the place of assembly, which is the point just before some crucial boundary—the imaginary line or the ocean, river, mountain, or other barrier—is crossed. This distance matters because it gives Pre-Invasion speechmakers time and opportunity to meet the first convention of Pre-Invasion Speeches: the Historical Review of the larger conflict. This review justifies the war in historical terms by giving the reasons for it.

Napoleon's speech featured above conforms to this convention by offering a Political Historical Narrative to justify the invasion of Egypt. His rationale is ostensibly commercial but is actually an appeal to his French soldiers' nationalism, as well as their presumed hatred of the enemy. (Perhaps in keeping with the French sense of the mission of spreading the Revolution's principles, Napoleon adds a liberation rationale to his justification.) "You are about to deal England the most certain telling blow she can suffer, until the time comes when you can strike her death-stroke," he declares. In the next sentence,

Napoleon explains to his men how they are to do this: "Not many days after our arrival," he confidently predicts, "the Mameluk beys, who have exclusively favored English commerce, who have injured our merchants and tyrannized over the wretched inhabitants of the Nile, will have ceased to exist." Enemy commerce is always a target in wartime, but for Napoleon, English commerce was doubly important—he famously considered England a money-obsessed "nation of shopkeepers" and believed that economic pain would always be more keenly felt there than it might be elsewhere.[3]

The second feature of Pre-Invasion Speeches is the Better Hopes Convention: the invasion must culminate in a better future. In explaining why the invasion is necessary, the speechmaker may present a historical narrative that draws on one or several of the four historical themes discussed in chapter 2—the military unit, religion, social group, or political entity. But whatever his source, the Pre-Invasion speechmaker is ultimately talking about *tomorrow*, not yesterday or even today. Past events will be discussed, including why the war began; present events will be considered, perhaps explaining why the war must continue or why the soldier-audience's confidence in their army is justified; but in the end, if the speechmaker talks about the past or the present, he must link them to what the invasion hopes to accomplish in the future. And the proposed accomplishment is rarely articulated solely in military terms, such as might occur in closed-door strategy sessions among senior planners. Thus the reason given will not be explained thusly: "If we capture this harbor the enemy's logistics will be compromised." Instead, the promised future must be equivalent to the invasion's dimensions, to the magnitude of risk that commanders are asking their soldier-audience to assume. In short, a "large" invasion that risks vast amounts of blood and treasure must be explained to soldier-audiences as having equally "large" consequences. Thus the harbor's value as a military objective may or may not be mentioned, but the value of winning the war as a result of capturing the harbor will always be mentioned: historic wrongs avenged, populations liberated or liquidated, the true faith restored, a permanent peace established, and so forth. In short, this second convention is usually characterized by a rhetorical symmetry between what is at risk in the invasion and the more conjectural, imagined future that will occur after the invasion succeeds.

By looking forward and backward, Napoleon's speech clearly offers his soldier-audience Better Hopes. His speech opens with the future: "You are about to attempt a conquest, the effect of which will be incalculable on civilization and the commerce of the world!" As he has done in other speeches, Napoleon here links his men's expected sacrifices with a larger, if rather grandiloquently stated, mission. But it is also a mission whose success promises vast if unspecified benefits for both "commerce" and "civilization." What he probably meant was *French* commerce and *world* civilization, a connection already intrinsic to the principles of the French Revolution: France would introduce Revolutionary, liberationist principles to secure its own borders, and revolution for the avowed purpose of liberating the world. At the same time, Napoleon reaches backward for a military paradigm that sets an example for how his army should behave in this invasion. The French fleet intended to land at Alexandria, named after Alexander the Great, whose martial prowess Napoleon especially esteemed: "Our every step will evoke memories of the past worthy of the emulation of Frenchmen." Here the imagined past of Alexander the Great, as related in biographies with which Napoleon was intimately acquainted, serves as a specific example for his own army's tomorrow—to become a great, but also an especially wise, army of conquest. The wisdom Napoleon probably referred to was Alexander's legendary (if often exaggerated) skill in governing his conquered kingdoms by respecting the natives' culture and religious practices. This theme is further discussed below in the fourth convention of the Pre-Invasion Speech, the ROE.[4]

No matter what type of rationale for the war is used, one important reason for offering it amounts to the third convention of the Pre-Invasion Speech (commonsensical in the extreme): Inspiring Confidence in the soldier-audience. First, the fact that the war is defended as just and necessary will by itself inspire confidence. The assumption is that soldiers who believe that they battle for the right will fight with greater assurance than those who believe that they are engaged in a bad cause, or no cause at all. Of course, confidence-building must transcend mere causes. Many a soldier has died in a

just cause because of friendly fire, incompetent officers, poor generalship, or nonexistent medical facilities, defects that can be as deadly
as a well-aimed enemy bullet. The soldier-audience facing an evil (or
worse, a militarily successful) enemy or some difficult terrain should
also be assured that victory will be achieved because of their side's
superior military, logistical, or technical capabilities. These may derive from several advantages, some or all of which may be noted in
a Pre-Invasion Speech. First, because the soldier-audience's cause is
just and necessary, the enemy's cause is unjust and usually unnecessary, unless it is compelled by the enemy's intrinsic evil. The soldier-
audience is superior in virtue to this enemy, who has, owing to some
defect, either never possessed virtue or at some point lost it. (Virtue or
lack of virtue is usually derived from one of the four historical narratives.) Second, the soldier-audience possesses superior fighting prowess; while this may derive from being more virtuous, it may also derive
from purely technical or logistical factors: its training, officers, and/
or equipment is superior to that of the enemy. In sum, the Inspiring
Confidence Convention attempts to answer the three great questions
presented by an invasion's unknowable future—the collective's question—"Will we win?"—and the individual's two questions—"Will
I be able to maintain self-control when the invasion begins?" and
"Will I die?"

Napoleon's Pre-Invasion Speech assumes rather than declares its
confidence in the army. This was probably because by mid-1798, Napoleon and the French Army (specifically the Army of the Orient for
the Egyptian conquest), by reputation or experience, "knew" one another quite well and in the best way—Napoleon's recently concluded
Italian campaign had been a resounding series of important victories.
Nevertheless, confidence-building gestures are present in this speech.
The cause for which the French invade Egypt is certainly just, as any
cause that benefits "civilization and the commerce of the world" would
be; the enemy is evil, although Napoleon finds no need to develop this,
other than to note that the English and their Marmaluke tools have
"injured our merchants and tyrannized over the wretched inhabitants
of the Nile." His confidence in the army's capabilities is implicit: when
he declares that "You are about to deal England the most certain telling blow she can suffer," there is no room for doubt; indeed, without

even mentioning the possibility of having to battle for that outcome, Napoleon simply assures his men that their debarkation in Alexandria may be all that is necessary, for "Not many days after our arrival" the Marmaluke tools "will have ceased to exist."

Pre-Invasion Speeches generally include ROE with enough regularity that they amount to another convention. ROE were discussed in the last chapter as a form of Instructional Speech, and there is no need to review their basics. ROE will often have an important place in Pre-Invasion Speeches, simply because one function of such speeches is to prepare soldiers for contact with the enemy or civilians residing in enemy lands. Yet there can be subtle differences between the ROE of Pre-Invasion Speeches and those contained in Pre-Battle Speeches, where engaging armed enemies or civilians is usually imminent: Pre-Invasion Speech ROE are more likely to contain something of a tutorial on dealing with enemy civilians or non-combatants. In this regard, Napoleon's speech has become a classic statement, an instruction to his men to remember that although they may be conquerors, they are, like Alexander the Great, best advised to respect the natives' beliefs (especially those that do not conflict with their own interests).

And Napoleon has reduced these natives to what he believes is their most salient characteristic. "The people among whom we are going are Mahometans; the chief article of their creed is: God is God, and Mahomet is his prophet." In Napoleon's view there is only one ROE worth noting: "Do not contradict them," he commands. Unstated is a bit of occupier's wisdom, and that is that the French should not court trouble on matters that are only peripheral to their interests. Napoleon vouches for this piece of conqueror's sagacity and cites ancient Rome as a historical example: "Deal with them as we have dealt with the Jews, with the Italians; show respect for their muftis and their imams, as you have for rabbis and bishops. The legions of Rome protected all religions. You will meet with customs different from those of Europe; you must learn to accept them." Armed engagements are to be restricted to armed enemies. In sum, the French are not at war with God but with the English and their supposed foreign lackeys. Thus did Napoleon tutor his army on why they were to fight, who they were to fight, what they were not to fight, and how they were to deal with the natives when the fight was over. And he conveyed it all in 185 words. However, remaining faithful to the spirit of this speech would prove much more difficult.

The Modern Pre-Invasion Speech

1ST MARINE DIVISION (REIN)

For decades, Saddam Hussein has tortured, imprisoned, raped, and murdered the Iraqi people; invaded neighboring countries without provocation; and threatened the world with weapons of mass destruction. The time has come to end his reign of terror. On your young shoulders rest the hopes of mankind.

When I give you the word, together we will cross the Line of Departure, close with those forces that choose to fight, and destroy them. Our fight is not with the Iraqi people, nor is it with members of the Iraqi army who choose to surrender. While we will move swiftly and aggressively against those who resist, we will treat all others with decency, demonstrating chivalry and soldierly compassion for people who have endured a lifetime under Saddam's oppression.

Chemical attack, treachery, and use of the innocent as human shields can be expected, as can other unethical tactics. Take it all in stride. Be the hunter, not the hunted: never allow your unit to be caught with its guard down. Use good judgment and act in the best interests of our Nation.

You are part of the world's most feared and trusted force. Engage your brain before you engage your weapon. Share your courage with each other as we enter the uncertain terrain north of the Line of Departure. Keep faith in your comrades on your left and right and Marine Air overhead. Fight with a happy heart and strong spirit.

*For the mission's sake, our country's sake, and the sake of the men who carried the Division's colors in past battles—**who fought for life** and **never lost their nerve**—carry out your mission and **keep your honor clean.** Demonstrate to the world there is "No Better Friend, No Worse Enemy" than a U.S. Marine.*

"Commanding General's Message to All Hands," March 2003, J. N. Mattis, Major General, U.S. Marines Commanding (printed proclamation)[5]

MAJOR GENERAL JAMES N. MATTIS'S SPEECH, distributed to his soldiers before the March 2003 invasion of Iraq, illustrates a more recent example of how Pre-Invasion Speeches conform to the four conventions just discussed. Precisely how these conventions appear in different Pre-Invasion Speeches may always be studied with profit, for they yield valuable historical insight not only about strategy and tactics but also about the invaders' expectations. Although Pre-Invasion Speeches never tell the whole story of any operation, they do reveal partial answers to some important questions: What were the invaders' declared objectives? How did they hope to accomplish them? Why were the soldiers told what they were told about the invasion?

The event prompting Mattis's speech was a genuine invasion in the sense used by this book: a line was crossed (Iraq's border with Kuwait); the action began a war or represented a genuinely different strategic or tactical phase in an existing war (regime change versus the earlier policy of regime containment); and the prelude to the invasion consisted of concentrating forces over time, which usually lends itself to creating Pre-Invasion Speeches (the months-long assembly in Kuwait of a large invasion force).[6] The invasion forces were thus separated in time and space from an actual battle. So distant were these forces from a battle that when General Mattis issued his speech, the nature of that battle (or battles), where it might be fought, and against precisely which forces armed with what kinds of weapons, was still conjectural.[7]

General Mattis begins by stating the invasion's rationale, and this conforms to the Historical Review Convention: "For decades, Saddam Hussein has tortured, imprisoned, raped, and murdered the Iraqi people," he immediately declares. "[He invaded] neighboring countries without provocation; and threatened the world with weapons of mass destruction." This review of the war's causes relies on a Political Historical Narrative that summarizes the enemy's crimes. Indeed, Mattis's main rationale for the war *is* the enemy's criminality, the evidence for which is liberally sprinkled throughout the speech: aside from the string of Saddam's past bad acts, there is a reference to his "oppression" and a chilling prediction about how such an evil man would behave in battle ("Chemical attack, treachery, and the use of the innocent as human shields can be expected, as can other unethical tactics"). Mattis had earlier shared his conclusion with his marines: "The time has come to end his reign of terror."

The claim was made earlier that Pre-Invasion Speeches usually draw their rationales from one or more of the four historical narratives. And General Mattis is certainly using history here—his references to Saddam's crimes are all based on past events, chiefly drawn from a political narrative of recent Iraqi history. Documented reports of mass murder and sexual abuse, the invasion of Iran in 1980, the 1990 invasion and pillage of Kuwait, and other crimes had already characterized most of the Western world's perception of Saddam at the time that Mattis's speech was given. But by historical standards of battle-speech indictments of enemies, Mattis's bill of particulars is curiously short. He does not indict Iraq as a social entity or attribute Saddam's evil to Arab ethnicity, Sunni sectarianism or supremacy, or the Muslim religion; unmentioned is Iraq's *system* of government, army, or (in contrast to Eisenhower's treatment of "Nazi tyranny" in his June 6, 1944, Order of the Day) adherence to Ba'athism or any other political ideology. On the contrary, Mattis instructs his soldiers that "Our fight is not with the Iraqi people, nor is it with members of the Iraqi army who choose to surrender." "Iraq" is thus differentiated from Saddam; as in Colonel Collins's speech, "Iraq" is not an enemy but a victim. This was probably not only an effort to reassure Iraqis that the only enemy was Saddam Hussein and his loyalists; it also carried a message to the Leathernecks that the "average" Iraqi is not the enemy. With this rationale, Mattis draws his Political Historical Narrative from a "bad men of history" model, in which the actions of millions are attributed to the evil or folly of a leader or small ruling clique. (This is actually a version of the "Devil made them do it" hypothesis of human motivation, with Saddam cast as Lucifer.)

By positioning an evil Saddam and his henchmen against blameless victims, Mattis confers a religious tint to his speech. He presents his argument within a stark Manichean frame of ancient origins and represents a binary that is first among equals in the conflicts appearing in the Hebrew Bible or the Book of Revelation. It is the argument of good versus evil, a conflict whose distinctly religious antecedents are so pervasive as to have become invisible in a more secular age. Mattis has already evidenced the existence of Saddam's Hell (torture, prison, rape, murder, invasion, threats) by his past evil acts. He also predicts what this evil might produce in the future: first could be a "chemical attack," a terrible war crime; "treachery" is to be expected as well, because intrinsic evil can only behave treacherously (Mattis probably refers here to the possibilities of feigned surrenders, combatants disguised as civilians, and homicide bombers garbed in civilian clothes or driving civilian vehicles); next is the "use of the innocent as human shields," another dastardly war crime, which, while not as murderous in mass as chemical weapons are, nevertheless has the potential of placing an anguished human face in some marines' gun sights; finally, there are "other unethical tactics." Here Mattis may refer to Saddam loyalists using civilian structures—houses, hospitals, and schools—for military purposes. Mattis wants his marines to remember that intrinsic evil is almost bottomless in depravity, although ingenious in application.

Mattis contrasts this evil with marine righteousness. The imagery is clear from the start: "On your young shoulders rest the hopes of mankind." At first, this seems a bit bombastic—after all, Saddam's regime may pose some serious threats, but few would really argue that the "hopes of all mankind" rest on regime change in Iraq. However, in the context of a submerged Religious Historical Narrative, the statement is entirely consistent with long-standing tradition. "Mankind" is only entitled to such grand "hopes" as are derived from God or His messiah. And messiahs bring with them millenarian reigns of peace that are defined by an absence of evil; historically, it is understood that such peace will reign only after evil has been vanquished. So it is with Mattis's marines: "The time has come to end his [Saddam's] reign of terror." Again, there is a need for rhetorical symmetry—Saddam's evil must be equivalent to marine righteousness. And the destruction of Saddam's evil is the messianic hope that the marines are to fulfill. (It is important to note that the messianism used by Mattis is not sectarian but ecumenical, a tradition found across the belief spectrum of Judeo-Christianity.)

But if Saddam is inherently evil, Mattis is quite clear that the marines' righteousness is instead conditional: it must be earned by good deeds and professional soldierly behavior. Thus the marines must be very careful, because goodness can be tempted by evil into committing depredations of its own. Here Mattis cleverly conforms to the ROE Convention of Pre-Invasion Speeches. The ROE will specify the conditions by which the marines can genuinely fulfill the hopes of mankind—as with Josephus's Galileans, the marines must be righteous, at least as this was understood in General Mattis's time and place. First, he makes it clear that "we will treat all others [that is, Iraqis who do not resist] with decency, demonstrating chivalry and soldierly compassion." In short, international conventions regarding EPWs (enemy prisoners of war) will be adhered to, and indiscriminate violence against civilians must be avoided. Next, despite Saddam's treachery, soldiers must remain calm, controlled, and professional. Soldiers will "take it all in stride"; they must retain the cool of the "hunter," not the desperation of the "hunted," because desperate men with deadly weapons are more apt to commit inhumane acts; they must not be caught "with [their] guards down"—that is, whatever the circumstance, they will act prudently and be ever mindful of their training. And if the enemy's proclivities for transgressing the rules of war create chaos, the marines will not reciprocate with lawlessness. In the absence of all order and respect for international law, the marines are to remember two guiding principles: use "good judgment" and always act "in the best interest of our Nation." But not necessarily the best interests of *themselves* as individual marines; for if they act selfishly, heedlessly, or vengefully against an unscrupulous enemy, they might do things such as call for an air strike on a schoolhouse that might kill two hundred innocents just to destroy twenty concealed enemy combatants. Instead, the marines are counseled to act in the "best interests of the Nation," which, in order to avoid the bad press resulting from the use of such violence (which would reflect badly on the "Nation," that is, the entity represented by the marines),[8] may require them to assume the far greater personal risk of clearing the schoolhouse room by room rather than calling for its complete destruction. *That* is how the marines will earn righteousness and thus fulfill their messianic role. As the next paragraph makes clear, General Mattis is confident that his soldiers will conduct themselves accordingly—in this struggle, the

Coalition is the force of Heaven. Consider the spiritualized language he uses about his marines: "feared . . . trusted . . . courage . . . faith . . . happy heart . . . strong spirit." As with so many battle speeches in the secular era, Religious Historical Narratives, while explicitly mentioned nowhere, are present everywhere.

Like most deeply submerged Religious Historical motifs found in battle speeches, Mattis's words are susceptible to multiple meanings. It is here that his speech conforms to the Better Hopes Convention found in most Pre-Invasion Speeches—the promise that a better future will result from the invasion. Not surprisingly, because messiahs are all about improved futures, the invasion's full promise is contained in the same sentence placing "on your young shoulders" the "hopes of mankind." These references are likely to appeal to several segments of the soldier-audience: one can be an atheist and still believe that Saddam is a bad man whose removal would benefit mankind. And in fact, there is present in Mattis's speech a strong element of secular idealism, the embrace of which requires no religion at all. "On your young shoulders" refers to *this* generation of marines, most of whom are still young, who must now shoulder the responsibility for making *their* future better (for the future belongs to the young), not just for themselves but for the world that will exist when the older generation has passed away. This appeal is universal; while some may not belong to a religion or a faith that believes in a messiah, everyone belongs to a generation that occupies a historical moment. And whether or not one believes in a messiah, everyone can agree with Mattis's conclusion: "The time has come to end [Saddam's] reign of terror." Here General Mattis has also created the symmetry present in most Pre-Invasion Speeches: the future resulting from this invasion must be of equal or greater magnitude in goodness to the sacrifices in blood and treasure incurred in mounting the invasion.

As with most Pre-Invasion Speeches, the general does not describe the invasion in the sterile terms of technical tactical objectives or broader strategic or geopolitical goals. Neutralizing specific enemy facilities, balancing regional powers, controlling natural resources, injecting democracy into the neighborhood, or projecting power into an unstable region do not exist in the world conjured by this speech.

Instead, Mattis offers ideals—bright, worthwhile things—for a successful invasion will mean liberating "people who have endured a lifetime under Saddam's oppression." Unlike battle speeches that emphasize revenge, this invasion derives from the worthiest motives. In Mattis's speech the afflictions of Saddam's Hell have not been visited upon marines, their country, or their families, but they have been endured by Iraqis, people largely unknown to the marines. The attacks of September 11, 2001, are nowhere mentioned; instead, there is a subtext intended to appeal to the religious and non-religious alike, involving one of the most moving figures in Western, and specifically Christian, history—the Good Samaritan. Whatever might be the interests of their nation or the Coalition they serve, the marines now go forth like EMTs to rescue a people that they do not know. In broader terms, this Religious Historical Narrative—kindness to strangers—may be found from Abraham to Jesus and beyond.

The Inspiring Confidence Convention is also present. Satisfying the first two conventions has already advanced the third—a justified invasion or war that promises a better future will by themselves inspire some confidence. But in a trained military, confidence must derive from considerably more than a just cause and a bright future. Life and death will be decided in the *here and now*; soldiers can die even in a just cause and might be maimed in ways that could darken the brightest futures. What matters is confidence in the factors that will mitigate casualties: thorough training that is relevant to the particular challenges likely to be faced in the invasion, wise planners, competent officers, the reliability of weapons, the dependability of supplies, and so forth. General Mattis addresses these issues in the same words already used to impart a moral fervor to the invasion. They can also be heard to reinforce the twin ideas of force competence and effectiveness.

First, soldiers are assured that the marines are preceded by an awesome reputation, an undeniable factor throughout their history that operates inversely in the morale of friendly and enemy forces: "You are part of the world's most feared and trusted force." Because marines are feared, some enemy combatants may refuse to engage, which increases survivability for the invaders; because marines are trusted, the civilian population may be more willing to cooperate rather than resist, increasing it as well. In a simple but cleverly effective sentence, Mattis suggests that the benefits of thorough training, long the pride of the marines, are present though completely under each soldier's control. "Engage your brain before you engage your weapon," he admonishes. In short, that his marines have their training, or "brain," is a given, but its proper use is their responsibility—ignoring it could, for example, result in soldiers foolishly provoking a firefight without adequate support or unthinkingly firing at people who are non-combatants. In short, as the marines contemplate an invasion in which so many factors are beyond their control, Mattis urges that perhaps the most important factor—their training—is entirely *within* their control.

Above all, the general emphasizes confidence in comradeship, for not only has the individual marine been thoroughly trained but the collective U.S. Marine Corps is also trained: "Share your courage with each other as we enter the uncertain terrain north of the Line of Departure. Keep faith in your comrades on your left and right and Marine Air overhead." This subtle but remarkable passage builds confidence by emphasizing two levels of comradeship. The first is the most intimate and arguably the most important level at which confidence can be inspired: among one's fellows. To "share your courage with each other" as marines cross into Iraq evokes the glances traded between soldiers packed into armored personnel carriers and the conversations passing among comrades on the eve of the invasion, after a firefight, or following the loss of friends. Mattis recognizes that as the invasion unfolds, confidence is something that must be established and then continually renewed in his marines' personal space. The second sentence—"Keep faith in your comrades on your left and right and Marine Air overhead"—addresses the second level of confidence-building, which envelops the U.S. Marine Corps as a collective. Here Mattis transforms the notion of confidence from the linear understanding occurring comrade-to-comrade into a geometric conception embodying the marine collective that exists to the left, right, and overhead. This is an important reminder to his men that the corps consists of much more than dusty infantry columns trudging or trucking north toward Baghdad—it is a complex fighting machine that is composed of many elements important to these columns' survival. Although Mattis only specifies one of those elements—"Marine Air," that is, the U.S. Marine Corps aviation component that includes attack aircraft whose missions encompass flying in support of the infantry—it is likely that "comrades on your left and right" may well have been "read" by some soldiers to include such combat specialties as marine artillery and armor, the truck drivers ferrying supplies, the engineers constructing pontoon bridges across Iraq's rivers, the corpsmen and doctors ready to help the injured, the chaplains to minister to spiritual needs, and so forth. In sum, Mattis suggests that the sources of confidence are many. And those in his soldier-audience who seek proof that individual endeavor is supported by many thousands have only to look around them to see these other elements performing their assigned tasks, each supporting the mission and reinforcing everyone's safety and well-being.

General Mattis's most interesting appeal resides in his final paragraph. A noun, "sake," is used three times in succession, each time coupled with another word on whose behalf the appeal is made: mission, country, and First Division marines from past conflicts. First, Mattis uses "sake" in its conventional sense: "for the benefit of" or "in the interests of" or "on behalf of" something. From the standpoint of succinctness, this use of "sake" is certainly justifiable—time and attention spans are often short before invasions, and battle speeches must always strive for concision. But the word "sake" has broader connotations too; it is not simply a neutral bridge-word but the bearer of a powerful emotional note of urgency or desperation, of very high stakes with permanent, potentially earthmoving outcomes. Its usage is especially dramatic in traditional English translations of Scripture, where "sake" appears often: "I will not again curse the ground anymore for man's sake," God assures Noah in Genesis 8:21 [KJV]; "He that findeth his life shall lose it: and he that loseth his life for my sake shall find it," Jesus declares in Matthew 10:39; "For ye know the grace of our Lord Jesus Christ, that, though he was rich, yet for your sakes he became poor," Paul proclaims in 2 Corinthians 8:9. In modern English, any sentence that begins with the words, "For the sake of" is almost certain to have a desirable object-word in the middle (peace, Christ, your country, our/your family) and some very emotionally compelling demands toward the end.

And so it is with General Mattis's speech. "For the mission's sake" is drawn from a Unit Historical Narrative: his soldier-audience is on notice that they will shortly hear an appeal whose weight justifies throwing their professionalism on the scales; "[for] our country's sake," a cue taken from a Political Historical Narrative, is likewise kept in the balance; "and [for] the sake of the men who carried the Division's colors in past battles—who fought for life and never lost their nerve" is drawn directly from a Unit Historical Narrative (that of the First Marine Division) and is the final weight deposited. Any one of these themes would have been a sufficient conclusion to his Pre-Invasion Speech. But Mattis insists on weighing them all against a two-fold instruction: his marines "[must] carry out [their] mission and *keep* [their] *honor clean*." (emphasis original) As a rhetorical device, it would at first seem that Mattis spends much for little return. First, "to carry out your mission" for the mission's sake is tautological. However, "to carry out your mission" because your predecessors successfully carried out theirs is eminently respectable—indeed, it is the stock-in-trade of Unit Historical Narratives—and pointing out that those predecessors never lost their nerve is also common in battle speeches. There is likewise a respectable pedigree to the demand that the mission be successfully completed for the sake of one's country.

But Mattis has already used the theme of "the mission" for the mission's sake, and one suspects that the phrase "keep your honor clean" was his real concern and also the object of the other two "sakes." He places "keep your honor clean" on a par with carrying out the mission, and here one's "honor" probably had two components: first, marines should remember that their predecessors in the First Division "never lost their nerve." In other words, a marine will lose his honor by cowardice. But cowardice is usually an internal matter, certainly an embarrassment but not an international war crime, and it is probably war crimes that are Mattis's chief concern. As he declared, First Division predecessors never lost their nerve but they also "fought for life." This is a curious phrase that, upon reflection, yields multiple meanings. First, one may "fight for life" by fidelity to one's training—that is, proceeding cautiously in general and aggressively where warranted, but always doing both in ways that mitigate comrades' casualties. But the First Division's predecessors presumably engaged in just wars for noble purposes, and thus "fought for life" in another respect as well— they liberated oppressed populations and overthrew death-dealing dictators. Now Mattis's phrase, saved for his last sentence—"No Better Friend, No Worse Enemy"—makes sense, because the lives for whom his marines fight are those belonging to this invasion's "real" clients: innocent Iraqi civilians, as well as those Iraqi soldiers who, by gesturing surrender, wish to transform their status from soldiers to EPWs. These are the people to whom marines will either make no better friend or, if they resist, no worse enemy. (Unlike the later battle against insurgents in Fallujah, there is likely to be less ambiguity during the invasion between friends and enemies.)

As was true in Colonel Collins's Pre-Invasion Speech, a soldier's clean honor was if not the whole mission then certainly a large part of it. The military outcome of the Iraq invasion was never in doubt; the only possibility of failure was political, as in the worldwide revulsion over real, misreported, or invented Coalition violence against Iraqi civilians that in turn might have provoked international calls for a ceasefire.[9] Media and enemy invention and misreporting of atrocities were probably understood as givens; the only variable absolutely under the control of Mattis's marines was to avoid committing depredations, intentional or accidental. Thus, once soldiers were advised to "keep [their] honor clean," Mattis wanted to emphasize that they were on an international stage with 360-degree media coverage, and there would be no curtain falling between acts: *"Demonstrate to the world* there is 'No Better Friend, No Worse Enemy' than a U.S. Marine" [emphasis added]. It would seem that the sakes of the mission, the country, and the unit were if not subordinated to then perhaps on a par with the sake of placating a watching world, one that just might have the power to halt the invasion altogether.

As noted above, Mattis's speech also embraces the ROE Convention. It is worth noting that the rules he emphasizes are not technicalities, nor are they the rules on ROE cards distributed to soldiers and intended to provide very specific guidance about when deadly force may be applied. Instead, Mattis, like Napoleon in his speech to the Army of the Orient, seeks a more philosophical understanding of the ROE. This larger view is characteristic of Pre-Invasion Speeches. The assumption is based on the rational expectation that soldiers who understand why a given set of ROE exists will be more likely to abide by them.

Pre-Invasion Speech Variations: Arise!

To the People of Western Virginia: The army of the Confederate States has come among you to expel the enemy, to rescue the people from the despotism of the counterfeit State government imposed on you by Northern bayonets, and to restore the country once more to its natural allegiance to the State. . . .

The commanding general appeals to all good citizens to aid him in these objects, and to all able-bodied men to join his army to defend the sanctities of religion and virtue, home, territory, honor, and law, which are invaded and violated by an unscrupulous enemy, whom an indignant and united people are now about to chastise on his own soil. The Government expects an immediate and enthusiastic response to this call. Your country has been reclaimed for you from the enemy by soldiers, many of whom are from distant parts of the State and the Confederacy, and you will prove unworthy to possess so beautiful and fruitful a land if you do not now rise to retain and defend it. The oaths which the invader imposed upon you are void. They are immoral attempts to restrain you from your duty to your State and Government. They do not exempt you from the obligation to support your Government and to serve in the army, and if such persons are taken as prisoners of war the Confederate Government guarantees to them the humane treatment of the usages of war.

> Excerpt from proclamation titled "To the People of Western Virginia,"
> September 15, 1862, by Major General William Wing Loring, C.S.A.[10]

BEFORE EXAMINING DEFENDERS' SPEECHES, it is worth briefly considering three important if less frequently encountered variations of the Pre-Invasion Speech. First discussed will be speeches that include an invader's appeal to all or some of the enemy's civilian population to arise and join them in fighting the enemy. These appeals are broadly similar to Recruitment Speeches but differ in two important respects. First, Recruitment Speeches are usually made within homogeneous groups, while the invader's appeal to revolt is typically addressed to a civilian population that differs from it in some important way—socially, culturally, politically, or religiously. Next, the invasion itself presents special problems in recruiting a potentially unfriendly or unknown group of civilians. The second variation of the Pre-Invasion Speech might be called the "Truth" Speech. Here the speechmaker seems to defy Western warfare's exhortatory tradition of battle speeches by offering a strikingly pessimistic assessment of what soldiers can expect during an invasion. In fact, Truth Speeches are exhortatory, but slyly so, and in sharp contrast to the standard, "Up, Guards, and at 'em!" exhortation of battle speeches. Last considered is the Speech of Lies, in which the battle speechmaker goes well beyond mere slant and intentionally deceives his soldier-audience in order to achieve some short-term tactical objective.[11]

An invader's call to arise hopes to inspire an enemy's civilian population to revolt, in the process adding civil war (or expanding an existing civil war) to the enemy's woes. These calls to arise obviously serve the invader's interest by increasing defender anxiety, forcing the enemy to divert resources from the main attack and occasionally inflicting actual damage on its war-making capacity. To succeed, the calls must exploit preexisting grievances between the civilian population and the enemy. One of the best known examples of this variation of the Pre-Invasion Speech is General MacArthur's broadcast to Filipinos discussed in chapter 2. There, the grievances were profound, for the would-be guerilla population had suffered three years of brutal occupation by a foreign power. The more obscure but equally illustrative example by Confederate General William Wing Loring is featured above. Here Loring appeals to Virginians from the state's largely non-slave-owning western counties who had become estranged from the seceded state of Virginia. Loring refers to Northern troops as the "invaders," though in truth most citizens of the mountainous western Virginia counties were probably inclined to see the Confederates as the invaders.[12]

In contrast to MacArthur's call to arise, which drew some powerful elements from both Religious and Political Historical Narratives, General Loring's call is drawn from a Political Historical Narrative. And the political history he uses is that of the state of Virginia, rendered dysfunctional by its 1861 vote for secession. That vote represented the will of its eastern, slaveholding counties; however, the mountainous, largely non-slaveholding western counties remained strongly unionist. Almost immediately, these western precincts seceded from the seceders and formed a competing, unionist state based in Alexandria. These counties would eventually become the state of West Virginia, but at no time did the seceded state of Virginia recognize its unionist counterpart. Thus Confederate forces operating in the western counties could only articulate their mission as liberating Virginia territory from Northern occupation. In General Loring's words (unexcerpted above), "We fight for peace and the possession of our own territory." The Confederacy never recognized the state of West Virginia when it formally joined the union in 1863;[13] moreover, it was apparently Loring's genuine belief that a majority of western Virginians favored restoring original ties with the seceded state; thus his speech was both heartfelt as well as reflective of his government's policy.[14]

By declaring his purpose as one of liberation, Loring offers a classic formulation of the invader's call to resist: "The Army of the Confederate States has come among you to expel the enemy, to rescue the people from the despotism of the counterfeit State government imposed on you by Northern bayonets, and to restore the country once more to its natural allegiance to the State [of Virginia, C.S.A.]." These kinds of formulations contain deeply embedded assumptions about the civilian population, which, regardless of the quality of intelligence data, always amount to a best guess rather than existing fact. Consider Loring's central assumption: that western Virginians regard the force he has come to expel as "the enemy." If the Northern troops are not so regarded by civilians, then in fact few people may feel the need for "rescue." If many locals believe that the new state government is legitimate, then they will not view it as "imposed . . . by Northern bayonets." Moreover, if the proposed creation of the State of West Virginia is deemed legitimate by a majority of the population, there is probably no longer any "natural allegiance" to the seceded State of Virginia. All of these assumptions flow from Loring's first assumption, that Northern troops are regarded as enemies; that is why his declaration of fact is actually a guess whose accuracy will reveal itself according to no higher wisdom than "only time will tell."

But Loring's speech is typical of Arise Speeches in that his call to join his army is not content to "wait and see." Instead, he uses dramatic rhetoric in an effort to stir passions, perhaps not a difficult matter (or even a necessary one) in cases where civilians have been genuinely oppressed by brutal occupiers. But Loring's speech leaves nothing to the imagination, and his call is expansive. He appeals to civilians to enlist in the grey ranks "to defend the sanctities of religion and virtue, home, territory, honor, and law." He declares that each of these things had been "invaded and violated by an unscrupulous enemy." It is in this sentence that another aspect of the Political Historical Narrative reappears: Virginia's western counties had been part of the state since colonial times; secession might exist as a state right, but not as a right of areas within established states; and since only Virginia could secede, no federal force had any right of occupation on any portion of the state. Thus, Loring's bill of particulars is premised on the illegal (from old Virginia's perspective) Northern occupation of the western counties.

A Political Historical Narrative does not require conjuring a story from the distant past; invented political histories about the present will also suffice. Loring uses a very recent invention drawn from a Political Historical Narrative about Confederate national identity: nationalism—that is, the ability of white persons living within the seceded states to imagine themselves as a people who are sufficiently different from Northerners in culture, religion, and history so as to justify a new national entity. "Your country has been reclaimed for you from the enemy by soldiers, many of whom are from distant parts of the State and Confederacy," Loring declares. In effect, he suggests that soldiers who, in the absence of a binding Confederate national feeling, would have no stake in liberating the western counties of Virginia have nevertheless come to fight for that purpose. But, he stresses, it is "*Your* country" [emphasis added] that has been thus partly liberated by these men. Loring's goal is not only to stir a presumed Confederate nationalism in western Virginians but also to stir it for a very specific purpose: to induce feelings of shame in his civilian-audience. After all, if western Virginians feel this national bond with other Southerners, they should feel bound by certain duties as Confederate citizens as well, the first of which is self-defense; if they do not assume this duty, Loring tells them, "you will prove unworthy to possess so beautiful and fruitful a land if you do not now rise to retain and defend it." Thus western Virginians who do not defend their land have defaulted on their obligation as citizens and as men and thus should feel ashamed.

It is worth dwelling briefly on Loring's "masculinization" of responsibility here, as it will also figure prominently in another proclamation considered later among Defender's Speeches. Loring's appeal to a masculine conception of duty is cleverly inserted in his list of things that the Northern enemy has "invaded and violated"—"religion and virtue, home, territory, honor, and law." The first three items on this list, religion, virtue, and home, were understood in American Victorian culture as a part of what has been called the "cult of domesticity"— a sphere thought to be entirely under the control of women. These things—church ("religion"), family virtue ("virtue"), and the family itself ("home")—might exist in a man's private space, but they were directed by women—wives, mothers, sisters, daughters old enough to assume the responsibility, and so forth.[15] Applying the words "invaded and violated" to these three items likely raised some disturbing thoughts in the minds of Loring's male citizen-audience, particularly around the sexual violation of their women. Men who have permitted other men to enter this private space unchallenged are less than men in a moral sense, for they have defaulted on a man's first duty—to protect his home, beginning with special protection for the "weaker sex." Moreover, Loring uses an interesting word to describe this violating and invading Northern enemy: "unscrupulous," a term indicating moral defectiveness. An immoral enemy who preys on the weaker sex must be confronted if defenders are to retain their manhood.

The remaining three items on Loring's list—"territory, honor, and law"—were likely considered intrinsically masculine. Territory is defended by armies, composed of men. The sense of honor Loring refers to here is the strictly redemptive sort, similar to that which informs the *code duello*—male western Virginians' private and public spheres have been insulted, and the insult must be avenged for the male honor to be redeemed. Finally, law must be upheld (after all, Northern occupation is illegal), and law, both in its formulation and in the election of those who formulate it, is an exclusively male prerogative. Thus is Loring's call for "all able-bodied men to join his army" perfectly symmetrical to both the call itself and the reasons for it: male civilians are being asked to arise (join his army) for exclusively male reasons: to protect their homes and women and redeem their honor by asserting control over the things that belong to them by gendered right—self-defense, personal honor, and control of society through the legal apparatus.

A final point that further supports this interpretation deserves mention. Because Loring appeals to male honor, he must also confront an issue that in his time would have greatly troubled an honorable man: "The oaths which the invader has imposed upon you are void," he assures his civilian-audience. "They are immoral attempts to restrain you from your duty to your [Confederate] State and Government." Loring here refers to the loyalty oath that federal authorities would have asked for and likely received (in fact, probably cheerfully, although Loring refuses to believe this) from many western Virginians. Oaths were extensively used during the Civil War to bind men to prisoner-of-war paroles, national loyalty, enlistments, and officer commissions, because it was generally believed, with reason, that an oath would morally obligate an honorable man. Because Loring must believe that his civilian-audience is honorable—after all, only an honorable man would recognize his duty as a citizen and bear arms in his country's defense—he must persuade them that the federal loyalty oath itself is not honorable; rather, it was forced upon western Virginians by an "unscrupulous" invader operating on an illegal premise, that their "Northern bayonets" could somehow negate the population's preexisting legal duties to the Confederacy. Thus, Loring declares an absolute "obligation to support your Government and to serve in the army." And insofar as conceptions of shame or honor are community constructs—that is, they depend upon how one perceives others perceiving oneself—Loring provides an escape: *he* personally, and his government (the only legitimate government of Virginia), will not think less of anyone for honoring their preexisting duty of bearing arms for the Confederacy, even if it means violating the federal loyalty oath.

But at the same time, he recognizes that others might continue to feel bound by the oath. This is where an old name for the Civil War—the "Brothers' War"—assumes literal significance; in these socially close-knit mountainous western counties, the chance of political conflicts rending families was likely very great, creating an added layer of complexity to the loyalty issue. If Loring were to follow his own reasoning, Confederate citizens who honored the loyalty oath and served in the federal army would be traitors and criminals, men who were not entitled to the customary protections of captured or surrendered soldiers. Yet Loring apparently concluded that provoking these kinds of tensions was counterproductive to his mission; perhaps he realized the effect that calling federal oath-fulfillers "traitors" might have on small towns and families. Thus he attempts to resolve these complex issues in a practical, if contradictory, way. First, as already noted, he absolves from shame all of those who will not honor the oath; next, he assures those who do decide to honor the oath and serve in the federal army that even if *they* are captured, they will still be entitled to the customary protections accorded prisoners of war. Thus, on one hand he declares, "[The oaths] do not exempt you from the obligation to support your Government and to serve in the army," but in the same sentence, he adds without a blush, "and if such persons [that is, those who honor the loyalty oath] are taken as prisoners of war the Confederate Government guarantees to them the humane treatment of the usages of war." Loring's answer might be illogical, but it was eminently sensible—civil wars are complex affairs, and consistency is not always the higher virtue.

Pre-Invasion Speech Variations: The Truth Speech

On 5 June 1944 at 1400 hours, General Norman Cota, who was in charge of a provisional brigade headquarters that was to serve as

the advanced headquarters for the 29th ID [Infantry Division], ad-
dressed his men: "This is different from any of the other exercises
that you've had so far. The little discrepancies that we tried to cor-
rect on Slapton Sands [an amphibious training center] are going to
be magnified and are going to give way to incidents that you might at
first view as chaotic. The air and naval bombardment and the artil-
lery support are reassuring. But you're going to find confusion. The
landing craft aren't going in on schedule and people are going to be
landed in the wrong place. Some won't be landed at all. The enemy
will try, and will have some success, in preventing our gaining 'lodge-
ment.' But we must improvise, carry on, not lose our heads."

General Norman "Dutch" Cota, addressing his officers before D-Day[16]

TRUTH SPEECHES SEEM to defy the usual conventions of Pre-
Invasion Speeches. Possible mishaps and hardships of the coming
invasion are emphasized instead of its benefits; exhortation, understood in the sense of encouragement, is minimized or absent; the content of the speech seems correlated with the soldier-audience's worst
fears, and it is difficult to see how a soldier, soon to be advancing into
grave peril, can draw much confidence from it. Of course, no commander, including those who deliver Truth Speeches, intends to de-
moralize his soldiers; instead, the Truth Speech is partially based on
a moral tradition of candor with those who are asked to assume potentially lethal risks in battle. And there are powerful practical considerations. Some Pre-Invasion speechmakers believe that reducing
expectations about the invasion proceeding smoothly or producing few
casualties is the best way to prepare soldiers for the shock of probable
outcomes; like General Cota above, they may sharpen this approach
by emphasizing that the rote methods perfected during training exercises likely will not be replicable during the actual invasion, where
chaos and confusion may prevail. Other battle speechmakers may believe that soldiers will repay a frank assessment with increased confidence; a commander who promises neither too much nor too little
but instead calls it as he sees it may create moral capital with his soldiers that will likely prove valuable later. Nevertheless, in sly ways the
Truth Speech remains exhortatory—by substituting hard probabili-

ties for soaring rhetoric, commanders are really offering their soldiers another tool for remaining in control of themselves and their efforts, and retaining confidence in leadership during actual combat. In this the Truth Speech shares the exact same goals as the most soaring or bombastic Pre-Invasion Speech.

General Cota's address was delivered just hours before the Normandy invasion and represents a good example of the Truth Speech. (There is every reason to believe that Cota's speech was heartfelt; he had in fact unsuccessfully opposed landing on Normandy in daylight, arguing instead for a nighttime or dusk invasion.)[17] The device he uses involves a simple contrast between training exercises and the actual invasion he believes will unfold: "This is different from any of the other exercises that you've had so far," he declares. "The little discrepancies that we tried to correct on Slapton Sands are going to be magnified and are going to give way to incidents that you might at first view as chaotic." From the beginning, he sounds a series of connected themes—first, the invasion will not proceed as planned; second, under the resulting stress, the things that inevitably will go wrong will be "magnified" in importance; third, the effect of this apparent magnification will be a *perception* of chaos. What Cota is attempting to do is to set the stage for his main advice, which he offers at the conclusion of his speech: "improvise, carry on, [and] not lose our heads." This is the formula for retaining control of one's company, platoon, squad, and, ultimately, self: when real combat has disrupted rote-learned routines, then adjust the routine to meet the reality ("improvise"); do not allow the sense of disruption to create paralysis ("carry on"); and *never* permit the disruption to create mental confusion or panic ("[do] not lose our heads").

Cota next discloses the probable sequence of how raised expectations are likely to be dashed on the real invasion beaches. First will come a false confidence, and Cota warns his soldiers not to be fooled. "The air and naval bombardment and the artillery support are reassuring," he states, but they are also largely irrelevant to the condition men will actually encounter traveling to and arriving on the invasion beaches: "confusion." He offers several reasons why things will be confused. The landing craft taking men from ships to shore will not operate according to the timetables drawn up months in advance in some distant headquarters. Some boats will "be landed in wrong place," and "some won't be landed at all," whether due to the chaos, mechanical malfunction, or destruction by the enemy (Cota leaves this last unsaid). But it is to the enemy that he next turns. Just as men should not be falsely reassured by the pre-invasion bombardment, so they should not be unnecessarily demoralized by enemy successes. Likewise left unsaid, but probably understood by Cota's soldier-audience, is the fact that this enemy is determined, well entrenched, well trained and well armed. Indeed, this enemy will have "some" success. (Cota's qualifier is very important as evidence of how the Truth Speech is actually exhortatory, albeit via different means than a conventional Pre-Invasion Speech.)

What successes will the enemy have? Here Cota does not go into great detail, either because reciting these details would be *too* candid, or because such things are likely already well embedded in the imaginations of his soldier-audience. All he discloses is that "the enemy will try, and will have some success, in preventing our gaining "'lodgement,'" or a permanent position on the beachhead. This is code for reminding his soldiers that the first wave of the invasion may be insufficient to gain the beachhead, and that additional waves will be necessary; that in process of landing, many soldiers will be killed and wounded by enemy action before even reaching the beach; and perhaps even more soldiers will become casualties on the beach and in the yardage between the beach and the first land objective. Indeed, by enjoying "some success" in preventing a lodgement, the enemy will make these outcomes highly likely. But Cota does not want his men to confuse "some success" by the enemy with that enemy's ultimate triumph; thus, he offers them a trinity of concluding advice: "improvise, carry on, [and] not lose our heads." By not losing perspective, soldiers will understand that dead comrades, din, destroyed landing craft, enemy mortar and machine-gun fire, and stalled advances toward the high ground do not equal an enemy victory. They are simply obstacles that must be overcome by cool-headed men determined to successfully wade ashore and capture the inland cliffs. In other words, Cota suggests that victory lies as much in his soldiers' *attitude* as in their equipment or their comrades' support.

The event bore General Cota out. In *Omaha Beach: A Flawed Victory*, historian Adrian R. Lewis notes that "General Cota's men were among the few soldiers who received a fair assessment of the coming battle. Cota forecast that naval gunfire would miss its targets, the aerial bombardment would be ineffective, and the beaches would be 'fouled up.'" For those of Cota's men who were listening and who, on the beachhead, would remember what he said, the general's few moments of speech in some respects probably equaled the many of months of training in their preparation of the men for the invasion. And it is in this sense that the Truth Speech is genuinely exhortatory in the negative meaning of the word, whose definition includes not only to "urge earnestly" but also "to . . . advise or caution earnestly; to admonish earnestly."[18]

The Counterpart: Defender's Speeches

The enemy is advancing in force into Pennsylvania. He has a strong column within 23 miles of Harrisburg, and other columns are moving by Fulton and Adams Counties, and it can no longer be doubted that a formidable invasion of our State is in actual progress. The calls already made for volunteer militia in the exigency have not been met as fully as the crisis requires.

I, therefore, now issue this my proclamation, calling for 60,000 men to come promptly forward to defend the State. . . .

I will not insult you by inflammatory appeals. A people who want the heart to defend their soil, their families, and their firesides, are not worthy to be accounted men. . . . Show yourselves what you are— a free, loyal, spirited, brave, vigorous race. Do not undergo the disgrace of leaving your defense mainly to the citizens of other States. In defending the soil of Pennsylvania we are contributing to the support of our National Government, and indicating our fidelity to the National cause.

People of Pennsylvania! I owe to you all my faculties, my labors, and life. You owe to your country your prompt and zealous services and efforts. The time has now come when we must all stand or fall together in defense of our State and in support of our Government. Let

us so discharge our duty that posterity shall not blush for us. Come
heartily and cheerfully to the rescue of our noble Commonwealth.
Maintain now your honor and freedom.

Excerpt from Pennsylvania Governor Andrew G. Curtin's
"Proclamation," June 26, 1863[19]

INVASIONS ARE USUALLY CONTESTED. One army crosses a line
while another army seeks to repel it. Just as commanders address
soldiers on the eve of invasions, so those defending against invasions
may also speak to their soldiers (or civilians who will soon perhaps be
soldiers). As history is replete with examples of brilliant and botched
invasions, it is likewise richly illustrated with examples of great or
tepid defenses. On June 26, 1863, Pennsylvania Governor Andrew G.
Curtin issued a proclamation calling the people of his state to resist
an invasion by the Army of Northern Virginia. This speech illustrates
the conventions of what this book calls the Defender's Speech—the
speech made by those who, still reeling from an initial attack, must
speak to both their their soldiers and would-be soldiers, informing
them about the invasion and then calling for resistance.

The first convention of the Defender's Speech is not a feature of
structure or topic but rather one of attitude: the Urgency Convention. The speech's voice or tone must convey this urgency and anxiety
in support of a fearful earnestness about prospects. This attitude is a
product of the suddenness of the invasion and the surprise with which
it is greeted. The speechmaker typically represents those responsible
for directing the defense, and he seeks to instill into the military (and
in modernity's total wars the entire civilian population) his own anxiety and fear; after all, it is from soldiers and citizens that resistance
must come. The people, whether in uniform or not, must be convinced
that the situation is emergent and dire, and that the very survival of
the entity—tribe, religion, party, or state—is at stake. Even invasions
that are widely anticipated nevertheless remain mysterious as to their
exact time and starting point, the identity of their initial targets, the
separation of feints from main movements, and their tactics or weaponry. Some of these mysteries may remain such until long after the
invasion has begun; this factor is usually a byproduct of the normal

"fog of war," which beclouds the speechmaker and almost guarantees that every invasion first appears as a profound crisis of unknown magnitude. Whether it reflects the speechmaker's personal anxiety or is meant to kindle the audience's fears, it is this sense of profound crisis that powers the Urgency Convention of the Defender's Speech.

The second convention of the Defender's Speech derives from the speech's second function: resistance. Resistance must be organized, and the audience instructed about what they must do to resist. Thus the Resistance Convention will contain recruitment appeals and instructions, blending elements of two speech genres already examined: the Recruitment Speech and the Instructional Speech. Particularly in modern warfare, recruitment is a necessary feature of resistance. First, whether the invasion initiates a war or further intensifies an existing war, the defender must usually increase the size of its armed forces; this means persuading civilians to volunteer, or at the very least not resist conscription. Second, like soldiers, civilians cannot simply be "ordered" to resist; they must be persuaded. Moreover, the speechmaker's actual authority over some citizens may have terminated in areas now occupied by the invader. Thus must the Defender's Speech contain the persuasive elements of the Recruitment Speech as well as elements of the Instructional Speech. Moreover, of course, an invasion may call into question the defending entity's very existence; one means of easing any doubts in this regard is to be seen as acting like a fully functioning government or military—exhorting for some cause, issuing orders, instructions, pleas, and demands, and so forth. Thus are the recruitment and instructional memes self-complementary in a Defender's Speech—an order-barking, proclamation-issuing, exhorting government or military is far more likely to inspire confidence and thereby stimulate resistance than is an entity from which little is heard.

The third convention is present in all persuasive arguments, whether or not they are battle speeches: the Motive Convention. The audience must be provided with an incentive to comply with the speechmaker's wishes. It is cited as a separate convention here because of its unusual importance in Defender's Speeches. This appeal seeks to answer a question that is existential to the defender and the

entity he represents—why resist? This question will never be explicitly posed in a Defender's Speech but nevertheless lurks behind its
every word. The answer is not as obvious as most Defender's speechmakers would prefer (or pretend) to believe; it is also the reason why
Defender's Speech appeals number among the most emotive of any
in the battle speech genres. First, the civilian (or military) population
might conclude that it is safer not to resist. Perhaps the enemy is only
transiting through and is not a force of permanent occupation; perhaps it may be appeased by no resistance; perhaps the enemy seeks
only forage and will satisfied with cleaning out the pantry before continuing on its way. Worse, the population (or some constituent element of same) may perceive the invader as a liberator who has come to
free them from the defender's shackles. Whether these attitudes stem
from a loss of confidence or outright hostility to the defender, the Defender's speechmaker must counter them. Two contrary instincts are
involved here—civilians and soldiers alike must weigh loyalty to the
defending entity against their concerns for personal survival and perhaps that of their family and homestead. It will take a powerful motive to persuade men, women, and occasionally even children to resist
an armed enemy when the course of least resistance might promise
the best measure of personal safety. Thus the third convention of the
Defender's Speech deals with the main appeal, which is always in answer to a question ("Why resist?") that the speech itself dare not pose.
While Defender's Speeches employ many motives, two common ones
are shame and nationalism.

Governor Curtin's speech to the citizens of Pennsylvania called for
militia volunteers to resist the invasion of his state by Robert E. Lee's
Army of Northern Virginia. Pennsylvania has already been "invaded"
by rebel cavalry; however, the most famous of these incursions was
no more than a raid.[20] By late June 1863 Governor Curtin was aware
that Lee's entry into his state was no mere foray, but June 26 found
the governor still unsuccessful in persuading enough Pennsylvanians
to join the state militia. Curtin's disappointment is patent—despite
his efforts to rally Pennsylvanians, he can only complain that his calls
"have not been met as fully as the crisis requires." The implication is
that Pennsylvanians do not yet appreciate the crisis's magnitude, and

indeed, they may not believe it is a crisis at all. Curtin's proclamation
now intends to remedy this.

The Urgency Convention of the Defender's Speech entails the voice
of urgency, anxiety, even terror. Governor Curtin's speech attempts to
answer this need by increasing gradually the emotional heat with each
succeeding paragraph; thus, the speech concludes quite differently
from how it begins, which is in the voice of a headquarters bulletin,
straightforwardly informing Pennsylvanians that the Army of Northern Virginia "is advancing in force into Pennsylvania," that a "strong
column" is only twenty-three miles from the state capital of Harrisburg, and that "other columns are moving by Fulton and Adams Counties." However, that this speech is definitely not a bulletin becomes
clear once Curtin, after stating the facts, begins interpreting them
for his audience. One fact—the proximity of "strong" rebel forces to
the state capital of Harrisburg (and thus Philadelphia)—probably sufficed to establish the situation's gravity in the minds of many Pennsylvanians. But Defenders' Speeches, like calls to arise, generally leave
little to the imagination. On the contrary, by communicating anxiety,
panic, and terror, the Defender's Speech hopes to crowd the audience's mind with as many disturbing details as possible.

The first disturbing detail in Curtin's speech is that this incur-
sion is not a raid; it is "formidable" and constitutes a "crisis." A raid
would not require "60,000 men to come *promptly* forward to defend
the state" [emphasis added]; only a large-scale invasion could demand
such a response. It is a general rule in Defender's Speeches that the
amount of desired audience anxiety is equivalent to the importance
of the stakes involved. And what does Curtin believe is at stake here?
Initially, he points out two things that are at risk: "the safety of our
people and the honor of our State." But as his speech increases the
anxiety-degrees, the stakes rise even above these—"I appeal to you
not to be unmindful," he implores his presumably patriotic but thus
far complacent public, "that the foe that strikes at our State strikes
through our desolation at the life of the Republic." Now Pennsylvania's cause is the nation's cause, and Harrisburg, though far north of
Washington, D.C., is somehow a steppingstone to the national capital. But Curtin now shifts from abstract patriotism to matters closer to

home. If Pennsylvanians were unwilling to fight for State or country, they just might be willing to defend themselves, their families, and their property. Here Curtin holds as a certainty that a failure to enlist in the militia will mean that "our people are plundered and driven from their homes solely because of their fidelity and loyalty to our free institutions." In emphasizing the image of refugees, Curtin was drawing on Northern propaganda (which does not necessarily detract from its truthfulness), which for years had claimed that when Confederate forces occupied an area, their first act was to expel whole families for unionist sentiments. Northern newspapers had written luridly of families evicted from their homes and forced onto the open road, taking with them no more than they could carry. The prospect that this might happen in prosperous southeastern Pennsylvania was probably enough to disturb many in the audience.[21]

The second convention of the Defender's Speech, Resistance, is normally manifested in calls for recruitment-instruction. Once a soldier- or civilian-audience has been sufficiently riled or frightened, the speechmaker must offer directions on how and where to resist; the audience must be told what to do. Curtin's proclamation offers many instructions. It specifies the number of men required (60,000), their length of service (ninety days), when they are needed ("promptly"), and where they are to report ("rendezvous at such points to be designated . . . by the adjutant-general of Pennsylvania"); moreover, it assures them of proper support ("which orders will also set forth the details of the arrangements for organization, clothing, subsistence, equipments and supplies"). Citizens wishing to serve in the militia have only to await the promised orders for an address to which to report for duty. The recruiting aspect of this convention is evident from the start—it is the point, in fact, of Curtin's proclamation. What differentiates this from an ordinary Recruiting Speech are the circumstances in which it is issued—those shocked by the immediacy of invasions lack the leisure to invent elaborate Religious, Political, or Social Narratives; there simply is no time to cite Tacitus or review God's history of the world or one's boyhood wanderings around Revolutionary War battlefields. Everything is compressed and terribly urgent.

And so the third convention of the Defender's Speech—the Motive for resisting—must be stark and powerful. By June 26 Governor Curtin had learned what many after him would also discover: resisting an invader cannot be assumed. For the reasons cited earlier, resistance may actually be the less rational alternative. So the motive force of the Defender's Speech must be powerful enough to persuade those soldiers or civilians who might have excellent reasons for surrendering, appeasement, or non-action out of fear of the invader's response. And the Motive Curtin uses—shame—is perhaps the oldest and most powerful appeal of the battle-speech genre since the days of the Hebrew Bible and Homer. "A people who want the heart to defend their soil, their families and their firesides," Curtin declares, "are not worthy to be accounted men."[22]

When battle speechmakers invoke shame, it is always in the context of a choice between acts of disgrace and a path to redemption. (In the shame meme this choice must always exist; otherwise it would be pointless to introduce shame as a motive.) In Governor Curtin's case, the continuing shame of a paltry response to his call for volunteers may still be reversed, and he now offers redemption. Pennsylvanians may yet "show [themselves to be] what [they] are—a free, loyal, spirited, brave, vigorous race" by volunteering to serve the ninety days' militia duty. In support of redemption, the governor draws from a Political Historical Narrative: "Pennsylvania has always heretofore responded promptly to all the calls made by the Federal Government," he reminds his audience. And what was true then should also be true now.

Shame arises from the breach of a social contract, although the "agreement" is not always voluntary or fair. One form of social contract relates to masculinity—men, because they are men, are expected to behave in certain ways, especially when confronting situations requiring physical strength or violence. In exchange, men were "granted" or just assumed primacy in many matters, but especially in warfare. Men who fail to fulfill these obligations, which are often expressed as warlike traits—bravery, courage, a willingness to confront violent death (their own or somebody else's)—are considered in breach of this gendered social contract. And it is this breach on which Governor Curtin chooses to base his appeal: the men of Pennsylvania should be

ashamed of themselves for their failure to respond to the rebel invasion. They have failed to act like men.

Curtin's concept of masculinity (shared with General Loring) can
be garnered by contrasting the emotive words or phrases used in the
shame sentence ("want [of] heart" to protect "their soil, families, and
their firesides," "not worthy," not "to be accounted men") with the
words used in the redemption sentence ("free, loyal, spirited, brave,
[and] vigorous"). Generally speaking, Curtin's comparison uses a metaphor of physicality with a hint of sexual virility. True men are strong,
healthy, and virile; men unworthy of their gender's privileges are the
opposite: weak-hearted (a metaphor that has both physical and spiritual implications), unworthy, not accounted as men (unmanned?), and
thus so impaired in spirit and flesh as to be unable to defend what
should be natural to a true man—his own soil (native state), fireside
(home), and family.

Here the political becomes personal. If eligible male Pennsylvanians shirk their civic duty of defense, Governor Curtin allows only
one explanation: it is because they are unmanly. Curtin next extends
the shame meme from among his fellow Pennsylvanians to beyond
the state's borders. "Do not undergo the disgrace of leaving your defense mainly to the citizens of other States," he warns, suggesting that
shame's burden is also collective; a failure to defend one's own state
breaks the social contract that exists between states—states are expected to first defend themselves. Here shame will attach not only
to individual unmanly Pennsylvanians but also to all Pennsylvanians,
presumably male and female, by virtue of state citizenship. It will
apply equally to those men who defended the state as well as those
who did not. All citizens will thus bear the shame of the collective's
failure to defend itself. While Curtin here extends a horizontal social
contract (citizen to citizen, state to state), he does not neglect its vertical dimension either: "In defending the soil of Pennsylvania we are
contributing to the support of our National Government, and indicating our fidelity to the National cause." The well-known philosophical
principle that the assertion of any statement implies the possibility of
its negative has no greater force than in matters of rhetoric; here, the
audience can imply that those who do not defend the soil of Pennsyl-

vania are not contributing support to the federal government, and thus are displaying infidelity to the national cause.

As suggested earlier, it would pointless to introduce shame without immediately offering redemption; after all, it is only through redemption (that is, enlisting) that the state's interests will be met. And like the skilled politician that he was, Governor Curtin applies his final words to charting the path for redemption. "Let us so discharge our duty that posterity shall not blush for us," he declares, adding an imagined future to the ranks of things standing in judgment of eligible but perhaps frightened or fence-sitting male Pennsylvanians. "Come heartily and cheerfully to the rescue of our noble Commonwealth. Maintain now your honor and freedom." In this last sentence, Governor Curtin has listed his priorities for this time and place: honor first, freedom second.

Defenders' Speech of Lies

[The] messengers sent to Pompey arrived back. Domitius read the dispatch they brought; and then, in his council of officers, he concealed its contents, and announced that Pompey would shortly arrive with help [in fact, the dispatch said that Pompey was not coming]; [Domitius] urged them to keep up their spirits and make all necessary arrangements for the defense of the town. He himself then held a secret conclave with a few friends and decided to attempt escape. When word of Domitius's plans got about, the soldiers in Corfinium gathered in groups in the early evening and, led by tribunes, centurions and the more reputable men of their own class, began discussing the situation. . . . Thereupon, the whole army unanimously had Domitius brought out and, surrounding him and putting him under guard, they sent a deputation from their ranks to Caesar, saying they were ready to open the gates and take orders from him, and that they would surrender Domitius alive into his hands.

Julius Caesar, *The Civil War,* 1:18–20

All day long the battle raged on the opposite side of the Chickahominy, and its progress could be distinctly seen from our camping ground. We could see that our men were apparently driven back. In fact nothing could have been more apparent. It was all a trap of Gen. McClellan to catch the enemy, so the officers said, and this served to allay apprehensions which might otherwise have produced serious evil. The Generals and their aides appeared remarkably tickled with the progress of events, and the course things were taking, and they even proclaimed that twenty-four hours more of such prosperous and successful strategy would open to us the way to Richmond. . . . We were only going to move our camp to a safer place, they told us, which was strictly true, though in a much different sense from what we expected. . . . While quietly sitting here discussing the peculiarity of our position and freely expressing opinions pro and con relative to the wisdom of the strategy which made such mysterious movements necessary, and inwardly doubting whether it was not forced on us instead of being planned at leisure by our Generals,—for the rank and file are by no means indifferent to these important matters.

Private Wilbur Fisk, July 15, 1862, from Harrison's Landing, Virginia[23]

EXAMPLES OF SPEECHES THAT LIE can be found in every genre of battle speech. It is appropriate to consider these in the context of Defender's Speeches, however, because the answer to the question posed here—why soldier-audiences react differently to some Speeches that Lie than they do to others—often reveals itself most dramatically when soldiers are asked to defend something. In general, a battle speechmaker's Speech that Lies intentionally misleads by deliberately concealing what he knows; he then either states the opposite of what is true or provides some other explanation that he knows to be false. If the lie is discovered, soldier-audiences seem to react in one of two ways—by mutiny or by a continued willingness to follow orders. The reasons for this difference illuminate something about the psychology of command as manifested in the battle speech—that, at bottom, truth is not the only measure soldiers use in judging what they are being told, and that what is paramount are the intentions of the battle speechmaker.

While both of the epigraph's examples are Defender's Speeches, neither was made in response to an invasion. Nevertheless, they usefully illustrate opposing responses to Speeches that Lie: mutiny and continued obedience. The first instance is that of Domitius, an ally of Pompey's during the latter's war with Julius Caesar. Caesar had encircled Domitius's army in the town of Corfinium, and Domitius had appealed to Pompey for assistance in breaking the siege but was refused. According to Caesar's account, Domitius was handed this message shortly before an officer's meeting. At that meeting Domitius "concealed its contents, and announced that Pompey would shortly arrive with help." In fact, Domitius did more: he "urged [his officers] to keep up their spirits and make all necessary arrangements for the defense of the town." Here Domitius not only lied but also successfully induced his officers to rely on the lie; pursuing this order, his subordinates probably spent some "personal capital" in exhorting their own men with promises of Pompey's reinforcements.

At this point—the moment when a Speech that Lies is made—it is useful to advance 1,911 years to Virginia's Peninsula during the American Civil War. Here on June 27, 1862, Private Wilbur Fisk and his friends in the Second Vermont Infantry watched as their distant comrades resisted a rebel attack at the battle of Gaines' Mill. "All day long the battle raged on the opposite side of the Chickahominy," Fisk reported to the *Green Mountain Freeman,* his hometown newspaper, "and its progress could be distinctly seen from our camping ground." No officer could conceal anything about the course of these events. "We could see that our men were apparently driven back," Fisk wrote. "In fact nothing could have been more apparent." And of course, no officer could try to conceal what was happening in plain view. Instead, perhaps during an assembly or in person-to-person conversations, the officers tried a different tack to explain events. "It was all a trap of Gen. McClellan to catch the enemy," the officers said—and here the officers lied or repeated someone else's lie. But as was the case with Domitius, the lie (temporarily) worked: "[This] served to allay apprehensions which might otherwise have produced serious evil." If the officers were ignorant of the real situation (in fact the Federal retreat was no ruse), the anonymous "Generals" probably did know better; however, they also joined the lie. "The Generals and their aids appeared remarkably tickled with the progress of events, and the course things were taking, and they even proclaimed that twenty-four hours more of such prosperous and successful strategy would open to us the way to Richmond." To support the lie, new explanations were given when the Vermonters were ordered to relocate their camp. "We were only going to move our camp to a safer place, they told us," a wiser Fisk wrote almost three weeks later, "though in a much different sense from what we expected."

Returning to Corfinium, Domitius's Defender's Speech was quickly exposed as a lie when his soldiers learned that at "a secret conclave with a few friends" he intended to escape and thereby desert his command. Likewise in Virginia, Fisk and his comrades seemed to know almost immediately that the Defender's Speeches they heard were also lies. And in both Corfinium and Virginia, the truth arose from the "bottom up," as soldier-audiences discussed their particular situations. But what differed was how these armies reacted to each lie. The Roman soldiers "had Domitius brought out, and surrounding him and putting him under guard . . . sent a deputation from their ranks to Caesar saying they were ready to open the gates and take orders from him, and that they would surrender Domitius alive into his hands." By contrast, Fisk and his comrades, although "inwardly doubting whether [the retreat] was not forced on us instead of being planned at leisure by our Generals," nevertheless obeyed orders and contributed their best efforts to making the Federal army's retreat a masterpiece of withdrawal. Why did one group of soldiers rebel and the others obey?

The answer will be found in how the soldier-audience perceives its speechmaker-commander's intentions. Speeches that Lie are tolerable, even if the lies are in plain view as the speech is given (as was the case with Fisk's group), as long as the soldiers trust the commander's basic intentions. No Federal officer personally benefited by falsely depicting McClellan's withdrawal strategy; while each individual might have disbelieved what he was being told, there appeared to be a sense that the lies "served to allay apprehensions," thus avoiding "serious evil." Soldiers might resent being lied to and will certainly question the competence of commanders who feel they must lie to extract themselves from tactical tight spots. But few in the Federal army questioned the underlying good faith of McClellan or his chain of command. Similarly, had Domitius limited his lie to the promise of Pompey's reinforcement and afterward explained that he did it to avoid panic, a mutiny might have been avoided. But when it became known that the lie was only to cover his personal escape, mutiny was probably unavoidable. Soldiers will tolerate an untruthful battle speech only as long as they believe that the battle speechmaker remains truthful to the unit's best interests, even if he is mistaken about them.

5

PRE-BATTLE SPEECHES

Alexander summoned the generals, squadron leaders and officers of the allies and urged them to be confident in view of the dangers they had successfully surmounted in the past; already conquerors, they were to fight men they had conquered, and God was a better strategist on their own side, putting it into Darius' mind to bring his force out of the open country and hem it into the narrow pass, an area just the size for the deployment of their phalanx; in the battle the Persians would have no benefit from their numbers, while their physique and morale were no match for their own. "We Macedonians,"
he continued, "are to fight Medes and Persians, nations long steeped in luxury, while we have now long been inured to danger by the exertions of campaigning. Above all it will be a fight of free men against slaves. And so far as Greek will meet Greek, they will not be fighting for like causes; those with Darius will be risking their lives for pay, and poor pay too; the Greeks on our side will fight as volunteers in the cause of Greece. As our barbarian troops, Thracians, Paeonians, Illyrians, Agrianians, the most robust and warlike races of Europe will be ranged against the most indolent and softest tribes of Asia. In addition you have Alexander commanding against Darius. . . ." Besides rehearsing these advantages they had in the contest, he pointed out the greatness of the rewards for which they were incurring danger. . . .

In addition, he reminded them of all they had already achieved with brilliant success for the common cause, and cited any noble act of personal daring, naming both the deed and the man; with the utmost delicacy he mentioned the dangers he himself had faced in battles.

Excerpt of speech by Alexander the Great to his troops
just before the Battle of Issus, 333 BCE[1]

IN THE LAST CHAPTER, we distinguished the Pre-Battle Speech from the Pre-Invasion Speech by the former's proximity to an actual battle. And because the Pre-Battle Speech is close to battle, its emphasis is usually different—looming battles can mean maiming, death, or disgrace, and very soon. Speechmakers must counter these prospects with something to soothe apprehensions or distract soldier-audiences from the carnage and personal testing that will shortly occur. Thus the dominant convention of the Pre-Battle Speech is the Confidence meme; Pre-Battle speechmakers use a variety of different themes that nevertheless all aim to instill confidence in the soldier-audience. A Pre-Battle speechmaker may simply declare his own confidence in victory or offer reasons why his soldier-audience is superior to the enemy ("Declaring Confidence"); a speechmaker may provide background, instructions, or intelligence data, including possibly assurances of God's favor ("Knowledge Is Confidence"); or the enemy may be taunted, insulted, or assessed as militarily, culturally, or racially weak ("Diminishing the Enemy"). The Confidence meme might also appear in other guises. The Conventions of Personal or Unit Recognition will be used by Pre-Battle speechmakers to strengthen bonds with their men by calling attention to individual soldiers' prior acts of bravery or a unit's past successes; the commander may use his own bravery to inspire soldiers ("Personal Example"); the commander may promise Rewards, where some spiritual or material gain will be conferred by fighting well or achieving victory. Finally, such speeches might incorporate Threats, which obviously lie outside of the Confidence meme. Here the battle speechmaker offers soldiers good reasons to believe that death at the hands of officers for cowardice is far more likely than death in battle.

A second convention found in both Pre-Battle and Pre-Invasion Speeches is the Stakes meme. Here the speechmaker declares what victory or defeat in the battle will decide. Battles can decide everything from family survival, the combatants' access to food, water, and shelter, or the fates of whole nations. (In contrast, the Pre-Invasion Speech is usually concerned with grander issues of strategy or why the war is being fought.) Stakes are sometimes expressed as an incentive: victory will bring Rewards. But sometimes, Stakes are presented as a

disincentive to defeat and will be expressed as an "if-then" proposition. Here losing the battle is the first premise that is linked to a conclusion of some unthinkable disaster; for example, if the battle is lost
then your families will be enslaved or the enemy will grant no quarter.
In short, while Confidence creates good feelings in soldiers, Stakes
are the "business end" of the Pre-Battle Speech, focusing on dire consequences. Stakes will be discussed at greater length below.

Alexander the Great's speech at Issus is a wonderful example of
the different guises in which Confidence Conventions can appear in
a Pre-Battle Speech. In relatively few words Alexander manages to
employ Unit Recognition, Knowledge Is Confidence, Diminish the
Enemy, Declaration of Confidence, Personal Recognition, and Personal Example. Many of his themes resonate to this day.[2]

He opens his speech with the Confidence meme of Unit Recognition. "[Alexander] urged them to be confident in view of the dangers
that they had successfully surmounted in the past," he declares first
at this officers' meeting. "Already conquerors, they were to fight men
they had conquered." Here Alexander places a recent Unit Historical
Narrative in the service of Unit Recognition. The year before Issus
his army had defeated the Persians at the battle of Granicus. By noting this victory, Alexander supports his Unit Recognition by using one
of Aristotle's proofs, found repeatedly in battle speeches: "[That] as a
rule the future resembles the past." Of course, if conceived literally,
many things must be true for the future to resemble the past: Alexander's army must be the same as at Granicus; the Persian army must
be the same as was defeated at Granicus; the tactical circumstances
and terrain of the new battlefield must resemble the old; finally, the
"X" factor—luck, divine favor, or random coincidence—must also be
replicable. But in his speech Alexander actually tells his officers that
now everything had *changed*: "It was not Darius' satraps whom they
were now to overcome, nor the cavalry that lined the Granicus, nor
the twenty thousand foreign mercenaries," he declares elsewhere. If
everything had changed since Granicus, what remains the same?[3]

Alexander will answer this question via Knowledge Is Confidence
and Diminish the Enemy. Alexander presents Knowledge Is Confidence by informing his officers not only that God favors them but

also how this favor is manifest tactically: "God is the better strategist than on [the Persians'] side" because He has "[put] into Darius' mind to bring his force out of the open country and hem it into the narrow pass, an area just the size for the deployment of their phalanx." Thus Alexander can conclude that "the Persians would have no benefit from their numbers." God's favor may be far more variable than the social and historical factors by which Alexander is about to diminish the Persians, but at least for now, He stands foursquare with the Macedonians/Greeks. The overwhelming majority of Alexander's officers probably drew at least as much confidence from this assurance as they might have from a more technical discussion of terrain, tactics, or weaponry.

Alexander next Diminishes the Enemy by comparing the social and political histories of the Macedonians/Greeks with those of the Persians. As to his enemy's social deficits, Darius's army will lose the battle because the Persian "physique and morale were no match" for those of the Macedonians/Greeks. The reasons lie not in racial but in social differences: "We Macedonians are to fight Medes and Persians, nations long steeped in luxury," he declares. (Later, he adds that Persians are "the most indolent and softest tribes of Asia.") Two assumptions operate here. The first is patent—men who live lives of wealth and ease cannot be good soldiers, because soldiering requires hard and strong men accustomed to campaigning and fighting and killing other men. Alexander proves this claim by asking each officer to look no further than himself: in contrast to Persians, "we have now long been inured to danger by the exertions of campaigning." This is an ingenious means of creating confidence, because its proof rests in the personal history of each soldier rather than some external fact that would require corroboration.

The second assumption is that Macedonians/Greeks are masculine men, while the Persians are less than masculine, if masculinity is enhanced by the ability to fight wars and endure hardship. In fact, he continues, Persians have definite feminine characteristics. In terms of physical size, Persians are to Greeks what women are to men—smaller ("[The Persians'] physique . . . [is] no match for [our] own"). And Persians resemble women, especially rich women, in morale.

Persians have historically been "steeped in luxury" and thus are "indo-lent"; their manliness has withered so that they and their mercenaries now number among the "softest tribes of Asia." In contrast, consider how Alexander describes the Macedonians/Greeks and their merce-nary allies: "Long . . . inured to danger by the exertions of campaign-ing. . . . Our barbarian troops [are] the most robust and warlike races of Europe."

Alexander next uses Diminishing the Enemy by comparing Political Historical Narratives: "Above all it will be a fight of free men against slaves," he declares. This directly refers to the contrasting political arrangements between Macedonia/Greece and Persia; the former prided itself on its democracy—after all, although Alexander ruled by inheritance and divine right, he had thus far established democracies in the wake of his march. "He ordered the oligarchies everywhere to be overthrown and democracies to be established," Arrian had earlier written. "[He] restored its own laws to each city and remitted the trib-ute they used to pay to the [Persians]."[4] Whatever these "laws" might have been, Alexander here recognizes the Greek predilection for each *polis* to have the freedom to decide its own form of government. But for Greeks, at least since the days of Herodotus, the Persians were a byword for cruelty and despotism. The underlying conviction here is one of the most durable in Western history: men who are free to choose their destinies (and presumably their allegiances) make better soldiers than those who are not. The reason lies in a missing prem-ise. Macedonians/Greeks will fight with greater resolution than Per-sians because such men were free to choose otherwise. And since their resolution is a matter of choice (and a product of persuasion), it is adhered to with greater energy, ingenuity, and fidelity during actual battles. Alexander flatters his men—they are the avatars of a superior political arrangement—and he belittles the Persians, who will not fight as well because they had no choice in the matter. This not only Diminishes the Enemy but also instills confidence, because free men who fight well have a greater chance of surviving a battle than slaves who fight poorly.

Alexander extends this political and social diminution of the Per-sians and elevation of the Greeks in order to resolve two obvious contradictions in his Pre-Battle Speech. First, Greek mercenaries, presumably free men and products of a martial culture, also serve in Darius's army. But Darius's Greeks lack something important—the right cause. Here Diminish the Enemy is applied to a motivation that has also proven extremely durable in Western military history: free men who fight for an *unselfish* cause are superior to soldiers who fight for selfish reasons, such as money. "And so far as Greek will meet Greek, they will not be fighting for like causes," Alexander declares. "[Those] with Darius will be risking their lives for pay" while "the Greeks on our side will fight as volunteers in the cause of Greece." We observed earlier that the assumption that "pure" soldiers—soldiers free from sin—make better warriors is an idea with Biblical antecedents. Alexander now argues its nearly identical twin: the "pure" motive. That love of lucre is far less self-persuasive than love of country also has ancient antecedents. Horace (65 BCE to 8 BCE) famously wrote *Dulce et decorum est pro patria mori* (usually translated as, "It is sweet and fitting to die for one's country/native land"—a sentiment impossible to imagine with mercenaries. But what of the mercenaries—the "Thracians, Paeonians, Illyrians, Agrianes"—who fight for Alexander? Lest his soldiers deem these paid allies to be unreliable comrades, Alexander resolves this second contradiction by explaining that these are *our* mercenaries, who happen to be "the most robust and warlike races of Europe." And of course, these manly soldiers-for-hire will be fighting Persians, whose feminized qualities have already been noted.

Alexander manages to employ another Confidence meme that is so audacious it could only work for either a cocksure leader or a fool willing to risk self-parody: the simple Declaration of Confidence. "In addition," he declares to his officers, "you have Alexander commanding against Darius." If all else has failed to instill confidence, Alexander uses his default argument: he is in command. Here he gambles that his men believe that certain qualities are bundled in the icon-word "Alexander," at least when coupled with the word "command." These qualities likely include personal courage, wise planning, effective tactics, concern for his soldiers' wellbeing, a tinge of divinity, and probably a lucky nature. In contrast, "Darius" becomes a metonym for "Persian," which Alexander has already defined (or more likely only reminded his officers of something they already believed) as cruel, decayed, feminized, and unfree.

But Alexander's speech also includes the additional Confidence conventions of Reward, Personal Recognition, and Personal Example. Either by word, deed, or both, these conventions build confidence by sealing the soldier-audience's acceptance of arguments just made using memes such as Knowledge Is Confidence, Diminish the Enemy, or Declaration of Confidence. Rewards, Recognitions, and Personal Examples are intended as rituals of adhesion, summarizing the great unilateral bargain of persuasion inherent in the Pre-Battle Speech. First, the commander asks for his soldiers' trust and loyalty; next, by accepting his offer of rewards, his compliments for past valorous deeds, or the worth of his personal acts of leadership, the soldier-audience also accepts his call to battle.

Alexander mentions Rewards but obliquely, having just excoriated Persian mercenaries who fight for pay: "[Alexander] pointed out the greatness of the rewards for which they were incurring danger," Arrian informs us, without specifying their nature. (While stakes are discussed further below, it is worth noting here that Alexander invests the Battle of Issus with two of them: the unspecified rewards just mentioned and the prospect that victory will end the campaign and thus allow his tired soldiers to return home.)[5]

However, in extending Personal Recognition, he is exuberant: "[Alexander] reminded them of all they had already achieved with brilliant success for the common cause, and cited any noble act of personal daring, naming both the deed and the man." Publicly acknowledging the contribution of individuals is strong cement between a commander and his troops. But in using his own conduct as Personal Example, Alexander demonstrated caution. He would not have had to stretch far for examples here—few commanders in Western history have rivaled him in their willingness to fight in the van of their army.[6] But proof that he means this as a morale booster and not a boast can be found in how he uses this theme: "[Alexander] with the *utmost delicacy* mentioned the dangers he himself had faced in battle" [emphasis added]. He understood that under these circumstances, recognizing his own bravery should go no further in degree than the recognition he extended to his most junior officer. His intent was to unify these officers for battle under his leadership, not to usurp his subalterns' self-esteem by vaingloriously emphasizing his own bravery. Alexander was brave, sometimes even foolhardy, but few generals loved—or needed—their army more than him, and perhaps none would ever rival him in establishing the military paradigm of Rewards and especially Recognition that continues to this day.

Declaring Confidence

In the briefing with his officers [Lieutenant-Colonel] Brandl said, "There's nothing out there that will defeat us. This is a right fight for us, a good fight for us. And we're going to win it. And we're going to do it with professionalism and honor." Brandl instilled confidence in his young officers, who passed it on down to the enlisted men.

> Lieutenant-Colonel Gareth Brandl, Pre-Battle Speech to his officers
> before the Battle of Fallujah, November 2004[7]

UNLIKE ALEXANDER THE GREAT, few modern commanders would simply utter their name as a surrogate for reasons to follow their lead. But as Lieutenant-Colonel Brandl's speech above suggests, Declaring Confidence continues to this day in Pre-Battle Speeches. By simply doing so (without providing any reasons) the battle speechmaker *is* the speech, and the soldier-audience must carefully weigh whether or not he possesses the legal, intellectual, and especially moral authority to merit confidence. After all, any person in uniform can declare "We will win," but it makes a difference whether the speaker authored the battle plan, is a private or a general, or has twenty years of combat experience or none at all.

Colonel Brandl's speech was made during a briefing with subalterns. "One of [Brandl's] main concerns on entering [Fallujah]," historian Gary Livingston wrote, "was the enemy ramming car bombs [Vehicle-Borne Improvised Exposive Devices, or VBIEDs] into the flanks of attacking Marines." This was a frightening prospect; except for the spontaneous acts of individuals and a brief experience with Japanese Kamikazes during World War II, enemies bent on suicide have not been the norm of America's military experience. Brandl's men might have been well drilled in tactics to defend against VBIEDs; but for most soldiers, the prospect of a VBIED's random appearance and its fearful consequences will always provoke anxiety. And as H-Hour approached, fears about this and other battle-connected prospects could only amplify. Brandl meant to fill the space between anticipation of the battle and the battle itself with something uniquely shaped to fit it—a Pre-Battle Speech (here remarks during an officers' briefing) that is meant to instill confidence.

Simply declaring confidence requires no proof, at least of a sort normally encountered in arguments. When Brandl declared "There's nothing out there that will defeat us," there was no need (and probably no time) to exhaustively detail how enemy weapons, numbers, and tactics compared with American capabilities. As an intellectual matter, Brandl's subalterns probably knew all about these things. But Brandl's men were almost certainly seeking other kinds of knowledge in the anxious hours before the battle. Regarding leadership, the soldiers' concerns might well come down to this: how does the commander feel about the prospects? Soldiers want to couple what they know, a few generalities about the battle and many details about their own missions, with what the commander is presumed to know: everything. Then they want to gauge his confidence to inform their own.

Understanding all of this, Brandl has thus to say confident things in a confident way. Indeed, what might appear to be mere platitudes long after a battle can be profoundly comforting words to soldiers on battle's verge. "This is a right fight for us, this is a good fight for us" is unlikely to rank among the greatest battle speeches ever made, but Brandl was not striving for eloquence but expedience. Such a battle can only have one conclusion, which Brandl supplies in the next sentence: "And we're going to win it." But consistent with other battle speeches given during the Iraq War, he doesn't stop there: "And we're going to do it with professionalism and honor." In this statement, Colonel Brandl means to establish confidence on two levels. First, in line with General Mattis and Colonel Collins, he wants to address the fact that fear should not be converted into the indiscriminate use of violence. Since any civilian vehicle can be a VBIED (although only a tiny fraction will be), Brandl wants his men to know that their "professionalism" and "honor" must prevent their own fears from inducing them to destroy *every* civilian vehicle. Although Brandl says nothing about grand strategy, his soldiers probably understood that the unnecessary deaths of innocents would only advance the enemy's objective of driving a wedge between Coalition forces and civilians. Thus "professionalism" and "honor" operate as code words for the need for focus, calmness, and restraint.

But these words also operate on another level directly related to the Confidence Convention. To remind these men that they are professionals and also honorable—that is, that they will adhere to the ROE—is another way of elevating their self-esteem. First, Brandl implicitly contrasts the enemy with his marines: jihadis who drive VBIEDs are not professional soldiers but indiscriminate killers; an enemy that fights this way is not honorable. Thus by boosting his marines, Brandl also diminishes the enemy. Second, Brandl hopes to remind them that they have been well trained for this battle, and that thorough training increases the odds of survival. After all, it is reasonable to assume that a "professional" soldier has a greater chance of surviving a battle with his honor intact than does an amateur or unprofessional soldier. And Colonel Brandl's remarks apparently achieved their purpose. "Brandl instilled confidence in his young officers," the battle's historian wrote, "who passed it on down to the enlisted men."

Knowledge Is Confidence

"A patrol has just reported to me that on top of Mount Austen, in a spiderweb of ridges, is a very strong Jap position," Carlson told his men. "The Jap position is unoccupied. If we get up there in a hurry, we can take those positions; we can relieve the pressure on Henderson Field. We can find out how strong the enemy is there. This will help our command to make a more accurate estimate of the situation. It may mean cutting down the time it will take to finish up Guadalcanal. It would be a good thing, wouldn't it? We're going to do it because it's important, because we're fitted to do it and in a position to do it."

Colonel Evans F. Carlson during Long Patrol,
Guadalcanal, December 3, 1942[8]

ALEXANDER THE GREAT used Knowledge Is Confidence by interpreting Darius's deployments as God's endorsement of the Mace-
donians/Greeks; he then described how those deployments were advantageous to his army. Pre-Battle Speechmakers often use disclosure
about these sorts of tactical opportunities to instill confidence in their
soldier-audience. The rationale is that if soldiers understand exactly
what the battle will accomplish, they will be more inclined to fight
in it. Two important points should be made about this Knowledge
Is Confidence approach. First, the disclosed details are rarely of the
"why we fight" variety. Instead, the results of a successful action are
portrayed in wholly tactical terms. By assaulting the bastion, capturing the hill, or completing the patrol along a dangerous route (the
background to Colonel Carlson's speech), the result will be the elimination of enemy artillery fire, the suppression of snipers, or the gathering of some important intelligence; none of this will win the war,
but it might shorten the larger battle in which this smaller action will
take place. Second, Knowledge Is Confidence should not be confused
with the Truth Speech discussed in the last chapter. While both approaches hope to increase confidence by emphasizing what is "true,"
the Truth Speech is an expectation-deflator and thus adopts a negative slant. As Colonel Carlson's speech suggests, Knowledge Is Confidence does not attempt to reduce expectations but instead tries to
fit them to the tactical opportunity presented. Often, this speech is
made by and to soldiers known to each other, still in the field, and long
after their baptismal fire. For example, Colonel Carlson's speech was
made near the end of his famed Guadalcanal Long Patrol, which had
already lasted nearly a month.

It is fitting that a speech of Colonel Carlson will illustrate the
theme of Knowledge Is Confidence. Carlson, a career marine who
had observed the Chinese Eighth Route Army during the 1930s, first
introduced the expression "Gung Ho" to the American military. "The
Chinese have two words for 'working together,'" he had explained to a
meeting of recruits for his Second Marine Raider Battalion. "'Gung,'
meaning work; 'Ho,' meaning harmony. *Gung Ho!* Work together. I
propose that Gung Ho be the spirit and slogan of our Raider Battalion." Under Carlson's command this would amount to more than a

slogan. Carlson believed that the relationship between the leader and the led should be founded on "knowledge and reason, not blind obedience. In a democracy, men must be thinking human beings, not puppets." Such a command philosophy would presumably always insist on the Knowledge Is Confidence convention when speechifying.[9]

The circumstances that gave rise to Carlson's speech demonstrate exactly the point when Knowledge Is Confidence is best applied. What has been nicknamed the "Long Patrol" was actually nearly four weeks of laying ambush in the jungles of Guadalcanal. Carlson had been ordered to stalk and harass the Japanese units that remained on island but had avoided or fled from the heaviest fighting earlier that fall. At the end, Carlson's six marine companies had wended through some 150 miles of jungle trails to cover only twenty-five to thirty airline miles; 488 Japanese had been killed and tons of supplies destroyed, while Carlson had lost only sixteen men, with nineteen wounded, although some 225 men contracted diseases including malaria, ringworm, jungle rot, and dysentery. And it was at the end of the Long Patrol that Carlson, having been ordered to return to American lines, received some intelligence that he immediately shared with his men. How Carlson used this intelligence to "persuade" his marines to include a very dangerous detour in their return route reveals how Knowledge Is Confidence themes work. Unlike Tennyson's Light Brigade cavalrymen, who do not "reason why" but merely "do and die," Carlson offers his men reasons for the risks they are about to assume.[10]

The structure of Carlson's appeal is logical. First, the knowledge is disclosed. "A patrol has just reported to me that on top of Mount Austen, in a spiderweb of ridges, is a very strong Jap position. The Jap position is unoccupied." What Carlson and presumably his men know is that their orders to return to American lines do not require them to ascend Mount Austen, a 1,514-foot eminence overlooking Henderson Field. There were good reasons for Carlson not to reconnoiter this mountain—his mission had been successful, many of his men were sick, and he had received no orders to do so. But Carlson was an aggressive commander. If there was an enemy position on critical ground that lay somewhere between his unit and the American lines, Carlson would investigate while still obeying orders to return. Thus, after sharing the knowledge, Carlson next makes a "proposal" to his men. "If we get up there in a hurry, we can take those positions," he declared. He then offers three reasons why it is worthwhile to march tired, unwell men up a mountain for yet one more possible battle with the enemy. The first reason was that "we can relieve the pressure on Henderson Field" (securing the airbase at Henderson Field was the main objective in the battle for Guadalcanal). The second reason was that "We can find out how strong the enemy is there," which would help "our command to make a more accurate estimate of the situation." This would in turn support a third reason for making the detour up Mount Austen: "It may mean cutting down the time it will take to finish up [the conquest of] Guadalcanal."

Thus far Colonel Carlson has placed himself in the grey area between fact and persuasion. He wants his men to willingly reconnoiter Mount Austen and has marshaled his facts accordingly; nevertheless, while facts may be framed persuasively, they remain only facts—a patrol has discovered enemy positions on Mount Austen, which does have a strategic position relative to Henderson Field, which has been attacked by an enemy on the mountain, information about which is likely to contribute to shortening the battle for Guadalcanal. But having stated the facts, Carlson, the most democratic of marines, now attempts to "close" (that is, persuade) his men to cheerfully do this project. "It would be a good thing, wouldn't it?" he asks rhetorically. However, his men remain marines, and no vote will be taken: "We're going to do it because it's important, because we're fitted to do it and in a position to do it," he concludes (orders). Of course, each one of these three propositions ("important . . . fitted . . . in a position") might be debated. But Carlson was a charismatic leader, a moralist and idealist who inspired great loyalty from his men. ("His eyes were stern," one marine recalled about an earlier episode. "They made me feel like my preacher was looking at me.") By the time of Guadalcanal, the Second Raider Battalion had already conducted its well-touted (although perhaps less than successful) raid on Makin Island, and most of the unit's men had already established the personal cohesion desirable for combat. Thus Carlson probably concluded that his men would follow willingly, but Knowledge Is Confidence was also already established in the battalion as the chief Confidence meme, especially in battle speeches. Carlson's pitch and style were no doubt expected by his soldiers.

It is tempting to think of Knowledge Is Confidence as a modern phenomenon particularly appropriate to Western armies drawn from democratic societies. However, its antecedents are actually quite ancient. Frontinus relates that in 468 BCE the Roman consul Titus Quincitius prepared his men to assault the town of Antium (present-day Anzio): "Accordingly, he called an assembly of the soldiers and explained how necessary this project was and how easy, if only it were not postponed." The approach worked: "Having roused enthusiasm by his address," he led the Romans in attacking the town.[11]

Diminishing the Enemy

"The hour of victory," [Vercingetorix] said, "has come. The Romans are fleeing to the Province and abandoning Gaul. But although this will assure our liberty for the moment, for future peace and security we need more than that; otherwise they will return in increased force and continue the war indefinitely. So let us attack them on the march while they are encumbered with their baggage. If the whole column of infantry halts to come to the rescue, they cannot continue their march; if—which I feel sure is more likely—they abandon the baggage and try to save their own skins, they will be stripped of the supplies without which they cannot live, and disgraced into the bargain. As for their cavalry, not a man of them will dare even to stir outside the column; you ought to know that as well as I do."

Excerpt from Vercingetorix's Pre-Battle Speech to cavalry officers before the attack on Caesar's legions, 52 BCE[12]

AT THE BATTLE OF ISSUS, Alexander the Great devoted considerable effort to diminishing his Persian enemy. After all, an enemy that is depicted as weak, stupid, or socially, ideologically, or racially inferior presents less risk to the soldier-audience than an adversary who embodies the opposite characteristics. But as the Gallic chieftain Vercingetorix would learn, there is grave risk in "over"-diminishing one's enemy. The reason is not only that one's assumptions about the enemy might be wrong, but that in making them one is also predicting enemy behavior (an attacked enemy will flee, surrender, or execute defensive maneuvers badly, and so on). Resting unlamented in military history's largest imaginary cemetery are all of the confident predictions about an enemy's behavior. The famous epigram attributed to Helmet von Moltke the Elder that "no plan survives contact with the enemy" can also apply to the assumptions buried in some Pre-Battle Speeches—particularly those that predict what an adversary will do.

One such Diminish the Enemy theme is featured above in Vercingetorix's Pre-Battle Speech to his cavalry officers as they prepared to attack one of Julius Caesar's legions. Vercingetorix's Gallic tribe, the Arverni, had been a reluctant part of the Roman Empire since their defeat by Quintus Fabius Maximus in 121 BCE. Sixty-nine years later, Vercingetorix, a twenty-three-year-old Arverni nobleman, would lead dissident members of his tribe in a rebellion against Rome. The revolt itself was based on poor assumptions. Unrelated political instability in Rome had compelled the senate to expand the army. Julius Caesar, who had been campaigning near the southern Rhine, returned to the Cisalpine Province to assist in recruiting. "The Gauls, drawing what they thought was the natural inference, invented a story that Caesar was detained by the disturbances in Rome, where political strife was so acute, they said, that he could not rejoin his army," Caesar wrote in his trademark third-person voice. "The prospect of such a chance spurred [the Arverni] into action." In truth, many Gauls, fearing Caesar, were divided about rebelling, and Vercingetorix did not lead a united Arverni tribe. Nevertheless, he successfully raised an army, joined with other tribes, and won the early battles despite the return of Caesar. However, Caesar would remedy his army's problems, especially his weak cavalry, by recruiting horse soldiers from loyal German tribes. Around the time of Vercingetorix's speech, Caesar had been reinforcing his army to (successfully) quell the rebellion.[13]

Vercingetorix foreshadows the flawed nature of his assumptions about his Roman enemy by opening his Pre-Battle Speech with two erroneous declarations of "fact"—that Caesar's redeployment was actually a flight and that the Romans were "abandoning" Gaul. In exhorting his cavalry officers, Vercingetorix argues that Rome's abandonment is only temporary and that permanent liberation for the Arverni will come only by destroying Caesar's legions as they marched away. By itself this was an excellent tactical insight. An army en route is vulnerable to flank attacks as well as being divided and then defeated in detail. And Vercingetorix's proposal to attack the Roman baggage train was also sound. Wagon drivers, haulers of supplies, and slaves composing the baggage train are less likely to be armed, trained, and maneuverable than infantry. While Vercingetorix might have mistaken Caesar's ultimate intentions, he still might have succeeded in his flank-attack strategy. And he asserts correctly that if "the whole column of infantry halts to come to the rescue [of the baggage train] they cannot continue their march." What Vercingetorix seems to be saying is that if the Romans are attacked in flank, they will have no choice but to fight.

But Vercingetorix does not believe that the Romans will respond by fighting, and it is here that he strays from the probabilities. Rather than provoke Roman resistance, he believes that his attack will produce the opposite result. "[If,] which I feel sure is more likely," Vercingetorix declares, "they abandon the baggage and try to save their own skins, they will be stripped of the supplies without which they cannot live, and disgraced into the bargain." Here he forecasts Roman ineptitude ("abandoning the baggage") and then cowardice ("try to save their own skins"). Of course, an Arverni cavalry officer might well question why any armed force would abandon the supplies necessary to its own survival rather than fight desperately to retain them. Vercingetorix's gratuitous characterization of Roman soldiers as being "disgraced into the bargain" was likely meant to complete an image of his enemy meeting the Arverni attack with disorder and indiscipline before scurrying away in the interests of personal safety. Moreover, Vercingetorix adds another, purely tactical judgment into the mix that is based on the ever fickle predictive value of past events: "As for their cavalry, not a man of them will dare even to stir outside the column," he assures his horse soldiers. "[You] ought to know that as well as I do." In sum, Vercingetorix has diminished his enemy in two respects: First, Romans have cowardly natures; second, in the past their cavalry arm has been weak.

And Vercingetorix's men appeared to accept these assumptions. "The cavalrymen cried that they should all swear a solemn oath not to allow any man who had not ridden twice through the enemy's column to enter his home again or to see his wife, children or parents," Caesar recorded. "This approval was approved and every man was duly sworn."

Vercingetorix's attack would fail, and his real error here was inaccurate predictions. First, neither Caesar nor his soldiers fled but instead resisted stoutly and with tactics that seemed to anticipate the Arverni attack. Second, Caesar's reinforced cavalry not only "stirred" from the column but aggressively fought Vercingetorix's horse soldiers. "At length the German horse gained the top of some rising ground on the right, dislodged some of the enemy, and chased them with heavy loss to a river where Vercingetorix's infantry was posted," Caesar reported. "At this the rest of his cavalry fled, afraid of being surrounded, and were cut down in numbers all over the field."[14]

But was Vercingetorix mistaken to exhort his men using a Diminish the Enemy theme? After all, he did inspire his men with confidence, which is the principal convention of the Pre-Battle Speech. However, the answer must be that his speech was certainly a mistake to the extent that any Arverni cavalrymen entered the fray expecting Caesar's infantry to scatter and his cavalry to remain idle. Historically, Diminish the Enemy seems to work better not by overcharging a soldier-audience's confidence with tales of enemy weakness but by dwelling on a good-versus-evil theme such as stoking hatred with atrocity stories about the enemy. Consider these assorted excerpts from a Pre-Battle Speech delivered by Walter of Espec (a member of Henry I's court and the founder of the Rievalux Abbey) before the Battle of the Standard (1138):[15]

> Necessity urges us [to fight against the Scots.] Recall what they have done elsewhere and do not hope for gentler treatment if the Scot should conquer us. . . . For who would want to live if the Scots win, to see his wife exposed to the Scots' lust and his little ones spitted on their spears? . . . I pass over the slaughter, rapine, burning which are practiced by the enemy. . . . I dread to say how they entered the temple of God, how they defiled his sanctuary. . . . [Saint] Michael will be present with the angels to avenge his injury, whose church they defiled with human blood, whose altar they polluted by placing a human head on it. Peter with

the Apostles will fight for us, whose churches they turned into stables and brothels. The holy martyrs whose shrines they burned and whose churchyards they filled with corpses will go before our army.[16]

Even if everything reported by Walter of Espec was an outright lie, they were not the kinds of lies that impair combat efficiency. Unlike Vercingetorix's cavalrymen, whose morale probably fell along with their unrealistic expectations the moment the Romans vigorously resisted, Walter of Espec's men might not discover that "real" Scots were different from these invented Scots until long after the war. Moreover, a ferociously resisting enemy may even lend credence to the atrocity stories. Atrocity stories do work to stoke hatred, aid recruiting, Diminish the Enemy, and fill soldiers with a desire for revenge. And tales of atrocities—real or imagined—continue to be used in just these ways. One has only to consider Colonel Brandl's speech after the Battle of Fallujah or Osama bin Laden's Recruiting Speech, discussed in the epilogue.

Stakes

[The] Carthaginians were urged to keep before their eyes all they held dear—the walls of their native city, their household gods, the tombs of their ancestors, their children, parents, and trembling wives—and to remember the dread alternative, death and slavery on one hand, world empire on the other, with no middle way, either for fear or hope, between those two extremes.

> Excerpt from Hannibal's speech exhorting the Carthaginian contingent
> before the Battle of Zama, 202 BCE, as paraphrased in Livy

Soldiers, here at last is the battle that you have so long expected! Victory now depends on your efforts, and is essential. It will give us abundance, good winter quarters, and a speedy return to our country. Do what you did at Austerlitz, at Friedland, at Vitebsk, at Smolensk, and let posterity point with pride to your conduct on this day: let people say of you: "He was at that great battle fought under the walls of Moscow!"

> Napoleon, Proclamation to soldiers from the heights
> of Borodino, September 7, 1812

On the Neptune, Thomas Fremantle [spoke] to his men at their dif-
ferent quarters. They were to think of their country, and all that was
dear to them. The fate of England, as Able Seaman James Martin
remembered Fremantle's words[,] "Hung upon a Balance and their
Happyness Depended upon us and their Safty also Happy the Man
who Boldly Venture his Life in such a Cause if he shold Survive the
Battle how Sweet will be the Recolection and if he fall he fall Covred
with Glory and Honnor and Morned by a Greatfull Country the Brave
Live Gloryous and Lemented Die.

> Pre-Battle Speech recollected by Able Seamen James Martin
> as spoken by Captain Thomas Fremantle of the HMS *Neptune*
> before the Battle of Trafalgar, October 21, 1805[17]

LIKE ALEXANDER THE GREAT, Pre-Battle speechmakers often include a reference to what is at stake in the coming battle. This "stake" is described as either a direct or a contingent consequence of winning or losing. Thus, when Hannibal, in the excerpt above, tells his soldiers that losing the Battle of Zama will mean the death or enslavement of their families, he is offering them a contingent possibility—nothing necessitates the enslavement of enemy civilians following the loss of a battle (and, in fact, no Carthaginian civilians were enslaved following Hannibal's defeat). But when Hannibal predicts that a Carthaginian defeat will end their "world empire," he is forecasting a direct (and accurate, as it turned out) result of the battle. What is important to note here is that the speechmaker defines "what is at stake." And in doing so, he inevitably returns to what might be called the Pre-Battle Speech binary: victory or defeat. Stalemates are almost never considered in the Pre-Battle Speech, nor are unintended outcomes.

The speechmaker's mission is exhortation; thus, he will reduce the "probable" outcomes to those that he believes represent an incentive for his soldiers to fight—or, if he is considering the consequences of a defeat, the outcomes that offer disincentives not to fight. This is why the stakes referenced in Pre-Battle Speeches are generally not of the rarified sort—for example, complex matters dealing with control of natural resources, geopolitical strategic outcomes, or commercial dom-

ination of sea lanes. It is not that these things are not worth fighting or
even dying for—quite the contrary, these matters may be central to a
state's or a people's existence. Rather, for battle-speech purposes, rarified matters defy concision and resist easy reduction to the "ideals" for
which one is prepared to sacrifice life or limb. The stakes contained in
the Pre-Battle Speech should combine "big pictures" (that is, Alexander the Great's speech at Issus, where he declares that the sovereignty
of Asia is at stake) with matters of importance to individual soldiers.
As will be seen, these may involve either material or intangible goods
in which the soldier-audience believes it has, or wants to have, a stake.
The three examples featured in the epigraph represent at least five
kinds of stakes: the personal stake of family and community survival
mixed with a "big picture" intangible stake of world empire (Hannibal/
Livy); the personal stake of survival or comfort (Napoleon); a stake in
an intangible quality such as prestige (Napoleon); and a stake in the
intangible qualities of nationhood, as reportedly spoken by Captain
Thomas Fremantle.

The first excerpt featured above is Hannibal's Pre-Battle Speech
to his Carthaginian soldiers, delivered just before the Battle of Zama.
This epic contest between Hannibal and the Roman general Publius
Cornelius Scipio Africanus, two of the most justly celebrated commanders of antiquity, was to decide the Second Punic War. Although
the precise location of the battle is unknown, Hannibal's paraphrased
remarks, including their suggestion that Carthaginian soldiers "keep
their eyes upon all they held dear," beginning with "the walls of their
native city," might suggest that Zama was fought within sight of Carthage itself. (Of course, Hannibal may have been speaking figuratively.) However, Livy's suggestion that this final battle was waged
close to Carthage does lend this speech a dramatic cast. For Carthaginian solders, the stakes of this battle could not have been higher
or more elemental, and Hannibal outlines them with brutal candor.
Whether his men could see Carthage's walls with their actual eyes or
only in their minds' eye, there is one terrifying assumption that informs this speech: in victory, Rome will do to Carthage what Carthage
had done to it during seventeen relentless years of a war waged mostly
on Roman soil. Hannibal urges his men "to keep before their eyes all

they held dear," and what follows is a catalogue of personal, family, and religious intimacy that would have touched every soldier in the ranks: "the walls of their native city, their household gods, the tombs of their ancestors, their children, parents and trembling wives." As Hannibal would have it, this is the list that was slated for Roman destruction, and it is not compiled at random. Hannibal means to predict a future of total annihilation, of the dead as well as the living, of household gods of stone as well as human flesh and blood. It would be dishonor as well as death—thus the reference to "trembling wives." In short, to lose the battle would mean the loss of *everything*, the past (ancestors, gods), the present (children, parents, and trembling wives), and the future (death and slavery, the end of Carthage's world empire.)

Real battles can end in many ways, and perhaps the most comprehensive binary would be "decisively" or "indecisively." But that is not how Hannibal wants his men to view the Battle of Zama's outcomes. He prefers a binary of absolute victory or abject defeat, and his language becomes almost rhythmic. He (or Livy) pairs various alternatives in couplet form as he urges his men to "remember the dread alternatives": "death or slavery on one hand/world empire on the other/with no middle way/either for fear or for hope/between those two extremes." Indeed, these words might have continued at greater length but for the fact that Hannibal was interrupted by the battle sounds of Roman horns and trumpets.

Given Hannibal's mission of winning the battle, he drew upon the ultimate stake in using this binary. As the commander, he had to persuade his soldiers that they in turn had to "conquer or die"—once men accept his definition of the stakes, they would have no alternative but to conquer, as all other choices are unthinkable. Of course, Hannibal lost the Battle of Zama. But Rome declined to sack Carthage, instead destroying its war-making capacity and levying punitive reparations on the city. The Carthaginian military camp was thoroughly plundered but the walls, household gods, tombs of ancestors, children, parents, and trembling wives of Carthage itself remained safe for another seventy years—until the Third Punic War.[18]

Where Hannibal creates the stake of family survival, Napoleon's Pre-Battle Speech (written proclamation) before the Battle of Borodino implies a different personal stake: "[Victory] will give us abundance, good winter quarters, and a speedy return to our country." Of these three values, food, good shelter, and a way home, it is clear that Napoleon's army was most interested in the first. One prominent historian has written that these men were "wanting to avenge the weeks of slogging march on mostly empty stomachs." Effective attacks on French communications by Russian Cossacks had resulted in "severe food shortages." Napoleon probably truly believed that once he had defeated the Russian army, the attacks on his supply chain would diminish and the countryside would be opened for uncontested pillage. Thus, for many French soldiers, victory meant dinner.[19]

So Napoleon's insertion of "abundance" as a battle stake for Borodino is not an invention but rather a simple recognition that his army was hungry. But Napoleon does invent at least one intangible good—the prospect of future prestige—which he also offers as a stake in the battle. Here he invents a vision of "posterity" when he declares, "let posterity point with pride to your conduct on this day." Of course, "posterity" does not exist at the time Napoleon delivers his speech; exactly what that posterity would resemble and precisely how it would regard his soldier's conduct, the Battle of Borodino, or Napoleon's entire Russian campaign is an unknown. And for some soldiers, of course, there would be no posterity. (Indeed, Borodino would be one of the bloodiest battles in European history.) But it is likely that many soldiers would value the prospect of imagining that one day, family and community would exclaim, "He was at that great battle fought under the walls of Moscow!" Essentially, Napoleon is creating value in imaginary goods, and indeed, enough value to induce some men to risk spending life and limb to attain it. Thus are some stakes tangible (food) while others are intangible (a well-disposed posterity.)

One of the most important intangibles for which soldiers will willingly die is that of nationhood. On October 21, 1805, the sense of nationhood was on full and lethal display in the waters off Cape Trafalgar, Spain. The War of the Third Coalition, pitting Russia, Great Britain, and Austria against Napoleon and his satellites, was well underway, and that morning two hostile fleets were closing. One was a Franco-Spanish flotilla under the command of French Vice-Admiral

Pierre-Charles Villeneuve, the other a British fleet under the command of Vice-Admiral Horatio Nelson. In the forenoon and with the enemy only two miles away, the HMS *Victory,* Nelson's flagship, signaled the fleet using special flags designated by Sir Home Popham in his book of signals. As each flag was hoisted, each ship translated as the words "England-Expects-Every-Man-Will-Do-His D-U-T-Y" appeared. (Because "Duty" had no single flag, it had to be spelled letter-by-letter.) This was Nelson's Pre-Battle Speech, one of the most famous in history.[20]

Less well known is Captain Fremantle's Pre-Battle Speech featured above, which was almost certainly delivered shortly after Nelson's. Both Nelson and Fremantle stressed nationhood, and this was no coincidence. These sentiments were in the breeze throughout Western civilization during the nineteenth century—one's nation-state had blossomed from a place to live into an enormously complex pattern of identity, language, culture, rights, and, as Nelson would signal, the occasionally lethal embrace of duties and expectations.

Aboard the *Neptune,* Fremantle moved from station to station, exhorting clusters of men with some version of the Pre-Battle Speech that Able Seaman Martin received when the captain called on his station. If Nelson had sternly stressed the nation-state's expectations of duty, Fremantle would embroider the same idea with the classical values of glory and honor; like Napoleon at Borodino, he would also conjure an imagined posterity that would continue to honor any that might die while performing his duty: "and if he fall he fall Covred with Glory and Honnor and Morned by a Greatfull Country." But what was probably of greater significance to these sailors than the whole Homeric swirl of "the Brave Live Gloryous and Lemented Die" was how Fremantle defined the stakes of the sea battle that was now only minutes away. As Battle of Trafalgar historian Adam Nicolson paraphrased Martin's recollection, it was all about "the fate of England." In Fremantle's usage, "England" is a metonym for a vast community of millions (including many that are not English but Irish, Scottish, or Welsh); moreover, according to Fremantle, the fate of this community "Hung upon a Balance and their Happyness Depended upon us and their Safty." Here Fremantle's metaphor of a scale is highly significant. What Nelson and Fremantle were heralding was the understanding that all modern soldiers and sailors willingly adopt, namely that the individual action of every man or woman is a fulcrum upon which rests the fate of the state or nation. This conviction has become a commonplace in modern battle speeches of all kinds; thus, each warrior's "stake" in modern battles is the felt connection between military service and the state's existence or prosperity. Thus, the conception adopted by Nelson and Fremantle at Trafalgar is far grander than that of Napoleon at Borodino, for their intangible of nation subsumes his intangible of posterity and community—and it would continue to do so for at least the next two centuries.

The Stakes: Hatred and Revenge

We must fight them with more hatred in our hearts than when we fought the Carthaginians; for against Carthage we felt but little anger, contending, as we were, for glory and empire; but these scoundrels here must be punished for the crimes of perfidy and murder. The time has come to avenge the brutal slaughter of our comrades and the treachery which would have awaited us too, if we had happened to seek refuge here; we must make an example of these traitors.

> Excerpt from the Pre-Battle Speech of Scipio Africanus
> before the attack upon Iliturgi, 206 BCE

"Picture to yourselves," [Josephus] concluded, "old men butchered, women and children slaughtered by the foe at any moment now. These impending disasters arouse fury in your breasts. Seize that fury and hurl it against those who will cause the disasters."

> Josephus, Pre-Battle Speech before Vespasian's
> final assault on Jotapata, 67 CE[21]

IN CONSIDERING THE EXAMPLES featured above an important question must first be answered: how should a stake be distinguished from a motive? This is especially important for intangible stakes, which are easily confused with motives—in fact, in battle speeches, stakes and motives are very close in meaning. Few people will have difficulty understanding a battle's stakes where the outcome is food for the victors. But where the motive is hatred of an enemy, distinguishing stakes from motives is more difficult. Where hatred is involved, one way to do so is clear in the Pre-Battle Speech delivered by Scipio Africanus above. The town of Iliturgi had changed its allegiance from Rome to Carthage as the two sides warred for control of Roman Spain. Rome was ultimately successful in restoring its fortunes, and a town's disloyalty might have been grounds for some sort of collective punishment. But in the interests of postwar stability Rome chose to forgive most of these places. Not Iliturgi, however, which had not only switched allegiances but also afterward murdered Roman soldiers who had already been granted refuge there. This was not considered mere politics or the changing fortunes of war but instead simply a crime. Now, as Livy concluded, "the time for exacting a penalty seemed to have come."

Scipio marched an army to Iliturgi and delivered a Pre-Battle Speech, excerpts of which are featured above. "We must fight them with more hatred in our hearts that when we fought the Carthaginians; for against Carthage we felt but little anger," he declared. "[But] these scoundrels here must be punished for the crimes of perfidy and murder. The time has come to avenge the brutal slaughter of our comrades and the treachery." Here Scipio demonstrates precisely how hatred is channeled into revenge, thus revealing the exact relationship between motive and stakes, hatred and revenge: in battle speeches, *the stake offered by hatred is revenge*. In short, hatred is the motive and revenge is the stake, the product of the motive. Mere anger—that which Scipio felt toward Carthaginians ("against Carthage we felt but little anger") erupts, as it inevitably will, whenever one fends off the blows of an armed enemy. But hatred is of an entirely different emotional magnitude. Anger is temporary, does not consume as much of the mind, and only flashes nearer its surface; genuine hatred has quiddity, is portable over long stretches of space and time, and has its own active intelligence. Anger is reactive, while hatred seeks expression and revenge is its satisfier, its best hope for release. And this is how the battle speechmaker functions as tribune—by converting hatred into revenge, as only someone can do who has the authority to seek tactical opportunities for that revenge. It was only when Scipio declared that revenge must be exacted from the Spaniards that his men had a genuine stake in the coming battle.

Scipio's speech had the desired effect. "All were fired by the general's speech," Livy reported, "and immediately [after] he ended, scaling ladders were issued to selected men from different maniples." And when his soldiers succeeded in entering the town they inflicted a horrific violence, rationalized, if not fully, by the lights of that sometimes savage age. "No soldiers took prisoners or had a thought for plunder," Livy claimed, "armed and unarmed citizens were butchered alike, women and men without distinction; they did not stop short in their beastly blood-lust even at the slaughter of infants."

Josephus's situation was the opposite of Scipio's. At the time he uttered the words featured here, he commanded the walled Galilean town of Jotapata, which was then besieged by Roman legions commanded by Vespasian. The town's walls had already been breached; on the day Josephus delivered his Pre-Battle Speech, he saw that the besiegers were organizing for the final assault: men carrying ladders to ascend the walls, archers strategically stationed to suppress any defense along the breached sections of wall, and cavalry stationed around the town to prevent escapes. The end was near and it threatened annihilation. By settled custom, towns that refused a demand to surrender or that harbored combatants (Jotapata had done both) were subject to a successful besieger's whim—and "whim" might include the massacre of soldiers and civilians, rape, enslavement, plunder, or the town's complete physical destruction. Faced with almost certain death at Roman hands, what could Josephus say to inspire his soldiers to resist? After all, a more rational calculus might have discouraged resistance and instead counsel that Vespasian be appeased, the town surrender, and its civilians beg for mercy. In sum, what stake does Josephus offer his men to continue to fight?[22]

In one sense, Josephus's speech mirrors Scipio's in that both seek to convert hatred into revenge, and then rely on revenge to provide their men with a reason to fight. But Josephus must be far more graphic than Scipio in conjuring hateful images. And this is the difference between the two Pre-Battle Speeches: Scipio relies on his soldiers' memory of the enemy's *past* crimes, while Josephus must conjure images of *future* crimes. The violence he wants his men to revenge has not yet occurred. After all, at the time he delivers his speech, the Romans are still outside Jotapata's walls.

First, then, Josephus creates the images. "Picture to yourselves," he implores, "old men butchered, women and children slaughtered by the foe at any moment now." To understand how his soldiers likely regarded this prospect, one must remember that Jotapata was not a military garrison but a civilian town. Its defenders were not stationed continents away from their homes; rather, their homes were only yards away, sheltering their families as they cowered from catapulted projectiles. "Within the town rose the terrible shrieks of the women, echoed from without by the groans of dying men," Josephus remembers at one point, suggesting just how demoralizing siege warfare can be for the defenders. Those women were the wives, mothers, daughters, and sisters of the soldiers. (Later, Josephus had them all locked in their houses, "for fear that their lamentation might weaken the resolution of their menfolk.")

Josephus then spells out the next step in converting hatred into revenge: "These impending disasters arouse fury in your breasts," he declares rhetorically. Of course, this response is not really as rhetorical as Josephus would have had his soldiers believe. Reacting with hatred to these imagined images is certainly one possible response; however, there are other possible responses too, including paralytic fear, a desire to flee with or without one's family, depression, suicide (as would be the case years later at Masada), or even mutiny against Josephus's authority (followed by an attempt to surrender to Vespasian). But for those soldiers who, picturing their families brutally slaughtered, do react with hatred, only a small final leap remains. "Seize that fury," Josephus orders, "and hurl it against those who will cause the disasters." Here then is the stake—according to Josephus's interpretation, the soldiers and their families belong to the walking dead, and the soldiers will probably die first, leaving them no opportunity to revenge the future murders of their families. Thus, the time for revenge is now, before a massacre that is all but certain. Thus does Pre-Battle speechmaker Josephus literally create a stake by imagining a future, provoking an emotional reaction to that future, and channeling the resulting passion toward his objective—resistance to the Roman besiegers.

Threats

The commanding general requests that previous to the engagement soon expected with the enemy, corps and all other commanding officers address their troops, explaining to them briefly the immense issues involved in the struggle. The enemy are on our soil. The whole country now looks anxiously to this army to deliver it from the presence of the foe. Our failure to do so will leave us no such welcome as the swelling of millions of hearts with pride and joy at our success would give to every soldier of this army. Homes, firesides, and domestic altars are involved. The army has fought well heretofore; it is believed that it will fight more desperately and bravely than ever if it is addressed in fitting terms. Corps and other commanders are authorized to order the instant death of any soldier who fails in his duty at this hour.

"Circular," Major General George Gordon Meade, June 30, 1863[23]

PRE-BATTLE SPEECHMAKERS use several methods to enhance or seal their soldier-audience's confidence in the arguments they make. "Carrot" methods might include intangibles such as a commander's personal recognition of soldiers or the unit's recognition of them through the awarding of medals, or tangibles such as cash, plunder, slaves, or rapine. "Stick" methods, to generate obedience if not enthusiasm, might include the gallows, a firing squad, an executioner's axe, or the brig. The most common threat in Pre-Battle Speeches is the promise to kill those who fail to obey orders during the expected battle, as with desertion under fire, disobedience of direct orders, surrender without just cause, or assorted acts of cowardice or treachery.

In modern Western armies, executions for cowardice—and the threat of executions contained in Pre-Battle Speeches—have virtually disappeared from public military discourse. This is attributable to the fact that many Western societies are unwilling to exact capital punishment for *any* reason. In addition, cowardice is today more likely to be understood in psychological rather than criminal or moral terms, and in the West the trend has been against the criminalization of behavior that is believed to be beyond the rational control of the actor. These various changes suggest that, for now, executions for cowardice or desertion under fire are no longer politically acceptable. Finally and decisively, this sort of discipline is not considered effective. As *The Marine Officer's Guide* observes, "Discipline imposed by fear of punishment will inevitably break down in combat or any other severe test. If you threaten your troops, discipline will also break." In sum, no Western commander today could announce (or allow himself to be quoted as announcing), what Colonel Edward Cross declares before leading his men into Antietam's Bloody Lane: "If any man runs I want the file closers to shoot him; if they don't I shall myself."[24]

Readers will note that Major General Meade's June 30, 1863, circular, issued the day before the Battle of Gettysburg commenced, combines elements of a Defender's Speech (discussed in chapter 5) and a Pre-Battle Speech. Three days earlier, Meade had replaced Army of the Potomac commander Joseph Hooker after the latter had requested his own relief. By June 30, Lee was well established in Pennsylvania, and the opposing armies were converging on the crossroads town of Gettysburg. Meade correctly believed that a major battle was imminent; Pennsylvania had to be defended and Lee's army expelled or destroyed. However, the tactical question of whether Meade's army would attack, defend, or combine the two somehow was as yet unsettled. Foreseen only was that the Army of the Potomac's forced march through Maryland and into Pennsylvania was ending, and that it would likely be followed by a climactic battle.

The most important contextual feature of the Threat is that it is rarely made in isolation. Rather, as is the case with General Meade's circular, the Threat is presented with other themes or conventions and almost always at the end of the speech. (Colonel Cross's threat also appears as his conclusion.) It is as if Pre-Battle and Defender speechmakers invoking the Threat assume that a certain percentage of their soldier-audience, worn out by fatigue or consumed by fear, has failed to grasp the confidence-building themes; thus, the speechmaker must conclude with some stunning attention-getter in order to obtain unanimous compliance with the orders to fight. The themes that Meade stresses are familiar by now: urgency ("The enemy are on our soil"); a call to resist ("The whole country now looks anxiously to this army to deliver it from the presence of the foe"); compelling motive ("Homes, firesides, and domestic altars are involved"); and, finally, like Governor Curtin's speech, shame ("Our failure [to defeat or expel the rebels] will leave us no such welcome as the swelling of millions of hearts with pride and joy at our success would give to every soldier of this army"). Meade's circular opens with an instruction to his subalterns that directly inserts the Confidence Convention at the center of his speech: "The commanding general requests that previous to the engagement soon expected with the enemy, corps and all other commanding officers address their troops, explaining to them briefly the immense issues involved in the struggle." And indeed, Meade makes no stronger endorsement for a citizen army's virtues than when he states his belief that if he is properly informed of these "immense issues," the citizen-now-soldier will fight. A few sentences later, Meade says as much. He believes that the army "will fight more desperately and bravely than ever if it is addressed in fitting terms." Indeed, there can be no stronger endorsement for battle speeches than a commander's conviction that his soldiers' willingness to fight depends in part on a "fitting" one. (Unfortunately, Meade does not define this for his officers.)

Given Meade's predilection for persuading armies, one is even more troubled by his speech. The Threat of "instant death" for disobedient soldiers seems in its context like a nonsequitur. Had Meade preceded the Threat with appropriate Rationalization—for example, noting that desertion under fire had become widespread, or that whole units were refusing to obey orders—his Threat would be more intelligible. Significantly, when Meade addressed the Army of the Potomac ten months later as the soldiers entered the Wilderness, he omitted Threat altogether. Before Gettysburg, Meade had been in command for mere hours; ten months later, his confidence in the army was high. One can conjecture that, absent some compelling Rationalization, the Threat might reflect the speechmaking commander's insecurities as much as his response to underlying realities. The Threat Speech will be considered again in the next chapter on Midst-of-Battle Speeches.[25]

Personal Recognition: Ancient and Modern

[Jugurtha] also addressed individually every man whom he had rewarded with a gratuity or honor for distinguished service, reminding him of the fact and pointing him out as an example to others; and finally, adapting his mode of address to each man's character—using in turn promises, threats, and entreaties—he sought to inspire courage in the soldiers at large.

Sallust's summary of Jugurtha's Pre-Battle Speech
near the Muthul River, 108 BCE

Riding up and down, [Marcus Petreius] addressed each soldier by name, encouraging them and bidding them remember that they were fighting against half-armed bandits in defense of their fatherland and their children, their homes and the altars of their gods. He was a good soldier, who for more than thirty years had served with great distinction as military tribune, prefect, lieutenant, and commander; and he knew many of the men personally and remembered their gallant feats of arms. By recalling these he kindled their fighting-spirit.

Roman commander Marcus Petreius before the Battle of Pistoria, 62 BCE[26]

SINCE ANTIQUITY Personal Recognition has been an important tool in the confidence-building kit of battle speechmakers, and perhaps never more so than in Pre-Battle or Pre-Invasion Speeches. If a speech allows the speechmaker to circumvent sometimes stultifying chains of command, Personal Recognition establishes an even closer connection between the leader and the led. It is not the final affirmation of comradeship, but it is certainly very close; here, the commander personally and publicly acknowledges the deeds of his soldiers, and in the process closes the distance between him and them. That these recognitions also have powerful symbolic significance to the many soldiers not singled out can be inferred from the numbers—while "riding up and down" Marcus Petreius would have addressed only a handful of the soldiers he commanded against Catiline; nevertheless, when Sallust observed that "he kindled their fighting spirit," he almost certainly meant the spirit of his entire army, not just those he recog-

nized. The other soldiers probably assumed that had *they* been standing in the front ranks, Marcus Petreius might have recognized them
as well; thus, under these circumstances, a general's informal recognition of one soldier's past bravery may, in the imaginations of his men,
illumine the past bravery of them all.

In this sense, an important element of Personal Recognition is the
Unit Historical Narrative. By recognizing a soldier's past deeds at
such-and-such a battle, the commander is literally writing the text of
a very different sort of unit history than the one he is likely to submit
to headquarters in an after-action report, describe in his memoirs, or
verbally relay later to his peers. In those reports, the clever or fortu-
itous movements of units, the lay of the land, an enemy's deployments,
or the foresight and skill of the commander are the factors behind victory; but when Personal Recognition is applied, past battles are instead won by individually named courageous footsoldiers, gruff-voiced
centurions, or once fresh-faced second lieutenants who have since become hirsute veterans.

However, the example of Jugurtha suggests that Personal Recognition is not limited to a commander's acknowledgment of past valor.
Because Personal Recognition in Pre-Battle Speeches is an intimate
personal interaction, undertaken at a time when a soldier's awareness
of his own mortality is likely to be acute, what passes between a leader
and one of the led may consist of many things. After Jugurtha had "addressed every man whom he had rewarded with a gratuity or honor for
distinguished service" and reminded "him of the fact and [pointed]
him out as an example to others," he deepened his acknowledgment
by "adapting his mode of address to each man's character." This pre-
supposed something that seems to have been more common in antiquity than today—commanders who had knowledge not only of their
soldiers' acts of bravery but also of their personalities. (This probably reflected smaller armies as well as some ancient armies' decades'-
long terms of enlistment.) Using this additional knowledge, Jugurtha
was able to employ "promises, threats, and entreaties"—probably
whatever he thought would work to "inspire courage in the soldiers
at large." It is easy to imagine Jugurtha, perhaps on horseback, riding along his lines of infantry or cavalry, and, remembering that one

man was greedy, another timid, and another vainglorious, calling out to each the rewards, threats, and honors that lay just over victory's horizon.

Marcus Petreius's approach represents a different model of Personal Recognition. First, although Petreius also "addressed each soldier by name," his purpose in doing so was to communicate a Political or Social Historical Narrative of the reasons why it was necessary to destroy the rebel Catiline. Presumably, it was between the calling-out of names that Petreius "[bid] them remember that they were fighting against half-armed bandits in defense of their fatherland and their children, their homes and the altars of their gods." This emphasizes Stakes, but it is a fainter form of Personal Recognition. By encouraging the soldiers to imagine that the battle is for *their* children, *their* homes, and *their* gods, they become personally invested in the larger struggle rather than their own accomplishments.

By summarizing Petreius's resume, Sallust gives reasons why soldiers valued their commander's recognition as well as why Petreius knew enough names to make Personal Recognition effective: he was "a good soldier, who for more than thirty years had served with great distinction as military tribune, prefect, lieutenant, and commander; and he knew many of the men personally and remembered their gallant feats of arms." Since the Marian Reforms, the Roman army, always relatively small in numbers, had evolved into a force of long-serving professionals—just the sort of men who would recognize in each other the kinds of qualities that Petreius could exploit in this Pre-Battle Speech. Thus, Sallust has laid ample groundwork to make believable his conclusion about Petreius's Pre-Battle Speech: "By recalling these," Sallust asserts, "[Petreius] kindled their fighting-spirit."

General [McClellan,] as soon as he was opposite our regiment, and saw the men with their clothes all muddy and torn, he rode straight to the colors, his horse pushed against me, as he took off his cap, waved and shook it over the colors, at the same time cheering, and all the rest of the officers joined with him, and he then turned around to the Generals who were with him and said, "These men with the colors

have seen service," and then rode on continuing his review. I shall al-
ways remember that event as being the most enthusiastic and happi-
est moment of my life.

Thomas Hollis, color-bearer of the Twentieth Massachusetts,
remembering General George B. McClellan, September 1862[27]

T HE FRENCH REVOLUTION inaugurated vast, short-term citizen
armies, and with these came weakened connections between senior commanders and the ranks. Unlike Marcus Petreius's long-serving professionals, few men in these citizen armies served more than
thirty months together, let alone thirty years. Yet these nineteenth-
and twentieth-century soldiers presumably craved as much personal
connection with senior leadership as did their ancient predecessors.
As Thomas Hollis's recollection suggests, a modern commander's
deeds, words, and symbols can supplant the ancient practice of calling soldiers by name and publicly recognizing their past acts of bravery. General McClellan was able to efficiently fuse speech and deeds
with the moment to produce a profound experience of loyalty, comradeship, and personal revelation for ordinary soldiers. This is especially remarkable given that McClellan probably knew few if any of
the Twentieth Massachusetts's rank and file or their individual acts
of bravery.

McClellan achieved this feat by using regimental battle flags as
surrogates for the individuals who marched behind them, enabling
soldiers to transfer their general's approval of their flag to themselves.
Of course, what allowed McClellan to do this was the fact that by the
time of the American Civil War (and among Western armies generally), the flag had achieved venerable status as the object of a civic
cult, the central metonym of government and, for most citizens, the
history, values, and customs of their nation. To Thomas Hollis and his
successors, the physical flag itself was "real" in a way different from
what it might be for civilians. The soldiers' flag was a daily presence
connected with special rituals that were constantly observed during
marches, in camp, and in the line of battle. For Hollis and every regimental color-bearer that lined the road to Antietam the very flag he

held had flown in many battles, had survived many comrades, and had waved over many corpses; some of Hollis's fellow color-bearers had even died trying to preserve it—that is, prevent its falling to the ground or being taken by the enemy.

General McClellan converted the road on which he traveled into a metaphorical stage on which he publicly could be seen to fulfill these special flag rituals. As he "rode along the lines," Hollis remembered, "[and] when he passed the colors of each regiment, he saluted them by raising his cap." Another soldier standing near Hollis testified to the effect of this gesture. "Far from the rear the cheers were heard, faintly at first, and gradually the sound increased and grew to a roar as [McClellan] approached. The weary men sprang to their feet and cheered and cheered; as he went the cheers went before him and with him and after him." McClellan had only to honor the flag to likewise honor the men.

McClellan's act of doffing his cap on its own electrified each soldier. But the experience became truly profound when it was coupled with words. McClellan rode up to Hollis, removed his kepi, waved it over the colors, and announced for all to hear, "These men with the colors have seen service." This was Personal Recognition that was just as meaningful to its recipients as the individual recognition extended by Marcus Petreius or King Jugurtha. Proof of this can be found in Hollis's narrative. "I had the honor of being complimented in a most flattering manner by General McClellan," Hollis remembered, adding later, "I shall always remember that event as being the most enthusiastic and happiest moment of my life." Interestingly, McClellan never mentions Hollis's name or even makes reference to him. In modernity, to compliment the symbol was to touch the soldier.

Personal Example

[As] we were formed into line of battle, expecting momentarily to be ordered to the front to take a more active part, Captain Baker made this little speech, "In a few moments we shall be where we shall see more active and more dangerous work, but no matter what we may meet let not a man of you run until I run, but when you see me run

then let every man run like the devil." Suffice it to say, no man was
seen running.

Pre-Battle Speech of Captain Otis H. Baker, Company H,
Third Massachusetts Volunteer Militia, before the Battle
of Kinston, December 14, 1862

For himself, he vowed that not one noble should England ever pay
in ransom for him, for in that fight he meant to win or die, but if any
of them had aught against his neighbor let him wash the mote from
out of his conscience with the priest, for if they should die unpro-
vided good could never come of it. At this all fell upon their knees and
clasped their hands towards Heaven, praying that God would have
them in his keeping, while the chaplains moved about from man to
man, shriving the weeping penitents and whispering comfort with
their last housel, in preparation for the death that might at any time
be on them.

Excerpt from the Pre-Battle Speech of King Henry V at Agincourt, October
24, 1415 (the day before the actual battle), as reconstructed by J. H. Wylie[28]

A SPEECHMAKER'S PERSONAL EXAMPLE —deeds under fire—
figures prominently in battle speeches and especially in Midst-
of-Battle Speeches, which are considered in the next chapter. However, as a Confidence Convention, a Pre-Battle speechmaker's *promise*
of deeds to be performed under fire can also help the cause. Here the
battle speechmaker publicly commits to assuming the same combat
risks as the soldiers (or even greater risks). Officers are metonyms incarnate, after all, standing in for cause, country, authority, the military's hierarchy, competence, and, in pre-battle situations, a soldier's
perception of combat risk. And it is with the latter than an officer's
Personal Example—ranging from facial expressions, tone of voice,
bearing, and gait all the way to real deeds of valor—can signify important things to his soldiers. First, he might imply that the risk of
death or injury in the expected battle will be manageable; after all,
if the officer is willing to assume personal risk when he could just
as easily (if not as effectively) "lead from behind," then perhaps the
prospects might not be as grim as they are feared to be. Second, an

officer's perspective carries extra weight because he is presumed to know more about plans, tactics, and enemy capabilities than those of inferior rank. Third, the officer's resume and character matter and inspire simply via their display. When the leader is a combat veteran who is known for good judgment, his personal example will mean more than just another soldier's (or an inexperienced officer's).

Consider the leadership skills and command credibility of Captain Otis A. Baker, whose speech is featured above. A successful mason and Massachusetts State Representative before the war, he had already served with a Rhode Island regiment during Bull Run, where he was wounded in the arm. He then joined another Rhode Island regiment for the highly successful Burnside Expedition, where he saw action on Roanoke Island and at the Battle of Newbern. Thus, when Captain Baker declared before the Battle of Kinston that "no matter what we may meet let not a man of you run until I run, but when you see me run then let every man run like the devil," William H. Luther, who heard this speech, was able to comment dryly in the regimental history that "Suffice to say, no man was seen running." Captain Baker's credibility, embodied in a Pre-Battle Speech that implicitly offered his Personal Example ("let not a man of you run until I run"), helped his solders march into battle, and his steadfastness under fire then helped them remain there. And this is how Personal Example differs in a Pre-Battle Speech from the same method used in a Midst-of-Battle Speech: in the Pre-Battle Speech, the words and the man are fused—the promise is only as credible as the person promising. In a Midst-of-Battle Speech, the identity of the person promising means less than the deed being performed—there, the man and the deed fuse. In sum, although Captain Baker's Pre-Battle Speech consists of forty-eight words, for the men of Company H the real speech was Captain Baker himself—his character, judgment, and experience. One way to understand the differences here between pre-battle and midst-of-battle leadership is to reinvent Captain Baker as a known coward. As such, his Pre-Battle Speech promise to lead his men would have been given slight regard. But once the firing started, if a cowardly Baker were to suddenly repent of his fears, seize a fallen color, and leap into the fray, shouting, "Follow Me!" there is a good chance that many men would indeed follow him. Before the battle, words matter if the speaker matters; during the battle, deeds trump all.

King Henry V's Pre-Battle Speech, delivered the day before Agincourt, illustrates another aspect of the Personal Example—the varied sources of confidence. Thus far in the discussion of Pre-Invasion and Pre-Battle Speeches, confidence has been narrowly defined in almost exclusively military terms—weapons, plans, commanders, comrades, and logistics. However, confidence is far more than the sum of these particular parts. What King Henry V recognizes, in a way that is very appropriate to his place and time, is that leading soldiers in battle requires more than a simple intention to do so. He certainly makes clear (so he says) that he is willing to lead, and to suffer the consequences if necessary: "For himself, he vowed that not one noble should England ever pay in ransom for him, for in [the upcoming] fight he meant to win or die." (In Henry's day, war had an entrepreneurial side, for it was a time when some soldiers—especially wealthy noblemen and monarchs—were worth far more alive than dead. The state had not yet monopolized war's proceeds, and a lucky captor could still make his fortune.)[29]

Yet the same passage in which Henry commits his personal example to combat concludes with a theme that might appear unexpected, at least to modern ears. "[But] if any of them had aught against his neighbor let him wash the mote from out his conscience with the priest, for if they should die unprovided good could never come of it." This theme is of Biblical pedigree; readers will recall the earlier example of Josephus urging that his soldiers to repent before God if they expected to be victorious. But a careful reading of Henry's words (or at least J. H. Wylie's reconstruction of them) reveals something different, more "modern," as it were. Unlike Josephus, Henry is not urging his soldiers to repent so that God will give them victory; rather, they should repent (confess) so that they may stride into battle fully confident that if death should come, their eternal souls will be fully "provided" for—that is, presumably in a state of grace. That his men should prepare their souls for death relates to victory only insofar as such readiness might bring about confidence that will make them more likely to win the battle. As Henry had essentially given an order for mass confession, his men immediately "fell upon their knees and clasped their hands towards Heaven, praying that God would have them in his keeping." Priests circulated through the ranks, "whispering comfort" and administering the Eucharist "in preparation for the death that might at any time be on them."

This interpretation should not be taken out of context. Henry's age was a devoutly religious one, in which faith framed most events. Earlier in the speech Henry had simply declared to his entourage that the English were "God's people," and that his side would win because of French sins, especially pride ("[God] can bring down the pride of these Frenchmen who boast of their numbers and their strength"). However, at no time does Henry connect confession, God's will, and victory. Rather, his men should "wash the mote from [their] conscience" so that with good prospects of dying in grace, they might fight like the devil. In short, God might favor the righteous army and the English His Chosen, but by Henry's day, He had ceased to be anyone's guarantor of victory.

Rewards

The prize would be great enough, were we only to recover by the strength of our hands the islands of Sicily and Sardinia which our fathers lost; but all the heaped wealth of Rome, won in her long career of conquest, will be yours; those rich possessions—yes, and the possessors too. Forward then, and win this splendid prize!

Excerpt from Hannibal's Pre-Battle Speech at Ticinus, 218 BCE

[Scipio] began by demonstrating to them that the operation was perfectly feasible, summed up briefly the damage which its success would inflict on the enemy and the advantages the Romans would gain from it, and went on to promise crowns of gold to the first men to scale the walls, and the usual rewards to those who showed conspicuous bravery.

Excerpt from Scipio Africanus's Pre-Battle Speech
before the assault on New Carthage, 209 BCE[30]

FOR MILLENNIA, one of the most persuasive angles of the Pre-Battle Speech (and the Recruiting Speech: see Gaius Marius's address in chapter 3) was the promise that victory could make ordinary soldiers rich. How the prospect of wealth adds confidence to soldiers confronting battle, and thus risking death, is a more complex matter. After all, one could argue that "all the money in the world" is insufficient compensation for risking one's life. Yet the historical record is absolutely clear on this point—from the beginning of organized warfare, far less sums *have* been more than enough to tempt men into battle. Whether the money is only a rationalization for soldiering's other advantages—the intense excitement, relief from creditors and bad marriages, thrill of risk taking, or temporary suspension of certain constraints from civilian life—is beyond the scope of this book. Likewise, other relevant possibilities—an escape from poverty, a break-out from oppressive class or social bondage, or simply a risk deemed acceptable for the price—also must be considered elsewhere. This book's thesis simply accepts the historical reality that the Reward is effective in recruiting men, retaining them in service, and inspiring them on the precipice of battle.

And for some war certainly did offer extraordinary opportunities for material gain. First, the enemy himself could be robbed—corpses and prisoners stripped of armor, weapons, and other valuables; abandoned or surrendered camps plundered, and enemy prisoners sold to slave traders (who numbered among antiquity's most devoted camp followers). Capturing an enemy town could be an even greater windfall. Civilians were wealthier than soldiers and were themselves available for bloodlust, rapine, and sale. In medieval Europe, warfare's material rewards had become remarkably businesslike, often governed by detailed contracts between a lord and his vassals or employers and mercenaries over the division of spoils. In Christendom, bloodlust, rapine, and slavery were, at least officially, discountenanced. But plundering the living and the dead continued and was joined by the newer opportunities of ransoming captives and privateering, for those who preferred to make war upon the waters.[31]

Hannibal's Pre-Battle Speech illustrates the most elemental model during antiquity (and probably long before) of how the Reward was used to inspire confidence. The Carthaginians had just crossed the Alps into Cisalpine Gaul and would momentarily confront Scipio Africanus's father at the battle of Ticinus River. Hannibal's lifetime project was to conquer Rome; having invaded Italy, that prospect now shone just over the horizon. Nurtured on revanchism, he might have been speaking personally when he declared that "The prize would be great enough, were we only to recover by the strength of our hands the islands of Sicily and Sardinia which our fathers lost." While material possessions mattered little to Hannibal—Livy attributes part of his greatness as a general to his common, soldierlike lifestyle—he understood that restoring Carthage's losses from the First Punic War was not the reason why every soldier had joined his army.[32]

After noting the opportunity to restore Carthage's control over the islands of Sicily and Sardinia (lost to Rome after the First Punic War), Hannibal inserts a strategic "but": "but all the heaped wealth of Rome, won in her long career of conquest, will be yours; those rich possessions—yes, and the possessors too." The "but" appears to acknowledge that if soldiers are only weakly motivated by abstract geopolitical advantages, there remains another spur to action—riches. And not the riches of some ordinary town but of Rome itself ("heaped wealth"), here further defined as things as well as people who will be transformed into things—that is, slaves. For Hannibal, whose hatred of Rome was profound, the prospect of enslaving Romans was probably irresistible; for some of his soldiers, it is more likely that the love of lucre exceeded any particular feelings about Rome or Romans.

Hannibal's Pre-Battle Speech is one model of Rewards. In promising them, Hannibal does not bother with the mechanics of distribution, or any particular division between Carthage and its soldiers, or a potential bonus for bravery, for example. Livy leaves the impression (perhaps intentionally) that when the looting and enslavement take place, it will be something of a free-for-all, with Carthaginians and their allies unleashed in the streets of Rome to do their worst. This impression would certainly have suited Livy, who included among Hannibal's faults his "inhuman cruelty [and] a more than Punic perfidy." And in fact, treating captured towns and cities in exactly this way did happen, and not just by Hannibal. Rome, too, could boast this sort of cruelty, although its army might, in the treatment of captured cities for example, proceed in a variety of ways, including setting unpleasant examples for others to contemplate before deciding whether to rebel against or submit to Roman authority, as well as clemency. However, as historian Paul Bentley Kern has observed in siege situations, "The laws of war more often justified violence than restrained it."[33]

However, there is another model of Rewards from antiquity that was used to inspire confidence or enthusiasm among a soldier-audience, and it is the opposite of the freebooting implied by Hannibal. When Scipio Africanus promised "crowns of gold to the first men to scale the walls, and the usual rewards to those who showed conspicuous bravery," he is evidencing the systematization of a genuine professional army. First, "crowns of gold and the usual rewards" were not only items of value but also of honor. Hannibal seemed to promise rewards to everyone; army membership was all that was necessary. But in Scipio's army, membership alone is insufficient to qualify for the reward. Instead, only two classes of soldiers are eligible: those who were first to scale New Carthage's walls, and those who demonstrated conspicuous bravery. Thus rewards would attach to behavior, not mere status; moreover, they would be used discriminately, for some behaviors were valued above others. In this sense, Scipio's Rewards point to a future time when a few dollars worth of ribbon and enameled metal might carry the "value" of a thousand times their weight in gold.

The Pre-Battle Speech: Fusing the Word and the Speechmaker

Caesar had everything to do at once—hoist the flag which was the signal for running to arms, recall the men from their work on the camp, fetch back those who had gone far afield in search of material for the rampart, form the battle line, address the men, and sound the trumpet signal for going into action.

Julius Caesar before a battle against the Nervii, 57 BCE[34]

IT IS FITTING to conclude this chapter by examining the Pre-Battle Speech in the environment for which it is best suited, and in a place that will assume even greater importance in the next chapter—

on the battlefield in the moments, even the seconds, before a battle is fully joined. The enemy is not only close but may have already discharged its weapons; it is here that the soldier-audience's spring is tightly coiled with fear and aggression, awaiting only the snap of command. And it is here that the word and the speechmaker move toward complete fusion. But adrenalin-powered energy should not be mania. As Caesar's example here suggests, the power unleashed by closing with the enemy must be controlled, carefully channeled toward the battle speechmaker's ultimate objective, which is to organize his soldiers to attack, withdraw, or defend.

First, the word and the deed in the Pre-Battle environment must be considered as linear phenomena, in which the act of speaking is only one in a series of acts unfolding rapidly but logically as soldiers are prepared for battle. Julius Caesar's legions were constructing their camp when the Nervii, a Belgic tribe whose lands roughly corresponded with present-day Belgium, unexpectedly attacked. "They suddenly dashed out in full force and swooped down on our cavalry, which they easily routed," Caesar reported later. "Then they ran down to the river at such an incredible speed that almost at the same moment they seemed to be at the edge of the wood, in the water and already upon us." The surprise was complete and Caesar reacted with a burst of energy. "[I] had everything to do at once," he remembered, some of which was probably accomplished via orders to subalterns. One can see a logical succession: first to activate the emergency alerts—flags hoisted as "the signal for running to arms"; second, to "recall the men from their work on the camp," that is, those who were engaged in surveying camp boundaries, digging, raising tents of hide, hewing wood, or drawing water, as well as those "who had gone far afield" in search of materials for the rampart. Force must be concentrated before it can be applied.

Once this was accomplished, Caesar then took the next step: to "form the battle line." Only now was it time to "address the men." And once the legions had formed, and men were properly instructed or exhorted, could Caesar "sound the trumpet signal for going into action." From this preparatory sequence we can begin to understand how words and deeds merge as part of a continuum of action, a se-

ries of connected acts most of which do not involve words but all of
which involve communication. Think of how many ways Caesar communicated: *hoist* the flag; *recall* men; *fetch* others; *form* a line, *address*
soldiers, and *sound* the trumpet. Each one of these actions involves
delivering messages necessary for the camp's defense; these messages
would include verbal orders for things to happen—for example, someone must be told to "recall the men"—and some of the messages, like
raising the flag or blowing a trumpet, are inherently communicative.

And then there was Caesar's speech. It qualifies only by seconds as
a Pre-Battle Speech: while the Nervii were already attacking, Caesar's
men, or at least his beloved Tenth Legion, had not yet engaged. (Had
Caesar waited to speak until his men were engaged, the following remarks would be a Midst-of-Battle Speech.)

> After giving the minimum of essential orders, Caesar hastened down to
> the battlefield to address the troops and happened to come first upon the
> 10th legion, to which he made only a short speech, urging them to live up
> to their tradition of bravery, to keep their nerve, and to meet the enemy's
> attack boldly. Then, as the Nervii were within range, he gave the signal
> for battle. On going to the other side of the field to address the troops
> there, he found them already in action.[35]

Here the Pre-Battle Speech conventions of Confidence and Stakes
reside in the same words: Caesar's plea that the Tenth Legion "live
up to their tradition of bravery." By failing to live up to that tradition,
they will lose that which distinguishes them in their own eyes and in
the sight of others—these are Stakes enough. By remembering that
tradition, they can draw confidence, because, since the future resembles the past, they will be brave now as they have been before. But in
this sequence something else unfolds that is centered in Caesar's person—constant detonations of energy that produce hyper-focused acts
of command. This becomes even more apparent moments later, in a
midst-of-battle episode that underlines the significance of Caesar's actions above. After leaving the Tenth Legion, what Caesar found when
he went to "the other side of the field" was incipient disaster: "The cohorts of the 12th legion were packed together so closely that the men
were in one another's way and could not fight properly. All the centurions of the 4th cohort, as well as a standard-bearer, were killed, and

the standard lost; nearly all the centurions of the other cohorts were either killed or wounded, including the chief centurion Publius Sextius Baculus." Here Caesar instantly diagnosed a potentially fatal but remediable problem: a breakdown in command owing to so many centurions being *hors de combat*. "Meanwhile the enemy maintained unceasing pressure up the hill in front," Caesar wrote of these critical moments, "and were also closing in on both flanks."[36]

In this crisis Caesar culminates the sequence of acts detailed in the epigraph. But his acts do not directly kill Nervii; rather, they inspire his soldiers to kill them:

> As the situation was critical and no reserves were available, Caesar snatched a shield from a soldier in the rear (he had not his own shield with him), made his way into the front line, addressed each centurion by name, and shouted encouragement to the rest of the troops, ordering them to push forward and open out their ranks, so that they could use their swords more easily. His coming gave them fresh heart and hope; each man wanted to do his best under the eyes of his commander-in-chief, however desperate the peril, and the enemy's assault was slowed down a little.[37]

Here the real significance of Caesar's passage in the epigraph becomes clear—a battle speechmaker who also commands fights by communicating. He will likely wage his war with both words and deeds—their sequencing will depend on circumstances—but in the end gestures, acts, and the omission of acts will be interchangeable with the spoken word. Caesar's most important deed here was simply to appear on the front lines. Just to stand silently in the van would have had value, for "His coming gave them fresh heart and hope." But of course he did much more—he acted by speaking and combined Personal Recognition with Instructional Speech. He was fully engaged in his soldiers' struggle, and they knew it: "[Each] man wanted to do his best under the eyes of his commander-in-chief."

6

MIDST-OF-BATTLE SPEECHES
The Word and the Deed

Hearing the commotion Titus, who was not far from the wall, exclaimed: "Now is your chance, men; why hesitate, when the Jews are ours for the asking? Seize your opportunity! Do you not hear the row? The men who have slipped through our fingers are fighting each other! The town is ours if we make haste; but we shall have to work hard and fight hard too. Great prizes cannot be won without taking risks. We must not wait for the enemy to make up their quarrel—necessity will reconcile them soon enough; and we must not wait for reinforcement either—we have beaten a whole army with a handful of men, and now we will capture the town by ourselves."

With these words he leapt into the saddle and led the way to the lake. Riding through the water he entered the town at the head of his men.

Titus exhorting his men during the assault on Tarichaeae, 67 CE

Marlborough, in the thick of the fighting, was perplexed to see one of his most senior officers making to flee the battlefield after this initial reverse. Not for him the knee-jerk justice of a shot in the coward's back, favored by [Prince] Eugene [of Savoy] across the valley; rather, the icy courtesy that leaves this most accomplished of generals a man of indecipherable character: "Mr—," he called, 'You are laboring under a misapprehension. The enemy lies that way. You have nothing to do but face him and the day is your own." This anonymous officer rejoined the battle, falling in with the other disordered troops as they regrouped.

The Duke of Marlborough at Blenheim, August 13, 1704[1]

THE MIDST-OF-BATTLE SPEECH includes a vast number of words and deeds that, though they arise in different tactical circumstances, all share the attribute of occurring during a battle. They might occur during an attack, a defense, or a retreat. And within each of these situations are myriad historical differentiators, each of which will further influence the type, length, and efficacy of the word or deed. Attacks may include everything from the blitzkriegs of mechanized warfare to the sometimes meticulously arranged set-piece battles of early modern Europe; defenses may include a quick volley of musketry delivered in an open field by retreating Civil War–era lines of battle or years-long sieges or trench wars of both ancient and modern combat; and an army may leave the field deliberately as part of an organized tactic or in disorder following some reverse in fortune. No single volume of battle speeches could completely capture the variety of tactical circumstances to which Midst-of-Battle speechmakers have responded with their words and deeds.

But amidst this blizzard of tactical circumstances, some common elements can be found via four important conventions that have helped to define the Midst-of-Battle Speech over the ages. The first of these is the use of an existing tactical circumstance—in Titus's case, for example, the divisions among his Jewish adversaries—to justify an appeal to the soldier-audience for some specific action. Borrowing a current military acronym, this is the SitRep Convention (short for "situation report")—that is, some information about the tactical situation that is shared with the soldier-audience. As Titus's example above suggests, this convention may be blended with other conventions already familiar to readers, such as Reward ("Great prizes cannot be won without taking risks") and a Unit Historical Narrative ("we have beaten a whole army with a handful of men"). Sometimes the soldier-audience can easily infer the "sitrep" from surrounding circumstances, thus obviating the need for the battle speechmaker to state the obvious. The case below of General Joshua T. Owen rallying Federal soldiers as a plainly visible enemy advances to the attack is one example of this.

The second convention of the Midst-of-Battle Speech is that which connects the word and the deed in the soldier-audience's mind: the

Moral Contract. Consider Titus's unilateral "sealing" of his Midst-of-Battle appeal via his own deeds. "With these words [Titus] leapt into the saddle and led the way to the lake," Josephus records. "Riding through the water he entered the town at the head of his men." Here the connection between the speech and the deed is clear: Titus's verbal proposal/command ("Seize your opportunity!") is immediately followed by his acting in a way that confirms what he has just explained to his soldier-audience. It is the ultimate unilateral contract, in which the speaker/actor (usually but not necessarily the commander) *symbolically* and *morally* obligates his already *legally* obligated soldier-audience by being the first to obey his own order.

Of course, the Moral Contract is not a genuine legal contract. After all, during almost any period in Western military history, when a soldier enlists or is conscripted he gives "constructive" consent to whatever his leaders might order, subject to certain timebound cultural and legal constraints (such as the duty to obey only lawful orders). But one of this book's premises is that if constructive consent were sufficient, there would be no need for most battle speeches. The commander would simply issue a terse order and receive compliance in return. Instead, and especially in the case of Midst-of-Battle Speeches and their distinctive interplay of words and deeds, the battle speechmaker must regularly unilaterally initiate and conclude a symbolic bargaining process with himself (as the leading symbol and representative of his unit); this process derives its force from certain moral—but not legal—assumptions shared with the soldier-audience. These assumptions should not be confused with the Judeo-Christian morals of Mount Sinai or the Sermon on the Mount. Rather, this is a special moral system steeped in the rituals and obligations of comradeship, perhaps established in the mists of pre-history but first extensively documented in the Greco-Roman period, one that in fact has little to do with the religion or morality of any particular period.

A good illustration of this Moral Contract involves Marcus Petronius, a centurion in Julius Caesar's army. In battle against the Gauls, Petronius found himself in advance of his men and surrounded by the enemy. The last few moments of his life represented a tug-of-war between his men and himself, as each vied to save the other. It was

Petronius who gave in first, offering his life to protect his comrades. As his situation worsened, he delivered a Midst-of-Battle Speech that is worth reproducing in whole: like so many reported speeches of antiquity, Petronius's words reveal by their length the arguments that similarly motivated modern speeches may not bother to explicate in full. They also lay bare the moral reciprocity of self-sacrifice that idealizes the Moral Contract.

> "I can't save myself and you," [Petronius said.] "It's my fault you're in this tight corner, because I was so keen to distinguish myself. So at least I'll help you to get away with your lives. Now's your chance: look after yourselves."
>
> With these words he charged into the middle of the enemy, killed two of them and forced the rest a short way back from the gate. [Petronius's] men still tried to rescue him.
>
> "It's no use," [Petronius] cried, "trying to save me. I've lost too much blood and haven't any strength left. So get away while you have the chance and fall back to your legion." So he went on fighting and a few moments later fell dead. But he had saved his men.

What is especially noteworthy here is the universality of the Moral Contract. Is there any doubt that Petronius's deeds (and some version of his conversation) have probably been reenacted in all wars before and after Caesar's time? As Petronius reveals, adherence to the Moral Contract can be at the risk of one's life, and at the risk of their own lives, his men attempted to save him until finally ordered back. And just as importantly, Julius Caesar the soldier-historian also values the Moral Contract. "But he had saved his men," Caesar concluded, the "but" indicating the positive estimation accorded Petronius for having redeemed himself thus.[2] Titus, too, invoked what might be called the "commander's clause" of the Moral Contract—like Petronius, he was out in front, obligating his men to follow not by mere orders but by personal example. And when deeds are performed at the risk or cost of the actor's life, they constitute the ultimate "earnest money" of the soldiers' Moral Contract.

A third convention of the Midst-of-Battle Speech, especially those intended to exhort soldiers for a burst of effort to secure some victory, is the Comrade Convention. Commanders such as Titus may have the absolute power of life and death over their soldiers, but in exhorting them for a final push, the preferred tone is not one of demand, orders, or threats, but rather the simple appeal of one soldier to another. Perhaps because something extra is asked of subordinates, something more must be given, if not in Reward then by a tone or words that suggest equality of circumstance if not of rank. Titus's tone abandons the legal verticality of command in favor of a more linear approach: "Now is your chance, men." Ranks are not addressed; rather, a situation that promises benefits to all is stressed. And the "I–you" paradigm for ordering subordinates disappears in favor of an undifferentiated mass that includes commanders and commanded alike: "[The] Jews are *ours* . . . The town is *ours, we* shall have to work hard . . . *We* must not wait for the enemy . . . *we* must not wait for reinforcement . . . *we* have beaten . . . *we* will capture the town by *ourselves*" [emphasis added]. Here the future Roman emperor makes his case not as a commander but, at most, as a first among equals.

The final convention in Midst-of-Battle Speeches will be familiar to most readers of military histories: Props. Flags, standards, pistols, swords, hats, whistles, trumpets, fifes, drums, and bugles have all been used to attract attention, signal for action, or inspire soldiers during combat. Their purpose may simply be communicative, as when a flag is waved as a gesture for troops to form around it for some action. But sometimes things serve as real props for a battle speech, as when the object is used to enhance or advance the speaker's message. At bottom the use of props actually comprises a deed, though one that is often accompanied by words. Obvious examples would be a commander waiving his sword in the air and shouting "Forward!" or (in the World War I trenches) an officer blowing his whistle, waving his pistol, and shouting, "Over the top!" Here weapons serve as props to enhance a verbal order to take offensive action.[3] The two examples discussed in the section below involve three props that have figured prominently in the history of battle speeches: the Roman standard, the flag of the modern nation-state, and the pistol.

Structurally, there are two types of Midst-of-Battle Speeches, differentiated by the identity of the speaker and the size of the soldier-audience. The following questions will help clarify the distinctions between them: Who is delivering the speech or performing the deed, and by whom are the words heard or the deed observed? Speaker-focused speeches are more typical. Because Midst-of-Battle Speeches are invariably made by soldiers, the issue of the speaker's rank becomes most relevant. The "top down" speech or deed involves a speaker/actor who commands the unit and a soldier-audience comprising that unit or an individual or individuals from it. The example of Titus exhorting his soldiers as they breached a wall of Tarichaea is typical of the "top down" genre. The "bottom-up" or "sideways" speech or deed involves the simple soldier, as in the example discussed below of the Roman standard-bearer whose words and deeds ultimately inspired his entire legion. The second type of Midst-of-Battle Speech centers on the size of the soldier-audience and seeks to understand when personal conversation—only one-to-one discourses will be considered here—becomes a battle speech.

Words, Not Deeds: A Modern "Top Down" Midst-of-Battle Speech to the Unit

Allied soldiers, sailors and airmen: Through your combined skill, valor and fortitude, you have created in France a fleeting opportunity for a major Allied victory, one whose realization will mean notable progress toward the final downfall of our enemy. In the past I have in moments of unusual significance made special appeals to Allied forces it has been my honor to command. Without exception the response has been unstinted and the result beyond my expectations.

Because this opportunity may be grasped only through the utmost in zeal, determination and speedy action, I make my present appeal to you more urgent than ever before.

I request every airman to make it his direct responsibility that the enemy is blasted unceasingly by day and by night, and is denied safety either in fight or in flight.

I request every sailor to make sure that no part of the hostile forces can either escape or be reinforced by sea, and that our comrades on the land want for nothing that guns and ships and ships' companies can bring to them.

I request every soldier to go forward to his assigned objective with

*the determination that the enemy survive only through surrender: let
no foot of ground once gained be relinquished nor a single German
escape through a line once established.*

Excerpt from General Dwight D. Eisenhower's
Order of the Day, August 13, 1944[4]

IN AMERICAN MILITARY HISTORY at least since the Civil War,
general officers have only rarely personally led troops under fire;
for supreme commanders, it is safe to say that they never have. Unlike so many generals in wars before the past century, the place of senior commanders is now almost universally understood to be in the
rear (or much further back) of frontline combat operations. As Victor
Davis Hanson points out, "[the] novel Greek idea—that the battlefield commander, along with his small staff of subordinates, should at
least be near the hard fighting, if not an active participant in the killing—survived in the West until the onset of the twentieth century."
The reasons why senior generals now lead from the rear are far beyond
the scope of this book, though the practice obviously affects the battle
speech.[5] For one thing, there are no more personally delivered Titus-
style speeches or deeds on the battlefield. Instead, commanders use
communications technology such as the printing press or the radio to
retail their appeals. General Eisenhower's above Order of the Day is
an excellent example of a modern commander's (top-down) Midst-of-
Battle Speech to his soldiers.

In the weeks following the Normandy invasion, the Allied offensive
had stalled in the face of tough German resistance, which had been
aided by the defense-favoring terrain of French hedgerow country.
Eventually, Allied soldiers broke out and attacked the Germans from
the north, west, and south, successfully trapping a large enemy force
in a pocket known as the Falaise Encirclement. The Canadian First
Army and United States Third Army advanced toward each other in
a partially successful effort to seal the gap along this pocket's eastern
line; while considerable German armor and infantry did manage to escape, the Allies captured or killed an estimated sixty thousand soldiers
and destroyed huge quantities of equipment. Eisenhower would later
describe the Falaise battlefield as "one of the greatest 'killing grounds'

of any of the war areas." But that assessment lay in the future. On August 13, 1944, Eisenhower wanted those German forces completely destroyed. To do so he needed to persuade his massive forces that a brief killing window had opened. Eisenhower thus issued the exhortatory Midst-of-Battle speech featured in the epigraph, which amounts to much the same thing as Titus's ancient call to "Seize the opportunity!"—albeit without the deeds.[6]

Each speech, after all, springs from the SitRep Convention; just as Titus premises his actions on informing his men about the opportunities presented by a momentarily divided enemy, so Eisenhower premises his speech on exploiting a similarly brief moment, the fruit of their recent attacks against the Germans. "Through your combined skill, valor and fortitude, you have created in France a fleeting but definite opportunity for a major Allied victory," he declares, complimenting his soldier-audience in much the same way that Titus did ("we have beaten a whole army with a handful of men"). Then Eisenhower adds to his appeal: "Because this opportunity may be grasped only through the utmost in zeal, determination and speedy action," he implores, "I make my present appeal to you more urgent that ever before." In fact, Eisenhower understood that the Falaise Encirclement was incomplete and some German forces were escaping through the gap. Because this leakage hurt the Allies and helped the Germans, destruction by any means became paramount—kill them while they were in range and in motion, for very soon neither condition might apply. Time was essential and immediate violence was required. Thus his exhortation is replete with the appropriate time-and-action words: "grasped . . . utmost in zeal . . . determination . . . speedy action . . . appeal . . . urgent . . . blasted unceasingly by day and by night, denied safety" and so forth.[7]

The Comrade Convention may also be found in Eisenhower's speech. He does not *order* his men to "grasp" the "opportunity" using the "utmost in zeal." (How can zeal be ordered?) Instead, each of his three "action" paragraphs, which are addressed to separate branches of his command, opens with the words *I request*. In part this reflects the fact that Eisenhower's command consisted of soldiers from many nations; as his own career as supreme commander amply demonstrated, in dealing with sometimes fractious foreigners (not to mention several of his own countrymen's outsized egos), he knew that more could be gained by tact than by threats. Moreover, the sentence preceding these "requests" clarifies that this exhortation is not an order but rather a plea: "I make my present appeal to you more urgent than ever before." The reason is somewhat paradoxical: whether soldiers volunteered or were conscripted, the enemy's maximum destruction can only occur through individual, voluntary efforts. When Eisenhower asks that "every airman . . . make it his direct responsibility that the enemy is blasted unceasingly by day and by night and is denied safety either in fight or in flight," he is really asking that pilots and mechanics alter "normal" procedures and schedule more sorties, perhaps in marginal weather or perhaps with less fuel, sleep, ordnance resupply, or equipment maintenance than usual. His request to his soldiers that "no foot of ground once gained be relinquished nor a single German escape through a line once established" is perilously close to a no-retreat order, something that is normally reserved for only the most dire circumstances; it is also something that is notoriously difficult to enforce and so becomes in effect entirely voluntary. Men must be persuaded to do these things, and persuasion is usually best achieved among comrades rather than ordered by distant superiors. Eisenhower's approach is thus soldier-to-soldier.

And for both Titus and Eisenhower the differences in ranks between the speaker and those spoken to go largely unmentioned: everyone is equal in the struggle. Of course, unlike Titus's legions, Eisenhower's army is a highly complex bureaucratic machine in which those who inventory supplies in rear-area stockpiles nevertheless also serve. Thus, the modern commander has if anything a greater incentive to adopt the collective approach in his appeals for victory. Eisenhower's final words make this point: "With all of *us* resolutely performing *our* special tasks *we* can make this week a momentous one in the history of this war—a brilliant and fruitful week for *us* and a fateful one for the ambitions of the Nazi tyrants" [emphasis added].

Evidence of a Moral Contract in Eisenhower's speech also appears in the Comrade Convention passages. It is a different sort of pact than that "proposed" by Titus—the Allied Supreme Commander will not personally drive the first tank into the Falaise line, confident that his loyal troops will abide by their end of the "agreement" and follow. Instead, Eisenhower relies on the comrade's preexisting rights in the Moral Contract. (An officer becomes a comrade, and thus a party to the Moral Contract, in part by force of law (rank) but also by behavior: his moral authority must be earned by bravery, good judgment, fairness, concern for his men's wellbeing, and so forth.) And here posing as a comrade, Eisenhower reminds his men not only that he has authority to order men into battle, but that *he* is also a member of the soldier-audience—Allied forces may be led by him, but they remain a collective, like the thousands of smaller collectives that his soldiers had already forged at the battalion, platoon, or squad level. Thus Eisenhower is entitled to ask for an extra push here, much as a squad leader might ask for extra covering fire while he or his fellow squad members proceed to execute some important task.

Eisenhower's plea is therefore not sealed with a Titus-like display of personal bravery. With a massive fast-moving army under his command, deployed along a front exceeding one hundred miles, there were few efficacious deeds that he himself could perform that would influence any but a tiny handful of soldier-witnesses, a poor tradeoff indeed for the risk. However, in support of Hanson's point (see note 4), Eisenhower was acutely aware of the importance of a commander's personal presence. Six days after the Normandy invasion he visited the beachhead, together with Chief of Naval Operations Admiral Ernest J. King and Army Chief of Staff George C. Marshall. "The importance of such visits by the high command, including, at times, the highest officials of government, can scarcely be overestimated in terms of their value to soldiers' morale," he later wrote. "The soldier has a sense of gratification whenever he sees very high rank in his particular vicinity, possibly on the theory that the area is a safe one or the rank wouldn't be there."[8] *Pace* General Eisenhower, the long history of battle speeches also suggests that soldiers may be gratified by these visits for another reason—the visits demonstrate a willingness of otherwise distant commanders to take the same risks that the soldiers themselves bear. Of course, such visits are not the same thing as leaping into the saddle, riding through a lake, and entering the town at the head of one's army. But they may be the closest modern equivalent.

Bottom-Up Midst-of-Battle Speeches to the Unit

Many of the men had already seen enlisted men fill a leadership void that an officer had left during the battle. One such was a veteran in the 17th Illinois who had already seen action at Fort Donelson. He somehow came over to the green, frightened recruits of the 53rd Ohio, whose colonel had abandoned them, and he helped them respond to the first Confederate rush. "He was a brave, cool man," one witness recollected. "First, he found some Enfield rifle cartridges. . . . Next he went along the line, telling the men he had seen the elephant before, and had learned that the way to meet him was to keep cool, shoot slow and aim low. He [told them] "why, it's just like shooting squirrels—only these squirrels have guns, that's all." Pretty soon he called out: "Good-bye" and . . . he hurried to rejoin his own company"

Anecdote related in Joseph Allan Frank and George A. Reaves, *"Seeing the Elephant": Raw Recruits at the Battle of Shiloh*, 147[9]

SOMETIMES IN THE MIDST of combat it is circumstances, not rank, that will determine who makes the battle speech and provides the leadership. Naturally soldiers would prefer their own officers, if they are trusted. But officers are as vulnerable as any other combatant to death, wounds, and cowardice; at the same time, ordinary soldiers can be quite resilient in fending for themselves when leadership falters or disappears. During the Battle of Shiloh, this was the situation with the Fifty-third Ohio Infantry. Their colonel had vanished and the men were unsure how to operate their muskets (which was not unusual for a novice Civil War regiment); now they faced an advancing battle line of rebels. Under these circumstances there would be no need for any battle speech to include the SitRep Convention.

Fortunately, an anonymous veteran from the Seventeenth Illinois came to the rescue just in time. Here one sees resiliency as a two-sided attribute—first, the anonymous enlisted man was sufficiently alert to recognize the Ohioans' peril and flexible enough to set aside

his own situation to help remedy theirs. Equally important, the Ohioans were able to instantly accept the Illinoisan's moral authority to
make an Instructional Midst-of-Battle Speech about how to fire an
Enfield rifle-musket. This mattered because acceptance was not the
Fifty-third Ohio's only alternative. They could have simply broken and
run, and many regiments in fact did exactly that.

The Illinois soldier's speech was of the "bottom up" variety, and a
close reading of this episode suggests that these speeches operate by
different rules than "top down" speeches. First, unlike officers already
known to the unit or boasting the emblems of higher rank, the "bottom up" speechmaker first must establish his authority to speak. Why
should anybody listen to *him*? Obviously, this temporary crisis of authority is mitigated in cases where an already familiar member of the
ranks steps up. But sometimes the speaker may not be known. Here
the Illinoisan's credentials were apparently announced and accepted
on the spot—he was a battle veteran who also knew the "load-in-
nine" firing drill for the Enfield rifle.

But would any veteran at all who was familiar with the Enfield rifle
have been found sufficiently reassuring by the Fifty-third Ohio so as
to persuade them to remain in line of battle and fight? The answer is
probably no. The Illinoisan had another special credential that was
inseparable from his speech, an attribute that was very clear to those
who shared the moment, though it was more difficult to describe afterward: "He was a brave, cool man." The Illinoisan obviously acted
as if he were not experiencing the same wave of dread as his soldier-
audience. He also made this persona visible to as many of the Buckeye
Staters as he could. In this respect, *he was the speech*. "Next he went
along the line, telling the men he had seen the elephant before, and
had learned the way to meet him was to keep cool, shoot slow and aim
low." This was excellent advice, and the fact that it was given in the
way it was given, as the enemy approached, enhanced its persuasive-
ness. The Illinoisan's message here was not only that he had survived
the siege of Fort Donelson but also that he had been assisted by the
competent handling of his Enfield. And now his presence, his walk
and his talk, assured them that the Enfield could help them too—one
had only to stay disciplined, take the time to fire, and aim low.

What the Illinoisan was actually doing in this Midst-of-Battle Instructional Speech is showing the Ohioans how to reassert control of a situation that was veering out of control. Some men might be killed, others injured, but the Illinoisan was a surety incarnate that there was a way to mitigate these outcomes—the proper, confident use of one's rifle. His final comment was an effort to convert the unfamiliar into the all too familiar, even the mundane, and to do so with a bit of unexpected humor, which always helps to break fear's grip: "Why, it's just like shooting squirrels," he declared, "only these squirrels have guns, that's all." For those Ohioans who were hunters the message was clear. At this distance, the enemy is a target much like any other, a moving form that could be shot using the same techniques already familiar to any Ohioan raised on a family farm. At the same time, the Illinoisan's speech makes no attempt to say that rebels are actually squirrels; quite the contrary, the rebels are armed and shoot back. Nevertheless, the Illinoisan is really reminding his soldier-audience that they are armed, can also shoot, and just might reduce the ranks of those who seek to shoot them. This speech seems utterly genuine and spoken in terms comprehensible to the soldier-audience by a man who, except for his regimental affiliation, must have struck the Buckeye boys as one of their own.

Personal Conversation as Midst-of-Battle Speech: Comfort

As we were rowing up to the vessel which we were to attack, amid a discharge of musketry, I was overpowered by fear, my knees trembled under me, and I seemed on the point of fainting away. Lieutenant Ball, who saw the condition I was in, placed himself close beside me, and still keeping his countenance directed towards the enemy, took hold of my hand, and pressing it in the most friendly manner, said in a low voice, "Courage my dear Boy! Don't be afraid of yourself! You will recover in a minute or so—I was just the same when I first went out in this way." . . . [It] was as if an Angel had put a new Soul into me. With the feeling that I was not yet dishonored, the whole burthen of agony was removed; and from that moment I was as fearless and

forward as the oldest of the boat crew, and on our return the Lieuten-
ant spoke highly of me to our Captain.

> Samuel Taylor Coleridge relating a story about Sir Alexander Ball comforting
> a young comrade during an assault on an enemy ship, as quoted in Adam
> Nicolson, *Seize the Fire: Heroism, Duty, and the Battle of Trafalgar*, 151[10]

THE MIDST-OF-BATTLE SPEECH that many soldiers remember might not be stirring words spoken to the unit but rather personal conversations they had with comrades or officers during the height of a battle. This is the second type of Midst-of-Battle Speech referred to earlier, and it varies depending on the size of the soldier-audience: is the speech or deed intended for a group, or for an individual? In the latter case, a speechmaker will exhort, comfort, or threaten another soldier once, or a series of soldiers one at a time. Traditionally, these speeches or deeds are not considered genuine battle speeches but instead mere anecdotes in a battle's history, something historians use to add life to otherwise lifeless expositions of unit movements or terrain features. The rationale is probably economic—for example, as an influence multiplier, a single word of Titus's army-wide Midst-of-Battle Speech would influence an event's outcome more than a thousand words exchanged between individual soldiers during the same event. However, this is actually misguided, because the one-on-one battle speech *can* have profound unit-wide consequences. General Mattis acknowledged as much in his Pre-Invasion Speech earlier, when he admonished his men to "Share your courage with each other" and "Keep faith in your comrades on your left and right." To understand how influential personal conversation can be, one need only speculate about the Duke of Marlborough's personal although private rebuke in the epigraph above. The duke addressed an audience of one, a man identified only as a "most senior officer," but some important aspect of the battle was probably influenced by the Duke's successful "remoralization" of him. And successful commanders have always known that under combat conditions, for good or for ill, the actions of one soldier can inspire or dispirit a great many others. Three common memes of personal conversation that sometimes function as Midst-of-Battle speeches are considered here: Comfort, Duty, and Threats.

The most important criterion for differentiating mere personal conversation from a battle speech is the purpose of the talk—does it
serve the same function as the grand battle speech, differing only
in the size of its soldier-audience? First of all, we should note that
in many ways, personal conversations better reflect the soul of combat leadership than speeches do. Conversations reveal the quality of
a leader's connection to those he leads, his skill at reading his soldiers, and the steps he will take to motivate, comfort, or steady them
under often horrific conditions. What makes these personal conversations especially remarkable is that while they represent the essence of
human empathy and sympathy, they are delivered at a time when the
speaker has as many (and perhaps more) reasons for fear, paralysis, or
self-absorption as the soldier to whom he speaks.

These may be "little" speeches, too, but when they are delivered
to enough individuals they can exercise an outsized influence. Here
the example of U.S. Army Lieutenant Richard Shea represents a typical situation where a personal conversation frequently repeated might
ultimately comfort an entire unit. During an especially tense time at
the Second Battle of Pork Chop Hill, as some soldiers became un-
nerved by Chinese propaganda blasted by loudspeaker into the American trenches each night, Lieutenant Shea sought to steady his men
not by discipline but by brotherly compassion. "When Shea saw or
heard the younger GI's expressions of fear, he would reassuringly put
his arm on their shoulders, giving them words of encouragement," one
man remembered. "'Don't let it get to you,'" [Shea said.] "'Everything's
going to be OK. We're in good shape.'"[11]

Most readers of military history, especially memoirs, diaries, and
letters, will immediately recognize this common anecdote of soldiers
comforting other soldiers in combat *tête-à-têtes* as a meme. As in Lieutenant Shea's case, these conversations may be equivalent to the unit
battle speech not only by their themes but also because, by the time an
officer has completed his "comfort rounds," the number of individuals
to whom he has spoken might equal an entire unit. And while fear can
grip combat veterans as well as novices, these speeches are usually remembered best by those for whom combat experience is new.

Such comfort seems to come in two varieties. The first is illustrated by Lieutenant Shea and depends for its success on the speaker having specific credibility due to some (mysterious) combination of previous combat experience, personal bravery, and even temperament. By all accounts, Shea, who was awarded a Medal of Honor posthumously, seems to have possessed these traits in abundance. This is really a Declaration of Confidence, and no reason for the reassurance need be given other than the fact that Shea offers it. Shea does not explain why "everything will be OK," nor does he offer any reasons why he believes the unit is "in good shape." No reasons are necessary. Shea's audiences simply assume that because he possesses superior knowledge and experience, his Declaration of Confidence must have a reasonable basis. A leader's ability to pull off this kind of speech moves inversely to the surrounding danger—the higher the danger, the more credibility a leader must possess. Thus under combat conditions, this approach would seem to be the sole prerogative of leaders whose personal credibility with their commands is near absolute.[12]

The case of Sir Alexander Ball featured above represents another important angle for the personal comfort speech: the battle speech-maker who explains why a soldier (or sailor) should feel, if not unafraid in combat, at least unafraid of his fear. This is not just a matter of socially constructed notions of honor. Fear is also physiological and can be accompanied by the kinds of embarrassing symptoms that Coleridge's interlocutor reported ("my knees trembled under me, and I seemed on the point of fainting away"), as well as paralysis and the loss of bowel and bladder control. Each of these reactions to fear undermines personal dignity and self-confidence in an environment in which such distractions can be lethal. Of course, Ball's motive for offering words of comfort can be understood either on humanitarian grounds or, more coldly, as a ploy to increase the odds of his own survival by maximizing his wayward comrades' fighting capacity.

The scene is indeed a vivid one. A British boarding party in an open boat is rowing toward an enemy frigate, a ship whose deck would have been higher than that of the approaching craft. Thus, the enemy, already alerted to the attack, has only to fire down from the frigate, perhaps behind some cover. Thus the British sailors are quite literally rowing into sheets of hellfire unleashed by the simultaneous discharge of a line of musketry. To boot, these perils are completely visible to Coleridge's interlocutor, who is "a very young midshipman."

Ball would later become one of the great admirals in the British Navy, a friend and confident of Lord Nelson and the man who helped bring British rule to the island of Malta.[13] However, on that day a much younger Ball acted toward his still younger charge as both an elder brother and a commander. The reason why the boy paid attention was because Ball had probably established his moral authority, less through rank than through his greater experience and his willingness to share it (quite like the Illinoisan at Shiloh). But Ball is not dispensing technical advice on firearms, he is offering something entirely different—presence of mind in the midst of hell. First, Ball takes the young man's hand and squeezes it—the counterpart to Lieutenant Shea's placing his arm around the shoulder of his soldiers. This is more than simple human contact: the seemingly instinctive gesture is a deed that prepares the boy for how Ball will use his own experience to steady him in the face of death. Ball will reenact a timeless ritual of the veteran using speech and deeds to comfort the novice, but his conclusions will nevertheless be supported by reason.

First of all, Ball favors very discreet staging. Taking the boy's hand and offering comfort "in a low voice" succeeds in not publicly calling attention to what must have been obvious symptoms of uncontrolled fear. As Adam Nicolson points out in *Seize the Fire*, Ball understands that these symptoms are not cowardice but rather a normal physiological reaction to combat; by offering comfort discreetly, Ball safeguards the young man's honor, an important strategy in rehabilitating his confidence. Indeed, as Nicolson notes, Ball does not even look at the boy as he speaks but instead "at the enemy . . . a gesture which itself preserves the young boy's honor." Nicolson concludes that Ball's actions represent the "community of honor vivified by an act of loving care" and adds that they comprise "one of the foundations of the British victory at Trafalgar: glory as an outgrowth of love." But understood in the long history of battle speeches, Ball's brief speech embodies principles that transcend this particular event.[14]

Ball's discretion immediately signals to the boy that what is to follow will not rebuke but support. "Courage my dear boy!" is Ball's opening gambit. "Dear" is affectionate and softens the immediately following admonishment, which contains a profound insight at a time when profundity is perhaps rare: "Don't be afraid of yourself!" While neither Ball nor the boy can control the immediate actions of the enemy—the next volley of musketry, an aimed ball, a lucky shot—each can control his own feelings and actions. After all, under the circumstances, inner thoughts and external deeds are all that remain *to* control. Ball makes no effort to deny or even minimize the dangers posed by the enemy without—such a tack would be instantly disbelieved and thus fail in its purpose, which is to steel his young charge for the task ahead. Instead, Ball focuses on the enemy within. Ball concludes his argument by presenting the most persuasive evidence of all—his own experience. "You will recover in a minute or so," he counsels. "I was just the same when I first went out this way."

This is comfort's very soul. Ball, an obviously brave man who is facing death once again, momentarily draws the boy into a place safer than the surrounding chaos—the comfort of personal (and survived!) experience. Thus Ball becomes proof incarnate of several important propositions. First, like the anonymous Illinoisan at Shiloh, he has previously faced this situation and has lived to tell the tale. Now he is here to share his surplus mental energy with the boy, giving the obvious impression that these situations are survivable and that combat does not mean (only) death. Second, Ball demonstrates that one can experience the physiological symptoms of fear and still not be a coward ("I was just the same when I first went out in this way"). Feeling afraid, or suffering the involuntary physical symptoms of overwhelming fear, is not cowardice; what's more, the moment will pass. Most importantly, Ball's entire speech shows the boy that he is not alone, either existentially or experientially. Ball has sailed this course before, is sailing it now as he holds the boy's hand, and will probably live to sail it again. Thus does the veteran Ball connect this boy with the universal experience of war: its physical and moral sensations as well as the prospect, factual or merely anecdotal, that in most combat situations, most sailors will not die.

The midshipman's reaction, at least as recalled by him years later as he related the incident to Coleridge, testifies to Ball's great success here. First, Ball understood not just the boy's fear but also how that fear was manifested in the specific social-military context of the eighteenth-century Royal Navy: fear of dishonor. "With the feeling that I was not yet dishonored, the whole burthen of agony was removed," the sailor recalled. (It is unlikely that Ball actually taught him anything new about honor; rather, Ball's speech dispelled any imagined connection between *experiencing* fear and dishonor.) Obviously, beneath this "burthen of agony" was the boy's willingness to do his duty and then some. "[From] that moment I was as fearless and forward as the oldest of the boat crew," he recalled. And however the boy behaved during the fray was obviously to Ball's satisfaction. "[On] our return," the sailor recalled with satisfaction, "Lieutenant [Ball] spoke highly of me to our Captain."

Personal Conversation as Midst-of-Battle Speech: Duty

[Specialist John "Brad"] Thomas's words ["Man, I really don't want to go back out there"] expressed how everyone felt. How could [Staff Sergeant Struecker] force those men back out into the fight, especially the men who had just come through hell to get back to base? The sergeant knew all the men were watching to see how he'd handle it. . . . Challenged like this, they expected Struecker to explode.

Instead, he pulled Thomas aside and spoke to him quietly, man to man. He tried to calm him, but Thomas was calm. As Struecker saw it, the man had just decided he'd taken all he could take. Thomas had just been married a few months before. He had never been one of the chest-beaters in the regiment. It was a perfectly rational decision. He did not want to go back out there to die. The whole city was shooting at them. How far could they get? However steep a price the man would pay for backing down like that, and for a Ranger it would be a steep price indeed, to Struecker it looked like Thomas had made up his mind.

"Listen," Struecker said. "I understand how you feel. I'm married, too. Don't think of yourself as a coward. I know you're scared. I'm scared shitless. I've never been in a situation like this either. But we've

got to go. It's our job. The difference between being a coward and hero
is not whether you're scared, it's what you do while you're scared."
    Thomas didn't seem to like the answer. He walked away.

Conversation among servicemen related in Mark Bowden's
Black Hawk Down: A Story of Modern War[15]

WORDS AND DEEDS may be used in personal conversation to
persuade soldiers to fight, by reminding them of their obligations to country, unit, each other, or themselves. In the previous section Sir Alexander Ball used comfort and his veteran's experience to
restore his comrade to the fight. Staff Sergeant Jeff Struecker's example above illustrates another approach. Here the sergeant had the un-
enviable task of persuading a fellow army ranger, a man who that day
had already performed bravely in combat, to return to the battlefield
(the city of Mogadishu) in order to rescue comrades who were trapped
by the enemy. However, unlike Ball's interlocutor, who suffered from
extreme anxiety, Specialist Thomas's emotional reactions to combat
were behind him. Earlier, on exiting a bullet-ridden Humvee that had
just returned from the battle, Thomas, blood-drenched from cradling
the body of a dead friend, had "lost it," shouting, "I can't go back out
there! I can't! They're shooting from everywhere!'" But by the time
Struecker spoke with Thomas, his state of mind, although not his conclusion, had changed. As narrator Mark Bowden describes it, Thomas
had "made a calculated decision, a perfectly rational one. He'd taken
all he could take. He'd just been married a few months before. He was
not going to go out there and die." In other words, Sergeant Struecker
had to persuade a self-possessed man to return to an extremely dangerous situation. The interaction between Struecker and Thomas illustrates how the Moral Contract—in this case, its provisions dealing
with duty—is addressed by one soldier and self-enforced by a soldier-
audience of another.

    Ball and Struecker's approaches are similar in one respect: both
use their personal experience to establish trust. Relating personal experience can be a powerful invitation for soldier-audiences to break
through their self-absorption and reconnect with peers. Struecker is

not trying to say that the return trip is necessarily survivable, but simply that Thomas is not alone: "I understand how you feel. I'm married, too. . . . I know you're scared," Struecker offers. "I'm scared shitless. I've never been in a situation like this either." It is by such time-tested strategies of personal identification that speakers of every variety have always gained the trust of their audiences, no matter the size.

But establishing personal trust is only the opener, not the argument. Ball used his remembrance of combat to establish the Rooseveltian proposition that the only thing the young midshipman had to fear was fear itself. But what Struecker has thus far conceded to Thomas is quite different. Unlike Ball, whose argument is based on his personal experience (that in combat the future will resemble the past), Struecker declares the opposite—he has never experienced anything like the urban warfare of Mogadishu and can offer no assurance whatsoever about the future.

All of Sergeant Struecker's assertions thus far—that he and Thomas are both married, frightened, and facing a novel experience of war— could just as easily justify abandoning the battle as returning to it. All Struecker has actually done is persuade Thomas to listen. But this is enough to allow Struecker to make his first argument: "But we've *got to go*," he implores. "It's our *job*" [emphasis added]. Here is the first of two calls to duty, framed by the Comrade Convention (Struecker includes himself in these calls to duty) but relying on a legal argument. By "our job" Struecker was likely referring to the kind of obligations contained or implied in the contract Thomas signed when he enlisted. After all, the sergeant's order was lawful, appropriate, and even laudable under the circumstances—to return to the battlefield and rescue comrades. Had Thomas's refusal led to some formal disciplinary action, a future court martial would probably have sustained Struecker as a matter of black-letter law.

But Struecker does not end his argument by appealing to legally required duties. His plea contains a second appeal to a higher duty, one that lies outside of any enlistment agreement or provision of the Uniform Code of Military Justice. It is even different from the one contained in the Moral Contract—the duty to rescue, if at all possible, endangered comrades. What Struecker argues in the end is that Thomas has a duty to himself. "The difference between being a coward and hero is not whether you're scared, it's what you do while you're scared," he counsels. The center of his argument is not "them" (the comrades in need of rescue), nor is it "I" (as in "I order you to do this"), nor is it the obvious understanding of "you" (as in "you will be punished or disgraced if you fail to obey"). Rather, the argument is made to a different understanding of "you"—the "you" of moral agency, the "you" that for soldiers must sometimes transcend personal survival to consider what "moral" quality life on any terms will have. (Few civilians are asked to make these choices. For example, an ordinary man fleeing a burning building generally is not expected by himself or others to first search every room for potential victims. It is enough that he tells the fire department about what he knows.) In short, if Thomas refuses to go, the most damaging consequence will be the potential of a lifetime of profound regret.

Perhaps also factored into Thomas's thinking at this point were the independent conclusions that two other comrades reached in deciding to join the rescue convoy. One soldier, whose arm was in a cast and who thus had a "legal" right to remain in safety on the base, was prompted by the Moral Contract to cut off his cast and demand a place on the returning Humvees. Another soldier followed his cast-unbound comrade not "out of passion or solidarity or patriotism" but because he "didn't dare refuse"—a case where peer pressure caused him to adhere to his legal obligations as a soldier. At first, of course, Thomas decided to emulate neither of these soldiers. Perhaps confused or put off by Struecker's argument, "He walked away." And while there may have been recriminations later, Struecker, in deciding for one-on-one conversation rather than a more public exchange, had no intention of embarrassing Thomas or trying to stimulate his moral agency by using peer pressure. In fact, nothing might have happened to Thomas, or in the blur of an extremely emotional circumstance, perhaps his refusal to return would have been forgotten (except, of course, by Thomas). Perhaps even if had been charged later with disobedience, he might have successfully ginned up a defense on the grounds of some emotional trauma—after all, the dead comrade whose blood drenched his uniform had been a close friend. As the convoy was about to return to Mogadishu's hellish alleys and streets, Sergeant Struecker probably had other things on his mind than Thomas's refusal to come. But despite his earlier objections, Thomas had quietly taken a seat in one of the Humvees. Perhaps moved by Struecker's words, he had apparently decided that in these circumstances, to rescue trapped comrades was also to rescue himself.

Personal Conversation as Midst-of-Battle Speech: Threats

En route to the bunker, [Lieutenant] Russell encountered a private from one of George Company's platoons. The soldier was sitting down alone in a roofless area midway in the communication trench, leaning against its wall. Russell stopped and, knowing the soldier's platoon needed him, asked the private, "Where's your platoon?" "I don't know," came the reply. Concerned the soldier had no support in sight, could give no support to any of the hill's dwindling number of defenders, and was exposed to persistent incoming artillery and mortar rounds, the company commander ordered, "Go find your platoon." Without hesitation, the soldier firmly replied, "No."

Russell didn't hesitate. He drew his .45 pistol and, moving to place the muzzle against the soldier's head, ordered again, "Go find your platoon. That's an order. See this pistol. You know what it can do." There was a brief frightening pause for both the soldier and his commander. Then the soldier got to his feet, turned, and walked up the trench line toward the area held by Pork Chop's defenders.

> Lieutenant Walt Russell, as quoted in Bill McWilliams's
> *On Hallowed Ground: The Last Battle for Pork Chop Hill*[16]

THE CHIEF PREMISE of this book is that what motivates men to join a military, learn to wage war, and finally do battle is persuasion, not force. And the vast majority of battle speeches and deeds from all ages support that conclusion. However, it would be foolish to deny that force has not sometimes been used to motivate men to fight. General George G. Meade's Pre-Battle Speech threat to kill disobedient soldiers was discussed in the last chapter. In that case, almost by definition, the threat is prospective and hypothetical; no instances have yet happened and it is possible that none will. But in a Midst-of-Battle situation the case is different—the offending act may have already occurred, or may actually be occurring, when the speechmaker applies Threat; moreover, because Midst-of-Battle Threat is usually invoked in the most dire circumstances, the Threat is likely to be followed by an immediate summary execution. If the historians and manual writers of antiquity are trustworthy on this point, Threat followed by death was perhaps more than occasional. Although the positive effects of summary executions were doubtful in the long term, Frontinus reports that Clearchus "used to tell his troops that their commander ought to be feared more than the enemy, meaning that the death they feared in battle was doubtful, but that execution for desertion was certain."[17]

In Western societies, as modern notions of the rule of law and due process were extended into military domains, summary executions became less frequent; at this point, as far as can be known, they have vanished. The current Uniform Code of Military Justice contains a variety of capital offenses but no express authority for a commander to summarily execute a soldier who, for example, in the face of an enemy refuses to obey a direct order, commits an act of cowardice, or leads a mutiny.[18] Nevertheless, as suggested by the previous epigraph, threats of death may occur in extreme circumstances. Perhaps because neither threatener nor threatened has any incentive to raise the issue later, most of these events are unrecorded. And in the U.S. military, there are no recent episodes on record where a commander has summarily executed a soldier for some willful failure of duty during combat. Thus, the use of credible death threats, at least in recent Midst-of-Battle Speeches, is almost unknown.

The episode recalled by Lieutenant Walter Russell is one instance of a relatively recent Midst-of-Battle Speech that did threaten summary execution for disobedience. The dialogue suggests what may be a pattern for these kinds of speech-deed events. Russell first establishes the facts, which in this case amounted to disobedience of a direct order during some very intense combat. ("Go find your platoon." "No.") What followed next was a deed coupled with a speech. The deed was probably necessary, as words alone had already been tried and had failed. For Russell to simply declare "Go find your platoon or I will shoot you" might have avoided the deed but just as likely would have only added an extra step—if the anonymous soldier had continued to disobey, Russell would then have been forced to proceed as he in fact did, drawing his pistol and making the threat real. Instead, the lieutenant acted more efficiently, immediately placing the pistol's muzzle against the soldier's head and thereby succinctly encapsulating what might be called the Clearchus Choice. The soldier now faced (he apparently believed) a more certain death from Russell's pistol than from the Chinese enemy.

But there is another, more interesting aspect to this speech-deed event. To be successful—that is, to act in a way so as to avoid having to act (and shoot the soldier)—the threat must be absolutely convincing. It must leave no doubt in the subject's mind that he faces not only death but, in particular, all that he fears about combat death— blood, pain, mutilation, bodily dismemberment. First, Russell conveys this message by adding what at first seem to be gratuitous words: "See this pistol. You know what it can do." Of course, the soldier, who has been through basic training, knows what a .45-caliber sidearm "can do." Moreover, having survived thus far the bloody combat of Pork Chop Hill, he would also have known what metal projectiles "can do" by simply looking around him. Yet these words now summon the soldier's apparent worst fears. And the words, combined with the tactile sensation of a muzzle pressed against his scalp, were obviously overwhelming. Russell was extremely ambivalent about this act—historian Bill McWilliams, who learned of it during an interview with Russell decades later, characterized the once-young lieutenant's feelings: "A shaken Russell wondered, and to this day, still wonders, what he would have done if the soldier again refused to obey his order." Nevertheless, the words and the deed worked, and the soldier returned to his unit.

Props and the Midst-of-Battle Speech

These perils [an amphibious landing in deep water off Britain] frightened our soldiers, who were quite unaccustomed to battles of this kind, with the result that they did not show the same alacrity and enthusiasm as they usually did in battles on dry land. . . . But as the Romans still hesitated, chiefly on account of the depth of water, the man who carried the eagle of the 10th legion, after praying to the gods that his action might bring good luck to the legion, cried in a loud voice: "Jump down, comrades, unless you want to surrender our eagle to the enemy; I, at any rate, mean to do my duty to my country and my general." With these words he leapt out of the ship and advanced towards the enemy with the eagle in his hands. At this the soldiers, exhorting each other not to submit to such a disgrace, jumped with one accord from the ship, and the men from the next ships, when they saw them, followed them and advanced against the enemy.

Related by Julius Caesar about the first invasion of Britain, 55 BCE[19]

GENERAL McCLELLAN, in the section on Personal Recognition in chapter 5, illustrated the use of physical objects in battle speeches, especially flags. There each soldier had invested the object —a regimental flag—with a double identity: the regiment's and his own. Thus, to compliment the flag was also to compliment the soldier. In this section we will discuss the somewhat different meanings of objects that are used in the Midst-of-Battle Speech, when things are typically displayed and combined with words during a battle in order to motivate soldiers to accept the increased risks of closing with the enemy. These objects are referred to here as "props," as the word is used in the theater: "Those objects that are necessary to the action of a dramatic work: (other than scenery, costumes, and fixed furnishings): weapons, documents, cigarettes, items of food and drink, etc."[20]

In this case the prop-wielder is usually the speaker. Thus, as was illustrated by Major (later Major General) Wadsworth in chapter 4, the speech may be "top down"—commander to subordinates—or, as illustrated above by the anonymous Roman standard-bearer, "bottom up" or "sideways"—subordinate to subordinate. But both of these Midst-of-Battle examples differ from the use of props in Personal Recognition: here props bundle a particular set of notions, often timebound, that might include ideas of divinity, comradeship, guilt, masculinity, national, tribal, or religious loyalties, which often stimulate peer pressure.

Caesar's tactical predicament was every amphibious warrior's nightmare—his fleet (eighty transports and warships) had such a deep draught they could not be beached close-in to Britain's shore. Armorclad soldiers were thus forced to disembark in deep water while under attack from the heavily armed British tribes that had gathered to oppose the landing. "[The Roman] soldiers, unfamiliar with the ground, with their hands full, and weighed down by the heavy burden of their arms, had at the same time to jump down from the ships, get a footing in the waves, and fight the enemy," Caesar later wrote. In response to this unfolding disaster, Caesar ordered only his warships ("swifter and easier to handle than the transports, and likely to impress the natives more by their unfamiliar appearance") to sail a short distance downshore and land hard on the enemy's unprotected right flank. "This maneuver was highly successful," Caesar reported. "Scared by the strange shape of the warships, the motion of the oars, and the unfamiliar machines, the natives halted and then retreated a little." But if Caesar sought to use psychology against his adversary, he quickly discovered that his legions had some psychological problems of their own—following their first landing attempt, his soldiers were now twice shy about entering the water at this new location. Thus was the scene set for the Roman standard-bearer's "bottom up" speech and deeds.[21]

To grasp the full import of what happened next one must first understand the Roman standard and its significance for Roman soldiers. Standards were specially decorated staffs whose exact appearance likely varied somewhat during the Roman army's long history but whose presence in the front ranks was a constant. In part, standards, like modern-era battle flags, served practical purposes. Some standards were topped by *vexilla* or flags (usually red) that are described by historian Adrian Goldsworthy as "suspended from a cross-bar to hang down in front of the main shaft" in order to locate "the commander's position in camp before a battle and on the battlefield." Each "century" within a legion (during Caesar's time, at least on paper, a legion consisted of ten cohorts with six eighty-man centuries per cohort) would have its own *signa,* poles "topped by either an ornamental spearhead or upraised hand" whose "shafts were heavily decorated with crosspieces, wreathes, and from two to six large discs." (The exact meaning of these decorations has been lost.) But the most important standards were those topped by the *aquila,* or eagle, an "object of massive reverence." And it is here that many of the Roman army's standards may have functionally and symbolically departed from the West's battle flags of a millennium and a half later—their potential religious significance. Tertullian, who lived two hundred years after Caesar, declared in his *Apology* that "The whole religion of the camp is a worshipping of standards, a swearing by the standards, a setting up of the standards above all gods." What this suggests about Caesar's anonymous *signifier* (standard-bearer) was that the symbol he carried as he leapt into Britain's waters was considerably more persuasive than the Western flag of the nineteenth century and afterward.[22]

Thus it may be significant that the Tenth Legion's *signifier* only spoke and jumped into the water "after praying to the gods that his action might bring good luck to the legion." Whether he prayed aloud or silently is not stated, but if standards had religious meaning, this man's prayers presumably carried more weight than those offered by ordinary soldiers. In any case, such prayers would also have evoked the standard's religious significance. Afterward the *signifier* made his Midst-of-Battle Speech: "Jump down, comrades, unless you want to surrender our eagle to the enemy," he shouted. "I, at any rate, mean to do my duty to my country and to my general." As was the case with Titus's Midst-of-Battle Speech, the *signifier's* words here become his pledge, one only he could fulfill by his own act: "With these words he leapt out of the ship and advanced towards the enemy with the eagle in his hands."

Caesar's description of how the *signifier's* soldier-audience responded to his words and deeds also indicates the spread of its influence throughout an army. First is the immediate experience of those closest to the *signifier*: "At this the soldiers, exhorting each other not to submit to such a disgrace, jumped with one accord from the ship." (Here is an example of a battle speech moving "sideways.") And what was the disgrace? The *signifier* had sealed a unilateral contract with his peers by pledging not only his own wellbeing but also the safety of the chief symbol of the legion's honor and perhaps the goodwill of the gods. Throughout Western military history, allowing a comrade to fight alone when help is available transgresses the Moral Contract; in this case, permitting the legion's honor to be besmirched (as well as perhaps risking the gods' grace) was apparently unthinkable. The *signifier's* speech was therefore suddenly replicated by many other speeches from comrade to comrade as soldiers "exhort[ed] each other not to submit to such a disgrace." By now the *signifier* and his prop had become inseparable—both required not so much rescue as redemption. Had the *signifier* jumped into the water alone, some comrades may have followed him; had he hurled his standard into the ranks of the enemy, some comrades might have jumped in and attempted to retrieve it. Placing both in harm's way simultaneously, however, was provocation of the noblest sort to every soldier who witnessed it.[23]

One can easily imagine Caesar's warships in parallel lines perpendicular to the shore. By looking off the sides of each vessel, most soldiers could easily see their comrades on at least two other ships. This facilitated peer pressure and explains what happened next: "And the men from the next ships, when they saw them, followed them and advanced against the enemy." Here the original words and deeds created significant ripples. The sight of comrades entering the water made it appear manageable and, of course, valiant. In all likelihood, the wider soldier-audience learned of the *signifier's* words and deeds only much later, if at all. But here Caesar provides a perfect model of how one soldier might influence the behavior of hundreds of others.

By 1861 *signa* had vanished. The conventional means for unit identification in camp, on the march, and during battles had become instead the flag. Although venerated from the standpoint of civic religion, some national flags, such as those of France or the United States, had no Christian (the majority faith in both countries) roots at all. Instead, these modern flags were the products of much more recent traditions, most of which were not yet beyond living memory at this time. Nevertheless, nationalism was a lesser faith, the dying for which might not assure the soul's immortality, though it would guarantee the continuance of the nation to a "grateful posterity." This flag had become the nation's emblem, symbolizing all of the attributes of that lesser faith—history, foundational myths, and exceptionalism. Thus readers will recall from chapter 4 that when a mounted Major James

S. Wadsworth appeared in front of the Fourteenth Brooklyn (readers will recall meeting this regiment in chapter 3) at First Bull Run with a "proposal" to lead them into battle, he counted on these attributes to persuade the New Yorkers to accept his leadership. Unlike the bottom up illustration of Caesar's *signifier,* Wadsworth provides a picturesque example of words and props-as-deeds emanating from the top down in a Midst-of-Battle Speech.

At least as preserved in memory, Wadsworth's presence is its own tableau of power and color. With the raging battle serving as the *mise-en-scène,* one can imagine him surrounded by the props of his rank, on horseback with a raised revolver in one hand and the flag's folds in the other, delivering a classic Midst-of-Battle Instructional Speech probably first uttered by some anonymous prehistorical warrior: "Follow me, boys." It would have been worthy of Jacques-Louis David, had he been alive to paint it.[24] Of course, as was discussed in the introduction, the difficulty with memory is its tendency to meld tenses. In 1861, James S. Wadsworth was neither a major general nor an "old veteran." Rank and combat experience would come later. Moreover, it is unlikely that Wadsworth was then a man whom "the soldiers all loved." Bull Run was his first battle, and in it he served as General Irwin McDowell's aide-de-camp, not as a field commander. But he *was* indisputably the largest landowner in the Empire State (fifteen thousand acres) and one of America's wealthiest men; at fifty-five years of age, he was also one of the army's older officers. Nevertheless, Wadsworth's "dash and courage"—or recklessness, as some would later describe his battle temperament—was a thing to be admired, if occasionally feared; on July 21, 1861, it was certainly the former.[25]

It is possible that Wadsworth considered his own elite background in deciding to perform deeds as well as speak words to motivate the Fourteenth Brooklyn to close with the rebels. His wealth, his Harvard and Yale education, and his training for the law could not be confused with military credibility, and at the time of First Bull Run, he had none. Instead, Wadsworth would use deeds—brandishing or holding the props of command—to compensate. He had his rank and his horse, but the flag and revolver were more persuasive props under the circumstances. Unlike situations involving Threats, Wadsworth's revolver was not aimed at the men he sought to persuade; rather, he used it to symbolically perform his end of the unilateral "contract" that he was about to propose. And his handling of the colors not only served to personalize an otherwise nonexistent personal connection with the Fourteenth Brooklyn but also linked the immediate cause represented by the flag (vindicating the nation by winning the battle) with the great violence required to achieve it (his revolver). Thus were cause and country, victory and violence connected in Wadsworth's physical person. It was left only for the stout, silver-haired major to utter his one-line Midst-of-Battle Instructional Speech. Indeed, anything beyond "Follow me, boys" would probably have been superfluous. The props added the rest of the content.

What the Fourteenth Brooklyn's soldier-audience was actually thinking just before and during Wadsworth's performance is no longer recoverable. But the narrator's recollection of the color-bearer stepping forward is significant, not only for its dramatic quality but also for the fact (think of Caesar's *signifier*) that whatever his comrades *were* thinking may have suddenly changed following his dramatic, probably timeless response: "General, I'll follow you anywhere." In the loose sense of moral contractual persuasion used in this chapter, Color Sergeant Frank Head's declaration amounted to an acceptance by the entire unit of Wadsworth's proposal. The revolver, the colors, the mounted major, and the color sergeant's response all forged a bond cemented by words and deeds.

Rallying Men

In this emergency Gen. Joshua T. Owen proved himself a hero. He was the only officer of note at hand. He sat on his horse, while the "rebel" batteries commenced to play pretty lively music. Their shells or shot seemed to be on a line with Gen. Owen's head. There appeared to be a sort of weakening in some parts of our line. . . . Gen. Owen never blinked an eye and seemed entirely unaware of the rebel shells . . . but he noticed the slight wavering of our men on the left, and he turned, and with ringing words, some of which I still remember, he said, "Men! If you are allowed to be driven from these works you are not worthy to be called Americans!" [He] shouted, "What is man if manhood has left you?" He stated how long he had been in the service, that if there was a point to be gained, he would notice and lead them to it. His words quickly and forcibly uttered could be heard above the din and there is no doubt they inspired confidence. The men seemed determined, Gen. Owen noticed it, and wound up his remarks with the words and what seemed a delighted countenance. "Now we'll wait for Johnny."

The recollection of the Battle of Spotsylvania contained in "James Donnelly, Late Corporal Co. D, 20th Mass. Vols. Sketch of his Life"

All the while, Carlson kept assuring his crew that everything was all right and that it was only a matter of time before they spotted the submarines. He reminded everyone of their motto, "Gung Ho," and of how important it was to work together. He had faith in them and they must have faith in him. Together they would get through this.

Lieutenant-Colonel Carlson's words to his men awaiting submarine rescue off Makin Island, August 1942, as quoted in George W. Smith, *Carlson's Raid: The Daring Assault on Makin*[26]

THE WAVE ACTION of military operations during a battle is often paralleled by the emotional state of its combatants. The experience of combat can be elating (Winston Churchill once said, "Nothing in life is so exhilarating as to be shot at without result") but also boring, terrifying, numbing, or abjectly depressing.[27] These swings can be pegged to tactical outcomes—victory, stalemates, and defeats all provoke different feelings. Many of this book's speeches represent exhilarating peaks or precipices of anticipation—the charged atmospheres of recruiting, pre-battles, or pre-invasions. But Midst-of-Battle Speeches made during tactical and mental troughs are just as important to the military enterprise. They come at times when victory is elusive or an exit from some dire tactical strait is impossible to imagine. These moods of despondency or panic can also spell great danger for an army. The circumstances are usually emergent and the stakes nothing less than survival. The battle speechmaker will usually say and do what he must in order to prevent panic or remoralize the soldier-audience.

Thus there are two connected memes found in many Midst-of-Battle Speeches meant to rally men from these troughs. The first is the Expedience Convention. Military emergencies can justify almost any words and deeds necessary to extract soldiers from destruction—that is, death or capture. The second convention is Hope. Unless death or capture is inevitable (and soldiers can be persuaded to accept them), a way out of the predicament must be shown or hinted at. In short, in order to prevent flight or destruction, soldiers must be given some hope that fighting on might produce a better result.

The examples featured in the epigraph illustrate two troughs often encountered in military literature. General Joshua T. Owen exhorting disorganized Federals to defend against oncoming Confederates during the battle of Spotsylvania is one example of the rallying word and deed. Here, a loud voice, the right words, and the appearance of self-possession demonstrated to those Federal soldiers within earshot and eyesight what they might expect of themselves while providing them with leadership that seemed unfazed by falling artillery shells or a rapidly closing enemy. By his cool example and exhortations, Owen succeeded in restoring order among frightened, disorganized men. In the case of Carlson's Raiders, the bloody attack on Makin Island was over and enemy reinforcements were expected soon. The Raiders had separated during the action; by nightfall, some had overcome the rain, high wind, and surf and successfully returned to their submarines, waiting offshore. But those under Colonel Carlson's immediate command found themselves in small boats, tossed about in rough seas at night, waiting impatiently at the rendezvous point for a late submarine. Here Carlson rallies his men in what seems to have been a far softer voice than Owen's, using unit slogans and dispensing confidence and hope. Although separated by seventy-eight years, both cases reveal how the Expedience and Hope Conventions govern what battle speechmakers will say and do to focus, inspire, or simply relax soldiers in the midst of battle.

The battle of Spotsylvania could serve as a paradigm of operational (and emotional) wave action. In the foggy predawn of May 12, 1864, Federal forces quickly overcame the surprised Confederates behind the strong entrenchments of Spotsylvania's Mule Shoe, the nicknamed salient in Robert E. Lee's otherwise impregnable line. The attack was successful and the stunned rebel defenders either retreated or surrendered en masse. The Federals, death locked in a bloody, running, inconclusive brawl with the Army of Northern Virginia for over a week, were elated. It looked like victory. But there were dangers in this particular kind of victory. The Federals continued their pursuit pell-mell after retreating Confederates. The blue lines, so meticulously arranged earlier that morning, became disorganized in the frenzied chase. And at the first sign of a rebel pushback, there was trouble. "We came right plum up to an advancing [rebel] line of battle before we were aware of it," Corporal Donnelly wrote. "It was our turn to fall back. And we fell back on the dead run." Retreating to the entrenchments they had captured just hours earlier, the fleeing Federals found that all was confusion. While some units had pursued the enemy, others had remained at the works, milling about, and were now "promiscuously mixed up with their regiments." With organization lost, the erstwhile victors suddenly found themselves on the defensive and facing the prospect of defeat. All that had been gained could be lost, and worse yet beckoned. It was here that General Owen met and mastered the moment.[28]

A glance at the fast-approaching rebel line of battle coupled with the sounds of bursting artillery shells comprised its own situation report, obviating the need for Owen to include any SitRep Convention. He had only to remind his men of the Moral Contract and demonstrate his personal adherence to the same; he would seal his expectations of them by his own conduct. And what Donnelly remembers before any words were spoken was the deed—Owen sitting impassively on his horse while shells passed by his head "with that terrifying schreech [sic]" (unexcerpted portion). "Gen. Owen never blinked an eye and seemed entirely unaware of the rebel shells." Owen's deed was simply to remain on horseback, an obvious target, and to beam perfect self-control amidst a situation as potentially deadly as that faced by any soldier in any war. But of course, Owen was not "unaware" of rebel shells or anything else that was happening on his stretch of the Federal line. Donnelly believed that the general saw the "weakening" and, as matters grew more critical, the "wavering" of parts of that line.

It was then that Owen decided that deeds alone were insufficient. They must be augmented by words.

But what words? Under these circumstances, Owen would say what he had to in order to steady men who were beginning to reveal unsteadiness. And the first words that Owen chooses—"Men! If you are allowed to be driven from these works you are not worthy to be called Americans"—might not have been the right words. It is unlikely that a native-born American speechmaker would have used this appeal to native-born American soldiers. To men whose social, political, and cultural identity had always been American, this challenge, or attempt at shaming, might have seemed puzzling. But Owen, nicknamed "Paddy," had been born in Wales, not America, and the first two regiments he had commanded, the Twenty-fourth and the Sixty-ninth Pennsylvania (which remained in the Philadelphia Brigade that Owen later commanded), were composed principally of Irish-born volunteers. To men probably eager to distinguish themselves as good citizens of their adopted country, such a challenge would likely be an effective stimulant.[29]

The words certainly resonated with the Irish Corporal James Donnelly, although he belonged to the Twentieth Massachusetts Infantry, a regiment not under Owen's command. But the Twentieth's brigade had become leaderless shortly before, when its commander was wounded. By the time the Twentieth and its eight sister regiments had retreated to the captured works, the nearest general officer was Joshua T. Owen. In short, "Paddy" Owen now technically commanded two brigades consisting of fourteen regiments, nine of which had never served under him. He must have recognized the need to broaden his appeal beyond his fellow Irishmen and any others already familiar with his command style. Thus he immediately altered his appeal, emphasizing a more universal theme, one likely to cross ethnic lines, as he stressed the one attribute shared by every soldier in both brigades. "What is man if manhood has left you," he demands, challenging his soldiers' masculinity. Then he burnishes his authority by reviewing his resume ("He stated how long he had been in the service"), a persuasive strategy he would only have employed with soldiers who did not know him.

Here the Hope Convention appears. First, Owen implies that the Federals' desperate defensive posture might only be temporary and that a reversal of fortune is possible. He declares that sometime during or after the rebel attack, "if there was a point to be gained, he would notice and lead them to it." Just as importantly, Owen keeps talking, and loudly, making sure that the one thing his soldiers hear above the shouts, crackling of musketry, and exploding artillery shells was the sound of his voice, still in command. Hopes begot hopes, as General Owen and his soldiers reciprocated each other's growing confidence. The order of Donnelly's recollection is revealing. First, Owen's words "inspired confidence," followed by his "men seem[ing] determined." Once Owen was aware that his speech was successfully rallying the soldiers, he beamed all the more, and in a show of confidence that would have been impossible just moments earlier, defiantly declared, "Now we'll wait for Johnny." This statement, implying as it does that the Federals were ready to receive and severely punish the enemy, may have been the most hopeful statement of them all.

Floating just outside a lagoon off Makin Island nearly eight decades later, Colonel Carlson also found the need to keep talking. But as battle speechmaker, he faced a different challenge than General Owen. The general had to prepare rattled soldiers to defend a fixed point; Carlson simply needed to keep his seventy-one marines calm until they could be rescued. Here overall circumstances, not just the enemy, fed anxieties. The sea was strong and the winds were high; to concentrate his small force at the rendezvous point, Carlson had their "four rubber boats and a wooden outrigger" lashed together, but choppy waters kept snapping tie lines; the rescue submarines were late; earlier that day the Japanese had sent fighter planes to strafe Carlson's force on Makin, so the enemy knew that the marines were in the vicinity. Carlson's assumption now was that the enemy would dispatch naval vessels that would search for the Raiders' boats as well as the rescue submarines; even if the submarines were nearby, some doubted that they would attempt a rescue in rough seas. And everyone's fatigue, coupled with the raid's high casualties (some of whom were in the rubber boats), only exacerbated the situation.

Carlson's circumstances might have been far less dramatic and pic-turesque than a line of soldiers braced behind barricades to battle a relentlessly advancing enemy, but these "quieter" situations are no less dangerous for having less drama. Anxiety and an overwhelming desire to simply conclude matters can impair the judgment of both the leader and the led. And in fact, this is exactly what happened within Carl-son's little command. The anxiety had become so intense that Carlson gave permission for one of the rubber boats to detach and "paddle off beyond the breakers and into the night" looking for the submarines. "It headed west—toward Southeast Asia."[30]

Expedience suggests that Carlson would say whatever he had to so as to elevate spirits. At bottom, of course, his real objective was to maintain discipline. He "kept assuring his crew that everything was all right and that it was only a matter of time before they spotted the submarines." Was everything all right? Certainly not, and there is some evidence that Carlson himself did not believe it. One crewmem-ber thought that Carlson was clearly "concerned . . . [and] worried" about various matters connected to the rescue. But what helped keep even this knowledgeable crewmember comforted was something else about Carlson, something that Corporal Donnelly had seen in battle speechmaker General Joshua T. Owen as well. "His expression never really changed the whole time we were on that island," the crewmem-ber recalled. "He would smile a lot, so you had to guess what he was really thinking." In battle, inspiring deeds come in many varieties: the raised sword, the brandished pistol, the self-assured smile amidst chaos, and, of course, the poker face.[31]

Aside from simply Declaring Confidence (see chapter 6), Carlson's paraphrased speech illustrates Expedience in another form, in that the meaning of the Raiders' motto, "Gung Ho," would prove very elas-tic (which is probably why such mottos endure). Months before, at an indoctrination session, Carlson had defined the two Chinese words as meaning "Work together." As mentioned earlier, there was a distinctly democratic tinge to this concept—something shared, the group con-sulted, a taking into account of what other men thought in formulating a final course of action. (A motto's elasticity is evidenced by the first definition of Gung Ho found in a recent dictionary: "wholeheartedly enthusiastic and loyal; eager; zealous"; "working together" is mentioned only etymologically.)[32] But being tossed about on high seas on a dark night in frail boats filled with even frailer men is apt to redefine a popular unit motto to meet the immediate crisis: "[Carlson] reminded everyone of their motto, 'Gung Ho,' and of how important it was to work together." Now Carlson offers a different meaning of the phrase: "He had faith in them and they must have faith in him." But here "Gung Ho" is used only to endorse the last part of that sentence—they must have faith in him. This was necessary because, for many crewmembers, there was no other faith left. "Some men began to grumble," historian George W. Smith notes, "whether there were any submarines out there at all. . . . The men were close to despair once again." All that remained was one of the Moral Contract's provisions: that because Carlson the commander shared their perils, he was also entitled to their faith, and his evidence-free assurances that "Together they would get through this" were entitled to credit. Thus Gung Ho became a gentler means of asking men to believe in what is probably one of the oldest command memes known: Trust Me. There was nothing democratic about *this* Gung Ho. Nevertheless, except for a moment's poor judgment in allowing that one boat to paddle away from the rendezvous point, Carlson did succeed in holding his little force together long enough to be rescued.

Retreat

Athenians and allies, even in our present position we must still hope on, since men have before now been saved from worse straits than this; and you must not condemn ourselves too severely either because of your disasters or because of your present unmerited sufferings. I myself who am not superior to any of you in strength—indeed you see how I am in my sickness—and who in their gifts of fortune am, I think, whether in private life or otherwise, the equal of any, am now exposed to the same danger as the meanest among you; and yet my life has been one of much devotion toward the gods, and of much justice and without offense toward men. I have, therefore, still a strong hope for the future, and our misfortunes do not terrify me as much as they might. . . . The safety and order of the march is for yourselves to attend to. . . . To sum up, be convinced, soldiers, that you must be brave, as there is no place near for your cowardice to take refuge in, and that if you now escape from the enemy, you may all see again what your hearts desire, while those of you who are Athenians will raise up again the great power of the state, fallen though it be.

Excerpt from Nicias's speech to Athenian soldiers
during the retreat from Syracuse, 413 BCE

When I got back to where the boat was swamped, I saw Col. Devins and quite a number of men were around him saying, "What shall we do." I heard him say, "Brave men of the 15th [Massachusetts], you have obeyed every order I have given you today. I have done all I can for you. I can do no more." . . . The solemnity in which these words were spoken, God knows will be as fresh in my mind the day I die as they were the moment they were spoken.

Private Roland E. Bowen, Fifteenth Massachusetts Volunteer Infantry,
recalling the Battle of Ball's Bluff, October 21, 1861[33]

AN IMPORTANT TACTICAL EVENT during some battles is the re-treat—an organized (or disorganized) withdrawal from the battlefield. Deliberate withdrawals in the face of an enemy are among the most difficult and esteemed feats in military operations. Here the battle speech is paramount, and the convention that must first be satisfied is the SitRep. "When a retrograde movement becomes necessary in combat, it is an invitation to disaster to move before men are told why they are moving," S. L. A Marshall observed in *Men Against Fire*. Even in situations where "the pressure has made that fact obvious"—that is, that a SitRep Convention is rendered unnecessary by what circumstances have made plain—Marshall declares that soldiers must "still be told how far they are to go and the line or point to which they are withdrawing must be made clear and unmistakable." Explaining why soldiers must retreat and instructing them where they are to go in part help to produce an organized and deliberate withdrawal.[34]

But a review of historical battle speeches suggests that there may be more to a retreat speech than this. In fact, the more desperate the withdrawal, the more likely it will be (assuming there is time and opportunity) that the two rallying conventions will also be used in retreats: Hope and Expedience. Nicias, quoted above, commanded an Athenian army sent to invade Sicily. After many reverses, his nearly defeated troops were forced to retreat from the outskirts of Syracuse. Nicias, although ill, nevertheless delivered a speech that turned on hope and included an entire range of appeals meant to strengthen his demoralized army's will to survive. It was a heroic if ultimately unsuccessful attempt to save his men from complete annihilation. Colonel Charles Devens, also quoted above, commanded the Fifteenth Massachusetts regiment in the American Civil War. After being routed at the Battle of Ball's Bluff, the Federal forces were sent scurrying down the cliffs above the Virginia banks of the Potomac River. The Fifteenth Massachusetts's soldiers were among the several thousand stranded men trapped between the wide, swift-flowing Potomac River and Confederate riflemen on the bluffs, who continued to shoot into the mass of panicked soldiers below. Devens's few words represent the final discharge of the Moral Contract between the leader and the led. Everything that defines a fighting unit—discipline, leadership, collective self-esteem, and the will to resist—is at an end.[35]

Nicias's situation, however, was far worse than Colonel Devens's 2,294 years later. In the summer of 415 BCE an Athenian invasion fleet consisting of 134 ships carrying 5,100 *hoplites,* 700 *thetes* (serving as marines), 750 mercenaries, 480 archers, 700 slingers, 120 Magaran light infantry, 30 cavalry horses, and more than 100 boats carrying grain, bakers, stonemasons and carpenters, and the tools for raising fortifications, as well as assorted camp followers, set sail for Sicily. Although the stated purpose for mounting this expedition was to aid a beleaguered Sicilian ally, Athens was also motivated by a desire to add the grain-rich island to its empire. The Athenian navy blockaded Syracuse's port while the army besieged the city. Ultimately, Syracuse would reorganize its army and ally with Sparta, and at that point even Athenian reinforcements would be insufficient for maintaining either the blockade or the siege. The Second Battle of Syracuse neutralized what was left of Athens's ships, and the army was trapped on the island. (Athenian command was divided between Nicias and Demosthenes, and the two men split over whether to attempt escape in the remaining ships or, as Nicias insisted, extricate the army by marching inland. Nicias prevailed.)[36]

According to Thucydides, this Athenian defeat was "by far the greatest reverse that ever befell a Hellenic army. They had come to enslave others, and were departing in fear of being enslaved themselves." His account is a vivid description of a demoralized army in retreat. When the Athenians left their camp, "the dead lay unburied," while those too ill or too wounded to march "were to the living far more shocking than the dead, and more to be pitied than those who had perished." They clasped their comrades and relatives around the neck, "begging them to take them"; as the army marched away they followed "as far as they could, and when their bodily strength failed them calling again and again upon heaven and shrieking aloud as they were left behind." Starvation was compounded by disgrace, then, and each soldier felt "a heavy burden, especially when they contrasted the splendor and glory of their setting out with the humiliation in which it had ended."[37]

The sight of this suffering spurred both Nicias and Demosthenes to words and deeds. Nicias "passed along the ranks and encouraged and comforted them as far as was possible . . . raising his voice still higher and higher as he went from one company to another in his earnestness." As Nicias spoke, he continued to walk the line, returning stragglers to their places while his co-commander, Demosthenes, "did as much for his part of the army, addressing them in words very similar." But the only words Thucydides actually offers are those of Nicias.[38]

The Greek commander will say whatever he must in order to keep his army on the march. The Hope Convention is dominant, propped up at every turn by arguments easily bundled by the Expedience Convention. Nicias first supports Hope by noting that as bad as things are, the possibility of salvation remains, "since men have before now been saved from worse straits than this." Next, the soldiers' hopes should not be extinguished because of a misplaced belief that they are especially cursed. After all, Nicias observes of himself, "in the gifts of fortune" he has been "the equal of any," yet here he is sharing his soldiers' fates now, while persevering in "a strong hope for the future."[39]

Nicias twists the concept of fortune to make many arguments in the name of lifting his soldier-audience's despair. Even if their misfortunes *are* the gods' punishment, surely they have suffered enough and a reversal of fortune can soon be expected; likewise, the Syracusans "have had good fortune enough" and their prospects can only change for the worse. Besides, other men "have attacked their neighbors and have done what men will do without suffering more than they could bear"—why should the Athenians now fare any different? His men may examine fortune from any angle they wish, but a change for the better must be due.[40]

Nicias gives additional reasons for hope to those soldiers for whom theology was insufficient: "And look to yourselves, mark the numbers and efficiency of the *hoplites* marching in your ranks," he admonishes, "and do not give way to too much despondency but reflect that you are yourselves at once a city wherever you sit down, and that there is no other in Sicily that could easily resist your attack." Their fate is under their own control, because "the safety and order of the march is for yourselves to attend to"; if every man thinks of the patch of ground he stands on as "his country and stronghold," then defends it as such, no enemy can prevail. In the meantime the army will quickly march to an Athenian ally, who will welcome them with food. After having exhausted the arguments of heaven's favor, reversal of fortunes, their own military prowess, mighty numbers, willing allies, and the promise of succor, Nicias concludes by combining what might be thought of as the first and last arguments of the Hope Convention—restoring imperial greatness, and having no choice but to hope:

> To sum up, be convinced, soldiers, that you must be brave, as there is no place near for your cowardice to take refuge in, and that if you now escape from the enemy, you may all see what your hearts desire, while those of you who are Athenians will raise up again the great power of the state, fallen though it be. Men make the city and not walls or ships without men in them.[41]

Of course, the battle speech was the Athenian commanders' last available weapon in the struggle with Syracuse. And it proved effective in motivating his army—for five days, until the last of the Athenians surrendered.

The small Federal army defeated at the Battle of Ball's Bluff would not have to wait as long or march as far as the Athenians to discover an end to their collective hope. More than seventeen hundred soldiers had been ferried across the Potomac River to Virginia, near the town of Leesburg. Once ashore, they traversed a switchback path up cliffs over 110 feet tall that bordered the riverbank. Atop the cliffs was a cleared field; while some companies marched inland, most of the soldiers took positions just yards from the precipice. Skirmishing sputtered intermittently that morning between the advanced Federal units and the Confederates; but later that afternoon a mixed force of Confederate infantry and cavalry confronted the Federals on the bluff and, after a pitched battle, decisively defeated them. This sent panicked men scrambling down the cliffs and swarming over the riverbank in search of a means of escape. With Confederates firing on them from the cliffs above, masses of hapless men overloaded and then capsized the few available boats. Some soldiers attempted to swim the river alone; a few made it, some were shot midstream, others drowned. Groups of men bolted up or down the riverbank, searching for other boats, or a ford; many managed to escape this way, but many were captured in the effort. And those soldiers who remained under the cliffs faced a stark choice—resist or surrender. Most would eventually surrender.[42]

As Private Roland E. Bowen of the Fifteenth Massachusetts hurried toward his comrades clustered around his regiment's colonel, he confronted sights that caused him to beseech Heaven "that I may [never] again witness such a scene." "Oh such terrible confusion, men running to and fro, others leaping into the river," the horrified private wrote several weeks later. "The horrid forms of the dead, the last struggles of the dying, the groans of the wounded and the heart rendering crys [sic] that would go up from a hundred drowning lips." A few moments later Bowen heard his comrades ask their colonel, "What shall we do[?]" It was a question that consumed hundreds of soldiers at that moment.[43]

Colonel Devens's reply was even more extreme than a naval captain's order to "abandon ship!" In this case, naval regulations stipulate that the captain be the last to leave a stricken vessel, thus implying that discipline and authority remain at some level to the very end.[44] But when Devens declares, "I have done all I can for you, I can do no more," he simultaneously asserts that the regiment's existence is suspended, at least temporarily, and that all distinctions of rank are nullified. Here is the absolute end of collective hope—that is, the hope that the command structure on which soldiers usually rely for their existence will continue to sustain them. In other words, "every man for himself." It is in this sense that Devens's brief speech represents the final battle speech, the speech that supersedes all other speeches until the regiment is somehow reconstituted in better circumstances.

However, what makes Devens's few words especially telling is his first sentence: "Brave men of the 15th, you have obeyed every order I have given you today." Why should he have prefaced his self-dissolution of authority with this compliment? There are probably several reasons. First, the vast majority of his regiment did behave bravely, and it was no fault of theirs that poor command decisions stranded them on the Virginia shore. Second, Devens may have felt some guilt—he and several officers under his authority had contributed to some of the poor decisions that unintentionally caused so much human carnage. But when his speech is considered as a whole, another reason emerges— it is not enough that Colonel Devens, a prominent lawyer before the war and a future attorney general of the United States afterward, terminates his legal authority over his men, he must also terminate the Moral Contract that binds military comrades. In declaring (in effect) that it is every man for himself, no man should feel bound to protect him (or each other) simply because he is a colonel or they are one another's comrades under arms. Men may ally themselves under some other source of authority (for example, religion, friendship, or a general regard for human life), but the Moral Contract rooted in comradeship is for now voided. And the immediate experience of hearing Devens speak ("The solemnity in which these words were spoken, God knows they will be as fresh in my mind the day I die as they were the moment they were spoken") suggests the pronunciation of an epitaph or the deliverance of a eulogy—which, in effect, it was. Devens was presiding over the death of his own unit, and in all likelihood, the deaths of many of its members. In noting his men's bravery, he acknowledges that until that very moment they had discharged their obligations under the Moral Contract as well as the legal duties imposed by the Articles of War. But now he was releasing them into a Hobbesian state of nature, of every man for himself and the devil take the hindmost.

7

THE POST-BATTLE SPEECH
Telling a Story

The general commanding takes this occasion to express to the officers and soldiers of this army his high appreciation of the fortitude, valor, and devotion displayed by them, which, under the blessing of Almighty God, has added the victory of Fredericksburg to the long list of their triumphs.

An arduous march, performed with celerity, under many disadvantages, exhibited the discipline and spirit of the troops and their eagerness to confront the foe.

The immense army of the enemy completed its preparation for the attack without interruption, and gave battle in its own time, and on ground of its own selection. It was encountered by less than 20,000 of this brave army, and its columns crushed and broken, hurled back at every point with such fearful slaughter that escape from entire destruction became the boast of those who had advanced in full confidence of victory. That this great result was achieved with a loss small in point of numbers, only augments the admiration with which the commanding general regards the prowess of the troops, and increases his gratitude to Him who has given us the victory.

The war is not yet ended. The enemy is still numerous and strong, and the country demands of the army a renewal of its heroic efforts in her behalf. Nobly has it responded to her call in the past. And she will never appeal in vain to its courage and patriotism.

The signal manifestations of Divine mercy that have distinguished the eventful and glorious campaign of the year just closing give assurance of hope that, under the guidance of the same Almighty hand, the *coming year will be no less fruitful of events that will insure the safety, peace, and happiness of our beloved country, and add new luster to the already imperishable name of the Army of Northern Virginia.*

General Robert E. Lee, General Orders No. 138, Headquarters,
Army of Northern Virginia, December 31, 1862[1]

POST-BATTLE SPEECHES must be specifically distinguished from Midst-of-Battle Speeches, for under some circumstances it may be difficult to tell them apart. For example, one could argue that Colonel Devens's "last words" to his regiment, which concluded the previous chapter, comprised a Post-Battle Speech. At the time he spoke, the main battle was over, and Confederates were really engaged in "mopping up" what was left of the disorganized Federals. But when Devens uttered his few lines, the battle was not really over—the bullets still flew, and panicked men were fleeing along and swimming or drowning in the river, or resisting however they could. The tactical situation remained ablaze, and battle speechmakers did not yet have the opportunity for perspective—that is, to reflect on the consequences of the just-concluded battle and then make a speech. In sum, a true Post-Battle Speech can only take place after the shooting has stopped or the arrows and spears have all landed, and enough time has lapsed to provide a clearer view not only of what happened during the battle but also of its results—victory, defeat, or stalemate. The dead and wounded must be counted, captured property and prisoners inventoried, and the battle's larger strategic and political consequences gauged.

What then is the function of the Post-Battle Speech? Unlike the Recruiting or Instructional Speech, whose function provides its name, the Post-Battle Speech, like its Pre-Battle, Pre-Invasion, or Midst-of-Battle cousins, has a purpose defined by the circumstances in which it is given. But unlike these other battle speeches, whose purpose is derived from circumstance, the Post-Battle Speech at first appears to serve no real military purpose. Indeed, for an army resting after a battle, there are few active tactical needs that require an exhortation. Yet Post-Battle Speeches *do* have profound purposes. Here the battle speechmaker tells a story that, like other stories, has a beginning and an end. Perhaps the Post-Battle Speech conveys lessons or wisdom, but always it seeks to lend meaning to the battle, and it usually includes a history that emphasizes the role of the soldier-audience in the fighting. This aspect of this speech will be referred to as the Story Convention.

Robert E. Lee's use of the Story Convention in his Post-Battle Speech illustrates how the battle speechmaker creates this history. First, Lee is clear that the battle of Fredericksburg caps the "long list" of the Army of Northern Virginia's 1862 "triumphs." This list will come as no surprise to Lee's soldier-audience, each member of which has personally contributed their efforts to driving the Army of the Potomac off Virginia's Peninsula (spring), decisively defeating John Pope's Army of Virginia (summer), and fighting to what many Southerners regarded as a "draw" at the Battle of Antietam (fall). (Lee's speech was delivered on the last day of 1862, a full eighteen days after the Battle of Fredericksburg. Probably no coincidence, this was perhaps meant to place the battle in the story of an eventful and ultimately successful year.)

Lee gives a "history" of the Battle of Fredericksburg that "proves," from the very fact that it is Lee himself speaking, what most of his soldier-audience knew already—that another decisive victory had been added to their army's resume. Why is it necessary to inform an army of something it already knows? Surely the soldiers of the Army of Northern Virginia collectively understood that the Battle of Fredericksburg was a decisive victory that inflicted terrible losses on the enemy. But in hierarchical organizations like armies (especially armies), official cognizance matters—for a thing to exist (and thereby influence pay, furloughs, promotions, future strategy, and so forth), superiors must first acknowledge that it exists. Lee's Post-Battle Speech fixes the past for the record and sets the future in terms of expectations. After all, it is the commander and battle speechmaker Lee who exercises greater control over this future than any other soldier. By declaring victory, the army should expect the fruits of victory, as measured (perhaps) in the above terms.

Lee begins by offering his version of the battle's pre-history: "An arduous march, performed with celerity, under many disadvantages, exhibited the discipline and spirit of the troops and their eagerness to confront the foe." Critical to the Story Convention (at least for victories) is Recognition, and here Lee uses unqualified, almost epic generalizations to describe his army's march from its two principal jump-offs in the Shenandoah Valley and at the Culpeper Court House to the town of Fredericksburg. Lee's characterization of his march does not pretend at an actual history. For example, he does not mention that Federal commander Ambrose E. Burnside skillfully stole a few days' march on him, or that initially Lee had only the vaguest idea of Burnside's final destination.[2]

And Lee's celebratory history continues in this vein. He insists that Burnside's army had every military advantage against the Confederates; preparing for the attack "without interruption . . . [it] gave battle in its own time" and on "ground of its own selection." The "immense army" of Federals faced "less than 20,000 . . . brave" Confederates. But despite the enemy's enumerated advantages, God, "who has given us the victory," only added to the existing "prowess" of Lee's army. As a result Burnside's columns were "crushed and broken, hurled back at every point with such fearful slaughter that escape from entire destruction became the boast of those who had advanced in full confidence of victory." The Story here is a straightforward narrative. By forced marches, an outnumbered Confederate army met a vast host who, besides having superior numbers, had the additional advantages of choosing the time, place, and tactics for the battle. But a combination of God's favor and the army's skill produced a great victory, a triumph that Lee's soldiers should especially savor because God was behind them.

Whatever General Lee might have believed when he scratched out or dictated General Orders No. 138, it is doubtful that he would have vouched for much of it later, perhaps excepting God's favor. First, few knew better than Lee that the Battle of Fredericksburg might have been a close thing had the Federals been able to sustain their breakthrough on the Confederate right. Lee also knew that Burnside's failure to adjust his tactics on the Federal right essentially created those "crushed and broken" legions that were "hurled back at every point," especially the points in front of Marye's Heights. And more than anyone else, Lee the combat engineer understood that the troop numbers he bandied about meant far less when one side was entrenched on hill-crests and behind stone walls, blasting packed, largely unprotected enemy ranks ascending an sloped open field largely denuded of cover. Moreover, while Lee is generous in congratulating his men—that is certainly one aim of this speech—he necessarily withholds mention of his own superior generalship, which essentially planned the defense (for which Lee had considerable time as well).

Of course, the "truth" is not the point of the Story Convention. In Post-Battle Speeches the battle events must be reprised in a way that allows the battle speechmaker (invariably speaking from the top down) to "prove" by his own public statements what the soldiers already know to be true—that victory (or some other desirable outcome) was achieved and they, with God's help, were largely responsible for it. Thus, Lee concludes, "That this great result was achieved with a loss small in point of numbers only augments the admiration with which the commanding general regards the prowess of the troops and increases his gratitude to Him who has given us the victory." Here is the recognition "proved" by the story. It is also very likely the one statement about which Robert E. Lee entertained no private doubts.

As Lee's Post-Battle Speech illustrates, the most important aim of the Story Convention is to recognize the valor of the army, which of course resonates with the Recognition Convention encountered earlier in other battle-speech genres. In Post-Battle Speeches, Recognition is usually group recognition, though it may be divided among units comprising the group; occasionally, Recognition will also be accorded to individuals. Lee's recognition is given to the Army of Northern Virginia: all its members have contributed "new luster to the already imperishable name of the Army of Northern Virginia." (Some of Lee's contemporaries had a different approach. Several months later, when Confederate General J. Bankhead Magruder wanted to congratulate his men after their victory at Sabine Pass, he complimented his "devoted and heroic men" but named only the officers.)[3]

Whether it is intended for groups or for individuals, Recognition is a form of congratulations for having behaved valorously during some moment in a just-fought battle. Less frequently encountered, especially after victorious battles (and unmentioned by General Lee after his lopsided victory at Fredericksburg), is the opposite of praise—the Criticism Convention. Here the battle speechmaker, after telling the story of the battle, will criticize the performance of units or individuals. This is another very important tactical function of Post-Battle Speeches: what the modern American military refers to as "Lessons Learned," or learning from one's mistakes. The Criticism Convention will be considered in greater detail below.[4]

The next two conventions that help to shape the Post-Battle Speech are Reward and Legacy. The Reward Convention, as mentioned, involves the promise of some material benefit for having served, fought, or been victorious in the battle. The Post-Battle Speech is an obvious opportunity for a successful commander/battle speechmaker to confer rewards. However, over the centuries there has been a decoupling of rewards from specific battle outcomes. As armies evolved, the material benefits of war began to flow exclusively to the corporate entity in whose name the army fought—the empire or nation-state. Symbolic awards such as medals or hierarchical benefits such as promotions, while present since antiquity, began to replace plunder as an incentive for fighting. (Consider Western armies of the twentieth century. While medals and promotions remain an important incentive for soldiers, the material "rewards" for service—such as enlistment bonuses, college tuition assistance, or pensions—are not linked to winning battles or even especially meritorious service. Undistinguished soldiers are equally eligible.) As the material benefits began to flow to the corporate entity, the purpose of the war or battle also became "corporatized" for the soldier-audience. A victory would no longer make individual soldiers rich, but it just might destroy the Papists, provide *lebensraum*, protect the sea lanes, or spread the True Faith. And once war's objectives became corporate, the benefits to the soldier-audience could likewise be articulated in corporate terms—victory meant not individual wealth but something more: purifying the world of some racial, ethnic, ideological, or religious pollutant, perhaps, or keeping the world safe for the values of the soldier-audience. Victorious battles helped achieve these objectives; thus amidst the increasing carnage and gradually replacing plunder was born the Legacy

Convention. Victorious soldier-audiences were now "rewarded" in Post-Battle Speeches by having their legacies enshrined. Here would be the summing up of what the battle accomplished and what the soldiers, through their participation, would forever remain known for.

The Legacy Convention may be expressed in intensely personal terms (discussed below) or, as in Lee's speech above, in the impersonal language of an imagined posterity. The victory at Fredericksburg had been the latest in a series of victories since the spring, and Lee explained to his soldiers that their legacy involved doing much to "insure the safety, peace, and happiness of our beloved country, and add new luster to the already imperishable name of the Army of Northern Virginia." Few might become wealthy from these victories, and no mention is made of personal prestige. Soldiers would have to draw satisfaction from the benefits received by having sustained the twenty-two-month-old government of the Confederate States of America. Implied in Lee's speech is that for true soldier-patriots this should be sufficient recompense.

The final convention of the Post-Battle Speech is especially prominent in speeches made after battles that do not end the war—that is, situations in which more battles are expected. This is called the Preparedness Convention, for here, soldiers are cautioned not to rest on their laurels—overconfidence, especially after a victory, has always concerned alert commanders, and the Post-Battle Speech made in the midst of an ongoing war is an excellent opportunity to remind soldiers that their legacy is not yet perfected; the enemy (and thus more fighting) remains. Robert E. Lee's words from his general orders perfectly illustrate the Preparedness Convention: "The war is not yet ended. The enemy is still numerous and strong, and the country demands of the army a renewal of its heroic efforts in her behalf." And Lee includes in his Preparedness Convention his continuing theme of Recognition. "Nobly has [the army] responded to [the country's] call in the past. And she will never appeal in vain to its courage and patriotism." The Preparedness Convention is a speechmaker's attempt to contextualize a battle (especially, but not exclusively, a victory) with a good news/bad news approach: we have won this battle but the war remains. *En garde!*

Other Elements of the Story Convention:
Remembering the Fallen

So, you would rather be taken prisoner by a brutal and avaricious enemy—have a price put on your heads . . . that another may be exalted by your misery and shame! No! No! Not at least if you belong to the same country as the consul Paullus, who preferred a noble death to a life of dishonor, or as all those brave men whose bodies lie heaped around him. Come then: before daylight is upon us and more of the enemy troops block our way, let us get out.

   Excerpt from Tribune Pulius Sempronius Tuditanus's speech
   following the Roman disaster at Cannae

In this field of battle the Northeast and Northwest mingled their blood on the field, as they had long ago joined their hearts in support of the Union. Michigan stood by Maine; Massachusetts supported Indiana, Wisconsin aided Vermont. . . . While we mourn the loss of many brave comrades, we who were absent envy them the privilege of dying upon the battle-field of our country under the starry folds of her victorious flag.

   Excerpt from General Orders, No. 57, Major-General
   Benjamin Butler, August 9, 1862

The tragic loss of Staff Sgt. Ryan Haupt, Sgt. Norman Taylor and Pfc. Nathan Frigo leaves our hearts heavy as we prepare to complete our mission. Any loss, but especially a loss this close to mission completion, is simply heart breaking; and losing three great Soldiers in one action is crushing. Our prayers are with their families, friends and comrades.

   Colonel Brian D. Jones and Command Sergeant Major David H. List,
   "Command View," *Iron Brigade Chronicle*, October 23, 2006[5]

WHETHER MARKING VICTORY OR DEFEAT, many Post-Battle Speeches include some tribute to the fallen. Of course, the dead are dead; but what matters to battle speechmakers and their soldier-audiences are the uses made of the dead. There is nothing inappropriate about this. In any war marked by religious, political, or cultural struggle, many of the dead originally joined or remained in service for some higher cause; even those who originally sought wealth, status, or adventure may have remained because they became personally devoted to friends and comrades. At bottom, it is safe to presume that whatever drew soldiers into service and sustained them while there, most acknowledged something greater than themselves, even if that were no more than the unit they served in. Whatever their motives, soldiers are much used in life, and it is difficult to imagine many objections to continuing their service after death. A soldier's duty never ends.

Three examples of how Post-Battle Speeches use the fallen are featured in this epigraph. In general, Post-Battle Speeches rarely refer to the dead much beyond a proto-eulogy; often, soldiers are not even mentioned by name but instead, as with General Butler's speech above, are described as "many brave comrades" or the like. Few details of the deceased are usually provided. However, an exception to this practice appears in the speech of the Roman tribune Pulius Sempronius Tuditanus. This "applied remembrance" is excerpted from his rallying Post-Battle Speech following the virtual annihilation of the Roman army by Hannibal at the Battle of Cannae.

The very name of Cannae became eponymous with the tactic of double-envelopment, or the surrounding and destruction of an adversary via a pincer movement. When Hannibal most famously used this technique in 216 BCE, his Roman adversary ceased to function as an army. The Roman solders who remained had escaped to one of two camps, themselves separated by Hannibal's army, which was exhausted by battle and the victory celebrations that had followed. A messenger was sent from one camp to the other, proposing that the two Roman remnants join forces and escape to Canusium (the present-day Italian town of Canosa di Puglia) and safety. But this proposal was received poorly; the men were simply too demoralized. Why should *they* have to steal through Hannibal's sleeping army, rather than the other camp? Some questioned the senders' motives—perhaps they were cowards and "preferred to risk other people's lives to risking their own." But the truth may have been what Livy attributed to another faction: they simply "lacked the heart to carry it out." Eventual surrender seemed preferable.[6]

It was Pulius's remoralizing speech that shook these comrades from their defeatist stupor and prompted them (more as individuals than as an organized group) to successfully make the dangerous journey. And the heart of Pulius's speech was a two-step, contrasting the shame of surrender with the martyrdom of the fallen. By effectively asserting provisions of the Moral Contract that posited certain obligations living soldiers have to dead comrades, Pulius illustrates this common meme in the Post-Battle Speech—the dead as martyrs to whom a duty is owed. This in turn is a variation of an ancient admonition that is perhaps best known in American history from Lincoln's Gettysburg Address: "that we here highly resolve that these dead shall not have died in vain." For Pulius, "these dead" come in two forms. The first and most important is the consul Lucius Aemilius Paullus. Despite being "severely wounded" by a "sling-stone" at the very beginning of the battle, Paullus was able to provide inspiring leadership and nearly succeeded in killing Hannibal himself. However, the effects of Paullus's wound eventually forced him to dismount, and he was followed by his cavalry troop. Even as the Carthaginians swarmed around them, "they made no attempt to escape, preferring to die where they stood." Livy gives the dying Paullus one of antiquity's most noble combat deaths. The wounded Paullus sits on a stone, bleeding out, refusing all efforts to help him flee ("As for me, let me die here amongst my dead soldiers"), and with his dying breaths he refuses to blame his co-commander, whose disastrous decision to engage Hannibal he had wisely counseled against.[7]

Clearly, Livy implies that this detailed knowledge of Paullus's death was widely known by Cannae's Roman survivors, for Pulius does little more than mention the consul's name, characterizing him in words that were probably hoary when Livy wrote them: Paullus, "who preferred a noble death to a life of dishonor." Pulius baits his men by challenging their self-esteem via the old strategy of shame: you would join me in escaping "if you belong to the same country as the consul Paullus." Of course, many of the soldiers do belong to the same country; they need only for Pulius to remind them, in the name of the fallen

Paullus, that obligations are owed to both that country and to Paullus's memory. Paullus honored the country by sacrificing his life. All Pulius is asking them to do is escape with their lives.

But this Post-Battle Speech also uses another type of fallen, one that is quite familiar from modern battle speeches—the soldiers who have died anonymously in combat and in such numbers that they simply cannot be listed individually. These anonymous fallen are described only as "all those brave men whose bodies lie heaped around [Paullus]." And like Paullus, the anonymous fallen have also preferred a noble death to a life of dishonor. The heaped bodies complete Pulius's imagined *mise-en-scène;* those in his soldier-audience who did not know Paullus might have known someone in those heaps, or perhaps in other heaps elsewhere on the battlefield. Pulius's point in including these fallen is to cast the net of Paullus's virtue over every soldier who fell, without inquiring whether death came while facing the enemy or fleeing him. In what has become a universal practice, virtually all of the deaths incurred during a battle are deemed heroic afterward, whether they were suffered by tragic accident, after great bravery, during desertion, or while simply doing one's ordinary duty.

While rallying his men for escape, Pulius's naming of Paullus and recitation of his deeds forms the backbone of his Post-Battle Speech's Story Convention. Two millennia later, in a Post-Battle Speech written after the Battle of Baton Rouge (August 5, 1862), Federal commander General Benjamin F. Butler's Story Convention uses the fallen in a very different way. Here, they are articulated not as individuals or as visually disturbing "heaps" of bodies but as residents of regions; here, they have no faces, only addresses. In fact, regions and the states that composed them become metonyms for these soldiers, living and dead; together, they comprise the Federal Union that is Butler's central metaphor. First, he declares that "In this field of battle the Northeast and Northwest mingled their blood on the field." Next he names several states belonging to those regions that also serve as metonyms for their soldiers: "Michigan stood by Maine; Massachusetts supported Indiana, Wisconsin aided Vermont."

In a war whose principal aim was the restoration of the Union, this use of the fallen is entirely logical. Only in life were the dead divided by region; having (presumably) fought for the Union, in death they were finally subsumed in it. Butler also extends this logic to the survivors of the Battle of Baton Rouge. They may come from different places, and they may all fight for the Union, but they also fight *as a union*. Here "Union" is not only a war objective but also a military tactic, a style of fighting in which formerly differentiated (by state citizenship) soldiers fight in one collective as "new" citizens—they have been reborn as Americans. The proof can be found in Butler's story of the battle, an event during which regiments from different states supported each other. Indeed, the battlefield itself is reborn; it is no longer ground near a city located in the seceded state of Louisiana but "the battlefield of *our* country" [emphasis added]. And the dead, however they may have died—valorously, cowardly, accidentally, or otherwise—are all defined as "brave comrades" who gave their lives for precisely the same purpose "under the starry folds of [the Federal] victorious flag." Butler's Story of the battle is Union, his Story of the living is unity of action, and his Story of the fallen is unity in death. Shrewd trial lawyer and experienced politician-turned-general Benjamin Butler certainly knew how to pitch a crowd, be it a jury, the electorate, or his soldier-audience.

The last example featured in the epigraph is excerpted from a Post-Battle Speech signed by both Colonel Brian D. Jones (whose Instructional Speeches were discussed in chapter 4) and Command Sergeant Major David H. List; it is explored at greater length in this chapter's coda. In each month's "Command View" Colonel Jones included proto-eulogies of this type for deaths that had been incurred since the prior issue; thus, there was nothing unusual about noting these deaths in what was really a Post-Battle Speech marking the end of his unit's mission. In prior issues, scrupulous care seems to have been exercised in expressing collective sorrow without attempting to "apply" the deaths to larger causes. (It should be noted that Colonel Jones is able to name individuals killed because in the Iraq War—in sharp contrast to earlier American wars—relatively few deaths occur in a given unit; thus, there are no anonymous "heaps" of dead.)

For the most part, Colonel Jones also frames the deaths of Staff Sergeant Haupt, Sergeant Taylor, and Private First Class Frigo as personal losses for his unit. He does so by using the metaphor of "heart," probably the most common figure employed to express personal emotion; Jones and List speak of hearts that are "heavy" and broken by the loss of these soldiers. That three men were killed "in one action" is "crushing." There is no talk of "starry flags" or exhortation of soldiers to some dramatic action. Instead, just as the emotions summoned here are highly personal (versus, for example, patriotic), there is an implied invitation for an action that is likewise the essence of personal: prayer. "Our prayers are with their families, friends and comrades," Jones and List conclude. Here is a classic, and largely secular, use of the word "prayer" that one would expect from an army representing a government in part based on the separation of church and state: a prayer for the deceased's survivors, which is roughly equivalent to a hope that the living do not suffer unnecessarily from these losses. (This should be contrasted with a prayer for the souls of the dead, which is a sectarian prayer, implying as it does some very specific religious beliefs.) As written, the Jones and List prayer is one to which even an atheist could subscribe.

However, there is one ambiguous line that could be read as applying these soldiers' deaths to the present tactical circumstances of the Third Heavy Brigade Combat Team. "Any loss, but especially a loss this close to mission completion," Jones and List declare, "is simply heartbreaking." Readers will recall from Colonel Jones's earlier Instructional Speech his concern about the contribution of complacency to injury and death. While there is nothing to indicate that these soldiers' deaths were the result of complacency, Colonel Jones's emphasis on timing, essentially connecting the "loss" with a moment so "close to mission completion" is likely to have raised the safety awareness of his soldier-audience. Men and women who had so far survived a complete rotation in Iraq would likely become even more careful in performing their jobs during the mission's final days.

Taking Responsibility

To conduct great matters and never commit a fault is above the force of human nature; but to learn and improve by the faults we have com-

mitted, is that which becomes a good and sensible man. Some reasons I may have to accuse fortune, but I have many more to thank her; for in a few hours she hath cured a long mistake, and taught me that I am not the man who should command others, but have need of another to command me.

Lucius Minucius's Post-Battle Speech after his defeat by Hannibal, 217 BCE

It's all my fault! I thought my men were invincible. . . . My fault! My fault!

General Robert E. Lee after the failure of Pickett's Charge,
Battle of Gettysburg, July 3, 1863[8]

FEW MILITARY HISTORIANS would argue with the Roman commander Minucius's self-assessment after he rashly attacked Hannibal and only narrowly avoided his own destruction. "I am not the man who should command others," Minucius declares, "but have need of another to command me." With that admission, he subordinated himself to his co-commander, erstwhile rival (and legendary general) Fabius Maximus. The acceptance of responsibility for failure is as rare for military commanders as it is for any other professionals. But like others, commanders sometimes do take responsibility for their failures, and occasionally, this will occur in a Post-Battle Speech.

Interestingly, the way in which commanders have taken responsibility for failure mimics the three basic stages by which many religions typically define genuine repentance. Admission is the first step. Here the commander admits that the battle was lost or that there was some other tactical or strategic failure. (When taking responsibility, commanders rarely discuss the tactical history of what caused the failure, probably because this might give the appearance of deflecting blame.) The second step involves the commander unequivocally Accepting Blame Personally. The final step comprises some combination of Genuine Regret and/or some action to assure No Repetition of the error. While this kind of repentance is usually associated with the Judeo-Christian tradition, its roots must be far older. Minucius was a pagan and Plutarch (his chronicler) a pagan's pagan.[9]

Minucius's Post-Battle Speech demonstrates this process. In re-producing (or inventing/reinventing) Minucius's Post-Battle Speech, Plutarch, like most of antiquity's historians, was at great pains to explicate all of the reasoning behind Minucius's decision to bow to Fabius's authority. Before his humiliating rout, Minucius was described by Plutarch as a commander "unseasonably eager for action, bold and confident," a leader who "humored the soldiery, and himself contributed to fill them with wild eagerness and empty hopes" about giving battle to Hannibal. Minucius's near-disaster was prevented only by the intervention of the older, wiser Fabius.[10]

Afterward, Minucius's reaction was probably all that the old man could have wished. "To conduct great matters and never commit a fault is above the force of human nature," the chastened general admitted to his troops, "but to learn and improve by the faults we have committed is that which becomes a good and sensible man." Here Minucius begins an Admission, the sincerity of which seems beyond doubt:

> Some reasons I may have to accuse fortune, but I have many more to thank her; for in a few hours she hath cured a long mistake, and taught me that I am not the man who should command others, but have need of another to command me. . . . Therefore in everything else henceforth [Fabius] must be your commander; only in showing gratitude towards him I will still be your leader, and always be the first to obey his orders.

Minucius's repentance is patent here—Admission, Accepting Blame Personally, and both Genuine Regret and an action that promises No Repetition. He proves the last by relinquishing his co-commandership to Fabius, thus assuring the world that he will not repeat his error, because in the future he will lack the authority to do so.

Given the sometimes imperious but usually cocksure confidence that so many commanders exude (indeed, it was this confidence that partly beguiled the Roman Senate to appoint Minucius as co-commander), Admission and Accepting Blame Personally are usually stunning when they occur. And when they are publicly voiced in a Post-Battle Speech, these things can be so jarring as to momentarily become *the* Story Convention, whatever spectacular events might have preceded them. Minucius and General Robert E. Lee, whose Admission and Genuine Regret featured above were expressed by him after Pickett's failed charge at Gettysburg, were both penalized by overconfidence. Minucius overestimated his own capabilities, while Lee overestimated the capabilities of his army. And both men's sense of self and sense of their armies were leveled by a harsh reality. (While few would argue that Minucius and Lee acted honorably here, it should always be remembered that in war the cost of a commander learning humility is usually paid with other men's lives.)

Robert E. Lee had physically positioned himself in order to greet his defeated soldiers as they ran, walked, or hobbled back to Confederate lines after their repulse by the Federals. He was there to rally their spirits, and he said, or was heard to say, many things to many soldiers, thus creating numerous reported versions of his actual words. This "Post-Battle Speech" is therefore not a set oration or printed proclamation later read to his assembled army. The general was understandably emotional; some of his remarks were made in personal conversation, others to the rank and file, or perhaps to no one in particular. However, they are worth considering if for no other reason than that they probably amount to the most famous Accept Blame Personally for failure in American history, military or otherwise. Aggregated, they amount to a Post-Battle Speech of considerable power.

As this ambulatory carnage streamed past him, Lee's reported remarks are at least particularly consistent. Responding to an understandably distraught General George Pickett, Lee declared, "Come, General Pickett, this has been my fight, and upon my shoulders rests the blame. The men and officers of your command have written the name of Virginia as high today as it has ever been written before." When a teary-eyed General Cadmus Wilcox, who had led a brigade against the Federals and was fortunate to return alive, began to lament his destroyed legion, Lee exclaimed, "Never mind, General, *all this has been* MY *fault*—it is *I* that have lost this fight, and you must help me out of it the best way you can." Lee was also overheard declaring, "It's all my fault. I thought my men were invincible. My fault! My fault!" Given human beings' limitless capacity for denial, it is difficult to argue with historian Earl J. Hess's balanced judgment that Lee "deserves enormous praise for [taking responsibility] in a war that saw many commanders try to save their careers by sacrificing others.

But in view of the tremendous suffering of his men, it was the least he could do."[11]

Lee's mini-speeches add up to an extended sequence of Admission, Accepting Blame Personally, and expressing Genuine Regret. But is there something more in the record by which Lee perfected his acceptance with some act or pledge of No Repetition, as Minucius had done by his own deed of relinquishment? The answer is yes, but not in a way that mattered for battle-speech purposes. On August 8, 1863, in a remarkable letter to Confederate President Jefferson Davis, Lee demonstrated in refined prose not only that he remained willing to Accept Blame Personally but further that he was fully prepared to offer No Repetition. "I therefore, in all sincerity, request Your Excellency to take measures to supply my place," he wrote. "I cannot even accomplish what I myself desire. How can I fulfill the expectations of others?" Davis wisely refused his request, and the Confederacy retained perhaps the one general capable of prolonging its existence for almost two more years. But private correspondence almost five weeks after the battle is not a battle speech.[12]

Post-Battle Speech: Defeat and the Criticism Convention

Back in camp, Marcellus addressed his men in such bitter and angry terms that a whole day's fighting followed by defeat was a lighter burden to bear than the words of their enraged commander. "Thanks and praise be to God," he said—if such words make sense in this situation—"that the victorious enemy did not actually attack our camp while you were hurling yourselves in panic onto the rampart and through the gates. You would assuredly have abandoned it as chicken-heartedly as you refused to stand up to him in the field. What is the meaning of this terror and fear? Of this sudden oblivion of who you are and with whom you are fighting? They are the same enemy as you spent last summer in thrashing on the field and in chasing off it, the same whom in these last few days you have day and night pursued in their efforts to escape you, whom you have skirmished with till they are sick of it, whom yesterday you would not allow either to keep going or to pitch a camp without molestation. Of the achieve-

*ments you may be proud of I say nothing: I shall speak only of what
you should be ashamed of and sorry for—that yesterday, in fair and
equal fight, you broke off the battle. That was yesterday, but now,
what have last night and today brought us? Have your forces been
weakened or Hannibal's increased in those few hours? I can hardly
believe I am speaking to my army, to Roman Soldiers; only your bodies and your weapons are recognizable as the same. If in these bodies
you have the same hearts, would the enemy have seen your backs?
Or taken the standards from a cohort or company? Till now he could
boast only about the destruction of Roman legions; today you have
given him for the first time the distinction of routing an army."*

Marcus Claudius Marcellus, consul, speech to his troops following
the Roman defeat at the Battle of Apulia, 209 BCE[13]

POST-BATTLE SPEECHES must account for a variety of tactical situations that come about after a battle. Victory—where the
enemy has been driven from the battlefield or its army has been captured, killed, dispersed, or surrendered—is the easy and obviously
most pleasant case. But except for draws, stalemates, or battles broken off, a winner usually entails a loser. And among the most difficult situations confronting a battle speechmaker is his address to a
defeated army. Marcellus's speech above was made after a relatively
minor engagement with Hannibal. Yet in many respects it thoroughly
illustrates the Post-Battle Speech of defeat.

According to Livy, Marcellus's Romans had "every day, punctually
at sunrise," been challenging Hannibal's army to leave camp and give
battle. Finally, in a Pre-Battle Speech, Hannibal indicated that he
had had enough Roman impudence. "Let the challenge once be accepted, let the enemy come out of a single battle with some bloodshed, and they would wage war more calmly and quietly in the future,"
Livy paraphrases Hannibal as speechifying to his soldiers. Hannibal's
army then succeeded in routing Marcellus's Romans. First, Marcellus's right *ala,* or wing, faltered; despite reinforcement by the Eighteenth Legion, the entire Roman army was soon moving in opposite
directions—one wing advancing and another retreating. "Confusion
turned to rout, duty was forgotten in panic, and [soldiers] fled for their

lives," Livy reported. The results, while less than catastrophic, were painful: "Some 2,700 men, citizens and allies, were killed; amongst them were four Roman centurions and two military tribunes." A total of six standards had been lost and presumably captured, which was an utter disgrace. Marcellus, who had begun the day by wanting to bloody Hannibal, had seen his own army bloodied instead. Later that day Marcellus presumably called a parade to deliver his Post-Battle Speech. The importance of command recognition (or censure) of the soldier-audience becomes obvious in Livy's first sentence. "Back in camp Marcellus addressed his men in such bitter and angry terms," he observed, "that a whole day's fighting followed by defeat was a lighter burden to bear than the words of their enraged commander." Men had known for hours that the battle had been humiliatingly lost, but seeing and hearing an angry Marcellus was the definitive "proof"—and soldiers probably shuddered, given the possible consequences.[14]

Like its opposite twin, the victorious Post-Battle Speech, Marcellus's remarks generally conform to Post-Battle Speech conventions. First, he presents the Story. But just as Robert E. Lee insinuated the Recognition Convention into his Fredericksburg story, so does Marcellus insinuate the Criticism Convention into his battle narrative. Marcellus's opening lines are barbed and sarcastic, and his first words could have been (but for two millennia) an angry parody of Lee's invocation of the divine. "Thanks and praise be to God," Marcellus declared, "that the victorious enemy did not actually attack our camp while you were hurling yourselves in panic onto the rampart and through the gates. You surely would have abandoned it as chicken-heartedly as you refused to stand up to him in the field." A few lines later he summarizes his history of that embarrassing loss: "Yesterday, in [a] fair and equal fight, you broke off the battle." And so Marcellus's history, considered alone, is highly critical of his soldiers, blaming everything on a panicked, "chicken-hearted" army that failed to do its duty.

But the real significance of Marcellus's Post-Battle Speech of Criticism is found not in this history but in the criticism itself. Like General Lee after Fredericksburg, Marcellus knows the war is not over and that he still needs his army; moreover, this army, despite its recent failure, was in fact a veteran army that had, until then, acquitted itself well on the battlefield. Indeed, much of Marcellus's criticism arises through comparing his soldiers' successes with this last defeat. "[Hannibal's soldiers] are the same enemy as you spent last summer in thrashing on the field and in chasing off it, the same whom in these last few days you have day and night pursued in their efforts to escape you, whom you have skirmished with till they are sick of it, whom yesterday you would not allow to either keep going or to pitch a camp without molestation [that is, before the battle]." Here Marcellus seeks to use a Unit Historical Narrative to sharpen his comments—the warriors that his soldiers were once are whom they must become again.

Marcellus uses their past as the first rebuke; but he drives the heart-stake home via the shame meme. Having offered the battle's history as his "proof," he suggests that his men are now something less than the Idea of Roman warriors:

> I can hardly believe I am speaking to my army, to Roman soldiers; only your bodies and your weapons are recognizable as the same. If in those bodies you had had the same hearts, would the enemy have seen your backs? Or taken the standards from a cohort or company? Till now he could boast only about the destruction of Roman legions; today you have given him for the first time the distinction of routing an army.

And it is here that Marcellus fulfills the Legacy Convention, albeit a very negative one: the distinction that his soldiers have earned—what their peers will learn and posterity will forever remember—is that they belonged to the first army entirely routed by Hannibal.

Unless the commander/battle speechmaker intends to liquidate his entire army (and the Post-Battle Speech becomes something like a death warrant read just before an execution), the Criticism Convention must, to be productive, contain something of a diagnosis of what went wrong, and more importantly, a remedy for it. After all, what is the point of a Criticism Convention without remedies? Punishment alone cannot suffice.

The war against Hannibal, already in its tenth year, had to go on, and Marcellus would continue to field this otherwise competent army. He has already hinted at what went wrong: the bodies and weapons might have been Roman (that is, the soldiers were properly fed, drilled, and equipped) but their "hearts," that is, their morale, had weakened. Battlefield incompetence from poor morale is quite different from cowardice, mutiny, or a refusal to obey orders. As Marcellus knew, poor morale is eminently fixable. And he began to do just that with his speech, the effect of which was to stoke his soldiers' sense of shame and (hopefully) create some overcompensation.

According to Livy, his troops followed this script. Marcellus had no sooner finished speaking than "from the ranks arose a cry for pardon for that day's sorry work, and Marcellus was besought to put his men's courage once more to the test whenever he might wish." *Now* Marcellus made a second brief speech, as today's Post-Battle Speech gave way to tomorrow's Pre-Battle Speech: "Yes, I shall do so, my soldiers," he answered the throng, "tomorrow I shall lead you into battle, so that as victors rather than vanquished you may win the pardon for which you ask." There was only the matter of punishment for the day's mishaps. Given what was within Marcellus's power to inflict, the sentence was quite light: those responsible for losing standards were given rations of barley instead of wheat (considered a humiliation) and in the presence of the entire army ordered to "fall out" from the line and thereby receive another unwelcome distinction.[15]

As narrated by Livy, Marcellus's approach worked. His soldier-audience, including those he singled out to be shamed, not only bore no grudge but willingly conceded their commander's wisdom. After Marcellus dismissed his men, "all admit[ed] that they had fully deserved censure and that in the day's fighting there had been not a single real man in the Roman line except their commander, to whom they owed the reparation either of death or of glorious victory." And in battle against Hannibal's army the following day, Marcellus's army prevailed.[16]

Victory and the Criticism Convention

Brave regiments of the division, you have won for us a high reputation. The country is satisfied. Your friends at home are proud of you. After two battles and victories, purchased with much blood, you may be counted as veterans.

1. *I appeal, then, to your experience, to your personal observation, to your high intelligence to put in practice on the battle-field the discipline you have acquired in camp. It will enable you to conquer with more certainty and less loss. . . .*

4. *Men! You brave individuals in the ranks, whose worth and daring, unknown perhaps to your superiors, but recognized by your comrades, influence more than others. I know that you exist. I have watched you in the fire; your merit is sure to have recompense. Your comrades at the bivouac will report your deeds, and it will gladden your families. In the end, you will be brought before the country.*

5. *Color-bearers of regiments, bear them proudly in the fight, erect and defiantly, in the first line. It will cast terror into the opponents to see it sustained and carried forward. . . . The noblest inscriptions on your banner are the traces of the balls.*

6. *Again, noble division, I wish you success and new victories, until, the cause of our sacred Union being triumphant, you return honored to your homes.*

Excerpt from General Philip Kearny's General Orders No. 15, June 5, 1862[17]

IN CONCLUDING this discussion, it is worth briefly noting that the use of the Criticism Convention does not require a defeat, only a perfection-seeking commander prepared to use any occasion to recommend improvements. General Kearny's speech above, issued after the Battles of Williamsburg and Fair Oaks—Federal victories of a sort—is one such example. It also illustrates how a speaker's personality can influence a battle speech. Why Philip Kearny in particular might have been inclined to join criticism and victory is suggested by his resume: he was a genuine man of war. At the age of twenty-five, he inherited the then-astronomical sum of one million dollars; but rather than join the industrial revolution or become a gentleman of leisure, he fulfilled his childhood dream of becoming a soldier, and the next year took a lieutenancy with the First United States Dragoons. One year later, at the behest of the War Department, he traveled to France and enrolled in the French Cavalry School at Saumur; in 1840 he served with the Chasseurs d'Afrique, contributing his efforts to the French conquest of Algeria. During the Mexican War he lost his left arm at Churubusco (1847), and in 1851 he left the service for world travel. But he did not leave war. In 1859 he traveled to France and again joined the Chasseurs d'Afrique, traveling with them on Napoleon III's Italian campaign. He charged with the French cavalry at Magenta and Solferino and during the latter battle was reported "holding his bridle in his teeth, with his characteristic impetuosity." As a result he was the first American to receive the Legion d'honneur. Naturally, such a man would not miss his own country's civil war, and May 1861 found him home again and in command of the First New Jersey Brigade. On April 30, 1862, he was commanding the Army of the Potomac's Third Division of Three Corps.[18]

Kearny recognizes but spends few words on the Story Convention ("after two battles and victories, purchased with much blood, you may be counted as veterans"), the Legacy Convention ("Brave regiments of the division, you have won for us a high reputation. The country is satisfied. Your friends at home are proud of you"), or the Preparedness Convention ("I wish you success and new victories, until the cause of our sacred Union being triumphant, you return honored to your homes"). Instead, in several of six enumerated paragraphs (only four of which are excerpted above), he weaves together Recognition and Criticism Conventions in a series of admonishments that are intended to increase efficiency and reduce casualties.

His comments have two threads: technical admonishments (not reproduced in the epigraph but well worth reading for their insights on Civil War–era infantry tactics) combined with morale enhancers. In paragraph 5, he admonishes and at the same time implicitly praises his color bearers, whose function was critical to the organization, battlefield communications, and morale of the regiment. First is the criticism, gently admonitory but identifying no specific color bearer or battle, and phrased maxim-like so as to transcend any cavils: "Color-bearers of the regiments, bear them proudly in the fight, erect and defiantly, in the first line. It will cast terror into the opponents to see it sustained and carried forward. Let it be the beacon-light of each regiment." Kearny's soldier-audience probably inferred from this that some color-bearers in one or both of the battles were not in the first line and did not carry the flags "erect and defiantly." Kearny is generous as to the reasons why this was so—perhaps his regiments' color-bearers failed because they did not understand the important advantages of psychological warfare ("terror into the opponents") and morale ("beacon-light of each regiment") conferred by carrying the colors ostentatiously in a battle.

But many, if not most, color bearers probably did carry the flags to Kearny's satisfaction, and for them he offers cleverly worded praise: "The noblest inscriptions on your banner," he declares, "are the traces of the balls." Again, no individual or specific regiment is singled out for praise; instead, what Kearny offers is a standard that can be self-proofed. Color-bearers have only to inspect their colors—flags rent by shot and shell were obviously those carried in the front lines, "erect and defiantly."

Kearny uses similar words of self-proof to emphasize a theme featured prominently throughout this book—the importance of commander cognizance of both individual and collective valor. Consider how Kearny addresses this issue in his paragraph 4:

> Men! you brave individuals in the ranks, whose worth and daring, unknown perhaps to your superiors, but recognized by your comrades, influence more than others. I know that you exist. I have watched you in the fire; your merit is sure to have its recompense. Your comrades at the bivouac will report your deeds, and it will gladden your families. In the end, you will be brought before the country.

Here, Kearny does not differentiate among individuals or specific units, although he is obviously not referring to every soldier in the Third Division. First, there are those "brave individuals [of] worth and daring" whose qualities are inevitably recognized by others ("your comrades"). By refusing to give names or units, Kearny leaves every soldier free to imagine that it is to him that the general now refers. Moreover, Kearny allows each man to fantasize that his peers have observed him ("recognized by your comrades"), that their commander has noticed him ("I have watched you in the fire"), and that soon his family and his country will also learn of his bravery ("gladden your families . . . brought before the country"). Thus each soldier may be secure in the knowledge that his deeds are being recorded by others for eventual redistribution elsewhere. Such a scheme relieves the commander, who had led this division for only sixty-five hectic days, from having to recite individual or unit bravery. And for those who skulked, fled, or pretended to be ill? No need to name them either, for they already know themselves to be outside the space Kearny has created for the brave and their comrades.

The Legacy Convention: Variations

Soldiers! When we have completed all that is necessary to secure the happiness and prosperity of our country, I will lead you back to France; there you will be the constant objects of my loving care. My people will hail your return with joy, and you will have to say, "I was at the battle of Austerlitz," to hear the reply, "He is one of the brave."

Excerpt from Napoleon's Post-Battle Speech after Austerlitz,
December 3, 1805

When all resistance was at an end the king gathered his men about him, and calling silence with uplifted hand thanked them for the valor they had shown on that glorious field, which would be to all men a proof that their cause was just. Yet let them not attribute their success to their own might but solely to the grace of God, who by the means of his little band had humbled this great host of Frenchmen in the dust.

King Henry V's Post-Battle Speech after Agincourt, October 25, 1415

Whoever lives past today and comes home safely will rouse himself every year on this day, show his neighbor his scars, and tell embellished stores of all their great feats of battle. These stories he will teach his son and from this day until the end of the world we shall be remembered. We few, we happy few, we band of brothers; for whoever has shed his blood with me shall be my brother. And those men afraid to go will think themselves lesser men as they hear of how we fought and died together.

Excerpt from Major General William F. Garrison's Post-Battle Speech
paraphrasing William Shakespeare, *Henry V*, act 4, scene 3[19]

IF THE PURPOSE OF the Story Convention is to flatter (after victories) or improve or criticize (after mediocre performances or defeats) the soldier-audience, then the Legacy Convention exists to console them amidst the otherwise inexplicable carnage of the battlefield. Little imagination is required to conceive of the reasons why Post-Battle speechmakers might want to broadly interpret war's seemingly insane leavings. The recent sights and odors of death in its most vivid forms haunt the memories of soldiers who themselves may have difficulty accounting for their own survival; chances are that this death was distributed randomly, chaotically, without regard to individual character, friendships, or merit; sooner or later, at length or briefly, even victorious armies will host large numbers of mourners. Facing all of this, battle speechmakers and their soldier-audiences require order from disorder and redemption from sin, even sin legally sanctioned; soldiers must have assurances that the object was worth the cost, that dead comrades died for something greater than just bad luck, and that the enemy dead, whether valiant, brave, or ruthless, nevertheless deserved their fate. It is through the Legacy Convention that higher reason descends upon the battlefield to remind combatants that the late struggle was about something, and that as human beings, they have been redeemed after so much bloodletting. Chaos is a metaphorical vacuum that invites an order-imposing narrative.

In the beginning of this chapter Robert E. Lee's Post-Battle Speech following Fredericksburg included a common Legacy meme: the recent victory redounded to the benefit of the nation and the army. But the Legacy Convention has many variations. While Lee's meme was impersonal, the excerpt from Napoleon's Post-Battle Speech after his great victory at Austerlitz is quite personal, inviting each soldier to visualize his own rewards from the hand of an imagined posterity. Lee, a religious man, filled his speech with gratitude to God, but the second example above, drawn from the real Henry V's Post-Battle Speech after the Battle of Agincourt, is almost Biblical in its Legacy Convention. The third example is General William F. Garrison's paraphrase of Shakespeare's fictional speech from his play *Henry V*. Garrison delivered his version following the October 1993 American military setback in Mogadishu, Somalia. A fictional speech would not normally be included in a study of "real" battle speeches, but by incorporating the Bard's *Pre*-Battle Speech into his own *Post*-Battle Speech, Garrison allows it to be considered here as the default meme of post-battle narratives: whether all is explicable or not, that which was done was done for the sakes of comrades.

Following his smashing victory at Austerlitz, Napoleon's Post-Battle Speech (a printed proclamation) sticks to the usual Story Convention (and then some) by giving special credit to his army. In an unexcerpted portion of the speech, Napoleon addresses them directly to further emphasize his soldiers' achievements in this battle: "Well done, soldiers! In the battle *you* have accomplished . . . *your* valor . . . *you* have crowned *your* eagles . . . What escaped *your* arms was drowned in the lakes . . . [The enemy], that outnumbered *you*, was unable to resist *your* attack, and henceforth *you* have no rivals to fear" [emphasis added]. According to Napoleon, his men defeated 100,000 enemy soldiers in "less than four hours," captured forty flags, the Russian Imperial Guard's standards, "120 guns, 20 generals, [and] more than 30,000 prisoners." However, the great victory, as all victories, came at a price. One historian suggests that Napoleon's claims of losses amounting to only 900 dead and 3,000 wounded "can safely be doubled." But whatever the final numbers, the emperor himself was characteristically sensitive to the plight of his wounded soldiers. With what remained of the daylight and well into the night he traveled the battlefield, often asking his staff "to keep quiet so 'that they could hear the cries of the wounded.'" He personally succored the wounded, "giving each a stiff drink of brandy and assurance that his wounds would soon be dressed and that he would soon be evacuated." The next day Napoleon wrote the speech excerpted in the epigraph.

Napoleon had described Austerlitz as "this eternally glorious battle." And of course by crediting his army with this great victory, he must also credit them with a reward commensurate to it. He makes three promises. The first is a reward probably most valued by most soldiers in every war ever fought—the promise that the army would be going home. "I will lead you back to France," he assures them, subject only to completing "all that is necessary to secure the happiness and prosperity of the country." (Whether the majority of his soldiers regarded this statement as a necessary contingency or resented it as weasel words is not known.) The second promise is that, once they have returned home, the soldiers "will be the constant objects of my loving care." This can only be interpreted as the promise of generous pensions, stipends for wounded soldiers, perhaps even bonuses of money. However, both returning home and enjoying material benefits are rewards, not legacies.

But Napoleon concludes his speech by informing his soldiers that they have also earned the right to the legacy of Austerlitz. And what is that? Earlier in his speech, Napoleon mentions two aspects. One was presumably permanent ("immortal glory . . . eternally glorious battle") while the other was likely temporary ("henceforth you have no rivals to fear"). Unlike Lee's post-Fredericksburg legacy, where he implied that his men could draw meaning from the slaughter by remembering that what was accomplished benefited both the government and their army, Napoleon does not define his legacy beyond asserting that it was "glorious." Instead, his appeal is based on a prophetic understanding of the very word "Austerlitz"; here, a mere one day after the battle, the history-obsessed Napoleon has already enshrined it as a celebrity event, one that will rank with Thermopylae, Cannae, or Issus. In passing he mentions that this newly minted highlight will also help "secure the happiness and prosperity of our country." But that is not the whole legacy, or even the most important one, which is instead social: his men can look forward to enjoying the prestige of having been part of it. Here Napoleon constructs an imaginary future conversation between an Austerlitz veteran and an anonymous French citizen. The veteran says "I was at the battle of Austerlitz," to which the civilian replies (to a caring audience, perhaps?), "He is one of the brave."

This imaginary conversation interprets Austerlitz's legacy in terms of each soldier's personal prestige and status. (It also assumes that the civilian community immediately shares Napoleon's understanding of Austerlitz's historical significance.) The Legacy Convention here, the thing evoked afterward to justify the battle, involves the gratitude of civilians at home and the reflected glory of the fighting itself. Beyond the personal importance derived from one's association with the celebrity name of Austerlitz, Napoleon does not invest his victory with much abstract or impersonal significance. "The signal manifestations of Divine mercy" that General Lee said made his victory possible are nowhere mentioned by Napoleon. Nor does he note higher causes of any kind. Austerlitz's legacy might be "eternal," but from each soldier's perspective it will be recognized in this world, not the next; in his lifetime, not his grandchildren's; for his benefit, not that of the perpetual state, the Grande Armèe, or the eternal God. Here, the battle is its own legacy.

How different is the Legacy Convention contained in Henry V's Post-Battle Speech! Of course one expects it to be so—the Battle of Agincourt was fought 490 years earlier, in an age that was as concerned with understanding God's hand in events as Napoleon was concerned with his place in secular time. Agincourt, though, was another smashing victory, this time for the English. Casualties for the latter are thought to have been low, only "some hundreds," according to historian John Keegan; the French fared far worse. While that army still threatened Henry's, he ordered that French prisoners of war be killed, and many were, until the Counts of Masle and Fauquemberghes finally withdrew and the English king was convinced that his victory was secure. For enemy wounded, Keegan speculates that the storms of English arrows and inherent weaknesses in French armor probably produced deep and dirty wounds; those unattended Frenchmen who were not killed immediately probably expired after the cold night of October 25–26 on the battlefield or were killed the next morning by the English. Keegan reports that the Bishop of Arras oversaw some six thousand burials, presumably mostly French.[20]

As Keegan points out in *The Face of Battle,* Henry V was "an experienced soldier and versed in the elaborate code of international law governing relations between a prisoner and his captor," whose "most important provision was that which guaranteed the prisoner his life." Henry was also a "Christian king," presumably bound by his religion, which held that "the prisoner's life was guaranteed by the Christian commandment against murder." However one interprets Henry's controversial order, then, between the horrific sights and smells of the battlefield and the fresh memories of killing both armed and unarmed men, it is entirely understandable that afterward many English soldiers sought additional rationales for why they had fought (or why the battle was worth fighting). Or perhaps they simply wanted fellowship amidst such extraordinary scenes. It may be important for a commander to accommodate this need in the hours and days after a battle, before any consensus of its tactical, strategic, or historic significance has been established. And as the passage in the epigraph suggests, King Henry obliged, and quickly.[21]

If Henry's words have the feel of a prayer, this is probably because his Post-Battle Speech is homiletic. It acknowledges God's sovereignty over worldly affairs, cautions his own men against the sin of pride, and chastises the enemy for being prideful. And perhaps some staging was involved. "When all resistance was at end the king gathered his men about him, and calling in silence with uplifted hand thanked them for the valor they had shown on the glorious field, *which would be to all men a proof that their cause was just*" [emphasis added]. Here Henry invokes the appropriate solemnity—prayerful intentions must be focused and prayers offered undisturbed—and simultaneously advances one central object of the Recognition and Story Convention by thanking his men "for the valor they had shown." But as the italicized words suggest, he also advances another important part of a Story Convention, one that begins to blend into Legacy. The very fact that Henry and his men stand as victors upon the battlefield should justify (though it cannot banish) the fresh sights, smells, and sounds of death. They are victorious, and only the just are favored with victory. (Although here, God was not the Biblical general as He was when advising Moses and Joshua about tactics, but rather the English soldiers were his instruments; but to properly qualify as divine instruments, they must first be righteous, which Henry suggests means avoiding the sin of pride. By Henry's time God's visible sovereignty over humankind had become hidden compared to the days of Moses and Joshua when He directly advised commanders. In those days soldiers could massacre a city's entire population [including domestic animals] and do so in good conscience because God Himself had approved, even commanded the action. But by Henry's time, the command to kill came from men and God's approval of such killing could only be learned by men's interpretations of His will.) The end does not so much as justify the means as redeem the sins incurred in attaining it.

And how does Henry interpret God's will? He provides an answer in the next sentence. "Yet let them not attribute their success to their own might but solely to the grace of God, who by means of this little band had humbled this great host of Frenchmen in the dust." These few words contain four mutually reinforcing messages, all of which strive to explain the victory and provide its legacy. First, Henry cautions his men against the sin of pride. This is a traditional religious message, but here it may play a special role. If Henry and his men had won the battle without God's help, then they might be personally answerable to God for certain actions during it—not just the killing during combat but also the killing of prisoners and, later, wounded men. But in Henry's second message (their victory was due "solely to the grace of God") he is also comforting soldiers who stand on (or near) the battlefield, enveloped by death's landscape itself, in whose creation they had played a part. And contained in the second part of this sentence is Henry's third message, which advances his religious interpretation still further: it was God "who by means of his little band [that is, Henry's army] had humbled this great host of Frenchmen in the dust." In other words, Henry's army was only God's instrument, and their actions were justified by Heaven's mandate. Finally, the army's/God's actions are further justified as retribution for French sin, especially the very sin that the king had just cautioned his men against—pride. In fact, based on James Hamilton Wylie's account of Henry V's various words before and after Agincourt, pride plays an important part in the king's feelings about the French. Before the battle, when Sir Walter Hungerford observed how badly the English were outnumbered and wished for "10,000 more good English archers," his king rebuked him with a reminder of just who the English really were and what their role was likely to be in the looming battle: "This people is God's people," Henry declared. "He has entrusted them to me to-day and He can bring down the pride of these Frenchmen who boast of their numbers and their strength." God would use his English instrument to punish the French for their pride.[22]

And so the Legacy Convention was likewise fulfilled. Those men who heard Henry's Post-Battle Speech and others who learned of it later came to understand that the battle's lasting consequence was additional vindication (if any were needed) that the English remained "God's people." They had fought to humble the French and demonstrate that it was God's will, not superior numbers, that determined the destiny of nations. It was a legacy that at least in Henry's mind clearly matched the battle's importance. Moreover, the narrative of having done God's justice was made in a time that welcomed them; thus it might also have calmed any doubters in the soldier-audience who questioned their individual acts and those of their commanders.

Napoleon and Henry V led their armies to triumphs that remain classic battles of their type, and the Legacy Conventions contained in their respective Post-Battle Speeches are also types, Napoleon's stressing the romance and glory of victory and Henry V's reminding his men that they acted as God's instrument. But what about those who lose battles or preside over setbacks? What Legacy Convention do they use in their Post-Battle Speeches? Assuming that such an unfortunate battle speechmaker's force survived, he will still likely deliver some Post-Battle Speech that attempts to convince his soldiers that the battle was worth fighting, that the dead died for something, and that the survivors will remember their participation as having some meaning beyond mere survival. The Legacy Convention contained in Major General William F. Garrison's Post-Battle Speech after bloody complications followed a "snatch and grab" operation in Mogadishu, Somalia, October 3–4, 1993, offers some insights here. In the last chapter this operation was the setting in which Sergeant Struecker appealed to Specialist Thomas to remember his duty.

The Mogadishu "battle" began when American soldiers attempted to kidnap key deputies of Somali warlord Mohamed Farrah Aidid. The details are beyond the scope of this book; suffice it to say that as the operation proceeded, Aidid's militia was alerted, and these forces then mobilized a heavily armed civilian population (some of whom were affiliated with the militia or other nationalist groups) to attack the American soldiers. Confidence in American air superiority, while not negated, was dented when Aidid's forces, equipped with shoulder-launched missiles, shot down two Black Hawk helicopters. Soon, the daylight "snatch and grab" operation became a desperate attempt to rescue soldiers trapped in Mogadishu's central city, which for Americans on the ground was an unfamiliar labyrinth of streets and alleyways bordered by low houses and shops. Adding to the urgency was that many men were wounded or short of water, ammunition, and medical supplies; moreover, expecting a short daylight operation, most of the soldiers left behind their night vision equipment; pinned down in Mogadishu overnight, these men found their defenses hampered and escape through the dark nearly impossible. And throughout this entire episode, General Garrison was at the base just a few miles away, monitoring anguished conversations on the radio and viewing televised images of wreckage and death as events slowly unfolded. Aidid's deputies had been arrested, but the cost was extreme: eighteen Americans and one Malaysian soldier had died and seventy-three Americans, seven Malaysians, and one Pakistani soldier had been wounded. Several days after the Americans were evacuated (except for one hostage), General Garrison assembled his command for a memorial service and delivered the Post-Battle Speech excerpted above.[23]

Garrison uses his own paraphrase of a portion of Henry V's fictional *Pre*-Battle Speech in act 4, scene 3, of Shakespeare's play bearing the monarch's name.[24] Much had changed in the two centuries' time between the flesh-and-blood Henry and William Shakespeare's fictional version. By the Bard's day, man had become the measure of many more things than was true of the real Henry's late medieval world; the fictional Henry's speech mentions God twice and Jove once, and all three as mere apostrophes; the fact that the battle falls on the religious feast day of Saint Crispin is pure coincidence, and Shakespeare uses it only as a fine-sounding calendrical reference point for future generations to mark the event. One of Shakespeare's concerns was the budding English nationalism of his time; the real Henry conceived nationalism only through the lens of religion, that is, the English as "God's people."

General Garrison's paraphrase is not concerned with God or nationalism; rather, he removes Shakespeare's lines from their original context and universalizes them, thus transforming the Bard's nationalist, rousing pre-battle sentiments into something reflective, tragic, and yet expressive of the warrior's code. Gone are the Lords, Saint Crispin, and the fact that the "gentlemen . . . now a-bed" are English; gone too is Shakespearian diction. For example,

> That he which hath no stomach for this fight,
> Let him depart. His passport shall be made,
> And crowns for convoy put into his purse
> We would not die in that man's company

is paraphrased by Garrison for his late-twentieth-century audience as follows: "Whoever does not have the stomach for this fight, let him depart. Give him money to speed his departure since we wish not to die in that man's company." What matters here is how Shakespeare's timeless formulation of comradeship ("We few, we happy few, we band of brothers") is now able to serve Garrison's need to make sense of—that is, to embrace—the Legacy Convention for a military action whose cost in blood exceeded its tactical or strategic benefits.

Garrison spoke directly to the operation's survivors, whom it would have been impossible to persuade via some tactical or strategic argument that the mission's cost was worth its price. First, such an argument would have been untrue; second, the soldier-audience was most likely in various stages of mourning, and such an argument might have been considered inappropriate. Instead, Garrison builds his Legacy Convention using Shakespeare's words. He is able to do this because Henry V's speech is a rarity among battle speeches (as a work of fiction, it can be). It is both a Pre-Battle and a Post-Battle Speech, and as such it has what few Pre-Battle Speeches possess: a Legacy Convention. This is so because when *Henry V* was written (1599), Shakespeare had the historian's advantage of knowing how the Battle of Agincourt ended; otherwise, the Bard's Henry could never have been able to assure the Lords Gloucester, Bedford, Westmoreland, and Exeter that "From this day to the ending of the world, / But we in it shall be remember'd" or that those sleeping English gentlemen "shall think themselves accursed they were not here." Although the Confidence Convention helps define the Pre-Battle Speech, few real Pre-Battle Speechmakers would ever venture this kind of confidence—after all, Henry's army might have done no better than a forgettable stalemate, or perhaps they would have ingloriously fled the field, or lost the battle and been captured and killed to the last soldier. In this last case especially, it is likely that no matter how some speechmaker glorified comradeship, many an English gentlemen would have thanked his God profusely that he was in bed and not in France.

But by knowing that the real Henry won, Shakespeare can universalize the fictitious Henry's ideas into a battle speech for every occasion. During a real battle, with victory still in the balance, not all soldiers prove worthy of joining the band of brothers. Some men kill themselves or each other through gross negligence, some flee or hide, some claim credit for deeds not their own, some cast blame to deflect from misdeeds, some exaggerate what they actually accomplished. But great victories tend to deodorize such unwelcome, embarrassing, or despicable behavior. After a victory, one is more inclined to deem a fellow battle participant to be a comrade without necessarily asking for too many details. The victory at Agincourt, coupled with Shakespeare's great gift, allowed him to formulate an ageless comrade's code that has since well served many a soldier, historian, and Hollywood screenwriter. And it succeeds equally well in speeches made before, during, and after battles. The principal reason is that while the destruction wrought in battle is often inexplicable, and the battles themselves may be initiated on foolish orders from faraway leaders whose policies of state and understanding of local conditions are detached from reality, the one thing whose existence is tangible is one soldier rubbing another's elbow in a line of battle. It is a thing as elemental and universal as human friendship, only more so. After all, war is an intensely social enterprise.[25]

Thus does Garrison's Legacy Convention reduce to just two words: each other. His reworked Shakespeare turns on the Bard's most famous lines: "We few, we happy few, we band of brothers; for whoever has shed his blood with me shall be my brother" [Garrison's version]. One is either in the band or out of it, and the band's first rule is the willingness to fight: "Whoever does not have the stomach for this fight, let him depart." The second rule is that those in the band will choose for themselves any others with whom they wish to spend—or end—their lives: "Give him [that is, the man who lacks the willingness to fight] money to speed his departure, since we wish not to die in that man's company." The band has other rules and customs as well. Members are set apart and grow in stature as time passes; they have even earned some license to exaggerate their role in the battle; accuracy matters less for participants than for non-participants, because the former, through membership in the band, have already become slightly mythologized, as had Leonidas's Three Hundred or Xerxes' Immortals. (Does it matter to myth that at Thermopylae Leonidas was joined by thousands of other Greeks or that Xerxes' Immortals proved to be less so?) "Whoever lives past today and comes home safely will rouse himself every year on this day," Garrison continues his paraphrase, "show his neighbors his scars, and tell embellished stories of all their great feats of battle. These stories he will teach his son and from this day until the end of the world we shall be remembered." Moreover, Garrison implies that members of the fighting band will not have to wait for the end of the world to reap the status deriving from their participation. Instead, they will benefit during their lives because "men [who were] afraid to go" to the battle "will think themselves lesser men as they hear of how we fought and died together." (Here one recalls Dr. Johnson's observation that "Every man thinks meanly of himself for not having been a soldier, or not having been at sea.")[26]

By definition, a universal sentiment is also a default sentiment. Shakespeare via General Garrison has provided a durable Legacy Convention that suits stunning victories such as Henry V's Agincourt or Robert E. Lee's Fredericksburg, battles of mixed results such as Mogadishu, and even outright defeats. It is the ultimate appeal because it appreciates the warriors on both sides of a battlefield regardless of the battle's outcome. The only requirement for inclusion in the band is survival, with some sense of honor intact.

The Post-Battle Speech after No Battle: Concluding a Modern Mission

We want to ensure that each of you understands what a tremendous impact the successful conduct of your assigned mission here has had on the people of Iraq, the American people and on the people of the region.

The selfless and impartial actions of you and your fellow Soldiers have demonstrated to the Iraqi people that there is hope for a democratic and impartial government. Your effective blend of combat and civic actions has brought many of the insurgents back into the political process. . . . Whether they can achieve such a lofty goal remains to be seen, but you have ensured that they have the opportunity and have provided them with an excellent example. . . .

Your relentless pursuit and destruction of al-Qaeda and related terrorists has been awesome. . . . Because of your determination to destroy these killers, the Iraqi people are safer and the American people are able to enjoy a life virtually uninterrupted by the threats and wanton acts of violence that these murderers employ. And that's why we serve. We could do no more in this area while we were here; but this is a fight that will continue to demand the attention and sacrifice of our Armed Forces for the foreseeable future. . . .

We could not be more proud of the manner in which you have conducted yourselves individually and as units. The sacrifices you have made and the losses we have suffered cannot be repaid or replaced; but they must be remembered.

Freedom isn't free, and your time here should illustrate vividly the very thin line between what we enjoy (and often take for granted) in our American way of life and the circumstances of others who lack the legacy and blessings of democracy. . . .

> Excerpt from "Command View" signed by Colonel Brian D. Jones and Command Sergeant Major David H. List, *Iron Brigade Chronicles,* October 23, 2006[27]

As was noted in the introduction to this volume, tactics can determine the type, duration, and content of battle speeches. While the epilogue contains a more detailed discussion of how current tactical developments might influence battle speeches in the future, it is appropriate to conclude this chapter with a recent Post-Battle Speech in which the mission, while replete with armed conflict, experienced no battle as that word has been traditionally understood since antiquity. In the above speech, Colonel Brian D. Jones joined with his senior noncommissioned officer to help their soldier-audience of the Third Heavy Brigade Combat Team [HBCT] (Fourth Infantry Division) understand the results of their unit's twelve-month tour in Iraq. That mission saw fighting aplenty, although attempts to capture the ultimate objective—favorable Iraqi public opinion—were as often made via doctors, the distribution of medical equipment, or the return of artifacts to an Iraqi museum as they were via guns.[28]

Here the Story Convention consists of a narrative that is different from the usual recounting of confronted enemies or damage inflicted. What the Third HBCT was meant to accomplish is stated early and, typical of Post-Battle Speeches, is couched in Recognition: "The selfless and impartial actions of you and your fellow Soldiers have demonstrated that there is hope for a democratic and impartial [Iraqi] government." To accomplish this, the unit's gun-toting warriors, while necessary, were not the only component required to complete the assignment. The task in fact required a twofold approach: an "effective blend of combat and civic actions" that ultimately, according to Jones and List, succeeded in returning "many of the insurgents back into the civic process." In short, in a departure from the purely military assessments of past Story Conventions, the narrative here must include a political assessment, for at bottom, that was the Third HBCT's mission. But as Jones and List indicate, to fulfill the mission, violence was still required: "Your relentless pursuit and destruction of al-Qaeda and related terrorists have been awesome," they declared. "Because of your determination to destroy these killers, the Iraq people are safer and the American people are able to enjoy a life virtually uninterrupted by the threats and wanton acts of violence that these murderers employ. And that's why we serve." Here the politics are disambiguated—the Third HBCT discloses two "clients," Iraqis and Americans.

This "Command View" column, like most Post-Battle Speeches, uses the Story Convention to support Recognition of the soldier-audience. As is readily apparent in the speech's passages thus far, the senior command expresses its approval of its soldier-audience's job performance with each accomplishment it mentions. And even more explicit approval appears toward the end of the speech: "We could not be more proud of the manner in which you have conducted yourselves individually and as units," the two men announce. "The sacrifices you have made and the losses we have suffered cannot be repaid or replaced; but they must be remembered." In military speech, the word "sacrifices" invariably refers to those killed in the line of duty, and in Post-Battle Speeches, any talk of death raises the all-important Legacy Convention.

The Legacy Convention is a species of Recognition, one that is articulated in terms more universal and transcendent than the immediate concrete results of enemy killed or miles marched. And here Jones and List deploy the Legacy Convention with great force. Their soldier-audience readers have probably already detected Legacy language in the Story Convention—for example, Iraqis having been made "safer" and Americans are "able to enjoy a life uninterrupted by threats and wanton acts of violence." But the two men also fulfill the Legacy Convention in ways that, given the political nature of the mission, reveals some ambivalence about it. Simply put, it is easier to destroy a column of enemy tanks than it is to change the way an ancient collection of tribes and ethnicities govern themselves; it is likewise easier to fight a war with undivided home-front support than a war in which a very few fight while most live as if there is no war. First, elsewhere in the column, in a passage of unusual candor, Jones and List posit a legacy of democratization, albeit one that has had very mixed results in the neighborhood:

> Your actions are also reverberating around the Middle East. Regimes in Syria, Jordan, Saudi Arabia, Iran and Egypt feel threatened by the possibility of a truly democratic government emerging in Iraq. They are taking an active role to defeat the chances of a democratic political success in Iraq. They may clothe this opposition in religious or political garb, but the fact is that they do not want the "dangerous" ideas of democracy to affect the ways they are able to exert control on their people. Your role in this is to provide a chance of democracy not only for the Iraqi people, but to allow them to serve as an example for their neighbors.

What makes this statement so striking is that of the five regimes mentioned, three—Jordan, Saudi Arabia, and Egypt—are (supposedly) bedrock U.S. allies in the region. On the other hand, from Jones and List's perspective, many of the fighters and much of the destruction that American soldiers contend with are coming from foreign nationals who are natives of these countries.

Readers are given another hint of ambivalence about the vital topic of the relationship of the home front to the war effort. Months earlier, Sergeant Major List published a poem in the *Iron Brigade Chronicles* entitled "The Price of Freedom" that his father, an army staff sergeant then serving in Vietnam, had written in 1970. It included these lines:

> There are people at home that don't understand
> The reason we are here in this land.
> There are some folks that yell in protest
> Because some coward said it is the best.
> Let them folks see a little boy,
> That never in his life owned a toy.
> Let them see a little girl in fear,
> And in each eye a great big tear.
>
> . . . .
>
> Those people back there who think we are wrong,
> Are not Americans and not very strong.
> The price of freedom comes very high,
> It is for certain many good men will die.[29]

Thirty-six years later, the son signs a Post-Battle Speech that concludes with this sentence: "Freedom isn't free, and your time here should illustrate vividly the very thin line between what we enjoy (and often take for granted) in our American way of life and the circumstances of others who lack the legacy and blessings of democracy." Thus do the Story and Legacy Conventions incorporate an ambivalence absent from the traditional Post-Battle Speech; while it may be true, to paraphrase Von Clausewitz, that war is a continuation of politics by other means, it is not always true that soldiers are also asked to serve as local politicians (though it has been so in Iraq).

Nevertheless, while the Third HBCT's civilian masters attempt to resolve exactly what kind of struggle the unit is fighting in — a war, as in the "Global War on Terror"; an "Intervention, Stabilization, and Transformation Operation"; or something akin to an older style police action — Jones and List understand that, whatever the case, "it" will continue for some time.[30] Thus the Post-Battle Speech's traditional Preparedness Convention appears, cautioning the soldier-audience that it has made only a down payment in what promises to be a longer struggle: "We could have done no more in this area while we were here," they conclude. "[But] this is a fight that will continue to demand the attention and sacrifice of our Armed Forces for the foreseeable future. Make no mistake: this threat is real and dangerous and it must be confronted."

What is striking about the conventions of Post-Battle Speeches is how adaptable they are. Tactics, missions, and circumstances change, but not the need to persuade the soldier-audience that the effort was worthwhile, that they performed well, and that more has yet to be done. The fact that soldiers must be told these things is itself a function of the "will to narrate," a human response to confronting that which is sometimes inexplicable.

8

ARRIVALS AND DEPARTURES
Assuming Command, Saying Farewell, Surrender, and Final Victory

Assuming Command

By direction of the President of the United States, I hereby assume command of the Army of the Potomac.

As a soldier, in obeying this order—an order totally unexpected and unsolicited—I have no promises or pledges to make.

The country looks to this army to relieve it from the devastation and disgrace of a hostile invasion. Whatever fatigues and sacrifices we may be called upon to undergo, let us have in view constantly the magnitude of the interests involved, and let each man determined to do his duty, leaving to an all-controlling Providence the decision of the contest.

It is with just such diffidence that I relieve in the command of this army an eminent and accomplished soldier, whose name must ever appear conspicuous in the history of its achievements; but I rely upon the hearty support of my companions in arms to assist me in the discharge of the duties of the important trust which has been confided to me.

General Orders No. 67, Major General George G. Meade's Assumption
of Command Speech to the Army of the Potomac, June 28, 1863

I don't remember word for word what I said to the Platoon [on taking command] but I am sure it had a lot of "fuck y'all," "mother fuckers," "it was bullshit that they were so fucked up that their Lt got relieved,"

and if they tried that same shit with me, "I would kick their mother
loving asses." So we got off on the right foot.

> Gunnery Sergeant Jason K. Doran recalls his Assumption of Command
> Speech, Second Platoon, Bravo Company, Iraq, April 10, 2003

Soldiers! The extraordinary decree of the Council of the Ancients
has placed me in command of the city and army. For two years past
the Republic has been badly governed. You had hoped that my return
would bring your afflictions to an end; you have hailed it with an una-
nimity that imposed on me the obligation I am now fulfilling; you will
fulfill yours and support your general with energy and firmness, and
with that same confidence which I have always reposed in you.

Liberty, victory, and peace will restore to the French Republic the
ranks she formerly held in Europe and that only ineptitude or treason
could make her lose. Vive la Republique!

> Napoleon's proclamation to his soldiers, November 9, 1799
> (Coup d'Etat 18–19 Brumaire)[1]

M OST OF THIS CHAPTER is devoted to speeches that mark
points of departure. First, however, we will briefly consider the
Assumption of Command Speech, the symmetrical opposite of the
Farewell Speech to be discussed later. Assuming command marks a
point of arrival: a new commander takes charge and with words (and
occasionally deeds) introduces himself to his soldiers. Of course, there
is typically more to these speeches than just salutations. For example,
Assumption of Command Speeches, like the Surrender Speeches also
discussed below, usually contain an Authority Convention. Especially
in modern armies, the assumption of command is an act of great legal
significance, something that must be "time stamped" to publicly sign
the transfer of authority. Soldiers must know whom to obey and from
what point exactly to do so. The new commander must therefore pro-
claim in some way his legal authority to command. Sometimes this is
done with lawyer-like precision: "By direction of the President of the
United States, I hereby assume command of the Army of the Potomac,"
General Meade announces in his speech quoted above. Gunnery Sergeant Doran also satisfies the Authority Convention, if somewhat less

grandiloquently. After being briefly introduced by another sergeant (who then walked away), Doran stood alone before his new platoon, an outfit with a difficult reputation. Napoleon's assumption of command illustrates a different twist: he was the sword's point in a conspiracy to replace the French Assembly with a consulship. After several unsuccessful appeals for support to different branches of the government, Napoleon and his co-conspirators decided to "persuade" the elected legislature by parading bayonet-wielding soldiers accompanied by an intimidating chorus of drummers beating the long roll. Although Napoleon's action concluded in the Coup d'Etat of 18–19 Brumaire, he obviously believed that the soldiers needed to hear that his Assumption of Command had legitimacy—that is, was properly authorized: "Soldiers!" he proclaimed. "The extraordinary decree of the Council of the Ancients [the upper house of the French Assembly] has placed me in command of the city and army." This was true, although Napoleon neglected to mention that he had helped coerce the council into appointing him.[2]

Another important feature of Assumption of Command Speeches is actually a subset of the Unit Historical Narrative: Acknowledge Predecessor(s). Most leaders recognize that their assumption of command is really an insertion—they usually succeed somebody and will eventually be succeeded themselves. Thus they are connected to their predecessor, whom the soldier-audience may have been accustomed to obeying and may even have admired. The predecessor may have been incompetent, brilliant, mediocre, or just lucky, and the incoming commander will usually carry a brief either to maintain the status quo or to change things in some way. But in any case, the predecessor must be acknowledged, and usually for one or more of three reasons: first, the incoming commander wants to co-opt any good will and loyalty that the soldier-audience has for the predecessor; second, the new commander wants to demonstrate continuity; third, the new commander wants to initiate change. Sergeant Doran's assignment was to create *discontinuity*—that is, spearhead change in the management of Second Platoon. Therefore, he acknowledged his predecessor only to inform his soldiers that things would now be very different: "It was bullshit that they were so fucked up that their Lt [Doran's predecessor] got relieved and if they tried that same shit with me, I would kick their mother loving asses," he succinctly explained. His predecessor had acted in ways that undercut his junior noncommissioned officers' authority, and Doran announced that he was going to have none of that.

But new commanders generally strive for continuity instead. One common means of accomplishing this is to link a courteous acknowledgement of the predecessor's service with an appeal for the soldier-audience's obedience and loyalty. Here the new commander seeks no more (or less) than what was given his predecessor: "It is with just such diffidence that I relieve in the command of this army an eminent and accomplished soldier, whose name [General Joseph Hooker] must ever appear conspicuous in the history of its achievements," General Meade declares, "but I rely upon the hearty support of my companions in arms to assist me in the discharge of the duties of the important trust which has been confided to me." Here Meade is pitching his soldiers not as their commander but as their comrade ("my companions in arms"). As discussed elsewhere in this book, appeals to comradeship are the surest basis for persuading soldiers to give that which can only be given freely—"hearty support," as General Meade would phrase it. This process also exploits the notion of comradeship from another angle: when the incoming commander declares that he feels the same about his predecessor as his soldier-audience does, this also evokes their common values. Of course, this especially applies in cases where continuity (or the initial appearance of continuity) is desired.[3] (In contrast, Napoleon acknowledges no predecessor, probably because in his mind none existed. However he obtained the Council of Ancients' authority, Napoleon, as one of the brand new consuls, may have understood his position as likewise brand new. Therefore, in this speech, Napoleon *was* the only precedent.)

As is perhaps evident from the foregoing, Acknowledging Predecessors can help shape what is arguably the most important function of Assuming Command Speeches: the Managing Expectations Convention. How the incoming commander characterizes his predecessor can signal the soldier-audience about any new expectations. In a crisis such as that confronting Meade when he assumed command several days before the Battle of Gettysburg, it may be wise to declare that there are no expectations other than what is expected of soldiers generally under the circumstances: "As a soldier, in obeying this order—an order totally unexpected and unsolicited," Meade reminds his soldier-audience, "I have no promises or pledges to make." He has thus "cleared the deck" of any concerns that some soldiers might have had that his assumption of command will result in potentially unwelcome changes in leadership, unit organization, or tactics. Now Meade is free to focus his army on "his" expectations, which in his case were not proprietary to him at all but simply consisted of what one would expect of any army seeking to repel an invader. "The country looks to this army to relieve it from the devastation and disgrace of a hostile invasion," Meade declares in the next sentence. "Whatever fatigues and sacrifices we may be called upon to undergo, let us have in view constantly the magnitude of the interests involved, and let each man determined to do his duty, leaving to an all-controlling Providence the decision of the contest." In short, the general manages expectations neutrally, in that he adds or subtracts little to what his army already expects to accomplish. Meade's approach might be contrasted with that of more charismatic generals such as Caesar, Napoleon, or McClellan, whose appeals were proprietary, in the sense that they sometimes sought to bind their soldier-audience through personal charisma, loyalty, or a reputation for brilliance, luck, or winning victories, as much as through devotion to an abstract cause or state.

For Doran, Acknowledging Predecessors also serves the function of Managing Expectations. By alluding to the events that led to his predecessor's relief of command, Doran figuratively clubs his platoon with what he does *not* expect: attempts by them to circumvent the chain of command. This is the "shit" that "if . . . tried . . . with me" would have him "kick their mother loving asses." In short, Doran serves clear notice of two related expectations: first, that he will support his subalterns; second, that he expects the platoon to obey these subalterns' valid orders without complaint, at least as far as complaints to him. And consistent with his views on respecting chains of command, Doran does not tell his platoon what he confides to his journal

—that the relieved lieutenant bore great responsibility for allowing this situation to take root and grow.

Napoleon first lays the basis for the Managing Expectations Convention by using a Political Historical Narrative. "For two years past the Republic has been badly governed," he begins. And this was true. External threats, French military reverses, internal anarchy, and corruption intensified national woes to a point that must have been widely recognized among men in the army (and in the civilian population from which it was drawn). This is probably why Napoleon felt no need to detail exactly what he meant by "badly governed"—his soldiers already knew. What links this Political Historical Narrative to Managing Expectations is the following question, implicit in Napoleon's statement: What will reverse the Republic's collapse, which is to say, in the immediate experience of his soldier-audience, what can we (you and I) expect from any action we might take today? And Napoleon is quick to answer: "You had hoped that my return [from Egypt] would bring our afflictions to an end," he continues, "you have hailed [my return] with an unanimity that imposes on me the obligation I am now fulfilling." According to Napoleon, here is the first expectation he manages: not what he expects from his soldiers but rather what they had expected from him. And (according to Napoleon) what the soldiers expected from him was a solution to the Republic's problems. (Perhaps for good reasons, Napoleon does not specify exactly what they expected him to do.) Napoleon now proceeds to exchange expectations with his soldiers and thus create the bargain that would survive to the Battle of Waterloo and beyond: "You have hailed [my return] with a unanimity that imposes on me the obligation I am now fulfilling," he declares. "You will fulfill yours and support your general with energy and firmness, and with that same confidence which I have always reposed in you." Here Napoleon has managed expectations, first by defining what his soldiers expected of him, and then by claiming that his Assumption of Command for this new enterprise (that is, the coup) was merely the fulfillment of his end of the bargain with them. Napoleon then attempts (successfully) to convert the soldiers' general expectations (assuming that his soldiers had such expectations) that he solve the national problem into specific acts toward doing so—to obey him "with energy and firmness." This is what Napoleon expects from them.

He concludes by "specifying" what fulfilling these exchanged expectations will yield: "Liberty, victory, and peace will restore the French Republic the rank she formerly held in Europe." He places this desired status not against slavery, defeat, and war but rather "ineptitude" and "treason," which he imputes to the government he is in the process of overthrowing. Here, he probably suggests that if this old government remains in power, slavery, defeat, and war will be the result. And he concludes his Assumption of Command speech with an ironic speechlet—*Vive la Republique!*—just one more illustration of how time-honored slogans can be hailed by the very speechmakers who seek to gut them.

Farewell

Decanters were handed round the room in what was described by Lieutenant Colonel [Benjamin] Tallmadge of the Second Continentals as "breathless silence." With glass raised, Washington waited until all had filled their own. "With a heart filled with love and gratitude," he began in a choked voice, "I now take leave of you. I most devoutly wish that your later days may be as prosperous and happy as your former ones have been glorious and honorable."

Overwrought, they mumbled confused responses to their chief's toast, swung their goblets about, and drank in some disorder to his health. Blinded by tears, his voice still faltering, Washington resumed, "I cannot come to each of you, but shall be obliged if each of you will come and take my hand." As the senior officer present, Henry Knox stepped forward silently and proffered his large cannoneer's fist. Weeping openly, Washington embraced his burly longtime chief of artillery and kissed him. . . . In turn, and by rank, each officer, [Baron] von Steuben following, came forward to be clasped, "suffused with tears," and unable to utter a single intelligible word.

> Washington's leave-taking of his officers at Fraunces Tavern, New York, December 4, 1783, quoted from Stanley Weintraub, *General Washington's Christmas Farewell: A Mount Vernon Homecoming, 1783*[4]

IN THE TACTICAL CYCLE OF WARFARE a battle speechmaker typically has three formal occasions on which to make one last speech to his soldiers before a final departure: saying farewell, announcing the unit's surrender, or proclaiming a war-ending final victory. Farewells can occur during or after a war; they may be voluntary or not—for example, Paullus's last words before his death might be considered a Farewell Speech—or, as discussed below, they might accompany the relief of a commander or the disbanding of a unit. Surrenders are what they are, whether wisely or foolishly made, and they are presumed to be involuntary, unless treachery is involved. A Final Victory Speech is also what it is, although in American history (and this is especially true of Farewell Speeches), these often contain unexpected extra material, such as a concern with the soldier-audience's conduct *after* demobilization. Fortunately, students of American battle speeches have abundant examples since the Revolution of superb Farewell and Final Victory Speeches. However, America is typical of other nations in not enshrining its Surrender Speeches. While the episodes that produced surrender are famous, what was said at the time is less so—while surrendered men often behave with extreme valor and must sometimes endure conditions that surpass combat in their brutality, surrenders are painful to recall and generate less national pride in recalling exactly what a defeated countryman-commander said at the time he submitted to the enemy.

We begin this discussion with what is probably the best known of the genre (or perhaps the second best, depending upon where one ranks Robert E. Lee's address to his army after surrendering at Appomattox) in American history: General George Washington's leave-taking at Fraunces Tavern in New York City. With the historian's advantage of knowing the whole story, we understand this event now as marking only the end of Washington's *first* great service to his country, that of military leader during the Revolution. Washington's second great service—his two terms as the infant Republic's first president—still lay before him. But at noon on December 4, 1783, none of this was known as senior Continental Army officers gathered in Samuel Fraunces's Long Room for lunch and a farewell to their commander.[5] The major point of beginning with this speech is its spontaneity. Neither Washington nor his speechwriter, Colonel David Humphreys, had written anything for the occasion. Instead, the general's remarks came naturally and were almost certainly not made with a nod to politics, army morale, or history. Unlike many Farewell Speeches, Washington refuses to aggrandize himself, and he minimizes the aggrandizement of his comrades as well; there is no triumphal review passing as a Unit Historical Narrative. He is merely a "first among comrades" initiating a sorrowful exchange of farewells with men among whom he had spent far more time in recent years than his own family. This is very important to some Farewell or Victory Speeches: at bottom, many are highly emotional events that are rarely driven by any tactical necessity (unlike Surrender Speeches, of course, which must often be demanded in order to occur at all or to occur peacefully), a commander's departure or an army's victory will happen whether or not any speech is made.[6]

Interestingly, Washington's speech (the above version of which was recollected by an eyewitness, Colonel Benjamin Tallmadge), spontaneous as it was, still includes several important conventions of the Farewell Speech that also characterize less spontaneous efforts by other battle speechmakers. (This reflects the fact that here, as elsewhere in battle speeches, most of the conventions are the product of tradition, necessity, and common sense.) There is the Gratitude Convention ("With a heart filled with love and gratitude"), arguably a species of Recognition, there is the Janus-like perspective that touches on times past ("your former [days] have been glorious and honorable") and times to come ("I most devoutly wish that your later days may be . . . prosperous and happy"). The latter perspective includes the Triumphal History Convention, a species of the Unit Historical Narrative, and the Future Hopes Convention.

A good place to begin analyzing these conventions is with another of George Washington's farewells, commonly known as the "Farewell Address to the Army." Delivered exactly thirty-two days before the leave-taking in Fraunces Tavern, it was addressed "for the last time to the Armies of the United States" in order "to bid them an affectionate and"—by Washington's own admission—"a long farewell." Unlike his remarks in the Long Room, this Farewell Speech was a prepared document that reveals by its length and contents his considerable deliberation.[7]

But before the Commander in Chief takes his final leave of those he holds most dear, he wishes to indulge himself a few moments in calling to mind a slight review of the past. He will then take the liberty of exploring with his Military friends their future prospects, of advising the general line of conduct which in his opinion ought to be pursued. . . .

It is not the meaning nor within the compass of this Address, to detail the hardships peculiarly incident to our Service, or to describe the distresses which in several instances have resulted from the extremes of hunger and nakedness, combined with the rigors of an inclement season. Nor is it necessary to dwell on the dark side of our past affairs. Every American Officer and Soldier must now console himself for any unpleasant circumstances which may have occurred, by a recollection of the uncommon scenes in which he has been called to act, no inglorious part; and the astonishing Events of which he has been a witness. . . .

Every one may rest assured that much, very much of the future happiness of the Officers and Men, will depend upon the wise and manly conduct which shall be adopted by them, when they are mingled with the great body of the Community.

He presents his thanks in the most serious and affectionate manner to the General Officers. . . . To the Commandants of Regiments and Corps, and to the other Officers for their great Zeal and attention in carrying his orders promptly into execution—To the Staff for their alacrity and exactness in performing the duties of their several Departments—And to the Non-commissioned officers and private Soldiers, for their extraordinary patience in suffering, as well as their invincible fortitude in Action. . . . With these Wishes, and this benediction, the Commander in Chief is about to retire from service—The Curtain of separation will soon be drawn—and the Military Scene to him will be closed for ever.

Excerpts from General George Washington's "Farewell Address
to the Army," November 2, 1783, at Rocky Hill, New Jersey

W ITH THE FIRST TWO SENTENCES from this excerpt, George
Washington established a precedent that subsequent generations of American Farewell Speechmakers would follow. In his final
speech as their uniformed commander, Washington would "indulge
himself a few moments" in a "slight review of the past" before taking "the liberty of exploring with his Military friends their future
prospects, of advising the general line of conduct which in his opinion ought to be pursued." Here Washington has embraced two of the
three Farewell Speech Conventions: Triumphal History and Future
Hopes. Triumphal History is a Unit Historical Narrative that recalls
the army's great achievements during a commander's tenure. Future
Hopes comprises what Washington wants for his soldiers, beginning
immediately and extending into the future. (The third convention,
Gratitude, is discussed below.)

To fully understand how Washington used these conventions, we
must consider how his personal style probably influenced this speech.
George Washington's public temperament was reserved and his battle style cool; this persona was coupled with a conviction that the
only leadership affect appropriate for a republic, especially one that
had just jilted its monarch, was austere modesty; thus, by inclination
as well as design, Washington was the antithesis of egoism. In his
long address, the word "I" does not appear once; instead, Washington
refers to himself in the third person, as either the "General" or the
"Commander in Chief." (The latter phrase was not yet exclusively reserved for a president.)

Given Washington's style, one would expect that although his generalship and cause has proved triumphant, his Triumphal History
would sound less so. He does not disappoint. He uses the rhetorical
device of introducing an important topic and then, by expressly refusing to discuss it, reminds his soldier-audience of its importance while
avoiding unseemly braggadocio: he declares that there is no need "to
detail the hardships peculiarly incident to our Service, or to describe
the distresses which in several instances have resulted from the extremes of hunger and nakedness, combined with the rigors of an inclement season." Of course there is no need to describe these—his
soldier-audience had suffered them all—but Washington obviously

feels the need to invoke these experiences, though without collective self-congratulation. And then he hints at something more ("Nor is it necessary to dwell on the dark side of our past affairs"), leaving to his soldiers the recollection of exactly what that "dark side" was. Does he refer here to lost battles? The winter army's suffering at Valley Forge? Or perhaps the petty backbiting among his generals, or the equally petty politicking with the young Congress? Was it friend Benedict Arnold's treason? Or the touring of freshly stinking battlefields, stepping gingerly over mangled bodies, the memories of which had already perhaps begun to produce some restless sleeps and jittery days? Washington does not feel the need to specify, and probably rightfully so, given the all-too-vivid recent experiences of his soldier-audience.

However, referring to these unspecified troubles does provide one half of the history Washington needs to prepare the background against which he will contrast what few of his army's triumphs he does mention. For Washington, at least in this speech, it is fair to ask the purpose of this triumph. Aside from its inherent value as a worthy cause redeemed, he links another possibility directly to its cost— the triumph is a balm to soothe soldiers: "Every American Officer and Soldier must now console himself for any unpleasant circumstances which might have occurred," Washington declares in words replete with psychological insight, the last of which are not excerpted above, "by a recollection of the uncommon scenes in which he has been called to act, no inglorious part; and the astonishing events of which he has been a witness. . . . Events which seldom, if ever before, have taken place on the stage of human action, nor can they probably ever happen again." (Washington will not say "glorious" but instead arrives obliquely at the same destination: his soldiers played "no inglorious part.")

Here, there is no boasting and no romanticizing of war; Washington seems to assume that his soldier-audience is filled with men who know better. Just as with "the dark side of our affairs," he has left the imagining of "unpleasant circumstances" to them. And it is likewise with his Triumphal History, which consists of unprecedented but unspecified "astonishing Events" which have never happened before and will never happen again but are once again left to his soldier-audience to remember. Thus the past's triumphs are acknowledged only as indefinite things, almost as if in the abstract. Perhaps in his mind (and in the mind of his soldier-audience) these "astonishing Events" are so bound up with the "dark side" that abstractions are not only the seemlier but also the less painful course. And here lies Washington's psychological wisdom. He makes no effort to beguile his men in their pain with vainglorious boasts of martial virtue that, if the experience of later wars is any guide, will quickly fade, even as war's painful memories (not to mention physical impairments) endure. Instead, Washington offers them a sensible consolation that may indeed be the only realistic one given their physical and psychological sacrifices—the suffering was endured in the name of the (right) historical cause and not in order to prove some personal qualities (such as courage or manhood) or to serve some collectively constructed virtue (such as glory or prestige). As will be discussed below, future commanders will have fewer hesitations in creating a Triumphal History that sounds more triumphant, however dubious these greater glories may prove to be as longer-term consolations or advantages.

Where Washington's Farewell Speech becomes more specific is in its embrace of the Future Hope Convention. What he deeply wishes, for the good of the soldiery as well as the new nation, is for his army to peacefully disband and then comfortably reassimilate into civilian life. His concern is neither sentimental nor hypothetical. Washington's soldiers had been long angry with Congress over broken promises for pay. Just eight months earlier, in Newburgh, New York, the American experiment might have ended abruptly with a coup d'etat had Washington not persuaded (by a speech, of course) his officers to abandon plans for a military solution to congressional inaction.[8] His Farewell Speech of November 2 is a continuation of these efforts: "tho' there should be some envious Individuals who are unwilling to pay the Debt the public has contracted, or to yield the tribute due to Merit," Washington observes, he implores his men not to "let such unworthy treatment [that is, by Congress] produce [any] invective, or any instance of intemperate conduct." In fact, he even proposes that the likelihood of Congress's redemption of its promises will be linked to his soldiers' behavior after demobilization: "Every one may rest assured that much,

very much of the future happiness of the Officers and Men will depend upon the wise and manly conduct which shall be adopted by
them, when they are mingled with the great body of the Community."
Here Washington emphasizes a need for continuing discipline, now in
the name of political rather than military objectives.

While this may be the heart of Washington's Future Hope Convention, it is not the end of it. First, in an obvious effort to mitigate
his soldiers' concern with short-term pay issues, he attempts to shift
their focus to the longer-term benefits of civilian life in a rich but un-
developed land. In a country "so happily circumstanced" in natural
resources as America, "the pursuits of Commerce and the cultivation
of the Soil" will yield its bounty to the competent. As for those "who
are actuated by the spirit of adventure, the Fisheries will afford ample
and profitable employment," and, here anticipating Frederick Jackson
Turner's thesis a century later, he adds that "the extensive and fertile
Regions of the West will yield a most happy Asylum to those who,
fond of domestic enjoyment are seeking for personal independence."

Aside from expressing his wish that his soldiers behave, collect their
promised pay, and earn good livings, Washington also has other hopes
for the future about matters that potentially affect everyone. These,
too, might have represented an effort to distract the soldiery from their
concerns about pay; but in a republican democracy, at least for many
of the white males that composed most of the soldier-audience, it is a
necessary distraction: "And altho', the General has so frequently given
it as his opinion in the most public and explicit manner, that unless
the principles of the Federal Government were properly supported,
and the Powers of the Union increased, the honor, dignity and justice
of the Nation would be lost for ever," he declares. He then charges
those in his army (but only those who agree with him) to help realize
these ends using democratic means: "[Yet I] cannot help repeating on
this occasion, so interesting a sentiment, and leaving it as [my] last in-
junction to every Officer and every Soldier, who may view the subject
in same serious point of light, to add his best endeavors to those of his
worthy fellow Citizens towards effecting these great and valuable purposes, on which our very existence as a Nation so materially depends."
Thus, he encourages his men to use legal means for redress as well as

general government reform. Washington's Future Hope Convention was filled to overflowing: fears of army disloyalty, questions about soldiers' behavior after demobilization and their adjustment to civilian life, and concerns about the powers and direction of the new government. It was a good deal for which to hope.

Finally, there is the Gratitude Convention, which in Washington's case flows from himself to his men. Elsewhere this can be otherwise in such speeches: the soldiery is (or should be) grateful to the commander. Napoleon's Farewell Speech to his Old Guard, delivered just before his first exile, included these lines: "Do not pity my fate; if I have consented to survive it is still to work for your fame; I mean to write down those great things that we have done together! Goodbye, my children!" Napoleon hints at martyrdom in these words; he endures his personal crisis for the sake of his men, or rather their future glory. Moreover, just as their past was made glorious by his sword, their future will be redeemed by his pen.[9]

In contrast, Washington's gratitude is a remarkably specific acknowledgment (the greater significance of which is discussed below) of the efficiency and skill that his soldier-audience has demonstrated during their service. To his generals, he is grateful not just for their advice but also for "their ardor in promoting the success of the plans [he had] adopted. Regimental and corps commanders and their subalterns are thanked "for their great Zeal and attention in carrying [my] orders promptly into execution." And to the rank and file, Washington is grateful for "their extraordinary patience in suffering, as well as their invincible fortitude in Action." In sum, Washington carefully phrases his expressions of gratitude to avoid connecting *his person* with his subordinates' loyalty; it is instead their loyalty to his plans, his orders, the cause, or duty that he singles out. And while he does express "his inviolable attachment & friendship" to his troops, he immediately limits their consequences: "[I flatter myself,] however, that [you will do me] the justice to believe, that whatever could with propriety be attempted by [me on your behalf], has been done." He makes no promises about the future or his usefulness to his soldiers. The following statement seems silly given Washington's subsequent history, but it is clear from his Farewell Speech that he does not anticipate any second acts in his public life, at least none that would directly effect the soldier-audience. The war is over, and he announces with remarkable finality that the time has come to leave the stage: "The Curtain of separation will soon be drawn," Washington concludes, "[and] the Military Scene to [me] will be closed for ever."

Farewell Speeches after Washington

The Lieutenant-Colonel commanding takes this, his last, opportunity to tender to you his congratulations that after more than four years of hard service, you are enabled again to go to your homes, and resume your peaceful avocations.

A brief review of your history in this regiment cannot fail now to interest you. . . .

With sadness you will bring to mind the appearance of this regiment as it marched out of Camp Andrew, July 8, 1861; and will think how many of the noblest and best officers and men comprising it now fill soldiers' graves. . . .

The Lieutenant-Colonel commanding thanks you for your adherence to your duties, and your fidelity to him, since he has had the honor to command you.

In conclusion, [I hope] that the lessons taught by this war will exert a beneficial influence on your future lives, and that you may become good citizens and worthy members of society.

> Excerpt from Lieutenant Colonel Charles F. Morse's Farewell Speech
> to the Second Massachusetts Volunteer Infantry upon its muster-out
> on July 12, 1865[10]

THE IMMEDIATE AFTERMATH of the American Civil War was probably the golden age of the American military Farewell Speech, as hundreds of units were disbanded and most commanders seemed moved to say something to mark the event. But there was much more to it than simply acknowledging some bureaucratically decreed exit. For several reasons, the bonds among Civil War soldiers were as strong as those of any long-serving professional army. States, and usually communities within states, raised their own regiments

(one aspect of this "Brothers' War" that merits more scholarly attention is the frequency with which actual brothers fought at each other's
side as well as against one another). Thus these citizen-soldiers often
shared hometowns, relatives, religious affiliations, and political affiliations. Indeed, in a war where many units had been enlisted as "Colored," "German," or "Irish," men also shared race or ethnicity, which
is just another way of adding that some were bound closer still by
sharing the experience of discrimination, immigration, or slavery. Furthermore, a long, bloody war produced high personnel turnover, and
many officers who had risen from the ranks were really chips from the
same sociocultural block as their soldier-audiences (although that was
less the case, perhaps, with gentleman Charles Fessenden Morse—
Harvard College Class of 1858—whose Farewell Speech is excerpted
above).[11]

Demobilization usually meant the permanent dissolution of the
regiment. A (very) lucky few soldiers had served all four years together,
with progressively higher percentages serving three, two, and only
one. Some of these units, like the Second Massachusetts, bore names
that had dominated newspaper stories for years; they would now cease
to exist with a single signature. Thus, at the end, there was a clear
sense of historical moment, which helps to explain why Farewell
Speeches proliferated after this particular war. But what is truly remarkable about these speeches, composed across the country by men
from every conceivable background, is their structural *sameness*. This
is consistent with a central contention of this book: speech conventions arise by some combination of tradition, necessity, and familiarity
with what other battle speechmakers have said in the past (although
that "past" may have been no hoarier than earlier that morning, when
an officer listened to a colleague deliver a similar sort of speech).

Lieutenant-Colonel Morse wrote the Farewell Speech excerpted
above as the Second Massachusetts Volunteer Infantry was mustered
out of service and out of existence. The unit had been formed in May
1861 for three years; due to reenlistments, it had persisted until July
1865. In the intervening four years and two months, some 1,687 men
passed through its ranks, of which 190 were killed in combat or died
later of wounds; another ninety-eight died from "Disease, Accidents,

In Prison, &c." The aggregate dead included sixteen officers, of whom thirteen were, like Charlie Morse, Harvard connected. These losses qualified the Second Massachusetts for inclusion on William F. Fox's famous list of the "Three Hundred Fighting Regiments," which ranked the Northern units by numbers of casualties; having served honorably in a unit on *this* list was the kind of distinction that even a member of Mrs. Astor's Four Hundred might have envied. And Charlie Morse, who had joined as a second lieutenant in May 1861, had been with the unit in almost every battle. Few men of the Second Massachusetts were as qualified or as deserving to write a heartfelt Farewell Speech.[12]

Each single-sentence excerpt from the epigraph is intended to compare Morse's uses of the Gratitude, Triumphal History, and Future Hopes Conventions with Washington's. The purpose here is not to repeat instances of these conventions but to demonstrate how they changed during the intervening eighty-two years. The largest change is simple excess: Washington's reflection, restraint, and modesty are now replaced by a much greater effort to define and control meaning. For example, as previously noted, Washington allowed his soldier-audience to consider for themselves such matters as "the dark side of our past affairs." By contrast, Morse specifies what he believes the darker side of his regiment's wartime experience was, and he details other matters as well. Morse lastly adds congratulations to the Gratitude Convention, and the regiment's battle itinerary and a proto-eulogy to his Triumphal History. While Washington's structural categories live on, Morse demonstrates how they can be changed to achieve different purposes.

Morse's entire speech is premised on gratitude, and he opens with a species of it—a congratulations: "The Lieutenant-Colonel . . . takes this, his last, opportunity to tender to you his congratulations, that, after more than four years of hard service, you are enabled again to go to your homes, and resume your peaceful avocations." Morse makes a significant exaggeration here—only a few soldiers being mustered out have belonged to the regiment for the full four years, and most in fact joined much more recently. But Morse is anticipating a modern trend by applying the Gratitude Convention to all soldiers without regard to rank, years of service, or actual accomplishment during the war: whether men carried a rifle in the front rank or clerked safely in the rear is not immediately relevant. By contrast, Washington's Gratitude Convention scaled down the Continental Army's ladder of rank in order to praise men by their individual functions.

Morse's lumping together of all soldiers is also accompanied by a somewhat related change—praise or congratulations based on the soldier's status rather than achievement. First, soldiers are praised for simply belonging to the regiment, the effective message conveyed by thanking them for their "hard service," which really required only their unit membership. Second, men are recognized for merely having survived the war: "The Lieutenant-Colonel commanding does most sincerely congratulate you who are now left in this command," Morse declares in the third person, "on having passed safely through this great struggle which has terminated so gloriously." Where Morse's embrace of the Gratitude Convention slightly resembles Washington's is in the penultimate paragraph. "The Lieutenant-Colonel commanding thanks you for your adherence to your duties," he declares, "and your fidelity to him, since he has had the honor to command you." Here the same aggregation of service observed above now extends to rank: officers and men alike are all heaped together as veterans.

What is the significance of these changes between Washington's time and the Civil War? For one thing, although we might not ordinarily think of the military as a democratic institution, it was probably true that by 1865 the Federal army had come to embody something of the Jacksonianism embraced by the public from which it was drawn. In other words, it reflected the same animating egalitarian spirit that had, since the first third of the nineteenth century, actuated mass political parties, high voter turnout, and intense citizen participation in politics. Students of the war have long observed the importance of politicking (with an eye on elections) in the appointments of senior regimental officers at the state level and general officers at the federal level. But the extent to which politics prevailed among the rank and file has been less intensively studied. From the first, company officers and NCOs were elected; even after this practice ceased, woe betide the officer who crossed too many of his men—he could expect a petition to the state governor who appointed him (and would approve most future promotions) and a complaining letter to his congressman or local newspaper editor denouncing his behavior and demanding a change; sometimes these epistles were signed by hundreds of soldiers within the regiment. By day, rank stood, but by evening, officers realized (to greater or lesser degrees in each regiment) that "consent of the governed" was still necessary. This was likely true even in a regiment whose officers had a reputation for being autocratic (such as the Second Massachusetts). By contrast, in the more hierarchical eighteenth-century world of George Washington, this presumed equality across ranks and social stations was still two generations away. Charlie Morse's habits of command probably reflected the world in which he lived—a vastly more politicized soldier-audience in which the army's principal actor was presumed to be the common soldier, celebrated by Morse's fellow Harvard warrior James K. Hosmer as "the Thinking Bayonet." Thus, Morse's command was also his constituency. And in talking to one's constituency, it is always wise to minimize offense and maximize praise.[13]

Morse's foray into Triumphal History is also an extended compliment to both the regiment and its soldiers. When he declares that a "brief review of your history cannot fail *now* to interest you" [emphasis added], Morse signals that the Unit Historical Narrative he is about to relate will be of the triumphal variety. The scene is easily imagined. Soldiers were likely assembled for final muster, anxious to start the journey for Massachusetts and home. Here, only one kind of history could not fail to interest them *now*—the kind that would ennoble each soldier's service and enfranchise him both as a participant in and a historian of the Second Massachusetts's glorious deeds (for soon he would be narrating these events for family and friends). And those deeds that soldiers did not personally experience (because so few had survived the regiment's entire four-year term), Colonel Morse had experienced on their behalf; through shared regimental membership, his Farewell Speech would vicariously endow his entire soldier-audience with a stake in the deeds of absent others. So Morse was something between a high priest and a living metonym, a stand-in for all that the unit had experienced, and a living channel between past glory and these current survivors.

The Second Massachusetts, Morse explains, had been organized virtually at the beginning of the war, and while "its first year of service was not an eventful one," it nevertheless "became famous for its good discipline and appearance." However, the regiment would soon need this discipline. The language he uses to describe the unit's combat resume is unconditional and epic: "On the night of May 24 [1862], your regiment, by its steadiness and bravery," Morse proudly relates, "beat back greatly superior forces of the enemy, and saved [General Nathaniel P.] Banks's little army from total destruction." Although the Federals lost this battle, what little credit accrued was the direct result of the Second Massachusetts's actions: "All of the honor that can be associated with the disastrous retreat of the next day certainly belongs to you," he claims. But as the summer and fall of 1862 unfolded and became 1863 and then 1864, the unit's resume became genuinely blood soaked, and Morse's language rises to these occasions: At Cedar Mountain, "with . . . determined bravery, this regiment faced and fought three times its numbers; and in twenty minutes, lost more than one-third its enlisted men and more than one-half its officers." Morse continues in this vein:

> Antietam, Chancellorsville, Beverly Ford, Gettysburg, and the great campaigns of the West, with their numerous battles and skirmishes followed in quick succession; and the war ended, leaving you with a most brilliant and satisfactory record, — a record of courage, gallantry, and tenacity in battle, of unflinching steadiness in defeat, of good discipline in camp, and of respect and prompt obedience to all superiors.

It is after concluding this section that Morse asks each man to be his own unit historian, albeit one endowed with Morse's version of its history ("[This] is the record which you can take to your homes"). He also explains that, since they have been enfranchised as incarnations of this history, they can expect personal honor after their return. This glorious and bloody past, Morse assures them, is "known and acknowledged throughout your State." All veterans will participate by association, whether or not they were present at a particular battle.

Here Morse sharply departs from Washington's Farewell. The "Father of His Country" did not mention specific battles, nor did he refer to casualties, other than (perhaps) alluding to them with the words "dark side." But in Morse's Farewell Speech casualties are a central theme: "It will not be with pleasure alone, that you recall the events of the past four years," he begins. "With sadness you will bring to mind the appearance of this regiment as it marched out of Camp Andrew [Massachusetts], July 8, 1861; and will think how many of the noblest and best officers and men then comprising it now fill soldiers' graves." A proto-eulogy of the type discussed in the last chapter then follows: "You will cherish the memories of these gallant men; and, though you lament their loss, you will remember that they died in battle, bravely doing their duty, fighting for their country and the right." Like Washington, Morse also offers consolation, but specifically in connection with the dead, not through some allusion that might be filled with all of war's horrors: "[You] will thank God, when you look about you, and see peace restored to this entire country, that the sacrifice of their lives has not been in vain."

Especially interesting are the differences between Washington and Morse over how to interpret all of this suffering and death. As noted above, Washington recommended that his soldiers understand victory as a balm for war's personal afflictions. But Morse sees his own war quite differently. For him, it has conferred a personal benefit beyond the satisfaction derived from a just cause vindicated. "[I feel] sure that no one of you will ever regret your part in this war," he announces. "As long as you live, and whatever your future in life may be, you will think of your soldier's career with the greatest pride and satisfaction: its hardships and sufferings, its dangers and glories, have made you all nobler, better, and more self-reliant men." For Morse's soldiers (at least, according to Morse) war has had a benefit that Washington never mentioned: it has enhanced their masculinity by hardening their self-reliance and ennobling their lives. In Morse's Farewell Speech, war becomes an extension of nineteenth-century patrician New England's obsession with "self-culture," defined by William Ellery Channing twenty-seven years earlier as "the care which every man owes to himself to the unfolding and perfecting of his nature." Whether or not many of his soldiers shared this view is unknown.[14]

Self-culture has also worked its way into Morse's use of the Future Hopes Convention. His concluding sentence links two ideas that together add something entirely new to Washington's hope that his men conduct themselves appropriately after demobilization. The revolutionary general was of course concerned that his soldiers behave themselves after discharge so as not to give Congress a reason to further delay honoring its promises of pay. But Morse looks upon the war itself as an important reason to both hope *and expect* that the newly minted veterans of the Second Massachusetts will behave themselves. The reason is that war not only perfects men but also citizens. Morse expects "that the lessons taught by this war will exert a beneficial influence on your future lives" but couples this thought with another: "[so that] you may become good citizens and worthy members of society." For Washington, good conduct is inherently virtuous and also serves practical ends—the men must make their livings in this vast new land and must also persuade Congress for their due. But Morse, in his Future Hopes, has idealized the experience of warfare and transformed it into a mode of self-perfection. In a sense, Napoleon's understanding of war as glory, romance, honor, and status might be different from Washington's, but it would certainly ring true to Charles Fessenden Morse.

Surrender and Farewell

After four years of arduous service, marked by unsurpassed courage and fortitude, the Army of Northern Virginia has been compelled to yield to overwhelming numbers and resources. I need not tell the brave survivors of so many hard-fought battles, who have remained steadfast to the last, that I have consented to the result from no distrust of them. But, feeling that valor and devotion could accomplish nothing that could compensate for the loss that must have attended the continuance of the contest, I determined to avoid the useless sacrifice of those whose past services have endeared them to their countrymen.

By the terms of the agreement officers and men can return to their homes and remain until exchanged. You will take with you the satisfaction that proceeds from the consciousness of duty faithfully performed; and I earnestly pray that a merciful God will extend to you his blessing and protection.

With an increasing admiration of your constancy and devotion to your country, and a grateful remembrance of your kind and generous considerations for myself, I bid you all an affectionate farewell.

General Robert E. Lee to the Army of Northern Virginia
after the surrender at Appomattox on April 10, 1865[15]

. . . And Just Surrender

By virtue of the authority vested in me by the President of the United States, I, as commanding general of the United States forces in the Philippine Islands, hereby resume direct command of Major General [William F.] Sharp's command of the Visayan-Mindanao force and of all troops under his command. I now give a direct order to General Sharp. . . .

Subject: Surrender. . . . The message: To fully stop the further useless sacrifice of human life on the fortified islands, yesterday I tendered Lt. General [Masaharu] Homma, the commander in chief of the Imperial Japanese Forces in the Philippines, the surrender of the four harbor forts in Manila Bay.

General Homma declined to accept my surrender unless it included the forces under your command. . . .

After leaving General Homma with no agreement between us I decided to accept in the name of humanity his proposal and tendered at midnight, night 6–7 May 1942 . . . the formal surrender of all American and Philippine Army troops in the Philippine Islands. You will therefore be guided accordingly, and will repeat will surrender all troops under your command. . . . This decision on my part, you will realize, was forced upon me by means beyond my control. [emphasis original]

Excerpt from Lieutenant General Jonathan M. Wainwright IV's radio
broadcast to subordinate commanders ordering the surrender of
American and Filipino forces to the Japanese, May 6, 1942[16]

"I AM A STUDENT OF the Civil War," General Wainwright wrote of his May 1942 surrender to the Japanese, "but not until then did I know how General R. E. Lee felt after Appomattox." Wainwright un-

derstated matters here a good deal; he and his soldiers faced brutali-
ties that a magnanimous victor spared Robert E. Lee and his army:
barbaric, killing years as prisoners of war held by captors who believed
that surrendered soldiers were shamed men deserving whatever they
got. Instead, Lee surrendered his army to generals much like himself,
indeed, men he had known, schooled with, superintended at West
Point, or served honorably with in an earlier war. His Federal counterpart, Lieutenant General Ulysses Grant, famously paroled Lee's officers and men and allowed the officers to retain their sidearms and
baggage; furthermore, any Confederate who owned a horse (or mule)
could keep it. Grant ordered Lee's hungry men fed; afterward, they
were free to return home. Needless to say, the surrenders of Lee and
Wainwright proceed from different galaxies. They are contrasted here
only to illustrate why Lee produced a Surrender Speech of great eloquence, assisted by a victor's magnanimity, while Wainwright's
complete speech reveals the blunt, business-like terms imposed by
a victorious general whose brutality (or failure to supervise subordinates) allowed the Bataan Death March and ultimately resulted in his
own execution for war crimes after Japan surrendered in 1945.[17]

The Surrender Speech might include a farewell but at bottom is a
special type of Instructional Speech. It is considered in this chapter
because it is also a departure speech—surrender marks the speechmaker's exit as a commander, whether forever (Lee) or not (Wainwright). Phrased with grace or with trepidation, the Surrender Speech
will still usually embrace three conventions. First, Authority: as was
true with Assumption of Command speeches, the speechmaker here
must establish (or remind) the soldier-audience that he has the authority to act (in this case, to surrender). This may be express ("By
the authority granted me") or implied, as when the speech belongs
to a speechmaker whose authority is already acknowledged. Second,
Justification: for the variety of reasons discussed below, Surrender
Speeches must explain *why* the surrender is necessary. Justification
generally adds moral authority to the commander-speechmaker's legal
authority. Third, Instruction: the speech must provide the soldier-
audience with critical information about the boundaries of their surrender—what the soldier-audience (and enemy) may do, must do,

and cannot do. And it is among these three conventions that Generals Lee and Wainwright meet, whatever their other differences of circumstance.

The Authority Convention is necessary because a Surrender Speech embodies a legally obligatory act. It is undertaken because the speechmaking commander is usually required by agreement (sometimes implied by the terms of surrender) to do it—in this case, convey to his soldier-audience orders that that will require them to perform some acts and to refrain from performing others. Practically speaking, for the surrender to take effect, each soldier must first be persuaded to do so. Subordinates who refuse to surrender or who continue to resist can jeopardize the entire arrangement. In smaller armies or units, where the commander is recognized on sight (or even in larger armies with especially ubiquitous commanders such as Robert E. Lee), the leader's authority to surrender may already be tacitly acknowledged by the soldier-audience, thus making its recitation in a Surrender Speech unnecessary. The fact that it is the commander who delivers the speech or signs the order is sufficient warrant. General Lee's signature ("R. E. Lee, General") on General Orders No. 9, which were distributed by a headquarters staff already well known to the soldiery, was persuasive—besides, dire circumstances, word of mouth, or personal encounters with Lee beforehand had probably predisposed most of the soldiers to accept Lee's act of surrender. For diehard rebels, Lee's say-so was enough, especially when personally conveyed as he rode through his army after his meeting with Grant. "Men, we have fought the war together and I have done the best I could for you," he explained from the saddle as the butternut-clad ranks crowded around him. "You will all be paroled and go to your homes until exchanged." In short, as was true of some commanders since antiquity, Robert E. Lee's person *was* his authority.[18]

The situation confronting General Wainwright was vastly different—his surrender may have ended a battle, but it was only the beginning of a war. He had assumed command over all American and Filipino forces after General Douglas MacArthur was evacuated by presidential order to Australia. But Wainwright anticipated the fall of his headquarters on Corregidor, and just hours before he surrendered, he assigned to General William F. Sharp the command of troops on the Visayan Islands and Mindanao. Here was an attempt at damage control: by limiting his own command to the almost eleven thousand soldiers and civilian refugees on Corregidor (and a few units on northern Luzon), Wainwright hoped to convince the Japanese that he could technically surrender no more than that. Sharp's forces could then fight on as guerilla units (which was MacArthur's hope), and in any case Wainwright's gambit might succeed in preserving a part of the army and thus buy more time.

But the Japanese commander, General Masaharu Homma, would have none of it. He refused Wainwright's limited surrender and demanded that he yield on behalf of all American and Filipino forces wherever located on the archipelago. Facing Japanese infantry just yards away from Corregidor's garrison, Wainwright was confronted with the choice of annihilation or total surrender. When he discovered that even his last redoubt on the island had been surrounded, he relented. "That was it," he later recalled. "The last hope vanished from my mind."[19]

Wainwright's circumstances were typical of modern warfare, with its more bureaucratic command structure and larger forces dispersed over wider areas. Here the authority question becomes paramount: the commander may not be recognized on sight and cannot personally visit each unit, and indeed, soldiers may well be confused about his actual authority to surrender. After all, it was only hours earlier that Wainwright had transferred command of some units to General Sharp. After addressing his Surrender Speech directly to General Sharp (other specific members of the soldier-audience are addressed later), Wainwright immediately asserts his personal authority to act: "By virtue of the authority vested in me by the President of the United States," he declares, "I, as commanding general of the United States forces in the Philippines Islands, hereby resume direct command of Major General Sharp's command of the Visayan-Mindanao force and of all troops under his command." Homma has thus forced Wainwright to retract his earlier delegation of authority to Sharp. Still, the Authority Convention is only partially fulfilled, for Wainwright must finish what he later termed "the disgusting job."[20]

"I now give a direct order to General Sharp," he begins, as if dictating a memo. "Subject: Surrender." Significantly, what follows is not just the surrender order but also a "history" of that order, which is intended to provide the justification for the surrender. Wainwright has already established his legal authority to surrender; what he must now demonstrate is his *moral authority* in yielding (here called the Justification Convention). *"To fully stop the further useless sacrifice of human life on the fortified islands,"* he continues, "yesterday, I tendered to Lieutenant General Homma, the commander in chief of the Imperial Japanese Forces in the Philippines, the surrender of the four harbor forts in Manila Bay" [emphasis added]. Establishing moral authority matters, because by agreeing to surrender, soldiers are ceding absolute control of their persons to a (it is hoped) *previously* killing enemy, but they are no doubt all familiar with instances of perfidious captors who will promise good treatment but then murder or torture prisoners or afflict them with savage privations (even in the case of a well-meaning captor, conditions can be harsh and the length of captivity indeterminate). If the most difficult task facing speechmakers is to persuade men to become fighters, then the second most difficult can be to persuade fighters to become prisoners of war.

Wainwright must tell a story to convince those not already convinced by their wounds, sickness, or hunger that surrender is morally justified. And for a rational commander leading a rational army, the best moral argument is one of necessity. First, Wainwright declares that he tried to spare them (that is, those under Sharp's command) from surrender, but Homma declined. Thus, Wainwright's first case is one of legal necessity. Next he makes a military case for necessity (not excerpted above): "It became apparent that the garrisons of [your] forts would be eventually destroyed by aerial and artillery bombardment and by infantry supported by tanks, which have overwhelmed Corregidor." And his next sentence contains a moral case for necessity: "After leaving General Homma with no agreement between us I decided to accept in the name of humanity his proposal and tendered at midnight, night 6–7 May 1942 . . . the formal surrender of all American and Philippine Army troops in the Philippine Islands."

Wainwright's case of moral necessity is summarized in one final argument, through which he converts the goodwill of his men (which was considerable and in sharp contrast to the low regard with which many then held MacArthur) into moral capital. After issuing his direct surrender order to Sharp ("You will therefore be guided accordingly, and *will* repeat *will* surrender all troops under your command"), Wainwright then personalizes his decision: "This decision on my part, you will realize, was forced upon me by means beyond my control." Why does Wainwright add this declaration, when he has already made his case for surrender based on legal, military, and moral necessity? Any surrender that is not prompted by a commander's treachery is assumed to be "forced" (though Lee also suggests that his surrender was forced, he speaks as a collective—it was "the Army of Northern Virginia" that was "compelled to yield" by an unforgiving disparity in resources). And in Wainwright's case, there was a profound element of force that was entirely absent at Appomattox, one that sadly foreshadowed the ensuing three years of his brutal treatment by Japanese wardens. First, despite the fact that the Americans had literally raised the white flag, enemy infantry, artillery, and air raids continued to attack Corregidor; next, attempts were repeatedly made to personally intimidate Wainwright and his staff, from their first contact with a Japanese lieutenant all the way to their negotiations with General Homma. Wainwright was also concerned with the fate of the thousands of civilian refugees that were harbored in his garrison and on the Allied-occupied islands. In a later paraphrasing of a contemporary conversation with his staff, Wainwright remarked that "a short period of continued warfare [by us] . . . would in no way compensate for the massacre of the men and women on the fortified islands." In his mind, the Japanese, already notorious for the "Rape of Nanking," would not hesitate to kill every civilian if some surrender arrangement was not made. Finally, there was the radio broadcast actually carrying Wainwright's speech: he had been forced to make it.[21]

By declaring that "the decision was forced upon me by means beyond my control," Wainwright becomes a metonym incarnate for the situation of every soldier under his command—as he is forced, so therefore are they. And this too adds to the Justification Convention, because human beings who are forced by means beyond their control to do a certain thing are no longer free agents, and thus are not personally responsible for the acts they commit. In most cases, a defense of compulsion is justification.[22]

Comparing the Justification Conventions used by Lee and Wainwright yields close similarities in structure, if not in eloquence. Lee has also woven into his statement of surrender his moral justification for doing so. (It does not injure his persuasive purpose to flatter his soldier-audience using superlatives and epic adjectives.) "After four years of arduous service, marked by unsurpassed courage and fortitude, the Army of Northern Virginia has been compelled to yield to overwhelming numbers and resources," he announces. Here Lee articulates the same case for military necessity (without the planes and tanks) that Wainwright would make seventy-seven years later. And the two generals make a similar case for the moral necessity of surrender: "But [despite his soldiers remaining "steadfast to the last"], feeling that valor and devotion could accomplish nothing that could compensate for the loss that must have attended the continuance of the contest," Lee argues, "I determined to avoid the useless sacrifice of those whose past services have endeared them to their countrymen." Stripped of tributes, this is much of Wainwright's case exactly: "further useless sacrifice of human life" and surrender "in the name of humanity" versus Lee's formulation of avoiding "the useless sacrifice" of his soldiers.

There are additional parallels between Wainwright and Lee regarding a Surrender Speech's most important tactical feature: the Instruction Convention. Of course, the very announcement of surrender, if it is believed, is for all parties a kind of instruction. Whether from the lofty heights of generals surrendering armies or the depths of a single forlorn soldier waving a white cloth, custom (and in more recent centuries, international law) imposes a whole series of required behaviors regulating the tendering and acceptance of a surrender and its aftermath. But whether done en masse or individually, surrender has always been a tricky business. Combatants might not end their hostility toward and fear of one another quite as easily as they can tie a white handkerchief to a stick.[23] Thus the Instruction Convention is critical, because it contains additional standards to which superiors can hold their subordinates at a spectacularly fraught time, and it provides this guidance for both the victors and the vanquished.

Lee realizes the Instruction Convention in two ways; he announces the fact of surrender, and then he discloses a single (and for most of his men, the most critical) term of that surrender: "[Officers] and men can return to their homes and remain until exchanged." That was the sum of their instructions in Lee's speech, although the real sum was far greater: except as noted above (officers to keep pistols and all men the horse and mules that they owned), there was actually a quite involved process that Lee felt no need to disclose in his speech. Confederate officers were to give written paroles on behalf of their commands, and military property had to be surrendered, including such items as muskets, ammunition, artillery, powder, and regimental flags. Interestingly, Lee never asked that Grant memorialize his promise about the rations—he simply assumed (correctly) that the Federal commander would honor his word. Some of the surrender details were handled at formal ceremonies (such as the deposit of flags and weapons) while other matters appear to have been dealt with informally. Either way, all of these details were outside both Lee's Farewell-and-Surrender Speech and the actual agreement signed between the Confederate and Federal commanders.[24]

If one tallies its actual words, Wainwright's complete Surrender Speech consists almost entirely of very detailed instructions. But before considering these, one must first account for the Japanese demand that Wainwright broadcast his speech in the clear. Aside from the propaganda value of having a surrendered enemy general publicly broadcast his submission, the Japanese likely had an important tactical purpose: Wainwright's words could now be heard by any American or Filipino soldier (or civilian) with a radio, thus the potential soldier-audience was expanded from General Sharp and the several other named officers to the entire allied force in the Philippines. Here broadcast technology converted a specifically addressed order into a Surrender Speech with the broadest audience imaginable.

Wainwright's precise surrender terms had been drafted by the Japanese, of course, and their expectation of strict compliance also became part of the speech: "[Let] me emphasize that there must be on your part no thought of disregarding these instructions," he warns. "Failure to fully and honestly carry them out can have only the most disastrous results." The instructions included details on where and how the widely separated commands should surrender: "Those [soldiers] remaining in northern Luzon to assemble at Bayombong or Bontoc and the commanding officer to present himself to the Japanese Army in Baguio and notify him of their surrender." They covered the disposition of weapons and other material: "It is absolutely prohibited that arms, materials, vessels or any other equipments or establishments be destroyed, burned or dispersed. . . . Easily movable portable weapons will be gathered in the vicinity of the assembly places of the troops. This refers to machine guns, small arms, and other equipment that may be carried by individuals." Mines and other defensive weaponry had to be fully disclosed: "Defensive installations of all types, especially in areas where land or sea mines are laid, will be reported accompanied by a sketch and the actual position indicated." In the end, Wainwright emphasizes that it will be the Japanese who will decide whether or not the instructions had been complied with. Despite Wainwright's surrender, the imperial forces "will not cease their operations until they recognize faithfulness" in obeying the orders. But even compliance is no guarantee of a peaceable surrender: "If and when such faithfulness is recognized, the commander in chief of the Japanese Forces of the Philippine Islands will order that firing will be ceased after taking all conditions and circumstances into consideration."

As revealed by his Farewell-and-Surrender Speech, Robert E. Lee was allowed to gracefully exit the Confederacy's rapidly darkening stage, and these circumstances were reflected in Lee's final salutation to his troops. "With an increasing admiration of your constancy and devotion to your country, and a grateful remembrance of your kind and generous considerations for myself," he wrote, "I bid you all an affectionate farewell." But reflecting his very different circumstances, there would be no surrender-farewells for Jonathan Wainwright. He could only tersely conclude his Surrender Speech, which was masked as an order, with the words "General Wainwright signing off." Unlike Robert E. Lee, there would be no college presidency in the offing, just thirty-nine months of humiliating and brutal captivity.

The Final Victory Speech

VICTORY ORDER OF THE DAY

Men and women of the Allied Expeditionary Force:

The crusade on which we embarked in the early summer of 1944 has reached its glorious conclusion. . . .

Your accomplishments at sea, in the air, on the ground and in the field of supply, have astonished the world. . . .

Full victory in Europe has been attained.

The route you have traveled through hundreds of miles is marked by the graves of former comrades. From them has been exacted the ultimate sacrifice; the blood of many nations—American, British, Canadian, French, Polish and others—has helped to gain the victory. Each of the fallen died as a member of the team to which you belong, bound together by a common love of liberty and a refusal to submit to enslavement. No monument of stone, no memorial of whatever magnitude could so well express our respect and veneration for their sacrifice, as would perpetuation of the spirit of comradeship in which they died. As we celebrate Victory in Europe let us remind ourselves that our common problems of the immediate and distant future can be best solved in the same conceptions of co-operation and devotion to the cause of human freedom as have made this Expeditionary Force such a mighty engine of righteous destruction.

Let us have no part in the profitless quarrels in which other men will inevitably engage as to what country, what service, won the European war. Every man, every woman, of every nation here represented has served according to his or her ability, and the efforts of each have contributed to the outcome. This we shall remember—and in doing so we shall be revering each honored grave, and be sending comfort to the loved ones of comrades who could not live to see this day.

Excerpt from General Dwight D. Eisenhower's
"Victory of the Day," May 8, 1945[25]

THE FINAL VICTORY SPEECH is an address by a commander or political figure that marks the conclusion of a war. In Eisenhower's speech above, we may recognize elements from other genres of battle speech: Story Conventions, Triumphal History, Remembering the Fallen, and Future Hopes, among others. Just as the Pre-Invasion Speech often discussed the larger issues of the war, the Final Victory Speech will often discuss the larger issues of the hoped-for peace— why the war was fought and what the peace is expected to achieve. Eisenhower's Victory Order of Day is a paradigm of the Final Victory Speech.

At 2:41 in the morning on May 7, 1945, Field Marshal Alfred G. Jodl, chief of staff of the OKW (Oberkommando der Wehrmacht), signed the document at Eisenhower's headquarters in Reims, France, that surrendered all German forces. By its terms the European war would be over at midnight on May 8, on which Eisenhower also issued his Victory Order of the Day. His intended Allied soldier-audience was probably the largest such in history: nine armies, twenty-three corps, ninety-one divisions, six tactical air commands, and two strategic air forces that together aggregated some 4,500,000 men and women. Recent losses had been steep as well. In the eleven months since the landings at Normandy, the total Allied deaths in Europe (excluding the Red Army) were approximately 195,500, of which 135,576 were American. At Appomattox, out of concern for the honor of his defeated adversary, Grant gave orders barring his soldiers from public celebrations. On May 8, Eisenhower simply recalled, "We had no local victory celebrations of any kind, then or later. When Jodl signed we merely went to bed for some much needed rest to get up the next day and tackle the multitude of tasks that followed upon the cessation of hostilities." And certainly one of those tasks was issuing the above order.[26]

Eisenhower opens his speech by embracing the Triumphal History Convention: "The crusade on which we embarked in the early summer of 1944 has reached its glorious conclusion." Readers will remember that in his Pre-Invasion Speech accompanying the landings at Normandy, Eisenhower also used the historical allusion to the Great Crusades. There, it had a coded religious significance. Here he transforms this significance into something like an instruction: as discussed more fully below, Eisenhower implies that with the conclusion of their crusade, the crusaders (that is, his soldier-audience) must now also conclude the righteous fury that usually accompanies such ventures. In other words, the war is over and the role of the soldier-audience as warriors for the Good and True will be changed into occupiers for the Good and True—a part that must follow a very different script.

As with any Triumphal History Convention, Eisenhower lavishly praises the soldier-audience's effort: "Your accomplishments at sea, in the air, on the ground and in the field of supply have astonished the world," he notes. Then he toasts their professionalism (unexcerpted above): "Working and fighting together in a single and indestructible partnership, you have achieved a perfection in unification of air, ground and naval power that will stand as a model in our time." The Allied forces not only conquered the Germans, they also vanquished those of little faith: "You have taken in stride military tasks so difficult as to be classed by many doubters as impossible." And also typical of Triumphal Histories, the value of his soldier-audience's efforts is heightened in light of the enemy's impressive capabilities (a "savagely fighting foe") as well as his own soldiers' suffering (enduring "every discomfort and privation") and their renowned intelligence and determination ("surmounted every obstacle ingenuity and desperation could throw in your path"). Eisenhower does not offer details here, so every soldier in his audience is free to insert his own experience.

But what of the purpose of the crusade? Eisenhower will answer this question via Remembering the Fallen. Here the dead will serve not only as a metonym for the very purpose of the European war but also as the link between the Allied forces' previous role as warriors and future role as occupiers. Eisenhower neatly segues from Triumphal History into Remembering the Fallen with a single sentence: "The route you have traveled through hundreds of miles is marked by the graves of former comrades," he declares. "From them has been exacted the ultimate sacrifice; the blood of many nations—American, British, Canadian, French, Polish and others—has helped to gain the victory." On hearing or reading these words, it would be natural for many soldiers, and especially the combat arm of his audience, to remember their dead comrades. Deaths had averaged over 16,500 per month since D-Day, and it is likely that every soldier in this audience segment knew someone that had been killed or injured.

Eisenhower first approaches the war's purpose horizontally, that is, from comrade to comrade and from the dead to the living. He constructs a chain of meaning that begins with the observation that the dead did not die alone; rather, they died as "a member of the team to which you [the living] belong." And the living audience is not severed from the dead; on the contrary, the living and dead are "bound together by a common love of liberty and refusal to submit to enslavement." Although both living and dead fought for freedom, there remains a profound difference between them in the meaning of their respective sacrifices, because the living, by virtue of having survived, now have an obligation to the dead, and it cannot be fulfilled through conventional postwar memorials: "No monument of stone, no memorial of whatever magnitude," Eisenhower declares, will be sufficient to vindicate the dead's sacrifice. He wants something more (and he wants it sooner): the sacrifice of the dead can only be vindicated by "a perpetuation of the spirit of comradeship in which they died"—that is, the spirit that arises from their mutual fight for liberty and against enslavement.

Eisenhower's use of the words "perpetuation of the spirit of comradeship" is highly significant. In asking that his soldier-audience perpetuate this spirit of liberty, he is really asking them to bring this spirit into the present moment (and on into the future). In sum, the best way to Remember the Fallen is to live today according to the principles for which they died. This is very much an expression of the Future Hopes Convention. But "perpetuation" also allows Eisenhower to add another link in his chain of meaning using this Future Hopes: a hint at the changed role of his military force. And here Triumphal History becomes sharply contrasted with Future Hopes:

> As we celebrate Victory in Europe let us remind ourselves that our common problems of the immediate and distant future can best be solved in the same conceptions of cooperation and devotion to the cause of human freedom as have made this Expeditionary Force such a mighty engine of righteous destruction.

The most striking feature of this passage is the binary it creates between two phrases: "the cause of human freedom" and the "mighty engine of righteous destruction." (They are opposed because "human freedom" cannot simultaneously occupy the same space as "righteous destruction.") For Eisenhower in May 1945, surrounded by the physical and human wreckage of the European war, this is the absolute paradox: that only "a mighty engine of righteous destruction" could achieve "the cause of human freedom." Destruction and freedom thus complement each other, for freedom could only take root amidst the complete ruination of Nazi Europe. But such freedom can only follow *after* righteous destruction has concluded.

In his quest to transition his force from warriors to occupiers, Eisenhower also shifts this binary from the present toward two very discrete futures: first, there is tomorrow or next week or next month ("the immediate future"), and then there is next year or next decade or perhaps posterity entire ("the distant future"). But these two futures share one key attribute: they both contain "our common problems." Except for the one instance discussed below, Eisenhower does not specify what these problems are. But one might glimpse them in his proposed solutions to them: "cooperation and devotion to the cause of human freedom." The meaning here is clear: an army devoted to the cause of human freedom cannot at the same time be an engine of righteous destruction. One cannot *both* occupy and destroy, at least when the objective is human freedom; destruction may have preceded occupation, but the common problem in the immediate future will be to occupy Europe in a way that testifies to the Allies' "devotion" to that objective.

Eisenhower subtly uses the comradeship trope to support his claim that the army *can* successfully make this transition from warrior to occupier. He does this by expanding an argument he has just made about the nature of his (living and dead) soldiers' comradeship, which arose from "a common love of liberty and refusal to submit to enslavement." Now he asserts that the "same conceptions of cooperation and devotion" that drove his soldiers to wage the crusade can be applied to a new mission: "the cause of human freedom." Will soldiers undertake this new mission for the same reasons they did the old mission—the "love of liberty"? Yes, because Eisenhower deftly connects the new mission with the old motive. Now, the comradeship ("cooperation and devotion") that made his force "such a mighty engine of righteous destruction" will be dedicated to the "cause of human freedom." And if human freedom cannot flourish while his army remains a "mighty engine of human destruction," then it must eschew revenge, victors' justice, punitive reparations, and the annihilation or mistreatment of POWs or the former enemy's civilians. Instead, this freedom-dedicated occupier must attempt to provide the conditions (for example, security, adequate food, clothing, and shelter) that make "human freedom"—that is, democracy—possible. A firm but humane occupation is the only way to insure that fascistic evil— one of "our common problems"—will not reemerge in the "distant future." One can occupy a country for the same reasons one originally used when waging war against it, and occupation becomes a continuation of the war's purposes by other means.

Eisenhower begins his concluding paragraph with what at first seems like an odd admonition: "Let us have no part in the profitless quarrels in which other men will inevitably engage as to what country, what service, won the European war," he urges. "Every man, every woman, of every nation here represented, has served according to his or her ability, and the efforts of each have contributed to the outcome." On the very day the hostilities ceased, could Eisenhower possibly already be referring to the kinds of arguments that usually emerge among historians long after wars are fought? Certainly not: at the moment, how the future will allocate praise or blame does not concern him. Rather, the "other men" he refers to are the political leaderships of the countries represented in his coalition, and a glance at the postwar map of Europe for May 1945 reveals the issue. At that moment, various Allied nations' infantries occupied different pieces of European territory; under certain circumstances, potentially *current* competing claims about who did what in the struggle against Germany or Italy could fracture the alliance of Great Britain, France, the United States, and Russia (and others). Such arguments could foster conflicts about Europe's postwar governance; economic disputes about matters such as reparations; legal disputes about victor's justice or even unleashing military forces to take revenge for German atrocities. (Eisenhower had surely received reports about the Red Army's "Rape of Berlin"; moreover, he also knew that compared to the United States, the other Western allies had suffered disproportionately (by many orders of magnitude) from the war and the German occupation. Indeed, in this respect, the situation resembled that in Europe following World War I. Thus Eisenhower is interested in insulating the diverse forces under his unified command from acting along narrowly national lines, warning against the well-known historical circumstance of "selfish interests" reemerging upon the defeat of a common enemy.[27]

And Remembering the Fallen will also serve to minimize these potential conflicts. Indeed, the very act of remembering "Every man['s], every woman['s]" contribution to victory is the best way of "revering each honored grave" of the fallen as well as "sending comfort to the loved ones of comrades who could not live to see this day." For soldiers, whatever the political future might hold, there will always be unity in reverence. Thus does Eisenhower argue that the "spirit of comradeship" will help keep his coalition denationalized. And comradeship is derived not just from the dead and their families but also from each other, and it must transcend national allegiances. Here the dead speak—just as the living coalition must be as dedicated to an enlightened occupation as it was to defeating a barbaric enemy, so must it also avoid destructive politics. Eisenhower entwines Future Hopes with what he probably believes are the past lessons of a more recently failed diplomacy—the Conference of Versailles following World War I.

EPILOGUE

My beloved brothers in Islam,

We have been struggling right from our youth; we sacrificed our homes, families, and all the luxuries of this worldly life in the path of Allah (we ask to accept our efforts). In our youth, we fought with and defeated the (former) U.S.S.R. (with the help of Allah), a world superpower at the time, and now we are fighting the U.S.A. We have never let the Muslim *umma* down.

We should realize that this life is temporary and eventually we have to return to Allah, the lord of the heavens and the earth.

Truly to Allah we belong and truly to Allah we shall return.

Muslims are being humiliated, tortured, and ruthlessly killed all over the world, and it is time to fight these satanic forces with the utmost strength and power. Today, the whole of the Muslim *umma* is depending (after Allah) upon the Muslim youth, hoping that they would never let them down.

The *jihad* has become an obligation upon each and every Muslim. We advise the Muslim youth not to fall victim to the words of some *ulema* who are misleading the *umma* by stating that jihad is still a communal duty. . . . The time has come when all the Muslims of the world, especially the youth, should unite and soar against infidelity and continue jihad till these forces are crushed to naught, all the anti-Islamic forces are wiped off from the face of the Earth, and Islam takes over the whole world and all the other false religions.

"And fight them until there is no more seduction and the religion will all be for Allah alone. But if they cease (worshipping others besides Allah), then certainly Allah is All-Seer of what they do." [Koran, 8:39]

We ask Allah to rank us among His truthful slaves.
• *Your brother,*
  Osama bin Laden

"Osama bin Laden's Message for the Youth of the Muslim *Umma*,"
December 2001[1]

I T SEEMS FITTING to close this study by briefly considering a battle speech given by America's chief adversary in the current Global
War on Terror. Thus far we have limited ourselves to speeches drawn
from Western military history. One characteristic shared by most of
these speeches is that they are the products of hierarchical organizations. Most descended vertically from superior to subordinate, while
a few moved horizontally between subordinates. But all were contained within a hierarchy and addressed to soldiers belonging to a
unit, which in turn was part of an organized military force sanctioned
by a higher government in whose name it acted. And, of course, this
hierarchy employed whatever means were available to communicate
these speeches: by voice, in print, or via electronic transmission.

But the West's adversaries, such as Al Qaeda (AQ) and its affili-
ates, franchisees, copycats, and wannabes, are often not organized hi-
erarchically. They reflect a force concept with flat management and
a vastly simpler org chart, and they are peopled by a minute fraction
of the operatives employed in the typical Western military model. As
discussed below, the battle speeches of these latter groups are apt to
move quite differently: the exact same speech, reproduced thousands
of times and heard by an audience numbering (perhaps) in the millions, will move vertically *and* horizontally, simultaneously and without boundaries. Also significantly, enemies as well as friends will
access these speeches. Thus far, partly as a result of this, AQ-type
groups have achieved outsized successes for chump change.

In fairness, AQ and its ilk are tasked with a much simpler mission
than that of Western militaries. The latter were originally organized,
armed, and fielded in order to fight counterparts that were similarly
organized, armed, and fielded. But AQ wages what Colonel Thomas X.
Hammes has described as "fourth-generation warfare" (4GW). Here
the AQ-type enemy is too weak to confront Western militaries directly;

instead, it "uses all available networks—political, economic, social, military—to convince the enemy's political decision makers that their strategic goals are either unachievable or too costly for the perceived benefit." In sum, the 4GW warrior's target is the adversary's decision makers—its political, media, business, and intellectual elites—who are not targeted for death as much as for persuasion that the war, occupation, alliance, natural resource, pipeline, international relief effort, charitable endeavor, or territorial presence is simply not worth the cost in blood, treasure, or, for some elites, simple inconvenience.[2]

As is the case with Osama bin Laden's above Recruitment Speech, this enemy's battle speeches prove very useful for what they reveal about the speechmaker's world—his strategy, assumptions, and problems. How these battle speeches are communicated to their recruiter- and recruit-audiences also reveals something about this particular antagonist's organization and recruitment methods and targets. Occasionally, as in the case above, such a speech may reveal internal complications and thus provide clues about vulnerabilities. But most importantly, battle speeches invariably speak to a vision. Especially in Recruiting Speeches, the battle speechmaker must announce what he is fighting for as he attempts to persuade others to join that fight. This vision will include both what he wants and what his enemy can expect if the speechmaker is victorious. People raised in societies saturated with commercial messages understandably tend to confuse exhortation with a sales pitch and thus automatically discount the former for its puffery. But one striking feature of many battle speeches is that while their facts may be stretched or even invented, and their emotional messages hyperbolized, their animating visions are usually candid, if not always successful. For Americans, in particular, accustomed as we are to the sometimes laughable propaganda speeches of World War II and Cold War adversaries, there may exist a tendency, now dangerous, to discount what an enemy says and question whether he really means it.

OSAMA BIN LADEN, the marquee warrior of 4GW, delivered the Recruiting Speech above in December 2001. It has two of the three conventions usually associated with the genre: Family Appeal and Speaker Identity. It appears to lack Staging—bin Laden was then (and still remains) unavailable for public tours of the *umma*—but, as discussed below, Staging is likely provided in the "aftermarket" by AQ's (and AQ-style) sub-recruiters.

Speaker Identity is the first convention bin Laden embraces. He leaves nothing to chance and is certainly not relying on the charisma and prestige that he enjoys across large swaths of the *umma*: "We have been struggling right from our youth; we sacrificed our homes, families, and all the luxuries of this worldly life in the path of Allah," he declares, reminding his audience of his resume: a professionally educated rich man's son who tossed it all away in favor of doing his duty to Allah by resisting the Soviet invasion and occupation of Afghanistan. But bin Laden does not rely on any enthymematic understandings— it all must be spelled out. "In our youth, we fought with and defeated the (former) U.S.S.R. (with the help of Allah), a world superpower at the time, and now we are fighting the U.S.A." This claim is probably intended less as a boast than as necessary historical background—it is almost 2002, and bin Laden is addressing "the Youth of the Muslim *Umma*," many of whom were perhaps too young to know of the *mujahidin*'s achievements in the 1980s.

How bin Laden uses Family Appeal is especially interesting and best understood in light of the type of struggle (and the probable outcomes) his recruits will face. If persuaded to undertake Offensive *Jihad,* there is a high likelihood of death or capture—death being an almost certain outcome for those persuaded to kill themselves in the act of killing others. Those who are not converted into ambulatory homicidals will still face a cruel life, fighting Western forces among bleak mountains, deserts, or urban areas; living covertly as members of killing cells in Western countries; or functioning as couriers or organizers, moving constantly, perpetually swapping identities in hostile societies where not even the *umma* is always trustworthy. This is not a life that comes naturally to most youth or has automatic appeal to family members, and bin Laden is probably aware of this. Thus he cleverly finesses Family Appeal by subsuming a youth's duties to his nuclear family into a larger duty owed to his imagined family of Muslims (the *umma*), the obligations of which bin Laden reinvents to accommodate his politico-military objectives. He then strengthens this transfer of duties by imputing to them Allah's imprimatur. The key equivalence is the imagined construct of *umma*: *umma* equals all Muslims, and all individual Muslims owe certain duties to the *umma*. The *umma*'s connection to the youth parallels the youth's connection to his blood relatives. "Today, the whole of the Muslim *umma*," bin Laden declares, "is depending (after Allah) upon the Muslim youth, hoping that they would never let them down." Just as a youth would not disappoint his mother or father, so a youth would not—at Allah's insistence, no less—"let . . . down" his larger Muslim family. After all, bin Laden, whose tone throughout this speech is that of a sage elder brother addressing a young person, is simply asking them to make the same sacrifices that he made once too. In short, bin Laden's overall tone, the speech's content, and the use of the customary salutation "brother" all contribute to the imagining of Islam as a large family to whom a duty of Offensive Jihad is owed. And perhaps as a challenge, or perhaps as an appeal to guilt (especially for those semi-Westernized Muslims already conflicted by juggling religious and ethnic identities with the adopted civic identities of newer homelands), he flatly declares: "We have never let the Muslim *umma* down."

Before introducing some of the explicitly 4GW aspects of this speech, two further points about its content must be noted. First, as was true with some of the Recruiting Speeches discussed in chapter 3, bin Laden assumes that idealistic appeals will resonate with the "youth" and thus he offers his audience the always-seductive eschatological vision: "Especially the youth," he declares, can "unite and soar against infidelity and continue *jihad* until these forces are crushed to naught." Once infidelity is eradicated, bin Laden exults in a burst of supremacist candor that "all the anti-Islamic forces [will be] wiped from the face of this Earth, and Islam [will take] over the whole world and all the other false religions." This is a heady assignment to entrust to any coming generation.

Where this Recruiting Speech differs from others discussed earlier is in how bin Laden uses it as a vehicle to combat a theological argument that he clearly regards as an obstacle to his recruiting. (Here one finds evidence that he does not in fact control the "real" *umma* but, as noted before, must reimagine both it and the duties owed it in order to further his politico-religious mission.) "We advise the Muslim youth not to fall victim to the words of some *ulema* who are misleading the *umma*," he warns, "by stating that *jihad* is still a communal duty." In other words, those clerics whose idea of *jihad* does not include flying hijacked civilian passenger planes into office buildings are wrong— they "mislead." Why this is so is not stated here, although in other speeches bin Laden, or his colleague Ayman al-Zawahiri, answers that question.[3] Clearly something is not right—given an *umma* thought to be just shy of one and a half billion Muslims, and one on whose behalf bin Laden has appointed himself to speak, we would obviously expect that he must have certain *ulema* in mind. (The fact that he does not name them suggests that such a list might be lengthy.) But what matters here is that bin Laden feels he must answer them theologically, thus suggesting a schism in the *umma* and, more generally (and significantly), evidence of a problem.

The means of distributing this and other AQ battle speeches cannot be disentangled from the nature and probable whereabouts of the recruit-audience (that is, everywhere). The diffuse nature of AQ and its cohorts suggests that bin Laden does not know himself the identities of those who will heed his call and "fight them until . . . the religion will be for Allah alone." In fact, as this speech is made, the actors who ultimately will take his advice *may not know themselves* that they are destined for Offensive *Jihad*. They do not yet exist as confirmed recruits; the conversion for Offensive *Jihad* in fact requires intense processing and substantial lead time. Thus bin Laden's Recruitment Speech must be virtually perpetual—useful now, useful next year, still useful in ten or twenty years. And the technological means do exist to ensure that this Recruiting Speech will be available almost anywhere and at any time: it may be distributed on websites, podcasts, cassette tapes, CDs, DVD recruiting and training videos, and satellite television broadcasts. This is how technology accommodates 4GW battle speeches—these adversaries have a parasitic relationship to "establishment" technology, adding little but thoroughly traveling these electronic highways, much like the barbarian invaders used Roman roads to ultimately overwhelm the empire. And it is here that Staging reappears. In the absence of bin Laden's person, his disembodied voice may be used as a voice-over in recruiting or training videos that feature inspiring imagery, for example, or as a podcast downloadable from an attractive website.

It is worth noting the two speeches already discussed in this book that bear very pale resemblances to bin Laden's. The first is General Douglas MacArthur's "I Have Returned" speech, broadcast to the Filipinos in October 1944, and the second is General William W. Loring's speech to western Virginians discussed in chapter 5. All three speeches call for uprisings, and MacArthur's is perhaps the closest to bin Laden's in its use of a Religious Historical Narrative. But for present purposes, what really differentiates these two speeches from bin Laden's is the matter of intended boundaries—both MacArthur and Loring have a limited, time-sensitive message, pinned to specific events and intended for a sharply defined, geographically and ethnically specific group. By contrast, bin Laden's speech is open ended; it is not limited geographically because the *umma* exists everywhere Muslims do, and it is not limited ethnically or racially because Muslims appear in every such group. Moreover, it has no time constraints: bin Laden probably believes that the conflict between Dar al-Islam and Dar al-Harb will be waged over many generations and across many civilizations.

But there is a flip side to using these kinds of communication technologies—if his recruiter- and recruit-audiences can access the weblogs, podcasts, CDs, DVDs, and so on, then so can Western media and security services. Clearly, AQ-type battle speeches are not intended to covertly circulate like *samizdat,* to be read in private and then secretly passed on. Here the secret to be guarded is not the speeches but rather the specific identities of the recruiter- and recruit audiences. And thus does a genuinely new development occur in the history of battle speeches: a battle speech that is written for both friends and foes.

Fortunately for bin Laden, there is a correlation of subject matter between what he wants to convey to Islam's youth and what he wants to tell his 4GW adversaries. Simply put, it is his eschatological vision of biblical (as in Koranic) scope: Manichean light and darkness has fallen over the world, large conceptual categories sweep the horizon, the future must be purged of evil and sanitized for the faithful. Thus the big-picture religious idealism: "We should realize that this life is temporary and eventually we have to return to Allah, the lord of heavens and earth." Thus the characterization of the enemy: "Muslims are being humiliated, tortured, and ruthlessly killed all over the world" . . . "satanic forces with the utmost strength and power" . . . "infidelity" . . . "anti-Islamic forces" . . . "false religions." Thus the actions available to righteous youth: "fight these satanic forces" . . . "unite and soar against infidelity and continue jihad" . . . "till [this evil] is crushed to naught" . . . "wiped off from the face of the earth." And the final vision: "Islam takes over the whole world."

It is probably not bin Laden's intent here to convert Westerners to Offensive Jihad. (Though many of his speeches do contain an invitation to convert to Islam, it is a tenet of Offensive Jihad to issue such invitations before waging war.) Instead, bin Laden believes that his Western, and especially American, enemies have become so morally degenerate that they are no longer willing to die in defense of their interests.[4] Thus this language also serves a very specific 4GW purpose—the intimidation of the enemy's elites via demonstrating a superior will to final victory. First, by December 2001 bin Laden has already demonstrated by deed what he believes is a greater willingness to die for his cause (for example, suicide attacks on the USS *Cole* in October 2000 or the nineteen hijackers' fates on September 11, 2001). While he is not yet ready to take credit for the attacks on the World Trade Center and Pentagon (a conclusive admission came in October 2004), in this speech he certainly boasts-by-implication (speaking only for his recruits, of course) of a greater willingness to die: "We should realize that this life is temporary. . . . Truly to Allah we belong and truly to Allah we shall return." Likewise, AQ has also demonstrated by deed (for example, the August 1998 East African embassy bombings or, of course, September 11, 2001) his policy of ignoring distinctions between military and civilian targets. In this speech, he reinforces the terror associated with that policy, also via intimidating language: "satanic forces . . . crushed to naught . . . wiped off the face of this Earth." According to the AQ script, the American elites will eventually give way. In this speech, as in others, bin Laden only implies his conviction that victory is not a function of sophisticated hardware but of superior will (and Allah's blessing). This Recruiting Speech may be little more than propaganda to Western ears, but when viewed in light of his entire speech-corpus to date, it is a safe bet that bin Laden believes that will to power and not technology will favor his side in this struggle.

VISION

To support security, peace, freedom, and democracy everywhere.

MISSION

Blackwater is committed to supporting national and international security policies that protect those who are defenseless and provide a free voice for all. We dedicate ourselves to providing ethical, efficient, and effective turnkey solutions that positively impact the lives of those still caught in desperate times.

We further are committed to the foot soldiers; the men and women who daily stand on the frontlines of the global war on terror and say, "not today," and who believe in a peaceful future for their communities and nations. Whether they serve in uniform or out, we will provide them the very best in training and tactical support to ensure they are fully prepared to meet current and future global security challenges.

"Blackwater Employment Opportunities," Recruiting Speech,
Blackwater USA website, October 2007[5]

WHITHER THE BATTLE SPEECH? One can discern two developments that might influence such speeches. As discussed above, the first of these developments, the rise of AQ and AQ-style groups, is already in play. As this book has emphasized throughout, changes in tactics and especially communications technology has always influenced the type, length, and content of battle speeches. Because AQ differs from the traditional Western military organization—it has a non-hierarchical management structure, a fluid membership, and an affinity for the public internet when distributing its battle speeches— it has changed such speeches. AQ's fluid force structure requires universal speeches—that is, ones that are not rendered obsolete by the passage of time. In addition, because its battle speeches will be read by friend and foe alike, they can be used as propaganda to service its larger mission of demoralizing Western and Muslim elites. But public distribution has also created a problem: battle speeches must also be used to silence internal critics, those in the Muslim community who disagree with AQ's means or ends.

The second development is not discussed above but merits a brief mention: the West's use of private security services for both conventional military functions and intelligence.[6] For example, private security firms are already used extensively in Iraq (and elsewhere around the world) to supplement (or even replace) "regular" armed forces. At present, the reason for this relates to budget and manpower. Private security firms may be more cost effective to use; moreover, as the demand for security has increased, governments have difficulty competing against private entities for experienced personnel. And private firms are an ideal security solution for clients who cannot use government resources to protect purely private interests (unless national and private interests happen to correlate).

Like their terrorist adversaries and Western armies, these private entities also create battle speeches posted on attractive websites. An example of a Recruiting Speech for one prominent firm is featured above. This speech is unremarkable and could easily have been written by any branch of the U.S., Australian, or British armed forces. Significantly, Blackwater USA has also instituted a professionally edited online monthly publication, the *Blackwater Tactical Weekly*, which in some respects imitates the brigade-level magazines discussed earlier.[7] *Blackwater Tactical Weekly* contains reprints from other media as well as various editorials that bear on the overall mission as featured above. These editorials can be exhortatory although not necessarily connected with a particular mission. In sum, whether the military force is private or public, battle speech genres and conventions will live on.

Whatever changes are in store for battle speeches—and here it remains as trite as it is true that change is the only constant—they will always need to persuade. Men and (increasingly) women must be convinced to undertake the work of soldiering, whether this means carrying a rifle overseas or operating an unmanned aerial vehicle flying over Iraq from an air-conditioned base in Arizona. And speeches will not be reinvented as much as slowly readapted, as some themes become obsolete and others arise. What will also remain constant are the battle speech conventions: recruiters will still have to stage, props will still serve their dramatic purposes, and commanders will still have to explain why the just-fought battle was fought and what it accomplished. War is a social activity, only more so; and in wars, speech remains the primary means of communicating, only with ever greater and more lethal consequences.

Notes

INTRODUCTION (pp. 1–26)

1. Onasander, *The General*, Proemium, 1:13, (Cambridge, Mass.: Harvard University Press, 2001), 379–81; Baron De Jomini, *The Art of War*, transl. G. H. Mendenhall and W. P. Craighill (Philadelphia: J. B. Lippincott, Co., 1862), 41–42; S. L. A. Marshall, *Men Against Fire: The Problem of Battle Command in Future War*, 1947 (reprint, Gloucester, Mass.: Peter Smith Publications, 1973), 138. In recent years *Men Against Fire* has generated enormous controversy for its author's methodology (or lack thereof) in supporting his claim that only 25 percent of World War II combat infantrymen actually fired their weapons; however, other parts of Marshall's book contain valuable insights, especially surrounding the need for greater oral communication during combat. For a recent article that contains an interview with a former member of Marshall's staff, as well as a listing of books and articles dealing with the controversy, see John Whiteclay Chambers II, "S. L. A. Marshall's *Men Against Fire*: New Evidence Regarding Fire Ratios," *Parameters* (Autumn 2003): 113–21, esp. n. 3.

2. Herodotus, *The Histories*, ed. Walter Blanco (New York: Penguin, 1992), 114.

3. David G. Chandler (introduction and commentary), *The Military Maxims of Napoleon*, transl. Lieutenant-General Sir George C. D'Aguilar (London: Greenhill Books, 2002), 242.

4. Thomas L. Livermore, *Days and Events, 1860–1866* (Boston: Houghton Mifflin Company, 1920), 133; S. L. A. Marshall, *Pork Chop Hill: The American Fighting Man in Action, Korea, Spring, 1953,* (1956; reprint, New York: Berkley Books, 2000), 26; *In the Words of Napoleon: The Emperor Day by Day*, ed. R. M. Johnston, with new material by Philip Haythornthwaite (London: Greenhill Books, 2002), 6.

5. Cotton Mather, "Souldiers Counselled and Comforted," September 1, 1689, p. 2; "To my Much Honored Friends; the Pious and Valiant Commanders Of the Forces now engaged against our Indian Enemies," (Boston: Samuel Green, 1689), p. 3. I am indebted to Susan Niditch's *War in the Hebrew Bible* (New York: Oxford University Press, 1995) for bringing this sermon to my attention. Niditch offers a more detailed analysis of Mather's sermon on pp. 3–4. William M. Fowler Jr., *Under Two Flags: The American Navy in the Civil War* (New York: Avon Books, 1991), 241.

6. Marshall, *Pork Chop Hill*, 26.

7. MacArthur and Wainwright's speeches can be found on *War on Radio* [sound recordings]: *The Pacific and European Theaters* (Thousand Oaks, Calif.: 2002) 8 CDs.

8. Trevor Royle, *Crimea: The Great Crimean War, 1854–1856* (New York: Palgrave Macmillan, 2000), 114–15. Russell's first war was actually the Schleswig-Holstein conflict of 1850—he was even wounded during the battle of Idstedt—but his reputation was made in the Crimea, where he spent almost two years covering British forces. See also Ilana D. Miller, *Reports from America: William Howard Russell and the Civil War* (Gloucestershire: Sutton Publishing, 2001), 7–8.

9. *Random House Dictionary of the English Language*, 2nd ed., unabridged (New York: Random House, 1987).

10. Henry Livermore Abbott to Charles Cushing Paine, July 28, 1863, Paine Papers, Massachusetts Historical Society. Abbott was explaining to a dead comrade's father why he could not recall any details about his son's death.

11. Field Manual, No. 22-51, *Leader's Manual for Combat Stress Control,* Section 1-5, Headquarters, Department of the Army, September 29, 1994. In section 5-3(d), "Signs/Symptoms of Battle Fatigue," memory loss is specifically named as one of the principal symptoms of battle fatigue, though the manual points out that "memory loss is usually less common, especially in its extreme versions. Mild forms include the inability to remember recent orders and instructions." Orders and instructions are one genre of battle speech discussed in chapter 4.

12. Journal entry for 17 Sept[ember 1862], *Stand Firm and Fire Low: The Civil War Writings of Colonel Edward E. Cross,* ed. Walter Holden, William E. Ross, and Elizabeth Slomba (Hanover, N.H.: University Press of New England, 2003), 47.

13. See *Stand Firm and Fire Low,* 47 n. 109, where Livermore reviewed Cross's journal and initialed marginalia.

14. *The Landmark Thucydides: A Comprehensive Guide to the Peloponnesian War,* ed. Robert B. Strassler (New York: Free Press, 1998), 1.22.1; *Polybius: The Rise of the Roman Empire,* transl. Ian Scott-Kivert (London: Penguin Books, 1979), 12:25b; Mogens Herman Hansen, "The Battle Exhortation in Ancient Historiography: Fact or Fiction?" *Historia: Journal of Ancient History* 42 (1993): Heft 2, 163, 172, 179.

15. Among the more distinguished opinions of the past century, see F. W. Walbank, *A Historical Commentary on Polybius,* 3 vols., (Oxford: Clarendon Press, 1957), 1:13–14; W. W. Tarn, *Alexander the Great: Sources and Studies,* 2 vols. (Cambridge: Cambridge University Press, 1948), 2:286–96; F. E. Adcock, *Thucydides and His History* (Cambridge: Cambridge University Press, 1963), 27–42. Also see P. A. Brunt's opinion on Alexander's speeches generally in *Arrian: Anabasis of Alexander, Books V–VII,* trans. By P. A. Brunt (Cambridge, Mass.: Harvard University Press, 2000), Appendix XXVII, 528–34; Doyne Dawson, *The Origins of Western Warfare: Militarism and Morality in the Ancient World* (Boulder, Colo.: Westview Press, 1998), 5.

16. Perhaps it is pertinent here that during the research and writing of this

book, I was repeatedly asked whether I would use certain battle speeches from films such as *Patton, The Longest Day, Gettysburg,* and *Glory* as examples. Apparently it does *not* go without saying that the battle speeches used in those and perhaps most other war films are at best composites of real speeches and usually pure fabrications, however compelling their contents.

17. Pritchett's responses to Hansen's article (see n. 14) may be found in his *Ancient Greek Battle Speeches and a Palfrey* (Amsterdam: J. C. Gieben, 2002), 1–80, and "The General's Exhortations in Greek Warfare," in *Essays in Greek History* (Amsterdam: J. C. Gieben, 1994), 27–109. Other responses to Hansen may be found in C. T. H. R. Ehrhardt, "Speeches before Battle?" *Historia: Journal of Ancient History* 44 (1995): Heft 1, 120–21; Michael Clark, "Did Thucydides Invent the Battle Exhortation?" *Historia: Journal of Ancient History* 44 (1995): Heft 3, 375–76. Reading history aloud appears to have been the rule in ancient Greece; see Alan L. Boegehold, *When a Gesture Was Expected* (Princeton, N.J.: Princeton University Press, 1999), 6–7.

18. Victor Davis Hansen, *The Western Way of War: Infantry Battle in Classical Greece* (New York: Alfred A. Knopf, 1989), 107–9; Adrian Goldsworthy, *The Complete Roman Army* (London: Thames and Hudson, 2003), 175, 184–85; Julius Caesar, *The Conquest of Gaul,* translated by S. A. Handford (London: Penguin, 1982), 2:21 and 2:25 (see also the introduction by Jane F. Gardner, p. 24); Pritchett, "The General's Exhortations," 105.

19. Hansen, "The Battle Exhortation," 166.

20. Tim Collins, *Rules of Engagement: A Life in Conflict* (London: Headline Book Publishing, 2005), 131–33.

21. Theodore C. Burgess, "Epideictic Literature," Ph.d. dissertation (University of Chicago, 1902), 212–14. To compare thematic historical continuities and discontinuities with Burgess (and the present book), see also John R. E. Bliese, "Rhetoric and Morale: A Study of Battle Orations from the Central Middle Ages," *Journal of Medieval History* 15 (1989): 201–26. Bliese's appendix A lists "motive appeals" by the number of times they appear in the 360 medieval battle speeches he surveyed for his article: "1. Show bravery, win honor; 2. Our cause is just; 3. God will help us; 4. Instructions and orders; 5. We have some military advantage; 6. You should not try to flee; 7. Plunder and booty; 8. Defend yourselves, family, country, etc; 9. Reminder of past victories; 10. Promise victory; 11. Vengeance; 12. Remember our 'nation's' reputation; 13. A small force can beat a larger one; 14. Promise eternal rewards of martyrdom; 15. Fight for Christ; 16. Follow my example; 17. Here is the battle we sought." Readers who can see the continuities and discontinuities between Burgess's ancients, Bliese's medievals, and the warriors from other periods discussed in the present volume will have been paying close attention.

22. For example, see Article 33 ("Pillage is prohibited") of the Fourth Geneva Convention, August 12, 1949, as well as the general provisions of the 1954 Hague Convention, "Convention for the Protection of Cultural Property in the Event of Armed Conflict," May 14, 1954.

23. Collins, *Rules of Engagement,* 130.

24. Ibid., 131.

1. THE HISTORY IN BATTLE SPEECHES (pp. 27–64)

1. *The Mind of Napoleon: Selections from His Written and Spoken Words* (New York: Columbia University Press, 1955), 50; *In the Words of Napoleon,* 217.

2. Had Napoleon cared about historical accuracy, he would have compared Xerxes's "armed hordes" with their adversaries, the tightly disciplined Greek phalanxes. See Victor Davis Hanson, *The Western Way of War* (Berkeley: University of California Press, 2000), 16.

3. The reporter of this speech, Gary Livingston, is mistaken here. At the time he spoke, Sergeant Major Kent was sergeant major of the First Marine Expeditionary Force, not the entire U.S. Marine Corps. Kent became sergeant major of the Marine Corps on April 25, 2007.

4. Gary Livingston, *Fallujah, With Honor* (Topsail Beach, N.C.: Caisson Press, 2006), 20; Richard Tregaskis, *Guadalcanal Diary* (New York: Modern Library of America, 2000), 24.

5. This category of metonymy, "The Place for the Event," is taken from Lakoff and Mark Johnson, *Metaphors We Live By* (Chicago: University of Chicago Press, 1980), 39.

6. The "Commandant of the U.S. Marine Corps' Official Reading List" may be obtained at www.mcu.usmc.mil/reading/ or from the Marine Corps Bulletin (MCBUL) 1500, "The Marine Corps Professional Reading Program," All Marine Corps Activities (ALMAR), 244/96. The U.S. Army, Navy, Air Force, and Coast Guard also offer reading lists. Good background about the various events that contributed to the public's understanding of the flag raising at Iwo Jima may be found in James Bradley and Ron Powers's *Flags of Our Fathers* (New York: Bantam, 2006), 207, 295. My conclusion about *Full Metal Jacket* figuring prominently in Iraq War memoirs is based on a wide but not complete survey of published books—new titles continue to emerge as the conflict persists. For references to the film, including one made by a soldier who was most likely a member of Sergeant Major Kent's audience, see Bing West, *No True Glory: A Frontline Account of the Battle of Fallujah* (New York: Bantam, 2005), 199 (the soldier quoted by West was a member of the First Battalion, Eigth Marine Regiment); Gunnery Sergeant Jason K. Doran, *"I Am My Brother's Keeper": Journal of a Gunny in Iraq* (North Topsail Beach, N.C.: 2005), 94; Jason Christopher Hartley, *Just Another Soldier: A Year on the Ground in Iraq* (New York: HarperCollins, 2005), entry for November 3, 2003; and Tim Pritchard, *Ambush Alley: The Most Extraordinary Battle of the Iraq War* (New York: Presidio Press, 2005), 209.

7. The full text of the Marine Corps Hymn may be found in Kenneth W. Estes, *The Marine Officer's Guide,* 6th ed. (Annapolis: U.S. Naval Institute Press, 2000), 461.

8. Estes, *The Marine Officer's Guide*, sect. 102, pp. 2–4.

9. Livingston, *Fallujah, with Honor*, 256.

10. Navy Department Communiqués: Commander in Chief, Pacific Ocean Arena (CINCPOA) Communique No. 300, March 16, 1945.

11. Josephus, *The Jewish War*, transl. G. W. Williamson (London: Penguin Classics, 1981), 319. The entire speech may found on pp. 317–22.

12. Walter Burkert, *Greek Religion*, transl. John Raffan (Cambridge, Mass.: Harvard University Press, 1985), 4–9.

13. For the entirety of Josephus's speech, E. Mary Smallwood has identified the following Biblical passages that Josephus apparently refers to: Genesis 12:10–20, 14:14; Exodus 7; I Samuel 5–6; 2 Kings 18:17–19:36; Chronicles 36:20–23; Ezra 1; 2 Kings 24:18–25:12; Jeremiah 27, 34, 37–39, 52. See Josephus, *The Jewish War*, 450 n. 17–22.

14. Josephus, *The Jewish War*, 404.

15. Ibid., 200–220 (defense of Jotapata), 221–22 (Vespasian's prisoner); Josephus's account of the siege of Jerusalem appears in chapters 17–22.

16. Ibid., 318, 317.

17. Ibid., 317–22.

18. Deuteronomy 28:15, King James Version [KJV].

19. *The War of the Rebellion: A Compilation of the Official Records of the Union and Confederate* Armies [hereafter, *OR*], Series 1, vol. 2, p. 574, Headquarters Army of the Potomac, Manassas, Va., July 25, 1861 (Washington, D.C.: Government Printing Office, 1880–1901); "Eisenhower Gives Battle Orders to His Armies," *New York Times*, June 6, 1944.

20. Josephus, *The Jewish War*, 319–20. Beauregard, a Creole, took communion and was buried as a Catholic; see T. Harry Williams, *P. G. T. Beauregard: Napoleon in Gray* (Baton Rouge: Louisiana State University Press, 1954), 2–3, 327. Johnston's antecedents were Episcopalian; see Robert M. Hughes, *General Johnston* (New York: D. Appleton and Company, 1897), 6. Eisenhower's mother was a fervent Jehovah's Witness (a name the movement did not adopt until 1931), and this was the religious standard of Eisenhower's childhood; see Carlo D'Este, *Eisenhower: A Soldier's Life* (New York: Henry Holt and Company, 2002), 33–34.

21. See also Psalms 77:20 and 105:26.

22. The Confederate Constitution may be found in Appendix K of Jefferson Davis's *The Rise and Fall of the Confederate Government*, 2 vols. (New York: Da Capo Press, 1990), 1:552–82. For Confederate Army religiosity, see Steven E. Woodworth, *While God Is Marching On: The Religious World of Civil War Soldiers* (Lawrence: University of Kansas Press, 2001), 178–79; and Robert N. Rosen, *The Jewish Confederates* (Columbia: University of South Carolina Press, 2000), 161.

23. Alfred J. Andrea, *Encyclopedia of the Crusades* (Westport, Conn.: Greenwood Press, 2003). Andrea's work is a handy reference to this often misunderstood topic. See his introduction for a brief summary of the Crusades and "Crusade," xvii–xxiii.

24. Several versions of this speech exist. The epigraph contains the version found in the *Rebellion Record*, as it appears to be the most complete—that is, the longest—version: Document 193, *Rebellion Record: A Diary of American Events,* edited by Frank Moore (New York: Arno Press, 1977), 12 vols., 1:273–74. It was reprinted there from the *New York Evening Post,* May 25, 1861. Another version may be found in the *New York Tribune* of the same day. The Seventh New York Regiment should not be confused with the Seventh Regiment New York State Militia Infantry, which had departed New York for Washington a month earlier; see Frederick H. Dyer, *A Compendium of the War of the Rebellion* (Dayton, Ohio: Morningside Press, 1978), 1408.

25. Few establishment figures in 1861 New York could rival Daly's qualifications to explain to new arrivals just what America or its struggles might mean for them. Born in the United States in 1816 to recently arrived Irish immigrants, Daly was a brilliant autodidact; appointed to the bench in 1844, Daly was awarded a LL.D by Columbia University in 1860 and later taught at its law school. His published works include *History of Naturalization and Its Laws in Different Countries* (1860) and *The First Settlement of Jews in North America* (1875).

26. The Seventh was a two years' regiment that saw service at Big Bethel, the Peninsula Campaign, South Mountain, Antietam, Fredericksburg, and Chancellorsville; Dyer, *A Compendium of the War,* 1407–8; *New York Tribune,* May 25, 1861.

27. The Southern argument indeed clearly carried weight with some of them. For a discussion of Germans who cast their lots with the South, see J. G. Rosengarten, *The German Soldier in the Wars of the United States* (Philadelphia: J. B. Lippincott company, 1890), 177–92.

28. For the passages about the "Allemanni," see Edward Gibbon, *The Decline and Fall of the Roman Empire,* 6 vols. (New York: Everyman's Library, 1993), 1:237–38, 286–87. "Countrymen" is used with a caveat—when Daly spoke, "Germany" in the modern sense had not yet been united.

29. Arrian, *The Campaigns of Alexander* (New York: Penguin Classics, 1976), 112–14. W. W. Tarn, writing in *Alexander the Great: Sources and Studies,* 2 vols. (Cambridge: 1948), 2:286, is convinced that Arrian invented this speech. Brunt seems less sure; see introduction, footnote 15. Arrian wrote his celbrated biography some four centuries after Alexander's death; thus unlike soldier-historians Caesar, Xenophon, or Josephus, who had their own imperfect memory texts for support, Arrian had only textual sources, which are today lost. Brunt observes, "Thus the speeches in [Arrian] cannot be *more* reliable than the contextual narrative, and they may be *less*" (emphasis original).

30. Livy, *The History of Rome from Its Foundation,* books 21–30; *The War with Hannibal,* ed. Betty Radice, transl. Aubrey De Selincourt (London: Penguin Books, 1972), 21:42–45. According to Livy, a nine-year-old Hannibal swore a sacred oath "that soon as he should be able he would be the declared enemy of the

Roman People," *Livy in Fourteen Volumes,* trans. By B. O. Foster (Cambridge, Mass.: Harvard University Press, 1919), vol. 5, XXI.1.4.

31. *In the Words of Napoleon,* 99–100; William Manchester, *American Caesar: Douglas MacArthur 1880–1964* (Boston: Little, Brown, 1978), 388–89.

32. Manchester, *American Caesar,* 388.

33. Bernard K. Duffy and Ronald H. Carpenter, *Douglas MacArthur: Warrior as Wordsmith* (Westport, Conn.: Greenwood, 1997), 5.

2. THE PRESENTATION AND THE RECRUITING SPEECH (pp. 65–103)

1. *Rebellion Record,* Document 263, "Fourteenth Regiment, N.Y.S.V., Arrived at New York, June 18," 1:413–15.

2. Modern U.S. Army procedures may be obtained from field manual FM-321.5, "Drill and Ceremonies." Gustavus B. Hutchinson, *A Narrative of the Formation and Services of the Eleventh Massachusetts Volunteers, from April 15, 1861, to July 14, 1865, Being a Brief Account of Their Experiences in the Camp and Field* (Boston: Alfred Mudge and Son, 1893), 53.

3. *OR,* ser. 3, vol. 2, "General Orders No. 91," p. 270; ser. 3, vol. 4, p. 810.

4. Dyer, *A Compendium of the War,* 1410–11. The Fourteenth Regiment Infantry should not be confused with the Fourteenth Regiment State Militia Infantry, also known as the "Fourteenth Brooklyn."

5. *Appleton's Cyclopaedia of American Biography* (New York: D. Appleton and Company, 1887), 6:151–52; 3:182–83.

6. Benjamin G. Shearer and Barbara S. Shearer, *State Names, Seals, Flags, and Symbols: A Historical Guide* (Westport, Conn.: Greenwood Press, 1994) 87.

7. Daniel George Macnamara, *The History of the Ninth Regiment Massachusetts Volunteer Infantry* (Boston: E. B. Shillings and Company, 1899), 23

8. The original statute may be found in *Supplement to the General Statutes of the Commonwealth of Massachusetts,* ed. William Richardson and George P. Sanger (Boston: William White, 1867), 87–88. The importance of this program to recruitment is discussed in Richard F. Miller, "For His Wife, His Widow, and His Orphan: Massachusetts and Family Aid during the Civil War," *Massachusetts Historical Review* 6 (2004): 70–106.

9. Shearer and Shearer, *State Names,* 82. Before the Massachusetts state flag was formally adopted in 1971, flags bore the "Seal of the Republic of Massachusetts," which had been formally designated in 1780.

10. Sergeant Fred C. Floyd, *History of the Fortieth (Mozart) Regiment, New York Volunteers* (Boston: F. H. Gilson Company, 1909), 188–89; "From United States General Hospital, Annapolis, Thursday, August 27, 1862," *New York Times,* September 1, 1862.

11. Several weeks after leaving the hospital, Fenton was reported killed in action.

12. *"A Grand Terrible Drama": From Gettysburg to Petersburg: The Civil War Letters of Charles Wellington Reed,* ed. Eric A. Campbell (New York: Fordham University Press, 2000), 375–79. Meade wrote his wife about this ceremony: "I don't think I told you that, day before yesterday, I presented to some soldiers of the Fifth Corps medals of honor, conferred upon them for good conduct on the field of battle. There was a great ceremony upon the occasion, and I made a few remarks, which I presume will appear in print." George Gordon Meade, *The Life and Letters of George Gordon Meade,* 2 vols. (New York: Charles Scribner's Sons, 1913), 2:227–28. The speech did appear in the *Philadelphia Inquirer* on September 23, 1864, and it is from this source that some of the quoted narration accompanying the speech was taken.

13. *OR,* ser. 1, vol. 42, part 1, "Medals of Honor awarded for distinguished services under Resolution of Congress, and &," pp. 848–50. The three men were Private Frederic C. Anderson of the Eighteenth Massachusetts Infantry, Private George W. Reed of the Eleventh Pennsylvania Infantry, and First Sergeant John Shilling of the Third Delaware Infantry. The flags were captured during the unsuccessful Confederate attack at the Battle of Weldon Railroad (Globe Tavern). E. B. Long, *Civil War Day by Day: An Almanac* (New York: Da Capo Press, 1971), 558–59.

14. The *Philadelphia Inquirer* reporter noted that the audience consisted of Brigadier General Samuel W. Crawford's division, which was the Third Division of the Fifth Army Corps. Before the Battle of Weldon Railroad, Crawford reported having "about 3,000 effective men." Deducting losses of approximately 1,900 men killed, wounded, captured, or missing from the battle would leave some 1,100 effectives. However, this figure does not take into account those on detached duty, ill, or absent from the battle for any reason, as well as replacements that may have been received since August 21. See *OR,* ser. 1, vol. 42, part 1, "Report of Brig. Gen. Samuel Crawford," p. 491, and "Return of Casualties," p. 124.

15. One of the sidebars to this Presentation Speech, omitted in the discussion here, was its use by Meade to quell any soldier politicking. Various state elections would occur in the next six weeks, capped by the contentious Lincoln-McClellan presidential contest in November. After stressing the Emulation meme, Meade immediately shifts into a lengthy non sequitur about the evils of soldiers even discussing politics: "With these [political] questions, as soldiers, we have nothing to do. Their discussion among you is not only useless, but pernicious. Our policy is to fight and the only question as to the conduct of the war pertinent for us to discuss is, how best we can defeat those who are in arms with the avowed purpose of destroying the Government."

16. Rick Atkinson, *In the Company of Soldiers: A Chronicle of Combat* (New York: Little, Brown, 2005), 238–39.

17. Ibid., 230, 238–39.

18. *Manual of Military Decorations and Awards,* September 1996, Incorporated Change 1, September 18, 2006, DoD 1348.33-M, API.1.2.21.

19. Sallust, *The Jugurthine War/The Conspiracy of Catiline* (London: Penguin Classics, 1963), 116–22.

20. Josephus, *The Jewish War*, 72; Mike Tucker, *Among Warriors in Iraq: True Grit, Special Ops, and Raiding in Mosul and Fallujah* (Guilford, Conn.: Lyons Press, 2005), 161–62.

21. Adrian Goldsworthy, *Complete Roman Army* (London: Thames and Hudson, 2003), 24.

22. Sallust, *The Jugurthine War*. For background, see S. A. Handford's introduction to Sallust's history, which contains a useful chart of the war's phases, 26–33. Sallust's observations about Marius and the senate appear on page 116.

23. *In the Words of Napoleon*, 311; Josephus, *The Jewish War*, 246–50; the entry "Pelopidas" in *Plutarch's Lives: The Dryden Translation*, 2 vols., edited with preface by Arthur Hugh Clough, introduction by James Atlas (New York: Modern Library, 2003), 1:392.

24. John D. Billings, *Hardtack and Coffee: The Unwritten Story of Army Life* (Boston: George M. Smith and Co., 1888), 38–39.

25. "A Message to Parents and Family Members," U.S. Marine Corps brochure, no date, no GPO information. Just as Marius recognized the connection between family and recruiting, so does today's military: the marines' recruiting website has a "Parents' Guide" section; the army's, a "For Parents" section; the navy's, a "For Parents and Advisors" section.

26. "Mass Meeting in Boston," *Boston Daily Advertiser*, April 22, 1861.

27. Proclamation of March 6, 1815, *In the Words of Napoleon*, 308–9; Proclamation of March 3, 1815, *Mind of Napoleon*, 214–15.

28. Aristotle, *The Art of Rhetoric, Volume XXII* (Cambridge, Mass. Loeb Classical Library, 2006), 1.ii.5.

29. George W. Smith, *Carlson's Raid: The Daring Marine Assault on Makin* (New York: Berkley Press, 2003), 44.

30. John G. Gammons, comp., *The Third Massachusetts Regiment Volunteer Militia in the War of the Rebellion, 1861–1863* (Providence: Snow and Farnham Co., 1906), 133–34.

31. "Special Notices, General Order No. 27," *Boston Daily Advertiser*, October 17, 1863; Alonzo H. Quint, *The Record of the Second Massachusetts Infantry, 1861–1865* (Boston: James P. Walker, 1867), 202–3.

32. See Bruce Catton, *Stillness at Appomattox* (New York: Doubleday, 1953), 37–38; Reid Mitchell, *Civil War Soldiers* (New York: Viking, 1988), 182.

33. Goldsworthy, *Complete Roman Army*, 77.

34. History Committee, *History of the Nineteenth Regiment Massachusetts Volunteer Infantry: 1861–1865* (Salem: Salem Press, 1906), 284.

35. William F. Fox, *Regimental Losses in the American Civil War: 1861–1865* (1888; reprint, Dayton: 1985), 156. A monument commemorating this ill-fated charge was erected at Gettysburg in 1879.

36. Quint, *Second Massachusetts*, 203.

37. Sergeant Kevin McSwain, "30 Illinois Guardsmen Reenlist During Ceremony," Multi-National Corps—Iraq, January 17, 2007, No. 20070117–01.

38. To understand just how complex reenlistment decisions can become, consider the maze of rules currently governing the U.S. Army's eligibility rules for a $15,000 bonus. A recent army statement declares, "The amount of their bonus depends upon several factors and is determined by the amount of time the person has spent in the Army; the zone they're in; the number of years in service they are being paid for and the length of their reenlistment." First time reenlisters have five separate reenlisting options; "mid-career" reenlisters have four. The various options include money, additional training, choice of postings, and changes in occupational specialty (MOS). See Sergeant Jon Cupp, "Retention NCOs, Career Counselors Dish Out Truth about Reenlistment," Multi-National Corps—Iraq, Release No. 20070123–05, January 23, 2007.

39. "Rolling to Warrior," *The Club: The Official Newsletter of the 1st Combat Brigade Team* 2(2): 11; "Reenlistment," 8. Sec. Joshua McPhie, "Cav Couple Take Oath Together," *Crossed Sabers: "Telling the First Team's Story,"* March 3, 2006, p. 2 (a publication of the First Cavalry Division).

3. Instructional Speech (pp. 104–44)

1. *In the Words of Napoleon*, 193; *Rebellion Record* 5:431.

2. In real armies (as opposed to media representations of armies), the process through which Instructional Speeches become set is rarely depicted. Even "final" instructions may invite comments from subordinates that will influence what the actual "final-final" instruction contains. And there is no better way to kindle these comments that to set forth the basis for an order. The process is not neat, and historians or other narrators do not always disclose (and may not actually know) what it is, but almost inevitably at some level most Instructional Speeches evolve from a discussion between a commander and his subordinates about the proposed orders.

3. Col. Brian D. Jones, "Command View," *Iron Brigade Chronicle* 1(8) (May 30, 2006).

4. Information about the distribution of the *Iron Brigade Chronicle* and the Third Heavy Brigade Combat Team, Fourth Infantry Division, was obtained in a written interview with the brigade Public Affairs Officer, Major Michael Humphreys, on October 3, 2006 [Humphreys interview]. The quotation is taken from the interview.

5. *Iron Brigade Chronicle* 1(8) (May 30, 2006): 12.

6. Humphreys interview. Other FARs include the following, all of which appeared in *IBC* on the dates given; italics and underlining are original: FAR #1 (February 4, 2006), "Make security and safety your first priorities (accidental/tac-

tical risk; drive safe not scared: seatbelts required; treat every weapons like it's loaded; 360 degree security 24/7 and 5/25." FAR #2 (February 25, 2006), "Be professional, be polite, be vigilant, be disciplined; and always be ready to kill. (*Never come off your weapons system or give up your personal weapon.*)" FAR #3 (March 20, 2006), "*Complacency kills. Do every TLPs, PCCs, and PCIs before every mission like it is your first.*" FAR #4 (April 1, 2006), "*Every Soldier is a sensor and a shooter . . . pay attention to constants and note change . . . and provide detailed patrol reports!*" FAR #5 (May 1, 2006), "*Always have comms and know your location (we can't help you if we can't talk to you or find you).*" FAR #7 (June 21, 2006), "*Always travel with a buddy (beside you or within eye contact): always take care of each other.*" FAR #8 (July 26, 2006), "*IO isn't everything but everything is IO.*" FAR #9 (August 31, 2006), "*Burn or shred everything that has writing on it. Don't make email that enemy's friend. Remember OPSEC!*" FAR #10 (September 24, 2006), "'*Perfect is good enough' when it comes to having your equipment ready for combat. Perform PMCS like your life depends on it . . . because it does.*" FAR #11 (October 23, 2006), "NCOs are the keepers of the standards!" As there were no subsequent *IBCs* published, FAR #12 was not reprinted. All FARs reprinted in the *IBC* are accompanied by bullet points as to how it applies in light of recent unit experiences.

7. A quick look into the origins of the phrase "Don't chase Apaches into rocks" yielded this passage from western writer B. M. Bower's *Cow-Country* (New York: Grosset and Dunlap, 1921): "Buddy at thirteen knew more of the wiles of Indians than does the hardiest Indian fighter on the screen to-day. Father had warned him never to chase an Indian into cover, where others would probably be waiting for him." Some version of the expression used by Colonel Jones is almost certainly of popular origin and antedates Bower's novel.

8. *In the Words of Napoleon,* 121; Estes, *Marine Officer's Guide,* 5–6.

9. *Random House Dictionary of the English Language,* 2nd ed., unabridged (New York: 1987); Carl Von Clausewitz, *On War,* ed. Anatol Rapoport (London: Penguin Classics, 1982), 255.

10. Josephus, *The Jewish War,* 180–81.

11. *The Life of Flavius Josephus,* 3.13–4.19 and 7.28–29, in *Josephus: The Complete Works,* transl. William Whiston (Nashville: Thomas Nelson Publishers, 1998), 2–3; Josephus, *The Jewish War,* 181.

12. *The Antiquities of the Jews,* 12.7.3, in *Josephus: The Complete Works,* 392.

13. *OR,* ser. 1, vol. 19, part 2, pp. 395–96.

14. Today, partisan political activities by active-duty members of the armed forces are tightly regulated. See Army Regulation 600–20, "Army Command Policy, 7 June 2006," especially Appendices B-2 and B-3, which offer guidance on permissible and prohibited political activities.

15. McClellan's complex relationship with the Democratic Party is finely detailed in Ethan S. Rafuse, *McClellan's War: The Failure of Moderation in the Struggle for the Union* (Indianapolis: Indiana University Press, 2005), 124–25, 84–85,

381. Secretary of War Edwin M. Stanton embodied the Lincoln administration's paranoia about McClellan. When Stanton removed McClellan from command, it was done under circumstances intended to minimize the general's possible "treachery," Stephen W. Sears, *George B. McClellan: The Young Napoleon* (New York: Ticknor and Fields, 1988), 340.

16. Rafuse, *McClellan's War*, 339–42; Allan Nevins, *The War for the Union: War Becomes Revolution, 1862–1863*, 4 vols. (New York: Scribner, 1960), 2:329; James M. McPherson, *Crossroads of Freedom: Antietam: The Battle that Changed the Course of the War* (New York: Oxford University Press, 2002), 66–67. McPherson believes that a majority of Union soldiers favored emancipation as a punitive war measure.

17. John Hope Franklin, *The Emancipation Proclamation* (Wheeling, Ill.: Harlan Davidson, 1995), 42–46, text of preliminary proclamation. The two congressional acts cited were the Second Confiscation Act of July 17, 1862, and the law of March 13, 1862, both of which prohibited soldiers from returning fugitive slaves to bondage.

18. *Revised Regulations for the Army of the United States, 1861* (Philadelphia: J. G. L. Brown, 1861); "Revised Regulations," 9; "Articles of War" (appendix), 500.

19. Romans 13:1–3 [KJV] reads "Let every soul be subject unto the higher powers. For there is not power but of God: the powers that be are ordained of God. Whosoever therefore resisteth the power, resisteth the ordinance of God: and they that resist shall receive to themselves damnation." This verse was used repeatedly by those opposed to secession. See Philip Shaw Paludan, *"A People's Contest:" The Union and Civil War, 1861–1865* (New York: Harper and Row, 1988), 346.

20. Rafuse, *McClellan's War*, 80. For example, "Blessed are the meek: for they shall inherit the earth" (Matthew 5:5); "Blessed are the merciful: for they shall obtain mercy," (Matthew 5:7) [KJV].

21. This heading is an inversion of Von Clausewitz's famous observation that "War is nothing but a continuation of political intercourse, with a mixture of other means." "War as an Instrument of Policy" in Von Clausewitz, *On War*, 402.

22. Smith, *Carlson's Raid*, 106; West, *No True Glory*, 50.

23. The following are the ROE *reportedly* issued sometime on or before January 2003 on laminated cards and distributed to infantry shortly to be engaged in Operation Iraqi Freedom-I:

> On order, enemy military and paramilitary forces are declared hostile and may be attacked subject to the following instructions:
>
> a) Positive identification (PID) is required prior to engagement. PID is a reasonable certainty that the proposed target is a legitimate military target. If no PID, contact your next higher commander for decision.
>
> b) Do not engage anyone who has surrendered or is out of battle due to sickness or wounds.

c) Do not target or strike any of the following except in self-defense to protect yourself, your unit, friendly forces, and designated persons or property under your control:

    Civilians

    Hospitals, mosques, national monuments, and any other historical and cultural sites

d) Do not fire into civilian populated areas or buildings unless the enemy is using them for military purposes or if necessary for your self-defense. Minimize collateral damage.

e) Do not target enemy infrastructure (public works, commercial communication facilities, dams), Lines of Communication (roads, highways, tunnels, bridges, railways) and Economic Objects (commercial storage facilities, pipelines) unless necessary for self-defense or if ordered by your commander. If you must fire on these objects to engage a hostile force, disable and disrupt but avoid destruction of these objects, if possible. The use of force, including deadly force, is authorized to protect the following:

    Yourself, your unit, and friendly forces

    Enemy Prisoners of War

    Civilians from crimes that are likely to cause death or serious bodily harm, such as murder or rape

    Designated civilians and/or property, such as personnel of the Red Cross/Crescent, UN, and US/UN supported organizations

f) Treat all civilians and their property with respect and dignity. Do not seize civilian property, including vehicles, unless you have the permission of a company level commander and you give a receipt to the property's owner. Detain civilians if they interfere with mission accomplishment or if required for self-defense.

CENTCOM General Order No. 1A remains in effect. Looting and the taking of war trophies are prohibited.

REMEMBER

    Attack enemy forces and military targets.

    Spare civilians and civilian property, if possible.

    Conduct yourself with dignity and honor.

    Comply with the Law of War. If you see a violation, report it.

These ROE will remain in effect until your commander orders you to transition to post-hostilities ROE.

24. Stephen C. Neff, *War and the Law of Nations: A General History* (New York: Cambridge University Press, 2005), 188–89.

25. West, *No True Glory*, 50–51. West reported that "Arab newspaper accounts of the new training circulated in Anbar Province. Insurgent leaflets nicknamed the Coalition troops *awat*, a sugary, soft cake that crumbles easily."

26. Ibid.

27. Wayne Mahood, *General Wadsworth: The Life and Times of Brevet Major General James S. Wadsworth* (Cambridge, Mass.: Da Capo, 2003), 67–68; Livingston, *Fallujah, With Honor*, 189.

28. Livingston, *Fallujah, With Honor*, 188–89.

29. "Gaius Marius," Plutarch's *Lives*, 562–63.

30. Hanson, *The Western Way of War*, 107.

31. Jason K. Doran, *"I Am My Brother's Keeper": Journal of a Gunny in Iraq* (Topsail Beach, N.C.: 2005), entry for March 23, 2003, pp. 66–67.

4. PRE-INVASION SPEECHES (pp. 145–85)

1. "Proclamation to the Army, at Sea," *In the Words of Napoleon*, 69.

2. Joshua 3:5 [KJV].

3. Napoleon reportedly explained his famous remark in an 1817 conversation with a doctor serving with the British Navy, Barry Edward O'Meara, who met the emperor on board HMS *Bellerophon* and later served as his physician on St. Helena. O'Meara published a memoir of that experience, *A Voice from St. Helena* (1822). Translation of the explanatory conversation may be found in *The Mind of Napoleon*, 193; this O'Meara biographical note is from *In the Words of Napoleon*, 396.

4. Napoleon famously numbered Alexander as one of the seven great commanders in history. The others were Hannibal, Caesar, Gustavus Adolphus, Turenne, Eugene of Savoy, and Frederick the Great. Maxim 78, *The Military Maxims of Napoleon*, p. 82. As a schoolboy Napoleon had been a passionate reader of Plutarch, and the latter's *Lives* contains a biography of Alexander the Great in which his occasional generosity and wisdom in ruling conquered peoples is often stressed. See Robert Asprey, *The Rise of Napoleon Bonaparte* (New York: Westview Press, 2001), 16 (Napoleon and Plutarch); "Alexander," *Plutarch's Lives: The Dryden Translation*, 2:139–99. Alexander's indulgence of foreign customs was often to his detriment, see especially *Lives*, 175–76, 186–87. However, Paul Bentley Kern in *Ancient Siege Warfare* (London: Souveneir Press, 1999) more accurately describes Alexander, at least in his treatment of captured cities, as a "brutal siege commander" (227).

5. "1st Marine Division (REIN) [Reinforced], Commanding General's Message to All Hands," Bing West and Major General Ray L. Smith , *The March Up: Taking Baghdad with the 1st Marine Division* (New York: Bantam Books, 2003), message reprinted opposite page 1.

6. The line between invasions and battles can easily blur; true invasions as defined by this book represent some strategic watershed in a war. Some invasions,

like the landings on Iwo Jima, are only extensions of existing tactical strategies (in that case, the Pacific island-hopping campaign).

7. The principal unknown variables included which of Iraq's forces would fight, the extent to which they would resist, and whether or not chemical or biological weapons would be used.

8. Note that Mattis speaks of "Nation," which combines the government and the governed, rather than just the government that has ordered the marines to invade. "Nation" is a far more powerful warrant of authority.

9. West and Smith, *The March Up*, 5.

10. "To the People of Western Virginia," *OR*, ser. 1, vol. 19, part 1, p. 1072.

11. The phrase "Up, Guards, and at 'em!" was taken from a letter by C. T. H. R. Ehrhardt of the University of Otago, Dunedin, New Zealand, which appeared in *Historia: Journal of Ancient History* 44 (1995): 120–21.

12. Indeed, invaders must be careful about indiscriminately calling for civilian resistance. First, such calls may simply be ineffective, as the enemy's civilian population may support its government's efforts to defeat the invader. But even where the invader has reason to believe that the civilian population is unhappy with its own government, caution remains necessary. MacArthur's speech succeeded because it relied on a favorable history at the time it was made: a trusted speechmaker, a willing Filipino audience, and established, well-organized native guerilla organizations that for years had been fighting the Japanese with American support. In contrast, President George H. W. Bush's February 15, 1991, call for Iraqi civilians to arise (largely understood to be directed at the Shiite population), while not technically a battle speech (by this book's criteria), is nevertheless useful as a comparison. Bush's speech, rebroadcast to Iraqis by the Voice of America, encouraged large uprisings by a population not well acquainted with Bush or the Americans, not well organized clandestinely, and worse, unsupported by the Americans when the resistance did occur. The result was disaster, as the still-empowered Saddam Hussein responded with a murderous and unchecked brutality.

13. The reconstructed state of Virginia attempted to undo the statehood of West Virginia by legal action *after* the Civil War. In 1870 the United States Supreme Court ruled in favor of the thirty-fifth state in *Virginia v. West Virginia*, 78 US 39.

14. That the majority of West Virginians were unionist can be scarcely doubted. But General Loring, like many an invader before and since, was misled by the reception his army received. See *OR*, ser. 1, vol. 19, p. 1068 (Loring to Randolph, September 1, 1862); p. 1071 (Loring to Randolph, September 15, 1862).

15. Nancy F. Cott, *The Bonds of Womanhood: Women's Sphere in New England, 1780–1835* (New Haven: Yale University Press, 1977), 1–2, 64–66, 88–89; Karen Halttunen, *Confidence Men and Painted Women: A Study of Middle-Class Culture in America, 1830–1870* (New Haven: Yale University Press, 1982), 58–59 (for a summary of some seminal works here, see footnote 11 on p. 58).

16. Adrian R. Lewis, *Omaha Beach: A Flawed Victory* (Chapel Hill: University of North Carolina Press, 2001), 9.

17. Ibid., 5.

18. Ibid., 9; Random House Dictionary.

19. "A Proclamation," *OR*, ser. 1, vol. 27, part 3, pp. 347–48.

20. This was Confederate cavalry wizard General J. E. B. Stuart's second "Ride around McClellan" of October 1862; see Douglas Southall Freeman, *Lee's Lieutenants: Cedar Mountain to Chancellorsville*, 3 vols. (New York: Charles Scribner's Sons, 1971), 2:291 map.

21. For typical examples of refugee stories, see the *New York Times*, April 27, 1862, "Union Refugees from Florida"; May 1, 1862, "Arrival of Union Refugees from Tennessee, BARABARITY OF THE REBELS: One Hundred East Tennessee Unionists Killed by Them"; and August 17, 1862, "Doings of the Guerillas."

22. The use of shame is so pervasive throughout Homer's *Iliad* as to be one of its central memes; for example, see 15:560–68. Shame is less frequently encountered in the Hebrew canon than in Greco-Roman literature, but see 2 Chronicles 32:21 [KJV]: "And the LORD sent an angel, which cut off all the mighty men of valor, and the leaders and captains in the camp of the king of Assyria. So he returned with shame of face to his own land. And when he was come into the house of his god, they that came forth of his own bowels slew him there with the sword."

23. *Julius Caesar*, The Civil War, *together with* The Alexandrian War, The African War, *and* The Spanish War *by Other Hands*, transl. Jane F. Gardner (London: Penguin Classics, 1976), 1:18–20; *Hard Marching Every Day: The Civil War Letters of Private Wilbur Fisk, 1861–1865*, ed. Emil and Ruth Rosenblatt (Lawrence: University of Kansas Press, 1992), 36–40.

5. PRE-BATTLE SPEECHES (pp. 186–230)

1. Arrian, *Anabasis of Alexander, Books I–V* (Loeb), with an English translation by P. A. Brunt (Cambridge, Mass.: Harvard University Press, 1976), book 2, 7:3–9.

2. Historian W. W. Tarn concluded that Arrian invented this speech. "This [speech] is as bad as it can be," Tarn declared. "It makes Alexander call Persians cowards, the last thing he would have done, and makes him talk about the levy of the Persian empire, which he knew was not there. . . . I take it to be part of a school exercise which Arrian adopted because of the allusion to Xenophon." W. W. Tarn, *Alexander the Great, Sources and Studies*, 2:286. However, P. A. Brunt, while conceding that few ancient historians recorded (or even could record) the *ipsissima verba* of any speech, remains critical of Tarn's view that Arrian simply invented the Issus speech. Rather, Brunt believes that Arrian derived most of this speech ("seems as likely to come") from his sources Aristobulus and Ptolemy, both

of whom were contemporary with Alexander but whose works are now lost. P. A. Brunt, "Arrian's Speeches and Letters," app. 27, Arrian, *Anabasis of Alexander, Books V–VII* (Cambridge, Mass.: 1983), 528–34. The speech is used here not because it is "genuine" but because several millennia of readers probably believed it was so; the same themes that Arrian placed in Alexander's mouth have echoed down through the ages. And it probably mattered that Arrian himself was a distinguished soldier whose works included, besides the *Anabasis*, a military tactics manual of which the section on cavalry still survives. Arrian had likely made more than a few battle speeches of his own; if the speech at Issus was his creation, it may have reflected words and deeds that, at least during Arrian's time, were actually said and done on battlefields.

3. Granicus was the first battle fought by Alexander after crossing the Hellespont. It is described in Arrian (Brunt), *Anabasis,* book 1, 13.1–16.7; Aristotle, *Rhetoric,* 2.xx.8.

4. Arrian (Brunt), *Anabasis,* book 1, 18:2.

5. Elsewhere in this speech, Alexander declares that "nothing remained after this final struggle [Issus] but to rule the whole of Asia and set an end to their long exertions." The desire of Alexander's soldiers to return home is an important theme throughout Arrian's account, and these words likely meant exactly that to them.

6. Alexander literature is immense, and the biographies surveyed for this book all concur about his extraordinary yet risky personal leadership. See, most recently, Paul Cartledge, *Alexander the Great: The Hunt for a New Past* (New York: Overlook Press, 2004), 185–86.

7. Livingston, *Fallujah, With Honor,* 21.

8. George W. Smith, *Carlson's Raid,* 201.

9. Ibid., 39–41. Some of Carlson's superiors believed that he was a communist, and "Gung Ho" command policies (not to mention Democratic leanings—he was close with the democratic Franklin D. Roosevelt) did nothing to ease these concerns (36–38). Furthermore, Carlson had become a media darling, which provoked jealousy within the corps (206–7).

10. Ibid., 203.

11. Frontinus, *The Stratagems,* (First Century, CE) ed. Mary B. McElwain, transl. Charles E. Bennett (Cambridge, Mass.: Loeb Classical Library, 2003), book 3, 1:1, "On Surprise Attacks."

12. Caesar, *The Conquest of Gaul,* transl. S. A. Handford, rev. with a new introduction by Jane F. Gardner (London: Penguin Classics, 1982), 7:66.

13. Caesar, *Conquest of Gaul,* 7:1.

14. Ibid., 7:67.

15. The Battle of the Standard was fought between King Stephen of England and King David I of Scotland, ostensibly over possession of Northumberland, though the larger issue was a succession crisis triggered by the death of King

Henry I. It was fought on August 22, 1138, in North Yorkshire, and the Scottish were defeated.

16. Aelred Squire, *Aelred of Rievault: A Study* (London: Society for Promoting Christian Knowledge, 1969), 77–80. Perhaps better known is the Battle of the Standard's Pre-Battle Speech by English medieval chronicler Henry of Huntingdon. See *The Chronicle of Henry of Huntingdon, comprising the History of England, from the Invasion of Julius Caesar to the Accession of Henry II,* transl. and ed. Thomas Forester (London: Henry G. Bohn, 1853), 267–69. There the speechmaker is the Bishop of Orkney. Some scholars believe that Aelred's version, while not the *ipsissima verba,* may be closer, at least in spirit, to what was actually said. See Michael Prestwich, *Armies and Warfare in the Middle Ages: The English Experience* (New Haven: Yale University Press, 1996), 312–14.

17. Livy, *The War with Hannibal,* 30:33; *In the Words of Napoleon,* 247; Adam Nicolson, *Seize the Fire: Heroism, Duty, and the Battle of Trafalgar* (New York: Harper Collins, 2005), 205–6.

18. The Third Punic War was fought between 149 and 146 BCE. The war ended when the city of Carthage fell after a three-year siege; the survivors were enslaved and the city burned for two weeks. According to tradition, following the leveling of the ruins, the Romans sowed the soil with salt, trying to assure that nothing would ever grow there again.

19. Robert B. Asprey, *The Reign of Napoleon Bonaparte* (New York: Basic Books, 2001), 259–61.

20. Nicolson, *Seize the Fire,* 127–29.

21. Livy, *The War with Hannibal,* 28:19; Josephus, *The Jewish War,* 210.

22. Kern, *Ancient Siege Warfare.* The sieges (and massacres) of both Jotapata and Ilurgia are discussed in chapter XIII, "Treatment of Captured Cities," 323–51.

23. "Circular, Headquarters, Army of the Potomac, June 30, 1863," *OR,* ser. 1, vol. 27, part 3, p. 415.

24. Estes, *The Marine Officer's Guide,* 316; Livermore, *Days and Events, 1860–1866,* 133.

25. "Circular, Headquarters, Army of the Potomac, June 30, 1863," *OR,* ser. I, vol. 27, part 3, p. 415.

26. Sallust, *The Jugurthine War/The Conspiracy of Catiline,* transl. S. A. Handford (London: 1963), 85, 231–32.

27. Account of Thomas Hollis, MOLLUS Collection, Houghton Library, Harvard University. This account was written thirty years after the events, and Hollis mistakenly remembered McClellan's acknowledgment as occurring at a grand review.

28. Gammons, *The Third Massachusetts Regiment Volunteer Militia,* 233–34; J. H. Wylie, *The Reign of Henry V,* 3 vols. (Cambridge: 1914–29), 2:132–36. I am indebted to Professor Victor Davis Hanson for references to Professor W. K.

Pritchett's works used in this book, especially *Ancient Greek Battle Speeches and a Palfrey* and the essays "The General's Exhortations in Greek Warfare" and "The General on the Battlefield," from *Essays in Greek History.*

29. See Prestwich, *Armies and Warfare in the Middle Ages,* 103–8.

30. Livy, *The War with Hannibal,* 21:42–45; Polybius, *The Rise of the Roman Empire,* (Second Century BCE) transl. Ian Scott-Kivert (London: Penguin, 1979), 10:11.

31. See section on "Contracts" in Prestwich, *Armies and Warfare in the Middle Ages,* 88–96. Regarding Christendom, soldiers fighting in "just" wars were required to assume extra measures of penance. In *War and the Law of Nations: A General History,* Stephen C. Neff observes, "Simply for fighting in a just war, a penance of three years was prescribed. One year of penance was required of a fighter for each enemy soldier that he knew that he had killed. If a soldier struck an enemy but was unsure whether death had ensued or not, the penance was forty days" (62–63).

32. Livy, *The War with Hannibal,* 21:4–5.

33. Kern, *Ancient Siege Warfare,* 324.

34. Caesar, *The Conquest of Gaul,* 2:19.

35. Ibid., 2:21.

36. Ibid., 2:25.

37. Ibid., 2:38.

6. MIDST-OF-BATTLE SPEECHES: THE WORD AND THE DEED (pp. 231–75)

1. Josephus, *The Jewish War,* 229–30; Charles Spencer, *Blenheim: Battle for Europe* (London: Phoenix Press, 2004), 277.

2. Caesar, *The Conquest of Gaul,* 7:50.

3. One might argue that swords and pistols are weapons being brandished in circumstances otherwise requiring them (that is, an assault), thus reducing their significance as props. However, in many circumstances but especially when an officer leads attacks over substantial expanses of ground, swords and pistols are of limited utility and indeed could not be used as weapons until the distance to the enemy has closed significantly. Why then draw and prominently display them half a mile away? For their effect rather than their actual use.

4. "Text of Eisenhower Order," *New York Times,* August 15, 1944. Eisenhower refers to the surrounding circumstances in his memoir, *Crusade in Europe* (Baltimore: Johns Hopkins University Press, 1997), 278.

5. Hanson, *The Western Way of War,* 108. It is worth quoting Hanson at length on the modern practice of commanding from the rear. "Justification for the general's absence from the field of fire has been found in his ostensible need to pay close attention to the myriad problems of planning and communication that modern battle requires. Yet the absence of the commander from contemporary combat has

often had a demoralizing effect upon the troops. A poor argument for this modern practice is the idea that the present-day commander's survivability is of utmost importance: his enormous staff has, after all, invariably planned for the very possibility of his demise, and his survival—even if he be a Rommel or a Patton—may ironically be less important to his men's immediate success on the battlefield than that of his ancient Greek counterpart, who had no replacement officers of comparable rank or status."

6. *The United States Army in a Global Era, 1917–2003,* Army Historical Series, ed. Richard W. Stewart, 2 vols. (Washington, D.C.: 2005), 2:151; Eisenhower, *Crusade in Europe,* 279.

7. Eisenhower, *Crusade in Europe,* 276–77.

8. Ibid., 254.

9. Joseph Allan Frank and George A. Reaves, *"Seeing the Elephant": Raw Recruits at the Battle of Shiloh* (Urbana: University of Illinois Press, 1989), 147.

10. Nicolson, *Seize the Fire,* 151.

11. Bill McWilliams, *On Hallowed Ground: The Last Battle for Pork Chop Hill* (Annapolis: U.S. Naval Institute Press, 2004), 245.

12. Ibid., 447.

13. Coleridge had served as Commissioner Ball's temporary secretary on Malta in 1804–5.

14. Nicolson, *Seize the Fire,* 152.

15. Mark Bowden, *Black Hawk Down: A Story of Modern War* (New York: Penguin, 2000), 160.

16. McWilliams, *On Hallowed Ground,* 102–3.

17. Frontinus, *Stratagems,* 4:1:17.

18. For example, see Section 899, Article 99, of the Uniform Code of Military Justice ("Misbehavior before the Enemy"), and note that by its literal terms, only a court-martial can order death for the given offenses:

Any person subject to this chapter who before or in the presence of the enemy—
(1) runs away;
(2) shamefully abandons, surrenders, or delivers up any command, unit, place, or military property which it is his duty to defend;
(3) through disobedience, neglect, or intentional misconduct endangers the safety of any such command, unit, place, or military property;
(4) casts away his arms or ammunition;
(5) is guilty of cowardly conduct;
(6) quits his place of duty to plunder or pillage;
(7) causes false alarms in any command, unit, or place under the control of armed forces;
(8) willingly fails to do his utmost to encounter, engage, capture, or

destroy any enemy troops, combatants, vessels, aircraft, or any other thing, which it is his duty to encounter, engage, capture, or destroy; or

(9) does not afford all practical relief and assistance to any troops combatants, vessels, or aircraft of the armed forces belong to the United States or their allies when engaged in battle;

shall be punished by death or such punishment as a court-martial may direct.

In modern armies, a leader's authority to execute soldiers without due process is probably implied and would almost certainly structurally parallel the defense of justifiable homicide traditionally available at law: the leader would have to demonstrate that the threat to the unit, cause, morale, or tactic was immediately lethal, dire, and emergent; that when he acted, he had a reasonable basis to believe that the threat was such; and that no disciplinary alternative existed at that time.

19. Caesar, *The Conquest of Gaul*, 4:24–25.

20. *The Concise Oxford Dictionary of Literary Terms* (New York: Oxford University Press, 2001), 2004.

21. Caesar, *The Conquest of Gaul*, 4:24–25.

22. Goldsworthy, *The Complete Roman Army*, 134–35; "The Post-Marian Roman Army," 46–48, 108–9. For more on the possible religious significance of the standard, see *Religions of Rome: A History*, 2 vols., ed. Mary Beard, John North, and Simon Price (Cambridge: Cambridge University Press, 1998), 1: 326. The authors note that in Roman camps "throughout the empire" the legionary standards were stored in a shrine that had both religious and patriotic significances. Of course, religion and the state were largely indivisible throughout most of the ancient world; see Tertullian, *The Apology*, translated by the Reverend C. Dodgson, M.A., 2nd ed., (Oxford: John Henry Parker, 1854), 1.16.

23. Risking the standard alone works too. Frontinus reports that when the Roman king Tarquinius fought the Sabines, he "seized a standard and hurled it into the ranks of the enemy" in order to better motivate his men. "To recover it, the Romans fought so furiously," Frontinus declares, "that they not only regained the standard, but also won the day." Frontinus, *The Stratagems*, 2:7:1.

24. Jacques-Louis David (1748–1825) painted *Napoleon at St. Bernard*, the definitive canvas rendering of the commander on horseback.

25. *Appleton's Cyclopaedia*, 6:312–13.

26. James Donnelly, "James Donnelly, Late Corporal Co. D, 20th Mass. Vols. Sketch of his life, Written by himself by request of Committee having in charge history and memorial of Regiment," MOLLUS Collection, Houghton Library, Harvard University, 45–46; Smith, *Carlson's Raid*, 172.

27. Winston S. Churchill, *The Story of the Malakand Field Force: An Episode of Frontier War* (New York: Thomas Nelson and Sons, 1916), 200.

28. Donnelly, "Sketch of his life," 43–44.

29. Ezra J. Warner, *Generals in Blue: Lives of the Union Commanders* (Baton Rouge: 1999), 353–54.

30. Smith, *Carlson's Raid*, 173.

31. Ibid., 172.

32. *Random House Dictionary,* 4th ed.

33. *The Landmark Thucydides,* 7.77.1–7; *From Ball's Bluff to Gettysburg . . . and Beyond: The Civil War Letters of Private Roland E. Bowen, 15th Massachusetts Infantry, 1861–64,* ed. Gregory A. Coco (Gettysburg: Thomas Publishers, 1994), 49, 51. In the same account Bowen provides two versions of Colonel Devens's words. The second version reads, "Fellow Soldiers, you have obeyed every command I have given today. I have done all I can for you. I can do no more."

34. Marshall, *Men Against Fire,* 140.

35. A first-rate recent study of Ball's Bluff is James A. Morgan III, *A Little Short of Boats: The Fights at Ball's Bluff and Edwards Ferry, October 21–22, 1861, A History and Tour Guide* (Fort Mitchell, Ky.: Ironclad Publishing, 2004).

36. *The Landmark Thucydides,* 6.43.1–6.44.1.

37. Ibid., 7.75.2–7.

38. Ibid., 7.76.1; 7.78.1.

39. Ibid., 7.77.1–3.

40. Ibid., 7.77.3–4.

41. Ibid., 7.77.4–7.

42. Morgan, *A Little Short of Boats,* 4, 1.

43. Bowen, *From Ball's Bluff,* 48.

44. See chapter 8, "The Commanding Officer," section 0852, "Loss of a Ship," subsection 2, *General Regulation of the U.S. Navy,* Regulation 1990.

7. THE POST-BATTLE SPEECH: TELLING A STORY (pp. 276–315)

1. *OR,* ser. 1, vol. 21, pp. 549–50, "Robert E. Lee, General Orders No. 138: HDQRS. Army of Northern Virginia, December 31, 1862."

2. Francis Augustin O'Reilly, *The Fredericksburg Campaign: Winter War on the Rappahannock* (Baton Rouge: Louisiana State University Press, 2003), 28. O'Reilly's account of the battle is now the standard, which I have used as context for Lee's battle-speech version of events.

3. *OR,* ser. 1, vol. 15, pp. 238–39, "General Orders No. 45, HQ, District of Texas, New Mexico and Arizona, Houston, Texas, March 11, 1863."

4. Indeed, so important is this function that the U.S. Army has established an official entity called the Center for Army Lessons Learned (CALL). "Lessons learned" also extend to health and safety matters outside of combat. For an example of how these are disseminated in Iraq, see Captain Mark Lappegaard, "Lessons learned from after action reviews," *Desert Bulls* 14 (March 7, 2006): 3.

5. Livy, *The War with Hannibal*, 22:50; *OR*, ser. 1, vol. 15, pp. 41–42, "General Orders, No. 57, Headquarters, Department of the Gulf, New Orleans, La., August 9, 1862, Maj. Gen. Benjamin Butler"; "Command View," Colonel Brian D. Jones and Command Sergeant Major David H. List, *Iron Brigade Chronicles* 1(13) (October 23, 2006): 3.

6. Livy, *The War with Hannibal*, 22:50.

7. *Abraham Lincoln: His Speeches and Writings*, ed. Roy P. Basler (New York: Da Capo, 1990), 734. The Bliss version of Lincoln's speech is used; the quoted line matches Basler's tentatively titled "First (?) Draft" and "Second (?) Draft" (734–37). Livy, *The War with Hannibal*, 22:49.

8. Plutarch, *Plutarch's Lives*, "Fabius," 1:244–45; Lee quoted in George R. Stewart, *Pickett's Charge: A Microhistory of the Final Attack at Gettysburg, July 3, 1863* (Boston: Premeir/Fawcett, 1987), 257.

9. Plutarch served as a priest at Delphi; see James Atlas, "Introduction," *Plutarch's Lives* 1:xi.

10. Ibid., 1:238–39.

11. The conversations with Pickett and Wilcox may be found in Stewart, *Pickett's Charge*, 256–57; however, the version of Lee's conversation with Wilcox used above (which features the original source's dramatic emphasis) is quoted in Earl J. Hess, *Pickett's Charge—The Last Attack at Gettysburg* (Chapel Hill: University of North Carolina Press, 2001), 329. Hess's judgment will be found on page 327.

12. Lee's letter to Davis appears in *OR*, ser. 1, vol. 51, part 2, pp. 752–53; Davis's reply in ser. 1, vol. 29, part 2, pp. 639–40.

13. Livy, *The War with Hannibal*, 27:14.

14. Ibid., 27.12–13.

15. Ibid., 27.13. According to Adrian Goldsworthy, the issuance of barley rather than wheat rations was punishment for behaving badly in battle. He notes that it numbered among those "public humiliations [that] were deeply felt" by soldiers. Goldsworthy, *The Complete Roman Army*, 101.

16. Livy, *The War with Hannibal*, 27:13.

17. "Document 58, General Kearney's [sic] Order," *Rebellion Record* 5:171.

18. *Appleton's Cyclopaedia*, 3:497; Warner, *Generals in Blue*, 258–59.

19. *In the Words of Napoleon*, 159; J. H. Wylie, *The Reign of Henry V (1415–1416)*, 3 vols., 2:178; Bowden, *Black Hawk Down*, 325.

20. John Keegan, *The Face of Battle: A Study of Agincourt, Waterloo, and the Somme* (London: Viking Press, 1976), 113–14 (casualties); see also "Killing of the Prisoners," 108–12.

21. Ibid., 109.

22. Wylie, *The Reign of Henry the Fifth*, 2:133–39.

23. Mark Bowden's gripping *Black Hawk Down* is now the standard account of the battle.

24. The following is Henry's complete speech from the play. *The Life of Henry*

the Fifth, Act IV, Scene III, by William Shakespeare, contained in *The Riverside Shakespeare,* 2nd ed. (Boston: Houghton Mifflin Company, 1997), 1004. For readers' convenience, the lines paraphrased by Garrison have been italicized. The point of noting these changes is to source General Garrison's speech, not to judge his paraphrase as a literary work. Suffice it to say that the general succinctly made his points about comradeship in language accessible to twentieth-century audiences.

> What's he that wishes so?
> My cousin Westmerland?
> No, my fair cousin.
> If we are mark'd to die, we are enow
> To do our country loss; and if to live,
> The fewer men, the greater share of honor.
> God's will!, I pray thee wish not one man more.
> By Jove, I am not covetous for gold,
> Nor care I who doth feed upon my cost;
> It yearns me not if men my garments wear;
> Such outward things dwell not in my desires.
> But if it be a sin to covet honor,
> I am the most offending soul alive.
> No, faith, my coz, wish not a man from England.
> God's peace!, I would not lose so great an honor
> As one man more methinks would share from me,
> For the best hope I have. O, do not wish one more!
> Rather proclaim it, Westmerland, through my host,
> *That he which hath no stomach to this fight,*
> *Let him depart, his passport shall be made,*
> *And crowns for convoy put into his purse.*
> *We would not die in that man's company*
> That fears his fellowship to die with us.
> This day is called the feast of Crispian:
> *He that outlives this day, and comes safe home,*
> *Will stand a'tip-toe when the day is named,*
> *And rouse him at the name of Crispian.*
> *He that shall see this day, and live old age,*
> *Will yearly on the vigil feast his neighbors,*
> *And say "To-morrow is Saint Crispian."*
> *Then will he strip his sleeve and show his scars,*
> *And say, "These wounds I had on Crispin's day."*
> Old men forget; yet all shall be forgot,
> But he'll remember with advantages
> What feats he did that day. Then shall our names,

Familiar in his mouth as household words
Harry the King, Bedford and Exeter,
Warwick and Talbot, Salisbury and Gloucester,
Be in their flowing cups freshly rememb'red.
This story shall the good man teach his son;
And Crispin Crispian shall ne'er go by,
From this day to the ending of the world,
But we in it shall be remembered—
We few, we happy few, we band of brothers;
For he to-day that sheds his blood with me
Shall be my brother; be he ne'er so vile,
This day shall gentle his condition;
And gentlemen in England, now a-bed,
Shall think themselves accurs'd they were not here;
And hold their manhoods cheap whiles any speaks
That fought with us upon Saint Crispin's day.

25. An example of how flexible Shakespeare's formulation is can be found in the U.S. Marine Corps's recruiting slogan: "The Few. The Proud. The Marines."

26. James Boswell, *The Life of Samuel Johnson* (New York: Everyman's Library, 1992), entry for April 10, 1778, p. 815.

27. "Command View," *Iron Brigade Chronicles* 1(13) (October 23, 2006): 3.

28. "Winning Hearts, Minds with a Medical Civil Action Project," *Iron Brigade Chronicles* 1(11) (August 31, 2006): 6–7; "Phoenix Soldier helps deliver 100 wheelchairs," *Iron Brigade Chronicles* 1(9) (June 21, 2006): 5; "$1 million worth of antique furniture returned to Iraqi control, placed in Baqubah museum," *Iron Brigade Chronicles* 1(7) (April 1, 2006): 4.

29. Staff Sergeant K. N. List, "The Price of Freedom," republished in *Iron Brigade Chronicles* 1(7) (April 1, 2006): 3.

30. "Intervention, Stabilization, and Transformation Operation" is taken from an article by Steven Metz and Raymond Millen, "Intervention, Stabilization, and Transformation Operations: The Role of Landpower in the New Strategic Environment," *Parameters* (Spring 2005): 41–52.

8. Arrivals and Departures: Assuming Command, Saying Farewell, Surrender, and Final Victory (pp. 317–55)

1. *OR*, ser. 1, vol. 27, part 3, p. 374, "General Orders No. 67, Headquarters, Army of the Potomac, June 28, 1863"; Doran, *My Brother's Keeper*, 124; *In the Words of Napoleon*, 88–89.

2. The story of the coup can be found in Asprey, *The Rise of Napoleon Bonaparte*, 327–39.

3. When Doran asked why his predecessor had been relieved, a fellow NCO told him that "[they] would try to correct the Marines and they would bitch to the Lt, and the Lt would change whatever [the NCO] had said. To the Lt it was a popularity contest. Leadership is not a popularity contest—that's called politics, and politics get Marines killed." Doran, *Brother's Keeper,* entry for April 10, 2003, p. 125.

4. Stanley Weintraub, *General Washington's Christmas Farewell: A Mount Vernon Homecoming, 1783* (New York: Free Press, 2003), 85–86.

5. This discussion relies on Stanley Weintraub's wonderfully written account from *General Washington's Christmas Farewell*. Weintraub states that of "the twenty-nine major generals commissioned by Congress during the war, only Knox, von Steuben, and McDougall were present. Most others had retired or resigned (or been discharged) since the war. Six had died, and one . . . had betrayed Washington—Benedict Arnold" (82).

6. This is not to say that Farewell or Final Victory Speeches serve *no* tactical purposes. For example, Farewell Speeches that occur during a war when a commander is replaced may be important as legal documents, both to formally identify the new commander and, as already noted, to "time stamp" the termination of the previous commander's authority. These speeches may serve important morale functions as well, such as when the departing commander vouches for the competence of his successor and urges the soldier-audience to proffer the same loyalty that he enjoyed.

7. This speech may be found in the indispensable "Papers of George Washington" at http://gwpapers.virginia.edu/documents/revolution/farewell (accessed on July 31, 2007).

8. The author is indebted to William M. Fowler Jr. of Northeastern University for a copy of his paper "An American Crisis: The Newburgh Address," delivered at Mount Vernon on July 20, 2006. This paper can be found at http://www.lehrmaninstitute.org/lehrman/newburgh.pdf (accessed on July 31, 2007). The author thanks Professor Fowler for his insights into Washington the man and the commander. His next book, *An American Crisis: The Near Fatal Years of the American Revolution,* is eagerly awaited. Washington's famous Newburgh speech is not included here because the tactical cycle of the mutiny is not covered in this book. As military historians well know, however, there are many examples of Speeches to Quell Mutinies from almost any period in Western history.

9. *In the Words of Napoleon,* April 20, 1814, "Farewell to the Old Guard," 302. The next day, Napoleon proudly declared to someone, "Well! You heard my speech to the Old Guard yesterday, you saw the effect it produced? That is the way to talk to them!"

10. Quint, *The Record of the Second Massachusetts Infantry,* 288–90.

11. *Harvard University: Quinquennial Catalogue of the Officers and Graduates: 1636–1920* (Cambridge, Mass.: Harvard University Press, 1920), 524. Morse graduated with a Bachelor's in Science degree.

12. Quick summaries of Massachusetts's regiments may be found in Francis Augustus Osborn, *Civil War Regiments from Massachusetts: 1861–1865*, 1908 (reprint, Pensacola, Fla.: Ebooksondisk, 2003), 37–38. Because the regiment's original term of service ended in August 1864, veterans who had reenlisted for an additional term were first mustered out of the old regiment and then remustered into a "new" regiment that bore the same designation (Second Massachusetts) but with one important change: the words "Veteran Volunteers" were added. Fox, *Regimental Losses of the Civil War*, 156; Quint, *Record of the Second Massachusetts*, 490–91. Though technically Morse was occasionally seconded for staff work, Quint declares, "Either with the regiment or on the staff of a general officer, he was in every action of the regiment."

13. The sometimes unruly democratic tendency of the Civil War recruit is a trite but accurate trope from the period. Further scholarly attention might be paid to the extent to which, following subordination, such recruits continued their resistance "by other means"—usually political. For some anecdotes on the Second Massachusetts's autocratic gentlemen officers, see Lorien Foote, "Rich Man's War, Rich Man's Fight: Class, Ideology, and Discipline in the Union Army," *Civil War History* 51(3) (September 2005): 269–87. Foote, however, does not account for how these gentlemen officers frequently softened their harsh "management" style through paternalism and benevolence. They loaned enlistees money, took on their legal woes, cared for their families during hard times, included them in their wills, and even raised funds for foreign-based charities on behalf of foreign-born soldiers against whom they might otherwise harbor strong prejudices. This too was politicking—of the older Federalist variety that Washington would probably have been familiar with. *The Thinking Bayonet* (Boston: Walker, Fuller, and Co., 1865) is the title of James Kendall Hosmer's book extolling the Federal rank and file. Hosmer, already a Unitarian minister with a pulpit, served as a corporal with the Fifty-second Massachusetts.

14. William E. Channing, "'Self Culture,' An Address Introductory to the Franklin Lectures, Delivered at Boston, September, 1838" (Boston: Dutton and Wentworth, 1838), 11. Some scholars have asserted that the egoism inherent in antebellum notions of self-culture gave way to the increased discipline and outward-looking demands of duty and country during the Civil War. For the seminal example of this, see George M. Frederickson's treatment of the war's influence on Ralph Waldo Emerson in *The Inner Civil War: Northern Intellectuals and the Crisis of Union* (New York: University of Illinois Press, 1993), 176–80. But if Morse's Farewell Speech is any indication, some men may have believed that the war experience actually served to advance their state of self-culture rather than belittle it.

15. "General Orders No. 9, 10 April 1865, Headquarters, Army of Northern Virginia," *OR*, ser. 1, vol. 46, part 1, p. 1267.

16. The Wainwright speech was assembled from two sources: Wainwright's personal memoir, *General Wainwright's Story: The Account of Four Years of Humil-*

iating Defeat, Surrender, and Captivity, ed. Robert Considine (Garden City, N.Y.: Doubleday and Co., 1946), 139–40, and Wainwright's original broadcast, available on the CD box set *War on Radio: The Pacific and European Theater* (Thousand Oaks, Cal.: 2002), disc 8, track 2.

17. Ulysses S. Grant, *Personal Memoirs of U. S. Grant,* 2 vols. (New York: C. L. Webster and Co., 1885), 2:491–94. The men forced to make the infamous death march had surrendered on the Bataan Peninsula the month before Corrigedor fell.

18. Douglas Southall Freeman, *R. E. Lee: A Biography* 4 vols. (New York: Charles Scribner's Sons, 1934). The nickname given to Lee by his men, "Marse [Master] Robert," tells considerably on the subject of his authority, especially given how such forms of address were typically used in the slaveholding regions of the South. "Paroled . . . until exchanged" refers to the practice of releasing prisoners of war on at least two conditions: that they not return to active service until "exchanged" for a POW of the same rank held by an adversary; moreover, paroled POWs pledged not to reveal sensitive information about their captors obtained during their imprisonment.

19. There is an interesting, if slightly strained, parallel to Lee's act at Appomattox here. Just after Lee had surrendered the Army of Northern Virginia, Grant asked him if he would "advise" that all Confederate armies (there were still large ones deployed) would surrender. Lee replied that "he could not do so without consulting [President Davis] first." Unlike General Homma, Grant simply let the matter rest: "I knew there would be no use to urge him to do anything against his ideas of what was right," Grant later remarked. This attitude is virtually inconceivable in more recent warfare. Grant, *Personal Memoirs,* 2:497; *General Wainwright's Story,* 120, 130–31, 135.

20. Properly satisfying the Authority Convention today has an important technological component, because a technologically advanced enemy could fake a commander's orders, voice, and even televised image. How then are soldiers to know when an order to attack, hold, or withdraw is genuine? This issue became especially pressing during the Cold War, when nuclear weapons were widely dispersed in response to political realities that might call for their use at any moment. Reportedly, the world's nuclear militaries have developed elaborate verification codes and procedures in order to validate proper genuine commands. But whatever the technology, it all remains subsumed under the Authority Convention.

21. *General Wainwright's Story,* 121–23, 126 (attacks continue after surrender); 124–25, 129–32 (intimidating treatment); 138 (concern for civilians). The view that Wainwright was forced to make the broadcast can also be found in *American Military History,* 2:92.

22. However, under most Western legal codes, compulsion is not a defense for the crime of murder.

23. John Keegan discusses exactly how tricky surrender became in the context of twentieth-century wars in *The Face of Battle,* 328–29.

24. Some sense of the formal and informal details of the surrender process is famously given by Joshua Lawrence Chamberlain in *The Passing of the Armies* (New York: Bantam Books, 1993), 188, 194–203.

25. This document may be found online at the (increasingly) indispensable Gilder-Lehrman historical archive: http://www.gilderlehrman.org/search/collection_pdfs/05/62/2/04//05622.04.pdf (accessed on July 31, 2007).

26. *American Military History,* 2:160–61; Eisenhower, *Crusade,* 428.

27. *Crusade* scrupulously avoids political issues in the same way Eisenhower's Final Victory Speech sought to avoid having politics affect his combined forces.

EPILOGUE (pp. 356–66)

1. *The Al Qaeda Reader,* ed. and transl. Raymond Ibrahim (New York: Doubleday, 2007), 268–69.

2. Colonel Thomas X. Hammes, *The Sling and The Stone: On War in the 21st Century* (St. Paul, Minn.: Zenith Press, 2006), 2. The author wishes to acknowledge his debt to Colonel Hammes's book, as well as to John Robb's book *Brave New War: The Next Stage of Terrorism and the End of Globalization* (Hoboken, N.J.: Wily, 2007). Together these thoughtful works represent superior attempts at developing a theoretical foundation for the war Americans face now and into the future. Regarding AQ, there can be no understanding of why this group has mobilized against American civilization without reference to bin Laden's October 2002 speech "Why We Are Fighting You: Osama bin Laden's Letter to Americans," which may be found in the *Al Qaeda Reader,* 197–208.

3. Perhaps bin Laden's most complete denunciation of "moderate Islam" will be found in an essay titled "Moderate Islam Is a Prostration to West," which translator/editor Raymond Ibrahim describes as "authorized or written by Osama bin Laden himself" (17). This essay may be found in the *Al Qaeda Reader,* 22–62.

4. In his October 2002 "Why We Are Fighting You" message, Bin Laden condemns the U.S. government and/or American society for, among other things, its support of Israel, the deaths of 1.5 million Iraqi children during the UN sanctions regime, Hiroshima, Nagasaki, gambling, usury, sexual promiscuity, homosexuality, the use of drugs and alcohol, racism, the spread of AIDS, Jewish control of the American economy, media, "all aspects of your life," President Clinton's dalliance with Monica Lewinsky, and the failure to ratify the Kyoto Agreement. Critics who sometimes point to the Islamists' broad and often topical indictments of the West may be missing the point. All of this really follows from one thing: "You are the nation who, rather than ruling through the *sharia* of Allah, chooses to invent your own laws as you will and desire," bin Laden declares. In his view and that of most

Islamists, *that* is the poisonous seed; all other present and future complaints are merely the predicted bad fruit. The larger point here is that bin Laden believes that a society this degenerate is not only indefensible but ultimately cannot be defended, even by its own military. See bin Laden statements, May and December 1998, *Al Qaeda Reader,* 260–61.

5. See http://www.blackwaterusa.com/employment (accessed on October 15, 2007).

6. Over the next century, of course, what constitutes "the West" is likely to change. For example, it could be assumed that demographic trends within Western Europe (native birthrates at levels far below population replacement), a failure to assimilate its Muslim minorities, and the likelihood of increased conversions to Islam will, in a half-century's time, render it something like a "border state" between East and West. Should this come to pass, Western Europe will be far less politically inclined to resist an Islamist movement that, according to its "newer" lights, will in turn be understood as less of a threat.

7. See http://www.blackwaterusa.com/btw2007/archive/010807btw.html (accessed October 15, 2007).

Bibliography

Abbott, Henry Livermore, to Charles Cushing Paine. July 28, 1863. Paine Papers, Massachusetts Historical Society.

Adcock, F. E. *Thucydides and His History*. Cambridge: Cambridge University Press, 1963.

Andrea, Alfred J. *Encyclopedia of the Crusades*. Westport, Conn.: Greenwood Press, 2003.

Appleton's Cyclopaedia of American Biography. 6 vols. New York: 1887.

Aristotle. *The Art of Rhetoric, Volume XXII*. Cambridge, Mass.: Loeb Classical Library, 2006.

Arrian: Anabasis of Alexander, Books V–VII. Translated by P. A. Brunt. Cambridge, Mass.: Harvard University Press, 2000.

Arrian: The Campaigns of Alexander. New York: Penguin Classics, 1976.

Asprey, Robert. *The Rise of Napoleon Bonaparte*. New York: Westview Press, 2001.

———. *The Reign of Napoleon Bonaparte*. New York: Basic Books, 2001.

Atkinson, Rick. *In the Company of Soldiers: A Chronicle of Combat*. New York: Little, Brown, 2005.

Beard, Mary, John North, and Simon Price, eds. *Religions of Rome: A History*. 2 vols. Cambridge: Cambridge University Press, 1998.

Billings, John D. *Hardtack and Coffee: The Unwritten Story of Army Life*. Boston: George M. Smith and Co., 1888.

Blackwater USA (now Blackwater Worldwide). *Blackwater Tactical Weekly*. http://www.blackwaterusa.com/btw2007/archive/010807btw.html.

Blackwater USA Recruiting Message. http://www.blackwaterusa.com/employment.

Bliese, John R. E. "Rhetoric and Morale: A Study of Battle Orations from the Central Middle Ages." *Journal of Medieval History* 15 (1989).

Boegehold, Alan L. *When a Gesture Was Expected*. Princeton, N.J.: Princeton University Press, 1999.

Bonaparte, Napoleon. *In the Words of Napoleon: The Emperor Day by Day*. Edited by R. M. Johnston, with new material by Philip Haythornthwaite. London: 2002.

———. *The Mind of Napoleon: Selections from His Written and Spoken Words*. Translated and edited by J. Christopher Herold. New York: Columbia University Press, 1955.

Boswell, James. *The Life of Samuel Johnson.* New York: Everyman's Library, 1992.

Bowden, Mark. *Black Hawk Down: A Story of Modern War.* New York: Penguin, 2000.

Bowen, Roland E. *From Ball's Bluff to Gettysburg . . . and Beyond: The Civil War Letters of Private Roland E. Bowen, 15th Massachusetts Infantry.* Edited by Gregory Coco. Gettysburg: Thomas Publishers, 1994.

Bowers, B. M. *Cow-Country.* New York: Grosset and Dunlap, 1921.

Bradley, James, and Ron Powers. *Flags of Our Fathers.* New York: Bantam, 2006.

Burgess, Theodore C. "Epideictic Literature." Ph.D. diss., University of Chicago, 1902.

Burkert, Walter. *Greek Religion.* Translated by John Raffan. Cambridge, Mass.: Harvard University Press, 1985.

Caesar, Julius. *"The Civil War," together with "The Alexandrian War," "The African War," and "The Spanish War" by Other Hands.* Translated by Jane F. Gardner. London: Penguin Classics, 1976.

———. *The Conquest of Gaul.* Translated by S. A. Handford, with an introduction by Jane F. Gardner. London: Penguin, 1982.

Cartledge, Paul. *Alexander the Great: The Hunt for a New Past.* New York: Overlook Press, 2004.

Catton, Bruce. *Stillness at Appomattox.* New York: Doubleday, 1953.

Chamberlain, Joshua Lawrence. *The Passing of the Armies.* New York: Bantam Books, 1993.

Chambers, John Whiteclay, II. "S. L. A. Marshall's *Men Against Fire*: New Evidence Regarding Fire Ratios." *Parameters* (Autumn 2003).

Chandler, David G. *The Military Maxims of Napoleon.* Translated by Lieutenant-General Sir George C. D'Aguilar. London: Greenhill Books, 2002.

Channing, Reverend William E. "'Self Culture,' An Address Introductory to the Franklin Lectures, Delivered at Boston, September, 1838." Boston: Dutton and Wentworth, 1838 (pamphlet).

Churchill, Winston Leonard Spencer. *The Story of the Malakind Field Force: An Episode of Frontier War.* New York: Thomas Nelson and Sons, 1916.

Clark, Michael. "Did Thucydides Invent the Battle Exhortation?" *Historia: Journal of Ancient History* 44 (1995): Heft 3.

Club: The Official Newsletter of the 1st Combat Brigade Team, The.

Collins, Lieutenant Colonel Tim. *Rules of Engagement: A Life in Conflict.* London: Headline Book Publishing, 2005.

"Commandant of the U.S. Marine Corps' Official Reading List." www.mcu.usmc.mil/reading.

Concise Oxford Dictionary of Literary Terms. New York: Oxford University Press, 2001.

Cott, Nancy F. *The Bonds of Womanhood: Women's Sphere in New England, 1780–1835.* New Haven: Yale University Press, 1977.

Crossed Sabers (a publication of the First Cavalry Division).

Cupp, Sergeant Jon. "Retention NCOs, Career Counselors Dish Out Truth about Reenlistment." Multi-National Corps — Iraq, Release No. 20070123–05, January 23, 2007.

Davis, Jefferson. *The Rise and Fall of the Confederate Government.* 2 vols. New York: Da Capo Press, 1990.

Dawson, Doyne. *The Origins of Western Warfare: Militarism and Morality in the Ancient World.* Boulder, Colo.: Westview Press, 1998.

De Jomini, Baron. *The Art of War.* Translated by G. H. Mendenhall and W. P. Craighill. Philadelphia: 1871.

Department of Defense. *Manual of Military Decorations and Awards.* September 1996, Incorporated Change I, September 18, 2006, DoD 1348.33-M, API.1.2.21.

Desert Bulls (publication of the First Combat Brigade Team, 34th Infantry Division).

D'Este, Carlo. *Eisenhower: A Soldier's Life.* New York: Henry Holt and Company, 2002.

Donnelly, James. "James Donnelly, Late Corporal Co. D, 20th Mass. Vols. Sketch of his life. Written by himself by request of Committee having in charge history and memorial of Regiment." MOLLUS Collection, Houghton Library, Harvard University.

Doran, Gunnery Sergeant Jason K. *"I Am My Brother's Keeper": Journal of a Gunny in Iraq.* North Topsail Beach, N.C.: Caisson Press, 2005.

Duffy, Bernard K., and Ronald H. Carpenter. *Douglas MacArthur: Warrior as Wordsmith.* Westport, Conn.: Greenwood, 1997.

Dyer, Frederick H. *A Compendium of the War of the Rebellion.* Dayton, Ohio: Morningside Press, 1978.

Ehrhardt, C. T. H. R., "Speeches before Battle?" *Historia: Journal of Ancient History* 44 (1995): Heft 1.

Eisenhower, Dwight D. *Crusade in Europe.* Baltimore: Johns Hopkins University Press, 1997.

Estes, Kenneth W. *The Marine Officer's Guide.* 6th ed. Annapolis, Md.: U.S. Naval Institute Press, 2000.

Fisk, Wilber. *Hard Marching Every Day: The Civil War Letters of Private Wilbur Fisk, 1861–1865.* Edited by Emil and Ruth Rosenblatt. Kansas City: University of Kansas Press, 1992.

Floyd, Sergeant Fred C. *History of the Fortieth (Mozart) Regiment, New York Volunteers.* Boston: 1909.

Foote, Lorien. "Rich Man's War, Rich Man's Fight: Class, Ideology, and Discipline in the Union Army." *Civil War History* (September 2005).

Fourth Geneva Convention, August 12, 1949.

Fowler, William M., Jr. "An American Crisis: The Newburgh Address." Delivered at Mount Vernon on July 20, 2006. http://www .lehrmaninstitute.org/lehrman/newburgh.pdf.

———. *Under Two Flags: The American Navy in the Civil War.* New York: U.S. Naval Institute Press, 1990.

Fox, William F. *Regimental Losses in the American Civil War: 1861–1865.* 1888. Reprint, Dayton, Ohio: Morningside Books, 1985.

Frank, Joseph Allan, and George A. Reaves. *"Seeing the Elephant": Raw Recruits at the Battle of Shiloh.* Urbana: University of Illinois Press, 1989.

Franklin, John Hope. *The Emancipation Proclamation.* Wheeling, Ill.: Harlan Davidson, 1995.

Frederickson, George M. *The Inner Civil War: Northern Intellectuals and the Crisis of Union.* New York: University of Illinois Press, 1993.

Freeman, Douglas Southall. *Lee's Lieutenants: Cedar Mountain to Chancellorsville.* 3 vols. New York: Charles Scribner's Sons, 1971.

———. *R. E. Lee: A Biography.* 4 vols. New York: Charles Scribner's Sons, 1934.

Frontinus. *The Stratagems.* Edited by Mary B. McElwain. Translated by Charles E. Bennett Cambridge, Mass.: Loeb, 2003.

Gammons, John F. *The Third Massachusetts Regiment Volunteer Militia in the War of the Rebellion, 1861–1863.* Providence: Snow and Farnham Co., 1906.

General Regulation of U.S. Navy.

Gibbon, Edward. *The Decline and Fall of the Roman Empire.* 6 vols. New York: Everyman's Library, 1993.

Goldsworthy, Adrian. *The Complete Roman Army.* London: Thames and Hudson, 2003.

Grant, Ulysses. *Personal Memoirs of U.S. Grant.* 2 vols. New York: C. L. Webster and Co., 1885.

Halttunen, Karen. *Confidence Men and Painted Women: A Study of Middle-Class Culture in America, 1830–1870.* New Haven: Yale University Press, 1982.

Hammes, Colonel Thomas X. *The Sling and the Stone: On War in the 21st Century.* St. Paul, Minn.: Zenith Press, 2006.

Hansen, Victor Davis. *The Western Way of War: Infantry Battle in Classical Greece.* New York: Alfred A. Knopf, 1989.

Hartley, Jason Christopher. *Just Another Soldier: A Year on the Ground in Iraq.* New York: HarperCollins, 2005.

Harvard University: Quinquennial Catalogue of the Officers and Graduates: 1636–1920. Cambridge, Mass.: Harvard University Press, 1920.

Herodotus. *The Histories.* Edited by Walter Blanco. New York: Penguin, 1992.

Hess, Earl J. *Pickett's Charge—The Last Attack at Gettysburg.* Chapel Hill: University of North Carolina Press, 2001.

History Committee. *History of the Nineteenth Regiment Massachusetts Volunteer Infantry: 1861–1865.* Salem: Salem Press, 1906.

Hollis, Corporal Thomas. "Account of Corporal Thomas Hollis." MOLLUS Collection, Houghton Library, Harvard University.

Homer. *The Iliad.* Translated by Richmond Lattimore. Chicago: University of Chicago Press, 1961.

Hosmer, James K. *The Thinking Bayonet.* Boston: Walker, Fuller, and Co., 1865.

Hughes, Robert M. *General Johnston.* New York: D. Appleton and Company, 1897.

Huntingdon. Henry of. *Chronicle of Henry of Huntingdon, Comprising the History of England, from the Invasion of Julius Caesar to the Accession of Henry II.* Translated and edited by Thomas Forester. London: Henry G. Bohn, 1853.

Hutchinson, Gustavus B. *A Narrative of the Formation and Services of the Eleventh Massachusetts Volunteers, from April 15, 1861, to July 14, 1865, Being a Brief Account of Their Experiences in the Camp and Field.* Boston: Alfred Mudge and Son, 1893.

Ibrahim, Raymond, ed. and trans. *The Al Qaeda Reader.* New York: Doubleday, 2007.

Iron Brigade Chronicle (includes all FARs).

Josephus. *The Jewish War.* Translated by G. W. Williamson. Edited and with an introduction by E. Mary Smallwood. London: Penguin Classics, 1981.

———. *The Life of Flavius Josephus* and *Antiquities of the Jews.* In *Josephus: The Complete Works,* translated by William Whiston. Nashville: Thomas Nelson Publishers, 1998.

Keegan, John. *The Face of Battle: A Study of Agincourt, Waterloo, and the Somme.* London: Viking Press, 1976.

Kern, Paul Bentley. *Ancient Siege Warfare.* London: Souveneir Press, 1999.

Lakoff, George, and Mark Johnson. *Metaphors We Live By.* Chicago: University of Chicago Press, 1980.

Lewis, Adrian. *Omaha Beach: A Flawed Victory.* Chapel Hill: University of North Carolina Press, 2001.

Lincoln, Abraham. *Abraham Lincoln: His Speeches and Writings*. Edited by Roy P. Basler. New York: Da Capo Press, 1990.

Livermore, Thomas L. *Days and Events, 1860–1866*. Boston: Houghton Mifflin Company, 1920.

Livingston, Gary. *Fallujah, With Honor*. Topsail Beach, N.C.: Caisson Press, 2006.

Livy. *The History of Rome from Its Foundation*, Books 21–30; *The War with Hannibal*. Edited by Betty Radice. Translated by Aubrey De Selincourt. London: Penguin Books, 1972.

Livy in Fourteen Volumes. Translated by B. O. Foster. Cambridge, Mass.: Harvard University Press, 1919.

Long, E. B. *Civil War Day by Day: An Almanac*. New York: Da Capo Press, 1971.

Macnamara, Daniel George. *The History of the Ninth Regiment Massachusetts Volunteer Infantry*. Boston: E. B. Shillings and Company, 1899.

Mahood, Wayne. *General Wadsworth: The Life and Times of Brevet Major General James S. Wadsworth*. Cambridge, Mass.: Da Capo Press, 2003.

Manchester, William. *American Caesar: Douglas MacArthur 1880–1964*. Boston: Little, Brown, 1978.

Marine Corps Bulletin (MCBUL), 1500. "The Marine Corps Professional Reading Program." All Marine Corps Activities (ALMAR), 244/96.

Marshall, S. L. A. *Men Against Fire: The Problem of Battle Command in Future War*. 1947. Reprint, Gloucester, Mass.: Peter Smith, 1973.

———. *Pork Chop Hill: The American Fighting Man in Action, Korea, Spring, 1953*. 1956. Reprint, New York: Berkley Books, 2000.

Mather, Cotton. "Souldiers Counselled and Comforted; To my Much Honored Friends; the Pious and Valiant Commanders Of the Forces now engaged against our Indian Enemies." Boston: Samuel Green, 1689 (pamphlet).

McPherson, James M. *Crossroads of Freedom: Antietam: The Battle that Changed the Course of the War*. New York: Oxford University Press, 2002.

McSwain, Sergeant Kevin. "30 Illinois Guardsmen Reenlist During Ceremony." Multi-National Corps—Iraq, January 17, 2007, No. 20070117-01.

McWilliams, Bill. *On Hallowed Ground: The Last Battle for Pork Chop Hill*. Annapolis, Md.: U.S. Naval Institute Press, 2004.

Meade, George Gordon. *The Life and Letters of George Gordon Meade*. 2 vols. New York: Charles Scribner's Sons, 1913.

Metz, Steven, and Raymond Millen. "Intervention, Stabilization, and

Transformation Operations: The Role of Landpower in the New Strategic Environment." *Parameters* (Spring 2005).

Miller, Ilana D. *Reports from America: William Howard Russell and the Civil War.* Gloucestershire: Sutton Publishing, 2001.

Miller, Richard F. "For His Wife, His Widow, and His Orphan: Massachusetts and Family Aid during the Civil War." *Massachusetts Historical Review* 6 (2004).

Mitchell, Reid. *Civil War Soldiers.* New York: Viking, 1988.

Mogens, Herman Hansen. "The Battle Exhortation in Ancient Historiography: Fact or Fiction?" *Historia: Journal of Ancient History* 42 (1993): Heft 2.

Morton, James A., III. *A Little Short of Boats: The Fights at Ball's Bluff and Edwards Ferry, October 21–22, 1861, A History and Tour Guide.* Fort Mitchell, Ky.: Ironclad Publishing, 2004.

Navy Department Communiques. Commander in Chief, Pacific Ocean Arena (CINCPOA) Communique No. 300, March 16, 1945.

Neff, Stephen C. *War and the Law of Nations: A General History.* New York: Cambridge University Press, 2005.

Nevins, Allan. *The War for the Union: War Becomes Revolution, 1862–1863.* 4 vols. New York: Scribner, 1960.

Nicolson, Adam. *Seize the Fire: Heroism, Duty, and the Battle of Trafalgar.* New York: Harper Collins, 2005.

Niditch, Susan. *War in the Hebrew Bible.* New York: Oxford University Press, 1995.

1954 Hague Convention. "Convention for the Protection of Cultural Property in the Even of Armed Conflict." May 14, 1954.

Onansander. *The General.* Cambridge, Mass., Harvard University, 2001.

O'Reilly, Francis Augustin. *The Fredericksburg Campaign: Winter War on the Rappahannock.* Baton Rouge: Louisiana State University Press, 2003.

Osborn, Francis Augustus. *Civil War Regiments from Massachusetts: 1861–1865.* 1908. Reprint, Pensacola, Fla.: Ebooksondisk, 2003.

Paludan, Philip Shaw. *"A People's Contest": The Union and Civil War, 1861–1865.* New York: Harper and Row, 1988.

"Papers of George Washington." http://gwpapers.virginia.edu/documents/revolution/farewwell.

Plutarch's Lives: The Dryden Translation. 2 vols. Edited with preface by Arthur Hugh Clough and an introduction by James Atlas. New York: Modern Library, 2003.

Polybius: The Rise of the Roman Empire. Translated by Ian Scott-Kivert. London: Penguin Books, 1979.

Prestwich, Michael. *Armies and Warfare in the Middle Ages: The English Experience*. New Haven: Yale University Press, 1996.

Pritchard, Tim. *Ambush Alley: The Most Extraordinary Battle of the Iraq War*. New York: Presidio Press, 2005.

Pritchett, W. Kendrick. *Ancient Greek Battle Speeches and a Palfrey*. Amsterdam: J. C. Gieben, 2002.

———. *Essays in Greek History*. Amsterdam: J. C. Gieben, 1994.

Quint, Alonzo H. *The Record of the Second Massachusetts Infantry, 1861–1865*. Boston: James P. Walker, 1867.

Rafuse, Ethan S. *McClellan's War: The Failure of Moderation in the Struggle for the Union*. Indianapolis: Indiana University Press, 2005.

Random House Dictionary of the English Language. 2nd ed., unabridged. New York: Random House, 1987.

Rebellion Record: A Diary of American Events. Edited by Frank Moore. 12 vols. New York: Arno Press, 1977.

Reed, Charles Wellington. *"A Grand Terrible Drama": From Gettysburg to Petersburg: The Civil War Letters of Charles Wellington Reed*. Edited by Eric A. Campbell. New York: Fordham University Press, 2000.

Revised Regulations for the Army of the United States, 1861. Philadelphia: G. L. Brown, 1861.

Robb, John. *Brave New War: The Next Stage of Terrorism and the End of Globalization*. Hoboken, N.J.: Wily, 2007.

Rosen, Robert N. *The Jewish Confederates*. Columbia: University of South Carolina Press, 2000.

Rosengarten, J. G. *The German Soldier in the Wars of the United States*. Philadelphia: J. B. Lippincott Company, 1890.

Royle, Trevor. *Crimea: The Great Crimean War, 1854–1856*. New York: Random House, 2000.

Sallust. *The Jugurthine War/The Conspiracy of Catiline*. London: Penguin Classics, 1963.

Sears, Stephen W. *George B. McClellan: The Young Napoleon*. New York: Ticknor and Fields, 1988.

Shakespeare, William. *The Life of Henry the Fifth, The Riverside Shakespeare*. 2nd ed. Boston: Houghton Mifflin Company, 1997.

Shearer, Benjamin G., and Barbara S. Shearer. *State Names, Seals, Flags, and Symbols: A Historical Guide*. Westport, Conn.: Greenwood Press, 1994.

Smith, George W. *Carlson's Raid: The Daring Marine Assault on Makin*. New York: Berkley Press, 2003.

Spencer, Charles. *Blenheim: Battle for Europe*. London: Phoenix Press, 2004.

Squire, Aelred. *Aelred of Rievault: A Study*. London: Society for Promoting Christian Knowledge, 1969.

Stand Firm and Fire Low: The Civil War Writings of Colonel Edward E. Cross. Edited by Walter Holden, William E. Ross, and Elizabeth Slomba. Hanover, N.H.: University Press of New England, 2003.

Stewart, George R. *Pickett's Charge: A Microhistory of the Final Attack at Gettysburg, July 3, 1863*. Boston: Premier/Fawcett, 1987.

Stewart, Richard W. *The United Stats Army in a Global Era, 1917–2003*. Army Historical Series. 2 vols. Washington, D.C.: Department of the Army, 2005).

Supplement to the General Statutes of the Commonwealth of Massachusetts. Edited by William Richardson and George P. Sanger. Boston: William White, 1867.

Tarn, W. W. *Alexander the Great: Sources and Studies*. 2 vols. Cambridge: Cambridge University Press, 1948.

Tertullian. *The Apology*. Translated by the Reverend C. Dodgson, M.A. 2nd ed. Oxford: John Henry Parker, 1854.

Thucydides. *The Landmark Thucydides: A Comprehensive Guide to the Peloponnesian War*. Edited by Robert B. Strassler. New York: Free Press, 1998.

Tregaskis, Richard. *Guadalcanal Diary*. New York: Modern Library of America, 2000.

Tucker, Mike. *Among Warriors in Iraq: True Grit, Special Ops, and Raiding in Mosul and Fallujah*. Guilford, Conn.: Lyons Press, 2005.

Uniform Code of Military Justice.

United States Army Field Manuals:
  Field Manual, FM-321.5, "Drill and Ceremonies."
  Field Manual, No. 22-51, *Leader's Manual for Combat Stress Control*, Section 1-5, Headquarters, Department of the Army, September 29, 1994.

United States Army Regulations. Army Regulation 600-20, "Army Command Policy, 7 June 2006."

United States Marine Corps. "A Message to Parents and Family Members," (recruiting brochure).

Von Clausewitz, Carl. *On War*. Edited by Anatol Rapoport. London: Penguin Classics, 1982.

Wainwright, General Jonathan M., IV. *General Wainwright's Story: The Account of Four Years of Humiliating Defeat, Surrender, and Captivity*. Edited by Robert Consodine. Garden City, N.Y.: Doubleday, 1946.

Walbank, F. W. *A Historical Commentary on Polybius*. Oxford: Clarendon Press, 1957.

Warner, Ezra J. *Generals in Blue: Lives of the Union Commanders.* Baton
    Rouge: Louisiana State University Press, 1999.
*War of the Rebellion: A Compilation of the Official Records of the Union
    and Confederate Armies, The.* Series I. Washington, D.C.: Govern-
    ment Printing Office, 1880–1901.
War on Radio [sound recordings]: *The Pacific and European Theaters.*
    8 CDs. Renton, Wash.: Topics Entertainment 2002.
Weintraub, Stanley. *General Washington's Christmas Farewell: A Mount
    Vernon Homecoming.* New York: New York Free Press, 2003.
West, Francis J. ("Bing"). *No True Glory: A Frontline Account of the Battle
    of Fallujah.* New York: Bantan, 2005.
West, Francis J. ("Bing"), and Major General Ray L. Smith. *The March
    Up: Taking Baghdad with the 1st Marine Division.* New York: Bantam
    Books, 2003.
Williams, T. Harry. *P.G.T. Beauregard: Napoleon in Gray.* Baton Rouge:
    Louisiana State University Press, 1954.
Woodworth, Steven E. *While God Is Marching On: The Religious World
    of Civil War Soldiers.* Lawrence, Kans.: University of Kansas Press,
    2001.
Wylie, James Hammond. *The Reign of Henry V.* 3 vols. Cambridge:
    Cambridge University Press, 1914–1929.

Films

Full Metal Jacket. Directed by Stanley Kubrick. Warner Bros. 1987.
Gettysburg. Directed by Ronald F. Maxwell. New Line. 1993.
Glory. Directed by Edward Zwick. TriStar. 1989.
Longest Day, The. Directed by Ken Annakin and Andrew Marton.
    Twentieth Century–Fox. 1962.
Patton. Directed by Franklin J. Schaffner. Twentieth Century–Fox. 1970.

Newspapers

Boston Daily Advertiser
New York Evening Post
New York Times
New York Tribune
Philadelphia Inquirer

Index

Specific speeches are indicated in **bold**.